FREEDOM FOR ALL

FREEDOM FOR ALL

AN ATTORNEY'S GUIDE TO FIGHTING HUMAN TRAFFICKING

KELLY HYLAND
KAVITHA SREEHARSHA

Cover design by Elmarie Jara.

Printed in the United States of America.

17 16 15   5 4 3 2 1

ISBN: 978-1-62722-647-9
e-ISBN: 978-1-62722-648-6

Library of Congress Cataloging-in-Publication Data is on file

Discounts are available for books ordered in bulk. Special consideration is given to state bars, CLE programs, and other barrelated organizations. Inquire at Book Publishing, ABA Publishing, American Bar Association, 321 N. Clark Street, Chicago, Illinois 60654-7598.

www.ShopABA.org

CONTENTS

Acknowledgments xi
Acronyms. xiii
Glossary. xv
Introduction 1

Chapter 1: What Is Human Trafficking? 9
Defining Trafficking 10
The Scale of the Problem 12
Trafficked Persons in the United States 13
The Industries Where Human Trafficking Is Found. 15
    Agriculture 15
    Manufacturing 15
    Domestic Servitude. 16
    Prostitution. 16
    Elder Care 16
    Country Clubs and Hotels 17
    Restaurants. 17
    Janitorial Services. 18
Root Causes 19
Traffickers' Tactics 21
    Force 22
    Fraud 24
    Coercion. 26
Misconceptions About the Term *Human Trafficking*. 30
The Impact on Trafficked Persons 32
    Financial Consequences 32

Physical Health.   33
Mental Health   34
Conclusion   34

Chapter 2: The Criminal Justice Response   37
Human Trafficking Task Forces   39
Federal Laws.   40
Trafficking Victim Protection Act   41
Related Federal Statutes   47
State Anti-Trafficking Criminal Statutes   47
Definition of Human Trafficking   48
Equity in Labor and Sex Trafficking Prosecutions.   48
A Victim-Centered Prosecution.   49
The Proactive Prosecution   50
Trust Building.   51
Law Enforcement Coordination   53
Coordination with Service Providers.   55
Prosecutors and Victim Services Attorneys Collaborating
for Immigrant Victims   56
Restitution and Asset Forfeiture   59
Restitution   59
Asset Forfeiture   60
Counterpart: Victim Services Attorneys   60
Civil Litigation   63
The Criminalization of Victims.   63
Arresting Victims   63
Post-conviction Relief.   66
The Role of Judges   67
Conclusion   68

Chapter 3: Corporate Law   69
Risk Mitigation   75
Damage Control.   79
Compliance and Risk Mitigation   80
California Transparency in Supply Chains Act   80
Foreign Corrupt Practices Act   84

SEC Regulation on Conflict Minerals. 85
Federal Acquisition Regulation (FAR) 88
Conclusion 92

Chapter 4: Labor and Employment Law Approaches to Human Trafficking 93

Myths and Misconceptions in the Labor Context 94
The Case for Proactive Identification 96
   Implementing a Screening Process 100
   Outreach and Collaboration 101
Building Civil Litigation Cases and Practices 102
   Civil Causes of Action 103
   Fair Labor Standards Act 106
   Discrimination Laws 107
   Racketeer Influenced and Corrupt Organizations Act 109
   Alien Tort Claims Act 111
State Civil Laws 111
The Practice of Civil Anti-Trafficking Litigation 112
   Building Trust with Trafficked Persons 112
   Safety Planning 113
   Coordination with a Criminal Case. 114
   Financial Implications of a Civil Judgment 115
   Diplomatic Immunity. 116
   Immigration Exposure. 116
Mitigating Against Human Trafficking
   and Resulting Lawsuits 117
Beyond the Lawsuit 118
   Coordination with Legal and Social Service Providers. 118
Conclusion 119

Chapter 5: Access to Immigration Protections. 121

The Nexus Between Immigration and Human Trafficking 122
The State of Play for Trafficked Immigrants 124
Identifying Trafficked Immigrants. 125
Immigration Relief and Protections. 130
   Immediate Access to Continued Presence 130

T Nonimmigrant Status (T Visa) for Victims of Trafficking .. 131
T Visa Adjustment of Status. 139
U Visa for Victims of Crime 141
Adjustment of Status 146
VAWA Self-Petition and Cancellation. 147
Special Immigrant Juvenile Status 148
Asylum. 149
Considerations in Representing Trafficked Immigrants 150
Language Considerations. 150
Culturally Appropriate Services. 152
Immigration Enforcement Victims Protections. 153
Coordinating with Law Enforcement 154
Investigation and Prosecution. 155
Conclusion 156

Chapter 6: International Law. 157
A Brief History 158
International Criminal Law 160
The Palermo Protocol. 160
Today's Lawyering 162
International Human Rights and Humanitarian Law 165
Women. 166
Children 167
Business and Human Rights 168
Migrants. 169
International Refugee Law 169
Asylum. 170
UNHCR Role. 173
IOs and NGOs. 174
International Labor Law. 175
In Practice. 176
Conclusion 178

Chapter 7: A Call to Public Interest Advocates and Attorneys 179

Understanding the Intersections with Human Trafficking 180
   Overcoming Misconceptions 180
Identification: The First Steps in Taking Action. 183
   The Benefits of Expanded Identification 183
   Leveraging the Public Interest Expertise 185
   Traditional Public Interest Lawyering. 186
   Domestic Violence and Sexual Assault Attorneys 187
   Immigration Attorneys 190
   Juvenile Justice Attorneys 193
   Labor and Employment Law Attorneys 196
Designing Legal Programs 198
   Providing Legal Representation 198
   Funding for Primary Services 199
   Ancillary Legal Services 200
   Collaboration. 200
   The Role of the Pro Bono Attorney 200
Conclusion 202

Epilogue 203
Resources for Attorneys 207
U.S. Government 207
Local Resources 209
Other Resources 209
Appendix 211
Palermo Protocol 212
TVPA and Reauthorizations 225
The Athens Ethical Principals 372
Luxor Implementation Guidelines to the Athens
   Ethical Principles 382
SB 657 California Transparency in Supply Chains Act 385
About the Authors 389
Notes 391
Index 407

ACKNOWLEDGMENTS

This book in many ways represents our collective experience within the range of anti-trafficking legal practice over the past fifteen years. Our broader work and this book have been a labor of love, which could not have been accomplished without the generosity, wisdom, and collaboration of so many talented colleagues.

Laurel Bellows made human trafficking the focus of her term as president of the American Bar Association, and the resulting work of the ABA Human Trafficking Task Force has brought the issue to the attention of attorneys nationwide. This book is an extension of that effort, and we are grateful for the support that has brought it to fruition, particularly from Jon Malysiak, Executive Editor at ABA Publishing, and Vivan Huelgo, Chief Counsel to the ABA Human Trafficking Task Force.

Over the years, we have had the great privilege to work with so many colleagues in social services, advocacy, legal services, corporate social responsibility, philanthropy, government, and law enforcement who have shared our same goal—to identify and prevent human trafficking. Many of them have lent their own voices in this book through interviews and quotations. They have all enriched our work with their tremendous contributions and perspectives, and for them we are thankful. Specifically, Christa Stewart, Suzanne Tomatore, E. Christopher Johnson, Kathleen Kim, Bridgette Carr and Abigail Price all contributed their time and talents to reviewing various chapters of this book; their insights were, as ever, insightful and spot on.

We also gratefully acknowledge everyone who has supported the Global Freedom Center, either as corporate partners, clients for our consulting and training, social media followers, donors, or moral supporters.

ACRONYMS

ABA—American Bar Association
ABA ROLI—American Bar Association Rule of Law Initiative
ARTIP—Asia Regional Trafficking in Persons Project
ATCA—Alien Tort Claims Act
CGRS—Center for Gender and Refugee Studies, University of California Hastings School of Law
CSR—Corporate social responsibility
DOJ—U.S. Department of Justice
DRC—Democratic Republic of Congo
DRL—U.S. Department of State's Bureau of Democracy, Human Rights and Labor
EICC—Electronics Industry Citizenship Coalition
FAR—Federal Acquisitions Regulation
FCPA—Foreign Corrupt Practices Act
ICE—U.S. Department of Homeland Security's Immigration and Customs Enforcement
ILAB—U.S. Department of Labor's Bureau of International Labor Affairs
ILO—International Labour Organization
ILRF—International Labor Rights Forum
INGO—International nongovernmental organization
NGO—Nongovernmental organization
OSCE—Organization for Security and Cooperation in Europe
SEC—U.S. Securities and Exchange Commission
TIP Report—Trafficking in Persons Report
TVPA—Trafficking Victims Protection Act of 2000
UNHCR—United Nations High Commissioner for Refugees

UNICEF—United Nations Children's Fund
UNODC—United Nations Office on Drugs and Crime
USCIS—U.S. Department of Homeland Security's Citizenship and Immi-
    gration Services
USG—U.S. government

GLOSSARY

Adjustment of Status—the change of immigration status to lawful permanent resident.

Alien Tort Claims Act—a federal law providing federal jurisdiction over certain tort cases violating a law of nation or U.S. treaty.

Asylum—a protection under U.S. immigration law available to certain immigrants who have experienced or fear persecution in their country of origin.

Continued Presence—temporary U.S. immigration status granted to victims of a severe form of trafficking in persons.

Human Trafficking—holding another in compelled service using whatever means necessary, be it physical or psychological.

Lawful Permanent Residence—an immigration status afforded to noncitizens lawfully permitted to permanently reside in the United States.

Limited English Proficient (LEP)—individuals who have a limited ability to speak, understand, read, and write English.

Mann Act—a federal law created to criminalize the interstate or foreign transportation of individuals for commercial sex purposes.

Palermo Protocol—Supplementing the Transnational Crime Convention in 2000, it is the seminal international law instrument that defines human trafficking and led to more than 140 countries' criminalizing trafficking.

Racketeer Influenced and Corrupt Organizations (RICO)—a federal statute criminalizing racketeering and organized crime.

Special Immigrant Juvenile Status—an immigration status afforded to certain immigrant minors for whom parental reunification with one or both parents is not viable because of abuse, neglect, or abandonment.

T visa—a nonimmigrant visa available to certain victims of a severe form of trafficking in persons.

Title VI of the Civil Rights Act of 1964—a federal law prohibiting discrimination by those receiving federal financial assistance, based on criteria including national origin, which has been interpreted by executive order and courts to include language discrimination.

Title VII of the Civil Rights Act of 1964—a federal law prohibiting employment discrimination.

TVPA (Trafficking Victims Protection Act)—Enacted in 2000 and reauthorized in 2003, 2005, 2008 and 2013, a federal law that creates the modern anti-trafficking infrastructure in the United States, including criminal provisions for investigations and prosecutions, benefits and services for victims, and prevention measures.

United States Citizenship and Immigration Services (USCIS)—a Department of Homeland Security agency overseeing lawful immigration to the United States.

U visa—a nonimmigrant visa available to certain victims of qualifying criminal activity.

Uniform Act on Prevention of and Remedies for Human Trafficking (Uniform Act)—Act passed in 2013 by the Uniform Law Commission (National Conference of Commissioners on Uniform State Laws) to provide a framework for state anti-trafficking laws.

VAWA Confidentiality—a set of federal laws protecting immigrant victims of crime from their perpetrators seeking to use immigration as a tool in their victimization.

VAWA Self-Petition and Cancellation—federal immigration provisions intended to assist certain abused immigrants to obtain lawful immigration status.

Introduction

[S]ocial scientists estimate that as many as 27 million men, women and children are trafficking victims at any given time. That means we're bringing to light only a mere fraction of those who are exploited in modern slavery. That number and the millions who remain unidentified are the numbers that deserve our focus.

—2013 Trafficking in Persons Report,
U.S. Department of State

Right now, an estimated 21 to 30 million people are enslaved around the world. They are in mines in the Democratic Republic of the Congo, fishing vessels off the coast of New Zealand, garment factories in Jordan, the forests of Brazil, carpet factories in Nepal, agricultural fields in Florida, and everywhere in between. That means that slavery is happening across the globe and it is in our backyard. It is within the products we buy and the services in our communities. It could in be the jewelry you are wearing, the shrimp you ate for dinner, the shoes on your feet, the phone in

1

your pocket, the nanny down the street, the night janitor at work, or the landscaper in your neighborhood. It is everywhere, touching everyone in very tangible ways whether we see it or not.

We have seen it firsthand. We were two of the first attorneys providing legal services to trafficked persons in the United States. Initially, when asked about our work, we often had to explain what human trafficking is as the starting point. No one had even heard of it. Most people thought it was a new term for smuggling. On more than one humorous occasion, someone thought we were talking about crowd control after sporting events and concerts.

What a long way we have come. Fifteen years later, it is rather telling that we no longer need to offer that explanation. There are still assumptions and misconceptions to rectify. But on the whole, the issue of human trafficking is now familiar to many more. From those early days to now, a plethora of organizations have emerged and have successfully raised awareness. These organizations focus on different aspects of human trafficking including child sex tourism, domestic servitude, and sex trafficking of U.S. citizen girls and boys, or they treat the issue broadly. They may be working in their local communities, on college campuses or nationally. Additionally, numerous cities have undertaken awareness campaigns complete with bus ads, public service announcements, and highway billboards. In roughly fifteen years we have gone from having virtually no information and knowledge about human trafficking to recognizing it as the top human rights issue.

Despite the apparent success of public awareness efforts, we are still not finding trafficked persons. Of the millions enslaved globally, over these same fifteen years of broad public awareness, we have consistently found *less than one percent* of trafficked persons. Put another way, that is only one person identified for every 2000 estimated to be enslaved. The number of victims identified has not risen along with the rate of public awareness.

Why do we continue to identify at such a low rate?

A person can only learn so much from a billboard or a 30-second public service announcement. In that short amount of time, a person may be exposed to the existence of human trafficking, but light touch awareness and mainstream media efforts are inadequate to convey how to identify one of the most hidden crimes.

Aside from a limited number of documentaries that deeply delve into the multiple forms of trafficking, mainstream news, television shows, and public awareness materials focus on sex trafficking. This focus succeeds in shock value and attention, but it also distances people from the issue personally because they do not see how commercial sex and sex trafficking intersects with their lives. Consequently, it becomes harder for them to understand what they can do about it. We therefore need much more beyond public awareness to increase identification.

There is also an information and training gap among those who unknowingly interact with trafficked persons; trafficking studies routinely cite training as an outstanding need. Few expect that they are likely to interact with trafficked persons, and as a result, do not know how to recognize or prevent trafficking. What knowledge they have may be based on stereotypes and misconceptions, which can misguide outreach and divert attention resulting in missed opportunities for identification of trafficked persons right in front of them. Identification requires training on when, where, and what to look for and what to do next, especially mindful that trafficked persons fear speaking out and are likely to be distrustful. Even a brief training targeted for the profession and role of the audience will prepare the professional to better respond.

Identification is also dismally low because of the hidden nature of human trafficking which we outline in great detail in Chapter 1. Trafficked persons are led to believe there will be serious consequences if they leave their job, run away, speak with anyone, or seek help. They are manipulated, shamed, misled, degraded, and threatened. Sometimes they are physically confined out of sight. Other times they are restrained by invisible but strong psychological bonds, allowing them to interact with many people unaware of their plight. Still, in both cases, trafficked persons are largely unable to reach out for help, so we need to reach out to them.

Another limiting factor is that we have been relying primarily on one sector to address the issue when, in fact, many sectors have an important role to play. Trafficking has been framed primarily as a criminal justice issue in the United States and perhaps even more so globally. To give some sense of the scope of the criminal justice effort, globally, roughly 4,000 traffickers are convicted annually. Last reported in the United States, approximately 138 traffickers were convicted federally and an unknown number, but perhaps dozens, were convicted at the state level; sex traffickers comprise the vast majority of these convictions. This is obviously barely scratching the surface given the estimates of the issue. One reason is that criminal justice professionals are more equipped to and adept at identifying sex trafficking than labor trafficking; existing criminal laws and infrastructure already respond to prostitution but not to labor violations. This means there is a great need for a complimentary enforcement effort and funding to address labor trafficking, which is estimated to comprise 78% of all trafficking. Additionally, criminal justice efforts are limited because law enforcement lacks the financial, linguistic, or cultural capacity to interact with the majority of trafficked persons.[1] Trafficked persons typically do not trust law enforcement therefore they are reluctant to report trafficking or seek help, leaving them unaware of the protections available to them under the law.

Overall, a criminal justice response is critical, but it is just one piece of the puzzle. To expand identification, we need to increase (needed a different word) the number and types of professionals who are looking and equip them through training. The best hope is to train the people who naturally interact with trafficked persons without knowing it. Studies show that trafficked persons encounter a range of additional professionals in the health, education, immigration, labor and employment, social services, and corporate sectors. The good news is that there are nascent efforts in each of these professions to address trafficking. A hospital in New York City implemented identification and response protocols for all employees. Educators, in limited areas, are beginning to recognize the signs of trafficking among their students in middle and high schools. More and more providers of social services are learning how to identify trafficked persons among their own clientele and communities. This is the type of expansion that needs to be fueled for even greater results.

We have met so many students and professionals who want to work on human trafficking in some way, some of whom are ready to leave their current jobs and start an organization or join an anti-trafficking NGO. But we have found that the majority, even though they would like to contribute in some way, simply do not see how trafficking is relevant to their work and where their skills can be applied to make a difference either in identification, services, or prevention. Our goal in this book is to demonstrate that relevance in addition to the intersection between multiple areas of the law and anti-trafficking interventions.

For instance, in criminal law, despite the majority of efforts to date happening within criminal justice, we have still only scratched the surface. Modern federal criminal laws are only as old as the year 2000, and state laws have slowly emerged in the years that followed. Many state laws are still completely untested. There is more legislative work to do as well as implementation of existing laws to ensure that investigators, prosecutors, and judges have the resources and training they need to take on these cases.

In the corporate sector, years of voluntary corporate codes of conduct are giving way to regulations and legislation that require corporations to maintain slavery-free supply chains. Corporate social responsibility (CSR) professionals as well as corporate attorneys see these first efforts as the tip of the iceberg. Beyond compliance issues, however, risk mitigation is necessary given concerns over litigation, NGO activism, rising consumer interest, and the possibility of a public relations disaster. Firms and in-house counsel are becoming engaged on all of these fronts. Given the extent of global supply chains today, where one brand can have thousands of suppliers worldwide, there is an incredible opportunity to prevent human trafficking on a massive scale with the right policies and procedures.

Employment law attorneys are also well-positioned to screen potential clients for human trafficking. Just as a discrimination claim may be hiding behind a contract violation, human trafficking may first present as a rather straightforward wage and hour issue or workplace injury. Legal aid attorneys working with immigrants, farmworkers, and the working poor can also identify human trafficking. A civil judgment provides a trafficked person with tremendous restorative effects. Trafficked persons have a federal private right of action, but regardless of whether a claim is brought at the federal or state level, both provide an opportunity to recover sometimes an incredible amount of lost wages and additional damages. When based on discrimination, these claims may be taken up by state fair employment agencies and the U.S. Equal Employment Opportunity Commission. An even broader effort to identify labor trafficking can occur through a fully engaged U.S. Department of Labor, with trained safety and health inspectors, wage and hour investigators, and inspector general fraud investigators looking into temporary worker programs. Moreover, the U.S. Department of Labor has tremendous potential to prevent trafficking through multiple regulations it issues to protect workers, including those at risk of trafficking.

Yet another example of attorneys critical to anti-trafficking involves those working in immigration law. Identification can happen in any number of ways including credible fear determinations at an airport, assessments of unaccompanied children at the border, intakes at immigration detention centers, in removal proceedings before an immigration judge, and within community-based organizations serving immigrants. Immigration enforcement officers are in the position to come across trafficking in the course of other investigations; their training, standard operating procedures, and policies can all make a difference in effective trafficking identification and assistance. Private, public interest, and pro bono immigration attorneys can add the T visa and U visa to their repertoire of services once human trafficking is identified. Advocates can document how their trafficked clients were recruited and compelled into service as a result of restrictions or vulnerabilities of certain visa categories. In turn, government attorneys can determine how to reduce the likelihood that those visa categories will be misused. There are a number of government attorneys developing and implementing anti-trafficking efforts in the immigration context from the U.S. Departments of Homeland Security, Justice, State, and Health and Human Services as well as a range of NGOs.

On the international front, attorneys practicing in transnational criminal law, refugee and asylum law, human rights law, rule of law, and international labor law have all found that their work intersects with human trafficking. It has been an exciting time for lawyers in these areas since the negotiation in 2000 of the Protocol to Prevent, Suppress and Punish Trafficking in Persons, Especially Women and Children (Palermo Protocol) supplementing United Nations Convention Against Transnational Organized Crime. They work within United Nations agencies, regional entities, international NGOs, and the U.S. Government implementing projects worldwide, strengthening government institutions and responses to trafficking, and protecting trafficked persons' rights.

Of course there are a number of other public interest attorneys within civil society and the public sector that can identify trafficked persons, provide services, or create policies geared toward helping victims and preventing human trafficking. To name just a few, anyone working on child welfare reform, comprehensive immigration reform, sexual assault and domestic violence, housing, and homelessness can all incorporate anti-trafficking into their issues, services, and policies.

Among all of these areas of law, the commonality is that working on human trafficking is rather cutting edge, affording an opportunity to develop areas of the law, employ creative arguments and thinking, and implement new policies and programs. Nationwide and grassroots, international and domestic, public and private, government and nonprofit, law firm and legal aid, litigation and policy, students and practicing attorneys—efforts at all levels are sorely needed to increase identification, services, and prevention.

Throughout the book we have infused our own experiences as well as those of other attorneys. We present the relevant areas of the law as well as where attorney efforts are required most. It is by no means a practice manual or how-to guide, but an introduction geared to help you take the first step to see how and where your legal skills are needed. For law students, we hope it is a career guide, demonstrating the breadth of opportunities that exist and helping you see the path you can carve for yourself.

We are often asked how it is possible to work every day on such a difficult issue. It is true that secondary trauma occurs to many service providers aiding trafficked persons, but it was minimized because we had the honor to accompany trafficked persons on their journey of rebuilding. We shared our clients' joy when they received their T visas and celebrated with them as they reunited with spouses and children after years apart. We have seen how our policy work afforded trafficked persons better protections. More recently, we have seen how corporate practices to prevent trafficking result from the supplier training we deliver. There has been progress, but the opportunities to make a difference are endless. The human trafficking response must be scaled to match the scale of the problem. Legal skills are a critical part of that response. You are the solution.

CHAPTER 1

What Is Human Trafficking?

The pain is something I will never forget. In the midst of your verbal and physical assaults, you worked the four of us to death.

—Teenage boy domestic worker in Michigan

Domestic Work

Jean-Claude (Kodjo) Toviave, a Togo native, was sentenced to eleven years in prison for enslaving and abusing four West African boys in his home for five years, pretending they were his own children after sneaking them into the country with fake documents. He also falsely claimed they were his own biological children and enrolled the three youngest in a public middle school. During the six-day trial, the jury heard from the four victims, who testified that Toviave regularly beat them with broomsticks, a toilet plunger, sticks, ice scrapers, and phone chargers if they failed to obey orders to do their house chores. Toviave also withheld food and sleep as punishment.[1]

Garment Manufacturing

Recruiters promised nearly 250 Vietnamese and Chinese laborers sunny beaches, life in the United States, and steady work in a garment factory for a wage they could never earn at home. Instead, the laborers found themselves in a dingy compound surrounded by barbed wire in American Samoa where they both lived and worked. They lived in cramped dirty quarters and were fed only broth and rice. There was very little work or pay. Managers also confiscated their passports. When the workers spoke up, asking about their pay and freedom, they were beaten and threatened with deportation. The owner, Kil Soo Lee, was sentenced to forty years in federal prison and ordered to pay $1.8 million in restitution. To date, it is the largest successful human trafficking prosecution in the United States.[2]

Commercial Sex

Justin Strom, age twenty-seven, of Lorton, Virginia, was sentenced to forty years in prison for leading the Crips gang in the sex trafficking of high school girls. Over six years, gang members attempted to recruit more than eight hundred teenage girls using fake social media profiles, contacts within high schools, and promises the girls would earn a lot of money from stripping. Once recruited, the girls were forced into prostitution through physical force, including chokings, beatings, and rape; bodyguards accompanying them to appointments throughout Northern Virginia; and drugs and alcohol to keep them compliant.[3]

Defining Trafficking

Human trafficking is also referred to as forced labor, labor trafficking, forced prostitution, sex trafficking, slavery, and modern slavery. We tend to use the term *human trafficking* unless there is need to distinguish between labor trafficking and sex trafficking. Controlling definitions vary depending upon your work—for example, whether you work as a district attorney, U.S. attorney, International Labour Organization (ILO) advisor, civil attorney, immigration attorney, or policy advisor. Those specific definitions are included throughout the book as necessary.

As an alternative to formal, legal definitions, it may be helpful to begin with an easily understandable, good working definition:

Human trafficking is holding another in compelled service using whatever means necessary, be it physical or psychological.

Sometimes human trafficking is used as an umbrella term broken down into distinct categories:

- Forced labor or labor trafficking often involves the use of a scheme, plan, or pattern, creating a climate of fear to make people believe there would be serious consequences if they attempted to leave their workplace.
- Domestic servitude is the forced labor of domestic workers, performing duties such as cleaning the home, cooking, and caring for children.
- Sex trafficking is the use of force, fraud, or coercion to compel an individual into commercial sex. Under U.S. law, if the individual is under age eighteen, force, fraud, or coercion is not required. It is manifested in street prostitution, brothels, massage parlors, and escort services.
- Debt bondage, debt servitude, or bonded labor is holding a person in compelled service by a real or alleged debt. Traffickers use debt as a coercive scheme to trap their victims—they create the initial debt through inflated recruitment and transportation fees. They may add to it by charging unreasonable amounts for room and board and other needs. They may also supposedly apply wages directly to this seemingly never-ending debt that must be paid before the worker can be released. In parts of Africa and Southeast Asia, people are also enslaved by ancestral debts.
- Child soldiering comprises boys and girls recruited or used by an armed force or armed group in any capacity, including as fighters, cooks, porters, messengers, spies, or for sexual purposes and marriage. In some countries, the use of child soldiers is systematic and pervasive.

The Scale of the Problem

Human trafficking claims an estimated twenty-one million people world-wide according to the ILO; other estimates range up to thirty million.[4] Because the ILO statistic is the one most often supported by governments and civil society alike as being the most rigorously produced and reliable estimates of trafficking made to date, we choose to rely on the twenty-one million estimate.

An estimated 78 percent of those being trafficked are held in labor trafficking and 22 percent in sex trafficking.[5] This statistic is enormously important given the widely held impression that all human trafficking is sex trafficking, when in fact sex trafficking claims less than one-quarter of trafficking victims, while labor trafficking claims more than three-quarters. Statistics guide policy, resources, and identification efforts. Therefore, a belief that sex trafficking is more prevalent means three-quarters of the victims remain hidden and unassisted.

According to the ILO, 55 percent of all trafficked persons are women and girls, and 45 percent are men and boys. Women and girls comprise the vast majority of sex trafficking victims at 98 percent, though 2 percent are men and boys. Women constitute 42 percent of labor trafficking victims compared to 58 percent for men. These statistics contradict the general impression of human trafficking; however, their use is critical to allocate resources and design identification efforts.

There are no reliable figures estimating the number of victims in the United States. The ILO did not provide statistics by country; the United States is grouped with the other developed economies, including Australia, Canada, and the European Union, with an estimated total of 1.5 million

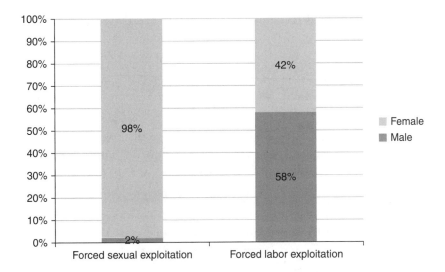

enslaved. The U.S. government no longer publishes or stands behind its earlier estimates. Unfortunately, those and other old and disavowed estimates are still in circulation. To make matters more confusing, media and nongovernmental organization (NGO) reports sometimes make claims that a particular state or city has the largest human trafficking problem or highest number of victims. Not all cities and states measure human trafficking, and certainly even those that attempt to measure it do not use a consistent definition or the same metrics. Therefore, these assertions are unreliable. Other estimates have been based on decades-old publications. The best data from which we can glean any numbers of human trafficking in the United States comes largely from service providers, who in Fiscal Year 2013 assisted just over one thousand confirmed trafficked persons.[6] Consider what the estimate could be knowing that we identify less than one-tenth of a percent annually.

Trafficked Persons in the United States

Trafficked persons identified in the United States have been male, female, and transgender; child and adult; U.S. citizen and foreign national; undocumented and documented. Their education has ranged from no schooling to master's degrees and specialized certifications such as nursing and teaching. Just as varied are their socioeconomic background, religion, and race.

Such diverse backgrounds paint such a broad picture that it may seem difficult to narrow in on a profile that would aid in identification. But that is precisely the point. If the profile of a trafficked person is narrow, we will continue to miss finding and assisting the vast majority of them.

Federal and state data continue to indicate a disproportionate number of investigations and prosecutions for sex trafficking, in spite of far greater numbers of victims in labor trafficking cases. One reason for this disparity is that one labor trafficking case in agriculture or a factory can have hundreds of victims, whereas sex trafficking cases tend to have smaller numbers of victims. For example, six federally prosecuted cases over a decade, all involving Florida agriculture, identified a total of more than one thousand victims.

A handful of trends can be observed about human trafficking in the United States.[7] A word of caution on these trends—they are based on extremely limited law enforcement data. We know that less than 1 percent of victims are identified and few come forward to law enforcement, so this data is not necessarily representative of the extent of the problem, but only what law enforcement has been able to uncover so far. However, it is the only data we have. Labor traffickers of U.S. citizens have successfully recruited people who are homeless, mentally ill, or drug addicted, all of which lend themselves to dependence on the trafficker. Sex trafficking of U.S. citizens has primarily involved minors who are runaways, homeless, gang recruited, or in foster care; Native American minors have also been sex trafficked and, as with other crimes, encounter jurisdictional barriers in identification and prosecution. Foreign national victims are both undocumented and visaholders with permission to be in the United States as domestic workers for diplomats, temporary skilled and agricultural workers, student exchange visitors, and workers on overseas government contracts. Most recently, the top countries of origin for foreign victims were Mexico, the Philippines, Thailand, Honduras, Guatemala, India, and El Salvador, but to date victims identified in the United States have hailed from more than seventy-five different countries.[8]

The Industries Where Human Trafficking Is Found

Confirmed human trafficking cases worldwide have occurred primarily within three broad areas:

1. Raw materials extraction and harvesting, including mining; fishing; and agricultural planting, picking, and packaging;
2. Manufacturing, including converting the raw materials into products such as garments, electronics, and bricks; and
3. Services, including child care, cleaning, landscaping, and commercial sex.

These categories are quite expansive, meaning that trafficking has been uncovered in nearly every industry imaginable. Here are a few illustrative examples from the United States.

Agriculture

Florida—Five individuals, four of whom were related, transported undocumented Mexican and Guatemalan nationals to agricultural fields in Immokalee, Florida. These traffickers forced the farmworkers into harvesting in tomato fields through beatings and ongoing threats of further physical harm and by creating and escalating their debt while paying them very little. To prevent their escape, traffickers locked the workers in trucks at night in the sweltering Florida heat. Two traffickers were sentenced to twelve years in prison and owe more than $240,000 in restitution to the victims.[9]

Manufacturing

Oklahoma—John Pickle, Inc., a Tulsa, Oklahoma–based oil industry parts manufacturer, recruited fifty-two skilled laborers from India. These welders, engineers, and electricians were promised certain wages and work conditions, but soon found themselves treated differently from the non-Indian laborers. The Indian workers received $1.00 to $3.17 per hour, while non-Indian employees made $14 per hour for the same work. Pickle managers confiscated the Indian workers' passports and forced these workers to live in a makeshift warehouse dormitory, watched by an armed guard. Managers subjected the Indian workers to ethnic slurs, food rationing, intimidation, and degrading tasks. A federal judge ordered $1.24 million in restitution in this case brought by the U.S. Equal Employment Opportunity Commission (EEOC).[10]

Domestic Servitude

Washington, DC—Alan Mzengi, a Tanzanian diplomat, and his wife, Stella, recruited a domestic worker to live in and clean their Washington, DC, home for monthly wages of $900. The worker's contract also stated she would work eight-hour days and would have two days off per week, receive two weeks' paid vacation annually, and collect overtime pay for additional hours worked. However, upon the worker's arrival, the Mzengis seized her passport and contract and forced her to work seventeen-hour days without a day off. The Mzengis emotionally and physically abused her, failed to pay her, prevented her from accessing medical care, and always accompanied her. The Mzengis failed to answer a civil complaint, and a default judgment was entered for the plaintiff.[11]

Prostitution

Illinois—Alex Campbell ran several massage parlors in Chicago, Illinois. He recruited undocumented foreign women from Ukraine and Belarus by claiming he could provide them with a job in his massage parlors, give them a place to live, and help them to obtain immigration status. He also feigned romantic relationships with them. He then branded them with a tattoo, took their passports, forced them to work long hours, did not pay them, and gave them little to no food. He forced one into prostitution and extorted $25,000 from another by threatening to send a sexually explicit video to her parents in Belarus. Campbell was sentenced to life in prison, having been found guilty of forced labor, harboring illegal aliens for financial gain, confiscating passports and other immigration documents to force the victims to work, and sex trafficking by force and extortion.[12]

Elder Care

California—Evelyn Pelayo recruited workers in the Philippines for two elder care facilities she owned in Long Beach, California. She paid $6,000 for each person she had smuggled into the country but then charged each of them smuggling fees of $12,000 to be paid off through their work over at least ten years. She confiscated their passports and threatened to contact immigration officials to have them deported if they tried to escape or told anyone about their working conditions. They worked up to twenty-four hours every day, only receiving minimal wages.[13]

Country Clubs and Hotels

Florida—Sophia Manuel and Alfonso Baldonado Jr., owners of Quality Staffing Services Corporation, recruited thirty-nine Filipino nationals for work at country clubs and hotels throughout South Florida. The company managers forced the workers to live in overcrowded, unsanitary conditions with insufficient food and water, confiscated their passports and then threatened them with arrest and deportation, and accompanied them at all times. Indebted before they even arrived in the United States, the workers received little to no pay for the work they did at the country clubs and hotels. After their guilty pleas, Manuel was sentenced to six years and six months and Baldonado to four years and three months.[14]

Restaurants

California—Trans Bay Steel, Inc., sponsored forty-eight skilled Thai welders on H-2B visas to retrofit the San Francisco–Oakland Bay Bridge. Contractors Kota Manpower Company and Hi Cap, Inc., managed the process. The contractors promised the workers wages six times higher than what the workers could earn in Thailand. In order to accept the job, the workers paid exorbitant fees to recruiting companies, creating a crushing indebtedness. Upon arrival, only nine worked as welders. The remaining workers instead worked in Kota- and Hi Cap–owned restaurants and other menial jobs. The contractors confiscated workers' passports and threatened the workers with arrest if they left. The workers were confined to small, shabby apartments without electricity, gas, or water and were forced to work without pay. The EEOC settled the case with Trans Bay Steel, Inc., for an estimated $1.4 million.[15]

Janitorial Services

Multiple Mid-Atlantic States—The Botsvynyuk brothers recruited villagers from their native Ukraine, promising them a salary of $700 to $800 per month, free room and board, and free transportation. Upon arrival, the men and women were told that instead they would have to work without pay to cover their recruitment and transportation debt of up to $50,000 cleaning Wal-Mart, Target, Kmart, Safeway, and other retail stores, along with homes and offices in Pennsylvania, Maryland, Delaware, New York, and New Jersey. Workers testified that the brothers raped, threatened, and beat them. When some workers escaped, the brothers threatened family members in Ukraine with mutilation, rape, and death if the workers did not return or pay off their debts. One brother received a life sentence and the other was sentenced to twenty years in prison.[16]

The Numbers[17]

- Estimates of human trafficking worldwide range from 20.9 to 30 million people.
- Of the millions enslaved, 44,758 were identified in 2013, less than 1 percent.
- In 2013, the number of victims identified globally decreased from 46,570 to 44,758. The most ever identified in a given year is 49,105 in 2009.
- The ILO estimates that of all trafficked persons 68 percent are held in forced labor exploitation, 22 percent in forced sexual exploitation, and 10 percent in state-imposed forced labor.
- In 2013, the number of criminal convictions of traffickers globally increased slightly from 4,746 to 5,776.
- More people are held in labor trafficking than in sex trafficking, yet of the 5,776 global criminal convictions of traffickers, 5,306 were sex traffickers and just 470 were labor traffickers.
- The ILO estimates that women and girls constitute 44 percent of all those in forced labor and 98 percent of all those in sex trafficking, whereas men and boys make up 56 percent of those in forced labor and 2 percent of those in sex trafficking.
- According to the ILO, 74 percent of trafficked persons are adults and 26 percent are children, defined as under the age of eighteen.
- Globally, 56 percent of trafficked persons are enslaved in a country other than their own; 29 percent are enslaved in the area where they normally reside; and 15 percent are enslaved elsewhere within their own country.
- More than 140 countries criminalize all forms of human trafficking.

Root Causes

Determining causation of a problem is essential to addressing it. That is the reason for many efforts to define the "root causes" of human trafficking. Depending on your frame of reference, there are a few different ways to view what the root causes are. One is that traffickers are the root cause because they seek profit via exploitation; they employ specific tactics to recruit and then compel labor or commercial sex. This puts the blame squarely on the responsible individuals. It does not blame the victims for having a characteristic that made them vulnerable and without which the trafficker would not have targeted them. It also demands a criminal justice response to investigate and prosecute the traffickers.

Another view is that there are broad, global systemic issues that create circumstances that make people more susceptible to human trafficking. Certain factors both push and draw an individual to migrate across a border or across the country. The major push factor of course is a lack of employment opportunities, and the major pull factor is the availability of a job elsewhere, which makes individuals to think about rural to urban migration or moving from developing to developed economies. Particularly when stories are circulating about a friend or neighbor who migrated and is doing well and sending money home, the pull becomes stronger. These are economic migrants. Pushing other individuals are widespread poverty, unavailability of education, armed conflict, climate instability, political repression, discrimination in various forms, or gender-based violence. The lure or pull of migration—economic opportunity, education, safety, self-determination, and peace—then is the opposite of the push factors.

These issues are complex. We cannot blame, for example, migration for human trafficking or limit migration in order to address trafficking, although we can take steps to ensure safe, educated migration. For example, approved U.S. visa applicants receive a booklet that describes their rights as visa holders and provides a hotline number if they need any assistance while in the United States; hundreds have called the hotline number to report contract violations and some have reported human trafficking. Similarly, we cannot claim that if we end war, global warming, and discrimination, we will end human trafficking, but we can look to see what additional protections we can provide to refugees, internally displaced persons, and stateless persons.

In other words, trafficking prevention requires narrower, targeted responses. For example, traffickers can easily threaten temporary foreign workers on H-2B visas with deportation because if the workers leave their employer, they are out of immigration status; they are tied to their one employer. The prevention response requires us to look for the vulnerability of various visa categories based on how traffickers are abusing them and then to respond appropriately. As another example, trafficked girls are often recruited while in foster care. Understanding that foster care may be a push factor, the Illinois state government revamped its child welfare system. Because root causes of trafficking overlap with so many other issues, anyone working within any of these intersecting fields, such as child welfare professionals, can look to integrate anti-trafficking-specific solutions where possible.

One systemic issue giving rise to human trafficking is the widespread consumer demand for inexpensive goods and the corresponding supply of those goods, fueling the need for sustained, cheap labor, sometimes only achievable at the expense of the workers. Another factor is the nearly impossible production schedules demanded by brands that suppliers can only meet, again, at the expense of the workers.[18] In order to maintain an often razor's edge profit margin, brands select suppliers and maintain factories in countries where wages are low, among other things. In these locations, worker protection can be weak, and regulation and oversight can be minimal. The best examples are the concentration of electronics factories in China and across Asia as well as garment factories in Bangladesh.

Another form of demand stems from the need for large numbers of migrant laborers for big projects in locations without sufficient worker protections. Nowhere is this more evident than the situation of migrant workers in Qatar, brought to build the infrastructure for the 2022 FIFA World Cup. Qatar's workforce is already made up of 94 percent migrant workers, and an additional one million workers are required to complete the massive construction and infrastructure projects for the World Cup.[19] Human Rights Watch has been closely following and reporting on the abuses, exploitation, and claims of trafficking linked to exorbitant recruitment fees and a restrictive immigration program.[20] In another example, the planned U.S. military buildup in Guam will bring thousands of foreign migrant laborers to the island for construction and the risk of human trafficking because there is no existing infrastructure that can support that number of workers. Prevention, therefore, is in the planning for everything from housing to social services and immigration to labor recruitment.

Root causes are complicated and nuanced, shedding light on why trafficking occurs and what targeted prevention responses are required. As lawyers, we are consumers, corporate counsel, policy makers, legal service providers, prosecutors, and more—all with the ability to craft solutions to address these causes.

Traffickers' Tactics

Popular culture would have us believe that traffickers are sheiks abducting American teenagers in Paris with Liam Neeson charging in to save the day. As discussed before, just as there is no single profile of a trafficked person, there is no single profile of a trafficker. As indicated by the few examples presented in this chapter alone, traffickers are citizens and foreign nationals, pimps, intimate partners, labor brokers, gang members, diplomats, subcontractors, company owners, and the neighboring family next door.

- Traffickers may be contractors and subcontractors in the corporate supply chain, whether at construction sites, at a farm or mine where the raw materials originate, or in a factory that manufactures, assembles, and packages the goods and products. They may be contractors providing services to businesses, such as landscaping, janitorial, and moving.
- They may be part of a large and sophisticated transnational organized crime syndicate, a small local business owner, or a private citizen with a domestic worker in his or her home.
- Traffickers may be members of a trafficked person's family, have a close personal relationship, or come from the same community.
- They may be brokers or other intermediaries assisting in the recruitment, document forging, smuggling, supervision, or transportation of workers. They may be regulated and unregulated labor recruitment agencies, even including government-run agencies.

Common among this diverse set of individuals is the desire to make a profit through free or low-cost labor without care or consideration for the worker. Whether they charge fees leading to indebtedness, undercompensate for services, provide inadequate housing and food, or deny access to health care, these traffickers use these tactics to make more money at the expense of another.

One of the more common questions we hear is, "Why didn't she or he just leave?" At first it can seem so implausible that someone could withstand horrendous treatment and not seek help at the first chance or run away. Yet the answer unlocks an understanding of what human trafficking really is as well as its devastating effects. Traffickers use force, fraud, and coercion.

Force

Especially when referred to as modern slavery, human trafficking conjures images of chains, handcuffs, locked doors, barbed wire, and beatings. Those are the most vivid examples of force because they are physically confining a person to a certain space or physically harming that person. In the United States, we have seen many examples of force used to compel service.

Physical Assaults—Traffickers have used beatings, dislocating or breaking bones, stabbing, strangling, burns, and more to compel labor and services. These assaults serve the same purpose as barbed wire and chains, conveying a trafficker's overt control over workers, making them fear another assault, and breaking the workers' spirit. In one particularly brutal case, sex trafficker "T-rex" Yarbrough would violently attack any victim who refused to perform a commercial sex act, including beating them with crow bars, padlocks and chains, belts, and wooden coat hangers, throwing them down stairs, smashing their heads in car doors, burning their legs with irons, and scalding them with hot water.[21] He even beat one victim, pregnant with his child, so badly that he induced her premature labor. In other trafficking cases, pimps have branded their victims with tattoos to demonstrate ownership; they have forced birth control and abortions. They have forced drug use to overcome resistance and facilitate addictions that must be paid for through their services. Andrew Blane Fields first enabled his victims' addiction to oxycodone and morphine and then purposefully subjected them to the physical withdrawal symptoms in order to force them to perform more commercial sex acts.[22]

Sexual Violence—Traffickers use sexual violence as initiation into prostitution, punishment, or breaking the spirit to ensure continual compliance. The examples used to compel labor abound—women in domestic servitude who endure intruders in their room every night, farmworkers in the fields or in employer-owned housing, men and women in manufacturing, women in entertainment clubs, and men at sea for months on fishing vessels.

Threats of Force—Threats of physical force can be just as powerful. When rape or physical assault is used to punish one worker, it intimidates other workers and the trafficker never has to utter a word. Other traffickers are quite explicit that if a person seeks help, tries to escape, contacts family, refuses to work, or otherwise disobeys a rule, there will be physical consequences. Traffickers convincingly threaten harm to others, either another worker or a family member. For those with family members who live far away and whose location is known to a trafficker, such threats of harm can be particularly effective: a trafficked person is already likely isolated and has no way to warn or protect the family member from this risk. In many of our cases, the trafficker threatened to harm a family member back in the country of origin. These threats are credible because traffickers may work with recruiters overseas and may be familiar with the local community and family members.

Surveillance—Just as effective as barbed wire can be the sense and often the reality that someone is always watching. The crew bosses in agriculture. Armed guards around a factory perimeter. Bouncers at a strip club. Security cameras, whether operational or not. At one massage parlor raid in Washington, DC, there was a video camera at every exit and in the small room with mattresses on the floor where the women slept; the women later explained that they were watched all the time and never permitted to go outside alone. Some trafficked persons may not be physically isolated but if permitted in public are always accompanied and transported. One of our domestic servitude clients accompanied the family to religious services and that was the only time she was ever outside the family home. Even when allowed to go home, some victims are continually monitored.

Physical Labor—Some types of strenuous physical labor can be a manifestation of force, which a number of our clients experienced. Some work is extremely arduous. Other times, working long hours, often without breaks or a day off, can be grueling and physically debilitating. One client described to us working eighteen-hour days, cleaning a house, prepping for and cleaning after dinner parties, and being on call through the night for an infant. Traffickers also use the duration or nature of the work as both a punishment and a reward—harder, longer, or more hazardous work for anyone resisting and easier work with breaks for anyone following the rules.

Malnutrition—Traffickers have also used food as punishment and reward. There are cases in which traffickers deny food for days to weaken their victims so they will finally submit, offering them food only after. We have represented clients who worked in factories subsisting for more than a year on nothing but vegetable broth and occasionally rice. We have also represented domestic workers who were only permitted to eat the family's leftovers.

Fraud

As we know, fraud is the misrepresentation of a material fact. Traffickers use fraud and deception primarily as a recruitment tool. Remember, for example, the Vietnamese garment workers who were promised sunny beaches and then were faced with an enclosed compound.

While some trafficked persons are abducted, the vast majority are looking for economic opportunity in their hometown, a nearby town, across the country, or in another country. They use traditional recruitment methods: newspapers, internet listings, and word of mouth. In many areas of the world, labor recruiters or labor brokers recruit workers for specific projects. These intermediaries present all of the information about the job opportunity, including the type of work, location, pay, days off, working conditions, housing, immigration requirements, and fees.

Unfortunately, bait and switch is a common tactic. People agree and sign on for new economic opportunities based on oral promises and even signed contracts, but after committing, a different reality awaits:

- A Russian company operating ice cream trucks near Kansas City, Missouri, promised a group of Ukrainian college students $10,000 to $15,000 for their summer work. Instead, the students earned less than minimum wage and were forced to work thirteen hours a day, seven days a week.[23]

- An Indonesian domestic worker held a contract stating she would be paid $1,300 monthly for her work six days a week, eight hours per day, but after arriving in the United States worked every day for far more than eight hours and her only pay was $160 wired to her family in Indonesia monthly.[24]
- More than six Vietnamese men and women were promised education and marriages to U.S. citizens but were put to work in a wedding boutique in Arizona.[25]
- In numerous cases, young women are promised work as waitresses, dancers, or masseuses, only to later be told that they must perform sexual services in brothels. Others are recruited for commercial sex but compensation and living circumstances are misrepresented.

Relying on what they think is a legitimate opportunity, trafficked persons may also not realize that they have been provided false identification documents. They may also not anticipate unsafe border crossings, differing job conditions, and an expectation that they will perform unlawful or criminal acts.

Sex traffickers have often posed as a boyfriend or a parental figure who lavishes attention, gifts, and promises. In cases of U.S. citizen minors, the trafficker may be a recruiter posing as a boyfriend or girlfriend, who then delivers the minor to a pimp or a larger crime syndicate boss. In multiple cases involving young Mexican women, the traffickers promised marriage, wealth, and life together in the United States.[26] These girls and women are often introduced into prostitution, presented in some cases as the only way the women and their trafficker can financially make their start together, and in other cases the trafficker uses violence.

Once defrauded, trafficked persons feel compelled to stay for a range of reasons, including the cost of returning home, fear of violating a contract, shame from being duped or because of the industry in which they have been working and acts they have performed, and the economic and other barriers that persist at home, potentially putting a trafficked person in a worse condition upon return. The initial fraud that ensnared them can then be coupled with physical force and coercion to ensure their continued labor.

Coercion

Psychological coercion has proven to be just as powerful as physical force and used more often, creating invisible barriers to a trafficked person's escape. It contributes to the trafficked person's feeling completely help-less, ashamed, having no control, and having no choice but to do what the trafficker says. The trafficker's goal is to break the psyche of the trafficked person and create a climate of fear that keeps the individual trapped, hopeless, and without help.

Withholding Identity Documents and Making Threats—Traffickers confiscate identity documents, including passports and other immigra-tion documents, required for workers to prove their lawful work status in the country and to legally exit the country. Document withholding can be coupled with related threats:

- "If you leave this job, you will have no legal status in this country. You can be picked up, jailed, and deported."
- "One phone call to immigration officials and I can have you arrested, jailed, and deported."
- "Do you know what law enforcement does to illegal immigrants?"

Trafficked persons often see implicit threats in the act of withholding documents, not even requiring a verbal threat. Most do not know that in the United States, it is a crime for someone to withhold another's docu-mentation. Trafficked persons fear that law enforcement will see them, instead of the trafficker, as the criminal.

Using Criminal or Unlawful Acts Against Them—Traffickers may have smuggled their victims into the country or obtained fake passports or fraudulent visas, with or without their knowledge and potentially in violation of immigration laws. They also may have forced their victims to carry drugs with them across the border, engage in prostitution, or per-form other criminal acts. Traffickers can then hold their victims' perfor-mance of criminal or unlawful acts against them to ensure they will not seek help from law enforcement. Traffickers may threaten to tell young women's parents so that the women are afraid to reach out for help. They may continually threaten to report their victims to law enforcement for arrest and imprisonment if they talk to anyone or try to escape. One of our clients entered on a tourist visa believing she had to work for an interim period before she could earn an employment-based visa, only to later be told that she was in violation of the visa for working and could be reported to immigration authorities at any time. Many clients in sex trafficking believed they were coming to work in restaurants and bars. Once they were in the United States, they knew if they reported their experience, they would be arrested for prostitution.

Inhumane Treatment—Traffickers demean their victims in order to reinforce a power dynamic. Two Nigerian domestic workers in Georgia were forced to bathe out of a bucket, eat spoiled food, hand-wash clothing, and cut the lawn with a long knife—all this despite having appliances available.[27]

- *Malnutrition*—There are multiple domestic servitude cases in which the worker was only allowed to eat the family's leftover scraps from their plates and a factory case where workers were only ever fed broth.
- *Unsafe living conditions*—Condemned structures, inadequate ventilation or heating and cooling, and infestations can all lead to serious physical harm and ailments in addition to the reinforcement that trafficked persons are not worthy of a decent living space.
- *Inadequate protection from hazards*—In sex trafficking, lack of condoms can lead to STDs and HIV/AIDS. In other situations, traffickers do not provide adequate clothing for extreme temperatures or protection from working conditions such as pesticides.
- *Verbal abuse*—Traffickers also break down their victims through derogatory slurs, insults, and name calling.

Shaming—The fear of rejection by family or community can be so strong that trafficked persons will continue to work, not complain, not try to escape, and become resigned to a life of exploitation or trafficking. Exploiting these feelings, traffickers sometimes make overt shaming comments, like "What will your family think of you after we tell them you have had sex with all of these men?" In other instances, traffickers know they need not even say anything to implicitly suggest that exposing the truth would bring shame to them and their families. Nearly all of our sex trafficking clients were terrified of their families' learning about the commercial sex. Others in both labor and sex trafficking feel the shame of returning home empty-handed after filling their family's heads with hopes and dreams. Family members who were expecting debts to be paid off, kids to go to school, and generally a better life will be bitterly disappointed and that weighs heavily on the mind of the trafficked person.

Blackmail—Particularly in sex trafficking cases, traffickers may have photographed or videoed their victims performing commercial sex acts, whether for prostitution or pornography. With photos and videos in hand, they may threaten to send them to family and friends or publish them publicly.

Social Isolation—Isolation, whether physical, cultural, or linguistic, creates a barrier that prevents trafficked people from even exploring the possibility of getting help out of the situation. Furthermore, it can make trafficked people believe that no one from their earlier life cares and has the capacity to help. Traffickers purposefully cut off their victims' access to the community.

- *Communication*—Sometimes trafficked persons have no access to radio, television, or newspapers. They may not have access to phones, mail, or internet to communicate with family and friends.
- *Physical*—Traffickers use a number of tactics to physically isolate individuals. Initially, they may transport trafficked persons to unknown locations. Traffickers also control transportation, shuttling individuals from living quarters to worksites and even accompanying them offsite. Especially when trafficked persons are new to the area, they may not know where they are or how to get around. Traffickers also place trafficked persons in rural and remote locations, making an escape improbable. Traffickers may even move locations periodically to keep victims disoriented and to prevent trafficked persons from developing trusting relationships or resources in the region. They may prohibit attendance at religious services, access to medical care, or a grocery store visit, unless accompanied.

- *Cultural and linguistic*—Simply being in a foreign country can be overwhelming and daunting. A trafficked person may not have the language skills or knowledge about his or her new country to know how to access help. In one case, the trafficker of a foreign domestic worker told her that Americans would pretend to help her and then kill her and sell her organs.[28] Many of our foreign-born clients told us that they have no 911 or free assistance from nonprofit organizations in their country, so it never occurred to them to seek help in that way. They also consistently said that they could not rely on police protection in their own country, so they had no expectation that U.S. law enforcement would respond any differently.

Religious and Cultural Beliefs—In some instances, traffickers take advantage of a person's religion and culture, which are so intrinsic to our identities. More than twenty West African girls were forced to work up to fourteen-hour days in hair and nail salons in New Jersey by traffickers who threatened to put voodoo curses on them, which was a very credible threat according to their cultural traditions.[29] Sex traffickers used witch doctors to threaten Guatemalan girls with a curse on them and their family members if they tried to escape.[30] Consider a trafficker's shaming of deeply religious people who might be condemned for participating in commercial sex by their religious leaders and community.

Economic Coercion—Traffickers most easily compel those whose savings are depleted, whose houses are mortgaged, and whose personal debts were incurred to pay for recruitment fees. They seize on those with families financially dependent on the worker and impose excessive fees and costs to accelerate debt. Imagine you are an agricultural worker in a remote area forced to buy everything from the company store at inflated prices, which adds to the debt.[31] What if you were threatened with a $25,000 penalty if you left your employment?[32] In what is a common scenario, traffickers in western New York deducted supposed charges for food, housing, transportation, and other items from migrant laborers' paychecks, leaving the workers with almost nothing and continually indebted; they were told they could not leave until their debts were paid.[33] Playing on the power and cultural dynamic, traffickers manage to validate these debts, despite their being unlawful. Many trafficked persons believe they will be killed or arrested if they try to leave without paying the debt. As a result, economic coercion, primarily through debt bondage, can prevent trafficked persons from seeking alternative employment.

Bonding and Dependency—Emotional connections that develop between traffickers and their victims are yet another reason victims feel they cannot leave or seek help. Somewhat akin to the Stockholm syndrome, whereby victims bond with their captor in hostage situations, traffickers create similar bonds with trafficked persons. In other situations, traffickers recruit girls by feigning romantic relationships and then the girls perform services with the expectation of love or support in exchange. It can be very difficult for the girls to later accept that the relationship was fake, so they defend their trafficker, not wanting any harm to come to the alleged boyfriend. We have also had clients who were recruited or held by family members, and there was still fierce loyalty to the family and an extreme reluctance to pursue any legal resource that would be detrimental to that family member. Domestic workers often feel very responsible for any children in their care, not wanting to be a witness for the prosecution if that means taking a child's mother or father away.

Misconceptions About the Term *Human Trafficking*

Throughout this chapter we have described and provided examples of human trafficking as one person compelling another physically or psychologically—through force, fraud, and coercion—to work or to perform a commercial sex act. It is equally helpful to understand what trafficking is not and where lines are blurred and contested, especially because trafficking has long been confused with other crimes and forms of exploitation. Misconceptions and misunderstandings divert our attention, efforts, and resources. In this book, we are particularly motivated to improve your ability to identify human trafficking, so the more questions we can anticipate and the more potential confusion we can address, the more successful your efforts may be.

Movement—The term *trafficking* makes us think of arms and drugs, where it does indeed mean the movement and sale of those goods. However, human trafficking does not mean or require movement or travel. Globally, 29 percent of trafficked persons are enslaved in the area where they normally reside.[34] Again, the focus is on the compelled labor or service.

Smuggling—Human trafficking is also not smuggling. Human smuggling is the unlawful transportation of a person across an international border, potentially a criminal and immigration violation. An estimated 56 percent of trafficked persons are enslaved in a country other than their own, so they crossed a border at some point either lawfully or unlawfully. How they crossed the border is not relevant to trafficking, only whether they were compelled to work or perform a commercial sex act. The confusion lies in the facts of cases when traffickers smuggle people as part of a larger human trafficking crime. For example, the Soto brothers and four accomplices engaged in both smuggling and forced labor.[35] They brought undocumented persons across the Rio Grande River, transporting them to Houston, Texas, then extorted money from their families before releasing them. However, they also held four women at a safe house, forcing them to work as domestic servants by day and raped and beat them at night.

Prostitution—U.S. law makes a distinction between prostitution and sex trafficking, with sex trafficking requiring the use of force, fraud, or coercion to compel the performance of a commercial sex act or involving a person under age eighteen. Because there are many adults in commercial sex not experiencing force, fraud, or coercion, raids of commercial sex establishments often fail to uncover sex trafficking.

Child Labor—Worldwide, there are an estimated 215 million child laborers. These are children under the age of eighteen performing work that is dangerous or harmful in some way and that interferes with their schooling. Without an education, the cycle of poverty continues. A portion of this 215 million—approximately 4.5 million—constitutes forced

child labor. Most children who fall within the child labor definition are
not compelled into labor and are therefore not trafficked.

Low-Wage Labor—Low wages may be an indicator of human trafficking but alone do not constitute trafficking. Some trafficked persons are
paid their contracted salary, even a living wage; other trafficked persons
are paid nothing. Conversely, many people work in the formal and informal economy in low-wage jobs; some of them are compelled into service
and therefore trafficked; many more are not. But the amount of wages
is not the determining factor for human trafficking. Many people out of
economic necessity accept jobs that are low paying, unsafe, or physically
demanding. It may be difficult for them to find another job, but if one
were available, they would be free. This freedom and mobility differentiates them from trafficked workers, who would be unable to seek and
accept another job.

The Impact on Trafficked Persons

It is hard to imagine what trafficked persons experience and how it affects them for the rest of their lives. Human trafficking is devastating to
an individual physically, financially, and emotionally. Putting yourself in
their shoes can help you provide better services, seek additional services
and referrals as needed, and even help identify trafficked persons. There
are service organizations throughout the country that can provide case
management and additional services.

Financial Consequences

Many trafficked persons were initially looking for jobs and opportunities
to earn money, send children to school, and pay down debt. Their financial needs remain and may even be more acute after the trafficking experience. Securing employment, therefore, becomes a priority out of financial
necessity, to make a new start, and to rebuild self-esteem.

Yet for many trafficked persons, this can be a difficult process. They
may lack educational, vocational, and language skills. Foreign-born
trafficked persons may lack legal permission to work or English language skills to earn a fair wage. Even prior to the trafficking, trafficked

persons may have been homeless, in debt, or lacking education. Sex-trafficked persons may not have any viable work experience as an alternative to commercial sex. Additionally, arrest records related to the trafficking could limit employment options. Given these difficult circumstances, job training and educational programs are therefore critical to assist trafficked persons to build skills to become economically self-sufficient.

Physical Health

To save money and avoid the public eye, not surprisingly, traffickers typically do not provide trafficked persons with access to health care. Injuries inflicted by the traffickers go untreated, the aches and pains of physical labor are endured, broken bones heal incorrectly, and infections from improper medical care may occur. Unless the conditions become particularly acute, traffickers rarely allow a hospital visit.

Traffickers are also extremely unlikely to provide access to other types of health care, so trafficked persons have no regular check-ups and no preventive, vision, dental, or reproductive care. One former client who had been recently freed from trafficking suffered tremendous headaches every day. A simple eye exam revealed that glasses would relieve this pain that she endured for more than a year. Another former client also suffering from headaches had four teeth pulled to finally relieve his pain. Yet another former client learned she had two sexually transmitted infections (STIs) but was able to begin treatment immediately once free from the trafficker. Pregnancy, HIV/AIDS, and STIs may have all gone untreated.

Chronic conditions may manifest, such as arthritis and back pain from repetitive motion or asthma from poor ventilation. Other illnesses such as hepatitis, tuberculosis, and diabetes may worsen or develop and go undiagnosed. A host of illnesses may arise from substandard living conditions, based on exposure to sewage, unsafe drinking water, and mold.

Substance abuse treatment is sometimes also required when traffickers have forced or encouraged drug and alcohol use. Drugs and alcohol may have been the victims' only payment. Other victims may have had a preexisting dependency issue that initially made them the trafficker's target.

Mental Health

Every trafficking experience is unique, as is the way each person processes and internalizes it. Some victims may feel overwhelmed, embarrassed and ashamed, helpless, fearful, or hopeless. They may have complete lack of trust in others because they were so betrayed and may have extreme fear of others because of the harm they experienced. The ways in which these feelings manifest can be quite varied and may surface when working with a trafficked person.

- *Memory problems*—Recounting the trafficking may be necessary for a criminal investigation, civil suit, or immigration benefits. However, some victims may have difficulty recounting the details of what happened. Gaps in the story from memory loss may be the brain protecting itself from retraumatization.
- *Avoidance*—This is another way in which the brain protects itself. Certain topics, places, and people may be triggers for the trauma to resurface, so they are avoided.
- *Flashbacks*—When negative memories are triggered, the trafficked person is likely to have a flashback. The feeling is so intense and real, it is as if the actual event is relived, which can be debilitating in the moment and thereafter.
- *Overwhelming sadness*—Many suffer from anxiety, depression, and even post-traumatic stress disorder. It can become so incapacitating that it interferes with daily activities and can cause suicidal ideation.
- *Sleep issues*—We have had clients who did not want to get out of bed as well as clients fearful to go to sleep because of nightmares and the potential for the traffickers' retaliation.
- *Physical symptoms*—Mental health issues can often manifest physically, for instance, with high blood pressure, increased heart rate, headaches, body pains, and ulcers.

The treatment is just as varied. Some victims may require medication, individual counseling, and hospitalization. Others may prefer support from their religious community or a small support group.

Conclusion

Undoubtedly you came to this book with some knowledge of human trafficking already, but we hope to have added to your knowledge by briefly illustrating how, why, and where it happens through examples and reliable statistics and information. What we have provided is a glimpse into the devastating crime and human rights abuse that is human trafficking. Hidden in plain sight, men, women, and children are physically and psychologically compelled into work in factories, agriculture, and other industries and into prostitution. Trafficked persons live and work in our communities, producing the goods and services we use every day. The scale is massive with an estimated twenty-one million people enslaved worldwide, 78 percent held in labor trafficking and 22 percent in sex trafficking. It affects every continent, race, age, industry, and sex.

Familiarity with traffickers' methods of force, fraud, and coercion now positions you to better understand both what compels a trafficked person's labor and services and what keeps such persons hidden in plain sight. Trafficked persons cannot leave because of threats, physical and sexual abuse, imposed debts, fear of law enforcement and immigration consequences, unpaid wages, and shame. These methods are what prevent trafficked persons from coming forward—self-identifying—even when they interact with community members or service providers and despite legal protections and services being available to them. This accounts for why identification is currently so low as well as why more people must learn how to identify trafficking.

As an attorney, reading through this first chapter you may have already seen a first glimpse at where your practice area intersects with trafficking. Criminal, corporate, employment, immigration, international, and public interest—these areas of law are all part of the required response.

How Attorneys Are Working on Human Trafficking

Civil Actions
Civil Litigation
Restitution
Federal Circuit Court
    Immigration Appeals
Civil Appellate Cases

Administrative
Public Benefits Claims and
    Appeals
Crime Victim Compensation
    Claims and Appeals
Disability Benefits Claims
    and Appeals
Federal Trafficking Victim
    Certification Requests
Unemployment Compensation
    Claims and Appeals
Workers Compensation Claims
    and Appeals
Employment or Labor
    Administrative Claims
School Expulsion Defense
Bankruptcy

Criminal
State and Federal Prosecution
Victim Witness Advocacy
Defense of Victims Charged as
    Perpetrators
Appeals
Post-conviction Relief

Family Law
Juvenile Dependency Actions
Emancipation
Adoption
Child Custody
Divorce
Name Change
Protective Order

Immigration Law
Humanitarian Parole
Continued Presence Request
U Visa
T Visa
VAWA Self-Petition or
    Cancellation
Special Immigrant Juvenile
    Status
Asylum
Lawful Permanent Residence
Removal Defense
Board of Immigration Appeals
Repatriation
Family Reunification

Corporate
Risk Assessments
Policy Development
Audits
Supply Chain Operations
Training
Philanthropy
Compliance
Public Relations

International
Diplomacy
UN Agency Implementation
Refugee Protection
Human Rights Litigation
Labor Organizing
Multilateral Policy
Project Implementation
Legal Reform
Human Rights Reporting
NGO Advocacy

Other
Academia
U.S. Government Policy
State and Federal Legislation

CHAPTER 2

The Criminal Justice Response

Trafficking in persons is a transnational crime with national implications. To deter international trafficking and bring its perpetrators to justice, nations including the United States must recognize that trafficking is a serious offense. This is done by prescribing appropriate punishment, giving priority to the prosecution of trafficking offenses, and protecting rather than punishing the victims of such offenses.

—Trafficking Victims Protection Act of 2000

The effort to address human trafficking has long been conceptualized using a criminal law paradigm through which traffickers are penalized and victims may be freed and protected. In 2000, Congress enacted the Victims of Trafficking and Violence Protection Act (VTVPA), the United States' first formalized effort to address human trafficking.[1] Adopting the *Three P* model of prevention, protection, and prosecution, Congress sought "to combat trafficking in persons, a contemporary manifestation of slavery whose victims are predominately women and children, to ensure just and effective punishment of traffickers, and to protect their victims."[2] The model has evolved through expansion and implementation of the TVPA over the years since the law's enactment.

Federal and state trafficking laws touch a range of criminal justice issues affecting attorneys contemplating their role in anti-trafficking efforts. In addition to increased criminal penalties for labor and sex trafficking, these laws offer mechanisms for crime victim compensation and protection. Crime victim measures provide services at a critical juncture, often as a victim newly emerges from trafficking or exploitation. They also create a necessary shield of protection intended to encourage victims to cooperate, thereby expanding the efficacy of human trafficking prosecutions. Congress also established a system to monitor the efforts of every country to meet specific minimum standards to eliminate human trafficking. These standards address the rigor of a country's effort to investigate and prosecute human trafficking, among other things.[3] In the wake of the TVPA, states updated and created new trafficking statutes as well.

These laws deter human trafficking, afford victims protection, and provide legal recourse to victims. However, despite the passage of federal and state laws, there still exists an uncomfortably large gap between the amount of human trafficking that continues and the number of trafficking victims who have been identified and who have accessed protections. State and federal human trafficking laws remain underutilized.

Law enforcement and prosecutors cite numerous challenges that may explain this gap. Some local prosecutors report feeling overwhelmed and under-resourced and prefer to turn human trafficking prosecutions to federal authorities,[4] while federal prosecutors similarly encounter resource limitations. Other state and local prosecutors cite untested laws and unclear legal standards, lack of guidance or training on how to use state anti-trafficking laws, and a lack of model prosecutorial tools specific to the anti-trafficking statute as obstacles they face in prosecuting trafficking violations.[5]

In spite of these ongoing challenges, increased attorney expertise on human trafficking criminal laws will increase and improve prosecutions, provide trafficking victims with the protection required to offer meaningful alternatives to being retrafficked, and successfully deter future human trafficking. This chapter addresses the role of the criminal justice system in anti-trafficking efforts, including the distinct and important roles that prosecutors, defense attorneys, victim services attorneys, and judges play at the intersection between criminal law and human trafficking. It offers an overview of criminal laws, systems that interact with the criminal system, and complex interventions required to protect human trafficking victims and prevent human trafficking.

Human Trafficking Task Forces

Human trafficking prosecutions require coordination with a wide range of stakeholders. In many cases, coordination is facilitated by Department of Justice–funded human trafficking task forces. Human trafficking task forces exist to coordinate and enhance the identification, investigation, and prosecution of human trafficking violations. Task forces that offer equal footing to members have the potential to create effective models and protocols that dictate identification and referral, guide effective prosecution, ensure minimum standards for protection, and provide cross-sector training.

Typically one criminal justice agency, the U.S. Attorney's Office, will convene the task force. Throughout this chapter, we discuss the benefits of effective stakeholder collaboration. A purposefully inclusive task force has the following members:

- Local Law Enforcement Agencies
- Federal Law Enforcement Agencies
- Local Prosecutors
- U.S. Attorney's Office
- Local Public Defender Agencies
- Federal Public Defender's Office
- Defense Attorneys' Bar Association
- Anti-Trafficking Victim Services NGOs
- Immigrant Community NGOs
- Tribal Governments (where appropriate)
- Violence Against Women Services NGOs
- Local Government Public Health Agencies
- State Labor Department
- Shelter NGOs
- Worker Rights NGOs

- Local Business Coalitions
- Local Public Benefits Agencies

Task forces allow prosecutors to work closely with a range of stakeholders who identify and refer human trafficking cases. Inconsistent applications of human trafficking definitions result in many victims' going unidentified. Some of the overlooked include male victims, labor trafficking victims, and LGBT-identifying victims. Task forces provide a structure for all stakeholders to apply a uniform definition of human trafficking, which expands identification and leads to prosecutions of cases involving all victims.

Task forces also create and implement policies that may lead to more referrals and prosecutions. For example, if all county public health workers had access to training on human trafficking, they would likely identify more victims from their extensive volume of clients and patients. They might also experience less trepidation in making referrals to victim service providers, who can screen potential victims before referring cases to prosecutors. Task forces also create referral protocols, which are necessary for the rapid-response nature of human trafficking cases.

Finally, a victim-centered criminal justice protocol outlines the various accompanying services and protections needed to coordinate with a prosecution. Prosecutors new to human trafficking may not anticipate the level of victim engagement and protection required for a prosecution to proceed. Without effective planning and service provision to accompany the prosecution, cases are likely to weaken. Federal but also local prosecutors can take advantage of the task force infrastructure to partner with victim service providers. A more extensive discussion of developing protections from the victim services attorney perspective is discussed later in this chapter.

Federal Laws

Federal laws provide the foundation for the prosecution of human trafficking in the United States. With state laws still in a state of evolution, federal prosecutors have led the way in utilizing federal criminal statutes and developing best practices for prosecuting these complex crimes and ensuring victim safety and protection in the course of prosecutions. The federal government coordinates the prosecution of human trafficking cases through the Human Trafficking Prosecution Unit (HTPU) of DOJ's Civil

Rights Division. The HTPU provides technical assistance and coordination with U.S. Attorney's Offices prosecuting federal trafficking cases. It also notably works to develop human trafficking case law in specific areas.

Department of Justice, Human Trafficking Prosecution Unit (HTPU): Coordinated Prosecutions

The HTPU leads efforts to coordinate human trafficking prosecutions by

- partnering with Assistant U.S. Attorneys and law enforcement agencies on investigations and prosecutions,
- ensuring consistent application of criminal anti-trafficking laws,
- directing victim services referrals, and
- coordinating related cases prosecuted in multiple jurisdictions.

Trafficking Victim Protection Act

Federal laws prohibiting human trafficking in the United States are rooted in the Thirteenth Amendment to the United States Constitution, which prohibits involuntary servitude and slavery.[6] Prior to the passage of the TVPA, human trafficking cases had long been prosecuted under federal criminal statutes against peonage, which prohibited holding, returning, or arresting persons with the intent of placing or returning them to peonage[7]; and involuntary servitude, which prohibited knowingly and willfully holding, selling, or bringing persons into the United States for the purpose of forcing them into service or labor.[8]

The TVPA built on these prohibitions and codified several crimes to be utilized against human traffickers. These crimes are broadly known as Chapter 77 offenses.

Forced Labor

Forced labor is defined as[9]

1. knowingly *or* in reckless regard
2. providing, obtaining, *or* benefitting from
3. labor *or* services
4. by means of force *or* threats of force; by means of physical restraint or threats of physical restraint; by means of serious harm or threats of serious harm; by means of abuse or threatened abuse of process;

or by means of any scheme, plan, or pattern causing belief that non-performance of such labor or services would result in serious harm or physical restraint.

The final element is designed to encompass the range of behaviors used to compel people, which often extend beyond physical force. Because so many cases of trafficking are manifested primarily through psychological coercion, prosecutors often frame human trafficking as a scheme, plan, or pattern. Such schemes, plans, or patterns need not involve recruitment or movement. They also need not affect a large number of victims, something often mistakenly perceived to be a forced labor requirement.

Tieu Tran recruited a woman from Vietnam to the United States by promising immigration sponsorship and high wages. Instead, the re-cruited woman was compelled to work long hours in a restaurant to pay down a smuggling debt, without receipt of promised pay. She was intimidated and manipulated due to her undocumented status and English language barriers. Tieu Tran pled guilty to forced labor.[10]

Sex Trafficking
Sex trafficking of children or by force, fraud, or coercion entails

1. acting or financially benefitting from
2. the recruitment, enticement, harboring, transport, providing, ob-taining, or maintaining
3. by means of force, threats of force, fraud, or coercion unless the person is not eighteen years of age
4. to engage the person in a commercial sex act.[11]

Sex trafficking is distinct from prostitution in several significant ways. First, sex trafficking requires a third party. Many people engage in commercial sex acting alone without any pimps.[12] Their participation in commercial sex would likely not satisfy the elements of sex trafficking. Sex trafficking also requires proof that the individual who engaged in a commercial sex act experienced force, fraud, or coercion or was under the age of eighteen. Not all adults engage in commercial sex due to force, fraud, or coercion. Prosecutors therefore must distinguish between commercial sex and sex trafficking.

While sex trafficking in the United States is neither limited to women and girls nor limited to particular races or socioeconomic levels, thus far it is found most often among U.S. Citizen minors and foreign-born adults. Prosecuting sex trafficking of minors requires an understanding of circumstances that lead to trafficking. Traffickers exploit the vulnerabilities of certain minors, including those who are homeless and runaways, those in foster care, and minors who lack family and economic support.[13] Abuse and neglect, lack of positive relationships with adults, parental abuse of alcohol and other substances, a history of emotional, physical, or sexual abuse, and school-related problems create additional vulnerabilities that traffickers target.[14] Despite a narrative that misleadingly describes sex trafficking resulting from abduction, trafficked minors are typically recruited by a boyfriend who evolves into a pimp, sometimes called a *romeo,* or are recruited directly by a pimp.[15]

Among adults, sex trafficking in the United States typically involves foreign-born individuals typically brought to the United States by those benefitting from their participation in commercial sex. These cases pose other unique challenges to prosecutors. Foreign-born sex trafficking victims are typically without lawful immigration status. They are also likely unfamiliar with the immigration protections that may be available to them. Therefore, they may fear immigration enforcement and know that without lawful status, their income-generating options are limited.

It is essential that prosecutors learn to build trust with sex trafficking victims. Those benefitting from the sex trafficking are incentivized to continue to manipulate relationships, often through emotional means. Prosecutors and victim service providers share the challenge of overcoming these controlling relationships, which are often the only relationships a victim has. In addition, sex trafficking victims may be concerned about the stigma of commercial sex, which can only be overcome by prosecutors and victim service providers building a relationship with the victim over time.

Before beginning to prosecute cases, prosecutors' offices should invest in building a collaboration with NGO service providers. Developing an infrastructure to respond to these needs of victims both for trust and relationship building and for services NGOs can provide will put a victim on a path that increases the likelihood of victim cooperation and comfort with the prospect of testifying. Prosecutors should therefore expect that a victim's testimony will evolve as trust develops. Specifically to respond to immigrant victims, prosecutors can partner with service providers offering assistance with immigration relief and services to access employment opportunities.

Some jurisdictions are responding to sex trafficking of minors by mandating services through the juvenile justice system or alternative secure facilities to prevent minors from returning to trafficking. However, confining a victim to mandatory services has yet to demonstrate effective outcomes and may retraumatize victims. Confinement also makes it harder for minors to access the education and job security they require to live a life free of retrafficking.

> Brothers Amador and Juan Cortes-Meza ran a sex trafficking ring, recruiting and transporting girls and women from Mexico to Atlanta, using the false allure of a romantic relationship and opportunity in the United States.[16] The brothers orchestrated psychological coercion, including isolation and using the victims' undocumented status to prevent them from reporting the crime. They also controlled victims through physical beatings and threats. The brothers, along with several others, either pled guilty or were convicted of multiple crimes, including sex trafficking.

Document Servitude

Another Chapter 77 crime targets document seizing as a specific criminal violation. Document servitude is the destruction, concealment, removal, confiscation, or possession of an actual or purported government document.[17] By distinguishing this particular method of coercion, prosecutors are able to try human trafficking cases where a trafficker has withheld a victim's documents, such as a passport, without having to prove that this act has the effect of coercion on the victim. Document servitude is a crime that has a particularly subjective impact on foreign-born victims who perceive a real threat to their safety if they try to leave the work without those documents. Without this unique crime, it may be difficult for a jury to understand this subjective fear imposed by traffickers who are withholding their victims' papers.

> John and Angelita Magat Farrell brought nine Filipino workers to the United States to work as housekeepers in their hotel in South Dakota.[18] Immediately upon arrival in the United States, the workers were forced by the Farrells to hand over their passports and other immigration documents. The Farrells never returned the documents to the workers even when requested by both the workers and the local chief of police. The workers testified that the Farrells held the passports as a means to control them, along with using debt servitude coupled with misrepresented wages, isolation, and threats of deportation and arrest.

Peonage

Peonage is another Chapter 77 crime that prohibits the use or threats of force on a person to compel work in debt servitude.[19] Debt servitude is common in cases where people are transported for the purposes of labor or commercial sex. Traffickers impose debts often characterized as the costs of transporting the victims, securing immigration documentation, and providing housing, transportation, and other services in the United States. Often these debts are inflated and misrepresented particularly with foreign-born victims who are unaware of the true costs. Undisclosed costs can lead to the increase of a debt's principal, which traffickers have also coupled with inflated interest rates, sometimes making it impossible to clear debts completely. Commonly featured in migrant work globally, these debts can easily be imposed by traffickers on foreign-born victims and used to make victims believe they will be harmed if they try to leave without paying the debt.

The Farrell case described above also highlights peonage as a method of human trafficking. In addition to document servitude, the Farrells imposed debts on their workers to cover costs of the transportation to the United States and the visa-processing fees. The workers understood they would owe a debt. The Farrells imposed additional debts to cover transportation, which had not been mentioned to the workers before. They also charged the workers for personal items that were not requested. The workers also received lower wages than anticipated and found themselves with increasing debt but more difficulty paying it off. The debt was affirmed through a contract with each worker, and the Farrells carefully scrutinized worker expenses to ensure payment.

This combination of practices makes it nearly impossible for victims to pay off the debt and requires them to continue in bonded labor, often for much longer than the victim originally anticipated upon recruitment.

Involuntary Servitude

As defined earlier in this chapter, involuntary servitude is a separate crime prohibiting the holding of a person knowingly and willingly or selling someone into servitude.[20] The means of involuntary servitude has been clarified as "the use or threatened use of physical restraint or injury, or by the use of threat of coercion through law or the legal process."[21] Involuntary servitude applies to both sex and labor trafficking cases. This crime primarily covers the acts of traffickers who use overt physical force or threats and may not reach the more subtle forms of coercion often present in human trafficking cases.

One of the most notorious human trafficking cases resulted in the conviction and forty-year sentence of Kil So Lee, who owned and managed a garment factory in American Samoa.[22] More than 250 workers were contained within a compound with barbed-wire fence, and Lee and his supervisors controlled the workers' ability to leave the compound.[23] The workers were practically starved. His managers also physically beat workers who did not obey orders.[24] The Kil So Lee case represents some of the most extreme facts but also illustrates some of the ways in which physical threats and injury are used to compel individuals into service.

Trafficking With Respect to Peonage, Slavery, Involuntary Servitude, or Forced Labor

One final crime covers a range of different crimes already discussed. It criminalizes the knowing recruiting, harboring, transporting, providing, or obtaining of a person for any of the Chapter 77 crimes.[25] It has been used in conjunction with other crimes described here.

Related Federal Statutes

In addition to anti-trafficking statutes, the Mann Act provides a tool to be used in federal sex trafficking prosecutions. The Mann Act criminalizes knowingly transporting any individual in interstate or foreign commerce for prostitution and other criminal sexual activities.[26] Enhanced penalties are available for the transportation of minors under the age of eighteen years.[27] The statutory provision entitled "Interstate and Foreign Travel or Transportation in Aid of Racketeering Enterprises" also criminalizes transportation, use of mail, or use of any facility in interstate or foreign commerce to carry out certain activities, including acts of prostitution in violation of law.[28]

State Anti-Trafficking Criminal Statutes

Criminal anti-trafficking law also rests with the states, and as of 2013 all fifty states had enacted a human trafficking criminalization statute.[29] There is no single unique model state anti-trafficking law; multiple NGOs promote somewhat varied laws. Therefore, prosecutors can contribute their knowledge and expertise and provide feedback to bolster their state's anti-trafficking laws.

Criminal Law–Related Provisions in State Laws

A comprehensive state anti-trafficking law will address the following criminal issues:

☑ Aligning definition of human trafficking with the TVPA
☑ Providing for equitable sentencing for sex and labor trafficking
☑ Establishing a comprehensive and mandatory victim restitution program
☑ Mandating law enforcement training
☑ Convening a state coordination body
☑ Ensuring proper treatment of victims as victims, not as offenders or perpetrators
☑ Granting eligibility for state public benefits and victim services

---

Definition of Human Trafficking

States with consistent definitions allow task forces made up of both local and federal agencies to work seamlessly on cases. More likely than not, however, one statute is going to be broader and have longer sentences, which may at the outset determine which agency is best suited to investigate and prosecute.

Equity in Labor and Sex Trafficking Prosecutions

Local and state prosecutors with equitable labor and sex trafficking definitions are better positioned to expand anti-trafficking efforts. Local law enforcement agencies mostly defer to federal agencies on labor trafficking cases.[30] Because trafficking is so clandestine and hidden, it will take time for even the most engaged prosecutor to build a volume of human trafficking prosecutions. Investigating and charging more labor trafficking cases can contribute toward building that expertise. Increasing the number of labor trafficking prosecutions communicates to the community that a local prosecutor recognizes the inhumane nature of both labor and sex trafficking. It may also generate more support from federal partners who want to support efforts to prosecute all types of human trafficking.

Thus far, local and state prosecutors have experienced unique challenges in addressing labor trafficking, resulting in less efficacy in enforcing labor trafficking at the local level.[31] Specifically, local law enforcement anti-trafficking efforts are often housed within vice or special victims units, which focus on prostitution, sexual assault, and domestic violence, more easily lending themselves to a sex trafficking investigation. Police departments do not generally have units to focus on labor violations. Consequently, members of law enforcement are less likely to encounter labor trafficking in the scope of their assigned work.

Other barriers are evident from the vantage point of labor trafficking victims. Mostly undocumented and without lawful immigration status, labor trafficking victims often view themselves primarily as undocumented and at risk of deportation rather than as a victim of a crime. Law enforcement partnerships with the federal government to enforce immigration laws only reinforce this apprehension to report crimes. Without affirmative and sustained efforts to overcome these complex trust barriers with local immigrant communities, direct reports of labor trafficking to police remain highly unlikely.

Expanding labor trafficking prosecutions requires proactive outreach to raise awareness and counter the conflation of sex trafficking with human trafficking that is prevalent in the media. Enhanced penalties for sex trafficking can also result in the allocation of resources primarily to sex trafficking prosecutions. Community stakeholders require increased understanding about labor trafficking to know what to look for.

Prosecutors developing an institutional response to this disparity in labor and sex trafficking prosecutions should consider several steps:

- ☑ Create a trafficking investigation unit that operates outside vice or special victims units.
- ☑ Support equitable state sex and labor trafficking sentencing policies.
- ☑ Discourage law enforcement immigration enforcement programs.
- ☑ Increase law enforcement and prosecutor partnerships with local immigrant communities and service providers.
- ☑ Ensure that anti-trafficking campaigns led by prosecutors' offices or partners address both labor and sex trafficking.

A Victim-Centered Prosecution

Despite prosecutions remaining a cornerstone of U.S. anti-trafficking efforts, the wide gaps in enforcement can be attributed not to lack of interest but rather to an evolving state of policy and infrastructure to respond. This coordination is at the core of a victim-centered prosecution, which acknowledges that effective prosecutions must first respond to victim trauma and harm in partnership with service providers.

An effective victim-centered approach addresses the following issues for victims:

1. Protection against traffickers
2. Information about and access to the criminal justice process
3. Access to services
4. Access to independent attorney representation

5. Restitution
6. Treatment with dignity and fairness
7. Privacy
8. Proceedings without undue delay

This approach reiterates a number of federally codified rights of crime victims.[32]

Most prosecutorial agencies have victim witness coordinators who liaise on behalf of criminal justice personnel with victims and their nonprofit victim services case managers. Often coordinators are more familiar with local service providers and victim compensation funds. They may assist prosecutors in building relationships and creating effective referral and protection protocols.

The Proactive Prosecution

With only a small percentage of traffickers having been successfully prosecuted, criminal penalties will not deter traffickers until prosecutors increase their capacity to prosecute cases. Prosecutors are immediately at a disadvantage due to the low number of trafficked persons who are identified. They will only be able to increase capacity when identification increases.

Increased identification strategies require a shift in stakeholder behaviors, which prosecutors can encourage. First, identification does not rest with just one type of stakeholder. Proactive outreach to a range of partners creates more touch points, any of which could be the one person with whom a trafficking victim interacts. Second, trafficking victims do not self-identify, and community stakeholders must have a better understanding of the definition and indicators of human trafficking to spot and begin conversations with trafficking victims.

Prosecutors' most immediate stakeholder partners are investigators. As prosecutors gain the skills necessary to identify trafficked persons under the elements of their laws, so too will law enforcement require the same skills to increase their capacity to identify human trafficking cases. The nature of human trafficking is so exploitative that many law enforcement officers initially disbelieve the prevalence of trafficking. Many law enforcement officials mistakenly believe that trafficking is not a problem in their state[33] and have not prioritized human trafficking investigations or training. Though human trafficking continues to gain political traction, some law enforcement agencies may only seek to enforce sex trafficking or only focus on minors, which only leads to other trafficked persons being overlooked and underidentified.

Trafficked persons are often unfamiliar with the term *trafficking* and therefore do not self-identify. Psychological coercion is so much harder to detect than physical force, leaving coerced victims presenting instead as commercial sex offenders, low-wage workers, undocumented immigrants, or sexual assault victims. Therefore, law enforcement human trafficking screening protocols should also apply to those who present to law enforcement either as victims of non–human trafficking crimes or as perpetrators of crimes.

Prosecutors and law enforcement who jointly invest in training key stakeholders on identification will see an increase in leads and referrals. For example, training will limit the number of leads that uncover prostitution or low-wage work that do not have the elements of human trafficking. In both examples, when untrained, these leads could also result in arrests of those engaged in commercial sex or workers who are undocumented, creating a chilling effect in their community where there might be victims of human trafficking.

Trust Building

Once trafficking victims are identified to law enforcement, prosecutors must build trust with trafficking victims. Prosecutors should expect for this to be a complicated and sometimes lengthy process. Facts to meet the threshold of human trafficking may not immediately emerge in an investigation, but law enforcement may be trained to notice enough indicators that they invest in a longer process of building trust. Consider a bystander who sees low-wage workers living onsite at a restaurant and thinks they may be trafficked. Fearful because they do not have immigration status, the workers do not disclose the details of their work or living situation. Without a process that anticipates these trust barriers, the workers likely return to their situation of exploitation and are never able to access victim protections. Their traffickers are not prosecuted, and others are trafficked.

A trafficker's psychological coercion is so powerful that victims are not always prepared to trust even those who offer assistance. Beyond general exploitation and control, traffickers typically instill the fear of law enforcement by reinforcing stereotypes and providing misinformation about the role of law enforcement. Many victims view also themselves as perpetrators of a crime, either in commercial sex or other crimes they are compelled to perform, or because of their unlawful immigration status, which would render them deportable if identified to law enforcement. Building trust also requires a culturally appropriate response from law enforcement. Victims are unlikely to believe that a law enforcement officer could understand their experience of being recruited and not abducted; although the circumstances may have ultimately been different than what they expected, at some point they *chose* to accept an opportunity for unsafe migration, unlawful status, low-wage work, or commercial sex.

A victim-centered prosecution might allow this referral and screening process, which allows victim service providers to overcome such trust barriers:

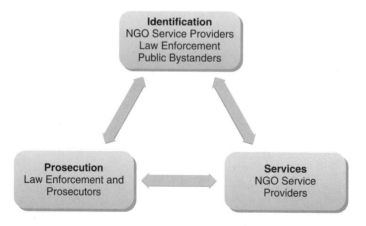

A key strategy for law enforcement and prosecutors is to partner early on with victim service providers who can advise trafficked persons about protections and services available to them and give them information about the criminal justice process. Informing potential victims about protections often helps overcome trust barriers. For example:

(a)   An undocumented labor trafficking victim who is worried about the risk of deportation may trust law enforcement once he or she knows about immigration relief available to trafficking victims.

(b)   A human trafficking victim who has experienced extreme trauma may not be able to articulate the facts of human trafficking until he or she has accessed mental health services.

(c)   Someone engaged in commercial sex is worried about being arrested but, after receiving case management and an overview of rights and protections, feels comfortable disclosing the victimization.

Failing to connect victims with available protections or even worse treating them as offenders may irreparably break any potential trust that victims may have had in law enforcement. Law enforcement and prosecutors can benefit from early and ongoing cross-sector collaboration with victim service providers, preferably those who are well-rooted in the same communities victims identify with, including communities of those participating in commercial sex, immigrant communities, low-wage worker communities and others."

Law Enforcement Coordination

As with other crimes, law enforcement collects evidence that may not offer prosecutors what they need to successfully prosecute trafficking cases. Because law enforcement and prosecutors have relatively little expertise on human trafficking cases as compared to other crimes, learning to build a case is necessarily a collaborative process. Law enforcement leads the investigation, collects evidence, interviews witnesses, and conducts surveillance. Prosecutors will have to build enough trust and rapport that they can share feedback on additional evidence required to overcome evidentiary gaps.

Once a trafficked person has been identified, building trust remains a priority. Though this typically starts with victim service providers, law enforcement and prosecutors also have a significant role to play in building trust. It requires law enforcement and prosecutors to develop culturally appropriate responses, recognizing the cultural context of their efforts to combat victimization and rebuild lives.

A trafficking victim's testimony may evolve over time. Trafficking victims often contradict their earlier accounts as they develop trust and learn more about the process. Some victims seek to protect individuals they fear will be implicated. Some victims simply do not understand the importance of being truthful in a court of law.

Trust Building

Li was recruited by a friend in China to work in a massage parlor in the United States. Upon arrival, she discovered that she would have to perform sex acts and not just massages. But she was in debt and saw no way out. Eventually, law enforcement raided the massage parlor. Many of the girls who had also wanted to escape the massage parlor were arrested. They were too scared to tell the police anything and eventually were deported. Li decided to tell the police that she had wanted to escape. She was the only one identified as a victim of human trafficking. Over the next several months, she cooperated in an investigation to prosecute the manager of the massage parlor. One day, upon probing from prosecutors, Li admitted to making up some of the facts around her recruitment in order to protect her friend. Though she was still a victim, the prosecutors had relied on her prior statements, and they had no other options and decided not to proceed with the prosecution.

Anticipating conflicting statements poses a challenge for prosecutors, but there are strategies to overcome this. As we saw in Li's case, multiple-victim cases should not rely on only one victim's testimony. Whether one victim's testimony or experience is stronger than another, it is also important that the victims are all treated equally. Victim-witnesses in multiple-victim cases often compare protections and benefits, and disparate protections can have a lasting impact on victims and on their willingness to participate in any investigation and prosecution.

Victims may also have relationships with their traffickers, which may be difficult for law enforcement to initially understand. Victims are recruited by friends and family and, as Li sought to do, protect those people through false statements. Prosecutors will benefit from understanding that cooperation for victims is subjective—they may want to partially cooperate and partially protect others. An ideal scenario would allow a victim time to disclose his or her entire experience to a service provider, who can work with a victim who might be reticent to share the details of the experience. Alternatively, prosecutors may seek to limit the amount of detail initially required to investigate a case and allow a longer investigation time.

A victim's trauma may also affect the victim's willingness to testify based on a mental state at a particular moment. Exploring the details of the violations and discussing the past can retraumatize trafficking victims, exacerbating their anxiety and reducing their ability to accurately recount events. Some may refuse to cooperate altogether, initially or later on.

Building trust is not only a means to ascertain the truth in order to seek justice but also a way to establish a relationship built on a shared goal of protecting the victim and creating new opportunities for the victim to live a life free of trafficking. Even for those cooperative testifying trafficking victims who are the means to a successful prosecution, victims ultimately look to prosecutors to watch out for all of their interests.

Coordination with Service Providers

Coordinating with service providers is necessary to any human trafficking prosecution. Victims emerging from human trafficking have a host of different needs. Prosecutions will only be successful if victims are stable, so it is important for prosecutors to ensure victim access to services from the outset. From a broader perspective, even a conviction without victim services leaves victims' trauma and other needs unaddressed, leaving them exposed and vulnerable to being trafficked again.

With these two critical outcomes, prosecutors should consider coordination with service providers as a core element in each case. Prosecutors' offices typically have victim witness coordinators, who liaise with victim services case managers. Since coordinators are resourced at different levels, prosecutors will have to ascertain their level of involvement in that process. For agencies without victim witness coordinators, prosecutors should anticipate and identify alternatives to perform these duties. Sometimes prosecutors themselves play this role.

Victim services case managers coordinate social and legal services. They coordinate a range of needs, including access to safe and confidential

emergency housing. Prosecutors' offices are often integrally involved
in securing immediate housing since many trafficking victims were in
trafficker-controlled housing. Victim witness coordinators should develop
partnerships with shelters that maintain confidentiality protocols that will
protect victims from being exposed to traffickers. Prosecutors should expect not to know the location of victims residing in one of these shelters.
There are a number of other services that victim witness coordinators
should anticipate facilitating for the victims in their cases. Understanding
the range of service needs for victims will lead to more successful prosecutions. As part of a task force protocol or otherwise, in advance of prosecuting any particular case, prosecutors should make sure that they can
identify service providers for a broad range of victim services needs.

Services Needs Checklist for Prosecutors and Victim Witness Coordinators

- ☑ Confidential Emergency Shelter
- ☑ Public Benefits
- ☑ Physical Health Services
- ☑ Mental Health Services
- ☑ Victim Witness Legal Representation
- ☑ Immigration Representation
- ☑ Emergency Food
- ☑ Dental Services
- ☑ Emergency and Long-Term Housing
- ☑ Crime Victim Compensation Fund Application
- ☑ English Language Classes
- ☑ Job Training
- ☑ Education
- ☑ Transportation
- ☑ Civil Litigation Representation
- ☑ Case Management

Prosecutors and Victim Services Attorneys Collaborating for Immigrant Victims

Foreign-born trafficking victims can have immigration as well as criminal
consequences requiring coordination between prosecutors and immigration lawyers and the courts and agencies that enforce these laws. Most

labor trafficking victims have some sort of irregular immigration status, whether they are undocumented or have a visa tied to employment by the trafficker. Still others have committed crimes in violation of federal or state laws as a result of the trafficking. Gaining their cooperation will require prosecutors to assist them in overcoming all of these administrative and criminal immigration violations.

Congress anticipated these concerns and created a shield of protection in the TVPA for those immigrant trafficking victims who elect to cooperate.[34] Those protections include continued presence and the T visa, both of which are extensively addressed in Chapter 5. However, these options create specific implications related to criminal prosecutions, which are discussed here.

Continued presence, the T visa, and the related U visa are premised on a victim's cooperation with an investigation or prosecution. Continued presence allows federal law enforcement to request permission to remain in the United States for victims of severe forms of trafficking who are co-operating with an investigation or prosecution.[35] A person with continued presence is certified as a victim of a severe form of human trafficking, triggering access to some refugee benefits, including cash assistance and access to ESL classes and job training, and an immigration employment authorization. Even for a victim who is not ready to work, the work authorization allows the victim to obtain identity documents, which facilitates access to numerous other services.

Continued presence is a valuable tool for law enforcement investigating a case of human trafficking involving victims who are undocumented or have visas tied to the trafficker. Continued presence is administered by federal agencies, which do not permit local and state prosecutors or law enforcement to request continued presence. However, local prosecutors have coordinated with their local Immigration and Customs Enforcement (ICE) counterparts to make that request and facilitate the process. Because it facilitates access to services and protection from deportation, continued presence is a tool that will engender a victim's trust in law enforcement. Therefore, victim services attorneys should work with law enforcement to secure continued presence at the earliest possible date.

By providing immediate access to work authorization and protection from deportation, continued presence is often a preliminary step before a victim applies for a T visa. The T visa allows a victim of human trafficking to seek temporary status with work authorization in the United States and to access a path to permanent residence.[36] T visa applicants are required to demonstrate cooperation with an investigation and prosecution of human trafficking or meet an exception to this requirement.[37] U.S. Citizenship and Immigration Services (USCIS) accepts either a law enforcement certification of cooperation or secondary evidence.[38] Victim services attorneys should work closely with prosecutors and law enforcement to secure this certification as early as possible, as T visas often have significant processing delays.

Direct and Indirect Benefits of T Visa Law Enforcement Declaration in a Victim-Centered Prosecution

- Shield from deportation
- Reunification with certain family members of victims who might be at risk overseas
- Access to cash benefits and food stamps
- Access to health care coverage
- Work authorization (permission to accept lawful employment)
- Identity documents
- Path to permanent status

Alternatively, the U visa was created within the same legislation as the TVPA and offers a parallel track for victims of enumerated criminal activities, which includes human trafficking.[39] U visa applicants must demonstrate *cooperation,* statutorily defined as "has been helpful, is being helpful, or is likely to be helpful."[40] U visa applicants must submit a certification in order to receive approval and may request a certification from a prosecutor. U visa benefits are very similar to T visa benefits, and if a trafficking victim elects to pursue a U visa, prosecutors should similarly view this request within a victim-centered context.

The T visa and, to a lesser degree, the U visa process is fraught with misconceptions regarding the role of law enforcement and prosecutors. Some prosecutors are reluctant to facilitate continued presence or sign a T or U visa certification because they are worried that victims will stop cooperating afterward. However, USCIS will accept evidence of nonco-operation from prosecutors while a T or U visa application is pending and may even revoke status once USCIS has approved status. T and U visa nonimmigrants also must demonstrate ongoing cooperation when they eventually apply for permanent residence.[41] The immigration process in-centivizes immigrant victims to continue to cooperate as an investigation and prosecution proceed and beyond.

Prosecutors may also be reluctant to sign a certification that may be construed by the defense as a benefit of cooperation. This defense argu-ment will always be tied to human trafficking prosecutions involving un-documented victims. Nevertheless, this has not deterred prosecutors who have been successful in securing convictions in cases involving victims who received certification as evidence of cooperation. Prosecutors should be prepared to argue that the certification itself does not offer any benefit and merely serves as a statement of fact. The benefit instead comes from USCIS, which adjudicates a number of additional requirements beyond the cooperation certification.

The T visa cooperation requirement only applies to individuals older than age eighteen.[42] Congress chose to exempt minors from cooperation requirements, anticipating the trauma and other barriers that make it difficult for minors to cooperate. This should signal additional consid-erations for prosecutors on child-victim–trafficking cases. Specifically, minors require additional services, including guardianship, school access, and shelter that they may not necessarily identify. They will also require the constant support of adults to help weigh their decision making in an investigation, in order to assess safety risks, trauma, and custodial issues.

Restitution and Asset Forfeiture
Restitution
The TVPA requires that restitution be paid for offenses that include vio-lence and for acts of sexual exploitation that often accompany trafficking in persons.[43] While courts determine how the restitution will be paid, prosecutorial decisions can impact the availability of restitution. The prosecutor's choice of charges against the trafficker affects the restitution rights available to the victim. While negotiating pleas, prosecutors must

also bear in mind agreements that accommodate adequate restitution. Prosecutors also help formulate the number of victims and amounts of restitution and modify those orders based on changed circumstances.

For example, in *United States v. Sabhnani*, the defendants Mahender and Varsha Sabhnani were charged with forced labor and other counts for conspiring to harbor in their home two domestic servants whom the couple brought to the United States illegally from Indonesia.[44] The jury found the defendants guilty of forced labor, peonage, and document servitude for forcing their victims to perform household chores without providing them with food, pay, or a proper living area.[45] The court also ordered the defendants to pay $936,546 in restitution to the victims and ordered forfeiture of the defendants' ownership interests in their home, where they held the victims.[46]

Asset Forfeiture

Asset forfeiture requires perpetrators to forfeit the assets used or acquired during the commission of the human trafficking offense. Because human trafficking is a crime motivated by economics, asset forfeiture allows the government to freeze assets and gain access to profits made through human trafficking, thus potentially not only deterring traffickers with a criminal investigation and sentence but also eliminating the profit margin that motivated the trafficking. Asset forfeiture funds may be distributed directly to the victim or to victim services agencies. Even if asset forfeiture provisions are not included in a state's anti-trafficking law, they should be available through general state asset forfeiture provisions.

Counterpart: Victim Services Attorneys

To complement prosecutors, effective prosecution and prevention require the participation of human trafficking victim services attorneys. Both federal and state laws specifically address and fund victim services and offer a range of protections. In addition to the human trafficking definitions included in the Chapter 77 crimes, the TVPA statutorily defines human trafficking for the purposes of victim services eligibility as follows:

(A) sex trafficking in which a commercial sex act is induced by force, fraud, or coercion, or in which the person induced to perform such act has not attained 18 years of age; or (B) the recruitment, harboring, transportation, provision, or obtaining of a person for labor or services, through the use of force, fraud, or coercion for the purpose of subjection to involuntary servitude, peonage, debt bondage, or slavery.[47]

States have designed victim services as a component of comprehensive state anti-trafficking legislation. New York, for example, passed legislation allowing the Office of Temporary and Disability Assistance to support victim services, including job training, English language instruction, and case management.[48]

For many victims, legal assistance is critical from the outset. Unlike many other crimes, the complex nature of human trafficking almost always necessitates access to a victim services attorney from the beginning of the investigation. Protocols designed in advance will reduce the risk that potential victims are detained by law enforcement. For example, when law enforcement conducts a raid, they will immediately try to classify someone as a victim or as a perpetrator. A victim may not necessarily disclose victimization and therefore may be detained. Someone who has been arrested or detained as if they have committed a crime is more likely to trust an outside victim services attorney over law enforcement. An immediately available victim services attorney can interview a potential victim, identify the individual as a victim or likely victim, and advocate for the victim's release and access to services as a victim. Any delay harms both the victim and the prosecutor. The longer the delay, the less likely a victim is going to trust anyone from law enforcement because of the victim associating law enforcement with that detention.

Beyond immediate access to inform victims of their rights, victim services attorneys can offer a range of critical protections to victims. Within the course of the investigation and prosecution, a victim-centered prosecution should allow victims to have attorneys present for all law enforcement interviews. Victim services attorneys should work with victims in advance to facilitate cooperation and even mitigate conflicting accounts. Attorneys may be able to draw attention to triggering circumstances, facilitate trust building with prosecutors, and reduce some of the victim's trauma and distrust. For example, facilitating more comfortable alternative interview locations reduces the distrust a victim might feel from being interviewed in a secure location typically meant for perpetrators.

The Immigrant Women and Children Project
of the New York City Bar Justice Center

In their representation of trafficking survivors, the City Bar Justice Center places client empowerment at the center of their work. They ensure that the decision to cooperate with law enforcement and how they cooperate are a matter of choice. The boundaries that they help a survivor establish in turn help their clients build trust with law enforcement. For example, by requesting that law enforcement not show up unannounced at home or work and by law enforcement's recognizing that request, survivors are empowered and made stronger witnesses, which ultimately benefits the prosecution.

Victim services attorneys also liaise with prosecutors, updating victims on the progress of the case and their personal role in the proceedings. Victims will be expected to testify and submit victim impact statements, with the assistance of attorneys. Participating in the criminal justice process can also be psychologically burdensome to the victim, and the attorney may be best positioned to monitor and respond to any resulting needs.

Victim services attorneys are also helpful in anticipating and responding to conflicts of interest among potential victims. Sometimes a potential victim may actually be a trafficker. In other cases, conflicts among victims emerge later in a case. Those with less understanding of complex human trafficking cases might assume that all victims have common interests. However, victims with varying loyalty to traffickers compete with other victims and seek different case processes and outcomes. Victim services attorneys may solve some of these conflicts by working with non-lawyer case managers to screen and refer out initial conflicts. Alternatively, victim services agencies and pro bono attorneys can anticipate conflicts by developing a list of alternative attorneys who are prepared to take on cases where conflicts emerge among victims in such case.

Among a victim services attorney's primary duties is advocating for the safety of a victim and the victim's family. Victim services attorneys should make sure that a victim's safety is the priority during the litigation by ensuring that traffickers are not given any information regarding the victim's location. Victim services attorneys may advocate with prosecutors for additional protection and safety planning. Collaboration between prosecutors and victim services attorneys also often results in increased referrals, with law enforcement trusting that a victim services attorney will provide a victim with the information needed to elect to cooperate with law enforcement.

Civil Litigation

Access to civil remedies is an important but sometimes overlooked aspect of victim protection. Prosecutors may have to coordinate with civil litigators pursuing a civil lawsuit against traffickers. Victims can use a lawsuit to restore the financial earnings, redress their injuries, and minimize risk of future exploitation by obtaining restitution and monetary damages to begin a new life. A lawsuit also offers them another avenue to justice on their own terms. While civil litigation generally proceeds on a long time frame, victims can feel some urgency in obtaining a civil judgment. Prosecutors should anticipate coordinating the timing, evidence collection, and victim services with civil litigators. Chapter 4 provides detailed information for civil litigators, but it will also inform prosecutors who are trying to navigate and anticipate challenges with parallel criminal and civil cases.

The Criminalization of Victims
Arresting Victims

Effective human trafficking interventions often focus on prosecution. But misconceptions and novelty associated with human trafficking continue to result in trafficked persons going unidentified and arrested as offenders, as perpetrators, and for administrative immigration enforcement, despite being victims. Such arrests have significant consequences. First, victims treated as criminals go unidentified and go without access to protections afforded to them under the law. Second, lack of identification allows traffickers to continue to commit crimes and violate human rights with impunity. Third, the arrest of victims reinforces the distrust of law enforcement among some of the most victimized communities, thereby preventing other victims from coming forward. Fourth, the impact of these arrests can be lasting and potentially foreclose an individual's opportunity to build a life free from slavery.

Minors engaged in commercial sex are often arrested and treated as offenders. But under criminal statutes, they are actually likely victims of sex trafficking. If the minor is arrested and not identified as a trafficking victim or sometimes in spite of being identified as a trafficking victim, the minor is at risk of entering the juvenile justice system. Such minors automatically have fewer choices as they move into adulthood. Juvenile justice programs sometimes move minors out of state into programs that isolate the juveniles, often like adults serving time in state prisons located far away from their personal support systems. Mandating a victim's participation in the juvenile justice system communicates to a victim that she is less deserving of protections and has to earn them through her participation. It also removes a victim's autonomy despite being victimized. This creates distrust and can prevent meaningful recovery. These victims are also economically disadvantaged because of their criminal records, impacting access to education and work opportunities.

Because adults can be engaged in commercial sex but not induced by force, fraud, or coercion, law enforcement may presume that they are violating criminal laws and arrest them. These arrest policies have resulted in a distrust of law enforcement. We have already seen that those in commercial sex are unable to report sexual assault or other crimes as a result of the commercial sex stigma. Those who experience force, fraud, or coercion in commercial sex may not realize that this characterizes them as victims, not criminals. Coupled with the existing distrust, trafficking victims are unlikely to self-identify to law enforcement.

In addition, undocumented trafficked immigrants are also arrested by local law enforcement partnering with federal law enforcement to enforce immigration laws. Without the knowledge to self-identify as a trafficking victim and without proactive efforts to identify a victim as trafficked, an unidentified immigrant will be treated as an immigration violator. This can result in local and federal immigration detention and ultimately removal from the United States. This returns a trafficking victim to the same circumstances under which he or she was originally recruited.

Finally, some victims also commit other crimes under the instruction of their traffickers. Because these victims do not fall into discernible categories such as engagement in commercial sex or being an undocumented immigrant, identification of these victims is even harder. Victims may be compelled to steal, transport or use drugs, and commit a variety of other crimes. If those victims do not feel safe sharing the entirety of their experience, they will be treated as criminals and not as victims.

In each of these scenarios, early identification of a trafficking victim could prevent all the unforeseen consequences involved with the arrest of a trafficked person. Law enforcement identification training that targets arrested populations can prevent charges from being filed. In the event that charges are filed, defense attorneys who better understand the context of human trafficking may be successful at getting charges dropped.

In the case of victims who are arrested, defense attorneys unknowingly represent victims. Defense attorneys have perhaps an even higher burden to identify trafficking victims because these individuals will almost never present as victims. Engaging defense attorneys and even juvenile justice advocates who work directly with incarcerated youth as active stakeholders adds in an extra layer of legal professionals positioned to identify human trafficking victims. Task forces have rarely included defense attorneys, but their participation is an important step in responding to victims who have been arrested. Defense attorneys have a pivotal role in informing their client who is arrested that he or she may in fact be a victim of trafficking. Particularly in cases where the crime is not easily associated with trafficking, defense attorneys, who are familiar with human trafficking indicators, will be better positioned to probe further.

Trained attorneys will be able to advocate for dropped charges, connect victims with critical services, and even lead law enforcement to investigate the traffickers. In the case of undocumented immigrants, public defenders and defense attorneys are responding to their duty to inform defendants of the immigration consequences associated with their criminal proceedings.[49] *Padilla* attorneys may be less familiar with trafficking-specific immigration remedies and should be provided training and participate in anti-trafficking stakeholder groups.

Under immigration law, an arrest will trigger immigration enforcement even if an immigrant does not face criminal charges. This process then subjects trafficked persons to immigration detention and removal from the United States. In such a case, an immigration attorney who is trained on T visa and victim issues can seek a T visa and secure an immigrant's release from detention and the immigration enforcement system. Defense attorneys can play a critical role of making prompt referrals to expert immigration victim attorneys.

When informal negotiations do not result in dropped charges, defense attorneys can move to dismiss charges based on the facts of victimization. A judge and a jury may be less familiar with the nature of human trafficking, but even for a defendant who has met the elements of a crime, human trafficking experts can testify to explain how a trafficker may compel a person to commit a crime. An expert can also describe to the court the impact of criminal punishment on a victim seeking a life free of trafficking.

Defense attorneys can also assert duress as a general defense for clients who have been charged with crimes related to trafficking. Duress requirements vary from state to state but would likely require defense attorneys to prove some threat of harm. Because traffickers threaten their victims in vague terms within a larger scheme of psychological control, experts can testify regarding the subjective fear of harm.

Post-conviction Relief

States are now beginning to respond and look back at the exposure of victims to conviction as perpetrators instead of victims. In some states, post-conviction relief is available to sex trafficking victims with sex trafficking related convictions. In 2010, New York State enacted the first statute in the United States that specifically allows trafficking victims to vacate prostitution-related convictions resulting from sex trafficking.[50] This statute allows defense attorneys to file motions to vacate convictions even after sentencing, giving victims of trafficking an opportunity for relief in case the defense attorney did not learn that the client is a trafficking victim until after plea or conviction.[51] The Uniform Law Commission, also known as the National Conference of Commissioners on Uniform

State Laws, also included a post-conviction relief provision in the human trafficking uniform state law,[52] thereby encouraging states to include this provision in future anti-trafficking legislation.

Sex Workers' Project of the Urban Justice Center (SWP)

SWP has been on the forefront of efforts to create post-conviction relief. After bringing forward stories of trafficked persons who had convictions related to prostitution, SWP advocated for the creation of a New York law that would offer post-conviction relief to these trafficked persons. Since the landmark law passed in 2010, SWP has also trained attorneys and begun to represent eligible trafficked persons.

Thus far, public interest and pro bono attorneys have led efforts to take on individual post-conviction relief cases. However, defense attorneys who learn more about these cases will not only bring their criminal defense expertise to the cases but also improve efforts to identify victimization in defendants who have not been convicted.

The Role of Judges

Criminal judges are uniquely positioned to have an impact on the state of human trafficking prosecutions. In a relatively new area, judges have an opportunity to streamline prosecutions, coordinate stakeholders, and even identify human trafficking. Because so many law enforcement officers remain less familiar with existing human trafficking laws, it may fall on a judge to identify an additional trafficking charge in a case and even recognize victimization in a defendant.

Outside of identification, judges and other court personnel play an important role in the efficacy of a prosecution, especially in witness tampering and safety. In addition to typical courtroom safety measures, traffickers can use a wide network to threaten the safety of victims and victims' relatives, even overseas. Admonitions that cover these extended risks may deter defendants from witness-tampering efforts. Judges can also honor efforts to maintain the confidentiality of victim locations. They can adopt procedures to provide victim law enforcement escorts both before and after appearing in court.

Judges associations have held conference and training sessions on human trafficking so that judges are more familiar with the nuances of the crime and they are better prepared when a case comes before them. Many state judges are also working to craft jury instructions based on new state laws so that prosecutions can proceed effectively once they come before the judge.

In many states, human trafficking laws remain untested, and courts will increasingly be making decisions of first impression on state laws. Since 2000, a significant body of cases has proceeded under the TVPA, offering interpretation of the federal anti-trafficking statutes. When judges finally preside over an anti-trafficking case, they will likely have many questions on proper application of their relatively new state law. In these instances, judges can look to the federal application of the TVPA for guidance, as this law has been properly tested and provides the necessary framework for anti-trafficking efforts.

Conclusion

Even in the context of criminal prosecution, human trafficking extends far beyond meeting the elements of a human trafficking law. Prosecutors have a role in collaborating with partners to proactively identify human trafficking and secure essential victim services that help to ensure victim cooperation. Victim services attorneys likewise have duties that extend far beyond the typical scope of crime victim representation. Finally, defense attorneys have a critical role that may perhaps result in the most impact in building trust of victims and prosecutors. Steady refinement of these practices by prosecutors, defense attorneys, judges, victim services attorneys, and other attorneys and legal professionals will ultimately result in increased prosecutions, deterring human trafficking and expanding victim protections. But most of all, the participation of more actors from the criminal justice system engaged in proactive efforts will bring about much needed justice and victim identification.

CHAPTER 3

Corporate Law

[E]very business can take action. All the business leaders who are here and our global economy companies have a responsibility to make sure that their supply chains, stretching into the far corners of the globe, are free of forced labor. The good news is more and more responsible companies are holding themselves to higher standards. . . . Human trafficking is not a business model, it is a crime, and we are going to stop it.

—President Barack Obama

Trafficking may occur at one point or multiple points throughout a product's life cycle—the supply chain—from the harvesting or extraction of raw materials, through manufacturing and transportation, to the retail shelves where products are sold. For example, men, women, and children in the Democratic Republic of the Congo (DRC) are forced to mine coltan. The mineral is then used in component parts for cell phones, DVD players, and video games, sometimes assembled by forced labor in China, Malaysia,

Vietnam, and elsewhere. Shrimp harvested using forced labor on Thai fishing vessels is sent to distributors and then served at restaurants, where dishwashers may be held in forced labor. Cocoa beans picked in West Africa using forced child labor might later become candy bars stocked on shelves by women and men also compelled to work. Goods known to be produced with forced labor in specific foreign countries include the following[1]:

Artificial flowers	Cottonseed	Pornography
Bamboo	Diamonds	Rice
Beans	Dried fish	Rubber
Brazil nuts/chestnuts	Electronics	Rubies
Bricks	Embellished textiles	Sesame
Carpets	Fireworks	Shrimp
Cassiterite	Fish	Stones
Cattle	Footwear	Sugarcane
Cement	Garments	Sunflowers
Charcoal	Gold	Teak
Christmas	Granite	Textiles
decorations	Gravel	Tilapia
Coal	Iron	Timber
Coca	Jade	Tobacco
Cocoa	Nails	Toys
Coffee	Palm oil	Wheat
Coltan	Palm thatch	Wolframite
Corn	Physic nuts/castor	
Cotton	beans	

Taking in that long list can become overwhelming, particularly when you consider, for example, how many thousands of products contain wheat alone; looking through our own pantries there is cereal, bread, pasta, cookies, spices, soups, condiments, and crackers. Even more disturbing, this annual list from the U.S. Department of Labor is just a starting point. It does not include goods produced in the United States and is not exhaustive; the authors concede that there are many more goods that may be produced with forced labor that they themselves did not document.

Regardless, the list demonstrates that forced labor is deep within corporate supply chains and in the goods that consumers purchase.

Human trafficking presents a great risk to business operations and not only for those with an extended supply chain. The consequences for a company with forced labor somewhere within its operations or those of its suppliers or contractors include

- *Supply chain disruption*—High-profile forced-labor incidents carry the same risk to operations as natural disasters, extreme weather, factory catastrophes, and cybercrime. Imagine the discovery of forced labor at a factory supplying one of the world's more visible brands. In some cases, the only appropriate response may be to terminate the supplier's contract. But how dependent are operations on this one factory? How quickly can another factory in the network ramp up to the meet the demand? How quickly can another reliable supplier be located? Lost time equals lost sales and profit. For this reason, suppliers' labor practices are a leading risk indicator for supply chain vulnerability.
- *Fines and lost contracts*—Regulatory risk is a common reality, and now companies must comply with a number of new requirements related to human trafficking. The noncompliance repercussions include financial penalties, loss of contracts, litigation, and administrative sanctions. For example, the U.S. government is ramping up enforcement of the Federal Acquisition Regulation on human trafficking. Government contracting officers now participate in mandated training and are required to conduct investigations and audits, particularly of high-risk contracts. Federal contractors found in violation risk suspension of their current government contracts and debarment from future contracts.
- *Litigation*—Forced-labor claims and noncompliance can result in administrative actions for debarment from federal contracts; criminal or civil litigation or administrative actions under the Foreign Corrupt Practices Act; criminal or civil litigation stemming from the Victims of Trafficking and Violence Protection Act (VTVPA); and civil litigation under the Alien Tort Claims Act, Fair Labor Standards Act, or numerous state torts. Litigation has financial costs but also causes corresponding reputational harm whether or not the suit is merited.

- *Reputational harm*—Consumers impart responsibility to a brand when something goes wrong, regardless of whether the brand's supplier was first, second, or third tier in the supply chain. All it takes is a label that can be tracked to a brand, and the reputational harm follows. Customer loyalty makes all the difference with a razor-thin profit margin. Whether it is a smartphone application grading a company's anti-slavery efforts, lawsuits over labor conditions, or headlines regarding slave labor found in a company's factories, the resulting reputational harm can damage the bottom line.

It is truly a fascinating and challenging time to be an attorney engaged in crafting a response to this reality, whether in a corporation, law firm, government agency, or nonprofit. Our corporate colleagues have described the nascent corporate response to human trafficking as just the beginning and the increased regulatory action as the tip of the iceberg.

The response to human trafficking—indeed to all forms of labor abuse and exploitation—is and will be very heavily influenced by several emerging areas within business. First, supply chain management has grown, along with the continually expanding network of suppliers and resulting complexities. Certain companies are mandated by health and safety concerns to be able to identify the source of a product. For example, agricultural companies are required to pinpoint the specific quadrant of a particular farm where produce originated. Many companies are working to map their first-tier suppliers in an effort to optimize efficiency, reduce risk, and realize significant cost savings. Although there are tremendous benefits, it is difficult work, and many corporations are reluctant to make the investment to make it happen, especially to go beyond the first tier. Their visibility into the depth and breadth of their supply chain operations therefore remains limited. Even those who have pursued increased visibility have tended to stop at the first-tier suppliers. Eileen Fisher, known as a socially conscious apparel brand, is one of the rare few that has gone beyond the first tier and is mapping their entire supply chain.

Second, corporate social responsibility (CSR) has taken a more prominent role within companies and larger corporate and supply chain discussions. Where once it was rare, now CSR departments are more commonplace in companies. CSR still means different things to different companies—environmental sustainability, labor and human rights practices, philanthropy, and/or ethical sourcing. The earliest CSR positions rooted in the green movement primarily focused on the environment in an effort to identify cost savings while highlighting the social benefit from environmental stewardship. As an example, in 2009, Wal-Mart established three environmental sustainability goals: (1) to be powered by 100 percent renewable energy, (2) to create zero waste, and (3) to sell products that sustain people and the environment. If its suppliers could not demonstrate their own sustainability practices, Wal-Mart would drop them as suppliers. Leveraged across 60,000 suppliers, this makes a huge difference. You can see how a similar response to labor issues within a supply chain could be managed in the future.

More recently, Wal-Mart, among others, has instituted an ethical sourcing initiative. There are no standards in this area; initiatives are voluntarily undertaken and individually designed. Generally, ethical sourcing aspires to minimize the company's impact on the environment, communities, and laborers at the source of a product. An initiative includes responsible purchasing practices with regard to environmental and labor standards. Starbucks claims that 93 percent of their coffee was ethically sourced in 2012, and its goal is to purchase 100 percent ethically sourced coffee by 2015. Coffee is the second largest internationally traded commodity, oil being the first. If this trend continues and expands as expected, it will revolutionize companies' understanding and oversight of their global supply chains, which will only serve to benefit anti-trafficking efforts as well. That mapping and infrastructure is instrumental to anti-trafficking efforts.

Likewise, the fair trade movement stands for similar labor and environmental principles but also carries a certification visible to consumers. Consumers have become more concerned and sensitive about the origins of their purchases, particularly in the case of food and apparel. Globally reported tragedies such as the 2013 Bangladesh factory collapse where more than 1,100 young workers lost their lives have forced consumers to think about the workers behind their clothing. Fair Trade USA opened its doors in 2013, citing a 20 percent increase in imported fair trade–certified

products. Companies therefore have options—fair trade, ethical sourcing, and/or industry-specific efforts.

Third, the emerging legal practice of business and human rights came
to the forefront following the 2011 introduction of the UN Guiding
Principles on Business and Human Rights,[2] also known as the UNGPs
or Ruggie Principles. Law firms and companies are increasingly creating business and human rights practice areas whose services comprise a
mix of impact assessment, policy development, and risk mitigation. The
companies ahead of the curve have established human rights programs,
such as those at Hewlett-Packard, or established human rights positions,
such as those at CH2M Hill. The aim is to minimize any negative human
rights impacts—from the lens of the rightsholders—from corporate operations, so it requires not only continual assessment and monitoring but
also operationalizing the findings and conducting remediation. Although
this work is far broader than combating human trafficking, such efforts
provide a framework in which companies can also address trafficking.

Finally, compliance itself has become a profession and business over the
last few decades. There are technology firms and tools specific to compliance, compliance officers and their associations, in-house counsel devoted to compliance, and law firms specializing in compliance for federal
contractors or for specific federal agencies. Their work entails the initial
creation of a compliance plan and program and managing and tracking
compliance within a company and its suppliers across large supply chains.

We are therefore witnessing a changing landscape, where a number
of corporate efforts have the potential to integrate anti-trafficking and
ultimately reduce the risk of human trafficking. But challenges remain.
We continue to hear from companies that they believe forced labor is
nonexistent in their supply chain. Many continue to rely on their singular
strategy using audits, despite evident flaws to unearth human trafficking in supply chains. Many express their confusion about what exactly
human trafficking is. Some are concerned that publicly disclosing anti-
trafficking efforts represents a concession about forced labor in their supply chains. Even more CSR professionals express that this is not yet a high
priority to consumers and stakeholders, so they are less willing to invest
in anti-trafficking efforts.

In our own work providing corporate consulting and training, companies have tended to seek our services in three situations. Sometimes a forced-labor incident, publicly known or privately discovered, has come to light, necessitating a reactive response. Or a company that has had issues in the past and has worked hard to rebuild now sees an opportunity to be a leader in the industry through proactive prevention. Or, the far more frequent occurrence, a company comes to us for help in meeting new compliance laws. All have been major multinational brands that stand to lose a lot or gain a lot; they have the biggest incentive. The vast majority of corporations, however, are those not yet addressing the issue.

It is in this context that the focus on anti-trafficking efforts arises. As we have pointed out, there are numerous professionals engaged in related work—supply chain management, CSR including ethical sourcing and fair trade, business and human rights, and compliance. However, in-house corporate attorneys and those in law firms primarily work on the issue of human trafficking through risk mitigation and compliance.

Risk Mitigation

It takes a lot more time and expense to manage a crisis than it does to identify and mitigate the risk up front. Human trafficking presents a variety of likely scenarios for those corporate attorneys focused on the worst-case scenario to consider and craft a risk mitigation strategy accordingly. Some of a corporate attorney's work, therefore, involves taking the following steps:

Perform Risk Assessments—A risk assessment is a necessary first step that guides tailored policy development. It is an examination of the circumstances in which forced labor may arise compared to the existing controls in place. Companies can then rate their residual risk to identify where additional controls, policies and procedures, and training are required in the immediate, short-, and long-term. In some industries, the risk may be high because of the prevalence of forced labor in particular goods, products, or countries. For others, the likely occurrence of forced labor may appear to be low, but the potential threat to the company when an incident occurs is high.

Although broad policies are necessary, known specific risks may require individualized remedies. Each company has a different risk footprint dependent upon the industry and location of operations. In financial services, it may be traffickers who are money laundering, whereas in construction it may be recruitment fees and debts incurred by migrant laborers. North Dakota oil fields carry different risks than do reconstruction projects in Iraq. Known high-risk categories include reliance on labor brokers/recruiters, a workforce from countries of conflict or instability, a workforce that is migrant, operations in countries ranked low in the annual *Trafficking in Persons Report*, and operations in countries or industries included in the *DOL List of Goods Produced by Child Labor or Forced Labor*.

Perform Supplemental Audits—Social auditing has come into question as safety and labor incidents have occurred in factories that had just been audited. Auditing alone is an insufficient strategy, particularly when trying to identify forced labor. Corporate attorneys are therefore working on risk mitigation by employing other strategies to supplement audits. For example, there are now a number of services, such as LaborVoices and Good World Solutions, which gather information anonymously from factory workers, obtaining a more accurate account of factory conditions than an announced audit under watchful managers' eyes will produce. Some corporations support their suppliers through technical assistance to strengthen business practices, minimizing the likelihood of cutting corners where labor is concerned.

Increase Transparency in Policies—Corporate attorneys weigh the risks and benefits of disclosing companies' policies. Fueled by emerging consumer tools that evaluate companies' efforts to address forced labor, consumers are increasingly demanding information on corporate policies related to human trafficking. Slavery Footprint, for example, allows consumers to calculate how many slaves work for a company based on the company's purchasing history, allowing them to learn about the prevalence of forced labor within the products they have purchased. The Free2Work application allows consumers to scan a barcode and see the product manufacturer's A–F grade regarding labor practices along with competitors' information to aid comparison shoppers. Still more NGOs are beginning to evaluate companies' efforts to address slavery and provide that information as a guide to consumers. The goal of these efforts is to encourage consumers to vote with their wallets on corporate policies against forced labor in the companies' supply chain.

Include Procurement of Services—Corporate attorneys are in the position to revamp the vetting process for contractors and to implement systems that monitor contractual services. Although manufacturing comes to mind first when thinking of forced labor, industries without supply chains are at risk as well. Remember from Chapter 1 the example of the Botsvynyuk brothers, who forced Ukrainian men and women to clean Wal-Mart, Target, Kmart, Safeway, and other retail stores, along with homes and offices in multiple northeast states. Human trafficking is possible within a number of contractual services, including janitorial, landscaping, security, call centers, catering, and travel. The contractual relationship typically reduces the level of oversight, which is what creates an opportunity for trafficking to occur without the knowledge of the company contracting for services.

Include Policy Against Purchasing Commercial Sex—A number of companies now have policies prohibiting employees' procurement of commercial sex in the course of business or at least during business travel. In part, these policies recognize that prostitution provides a financial environment for perpetuating sex trafficking. From the risk mitigation standpoint, these policies anticipate the scandalous headlines likely to emerge if corporate employees patronized a person later determined to be a sex trafficking victim.

Strengthen Corporate Policies—At a minimum, corporate policies should include a prohibition against human trafficking in addition to the core International Labour Organization (ILO) labor standards. The ILO reports that the majority of the top five hundred corporations in the United States and United Kingdom have adopted supplier codes of conduct based on ILO conventions and recommendations.[3] Corporate attorneys may need to strengthen existing policies based on their risk assessment, the need to supplement audits and increase transparency, and the need to spell out how to handle procurement and how to report violations. Additionally, policies should set forth any remedial actions available, both to the individual harmed and to any supplier. Incentive structures can be created. New policies may guide employees, translate into a supplier code of conduct, or become new contract clauses. The Coca-Cola Company's established global workplace rights division, for example, is often heralded as an example for its comprehensive policies.

Conduct Training—A policy will only be effective if it is implemented. In fact, compliance without training is often meaningless and deemed as noncompliant. Training is the vehicle to reach employees and suppliers with this critical information that guides behavior and increases skills. Advances in "e-learning" make it easier to bring training to corporations large and small as well as their suppliers located worldwide. Our clients, for instance, have implemented a range of training methods. Some may focus exclusively on employees and policies. Some may focus on suppliers and their code of conduct. Others update existing ethics and compliance training with a trafficking module. Still others focus on do's and don'ts specific to hiring migrant laborers and how to identify forced labor. Beyond supply chain training, Carlson Companies was the first in the hospitality industry to train its management and employees on the signs of potential child sexual exploitation, including child sex trafficking, on its properties. Additionally, Delta has trained its flight crews to report suspicious behavior that may be indicative of human trafficking.

Harmonize Public Effort—A company with transparent policies, philanthropic support of anti-trafficking organizations, and a public anti-trafficking commitment will be in a much better position to handle a forced-labor incident that becomes public. In such companies, accusations of willfulness or nonprotection of workers are unlikely to garner any support when so much has been accomplished internally and communicated externally. These public anti-trafficking efforts can also help increase market share as customers become more loyal to the brand because of the companies' very public commitment. At a time when a number of online websites were criticized for facilitating sex trafficking, Google convened stakeholder meetings to determine how it could contribute to anti-trafficking efforts with its technical expertise; it also made a $12 million philanthropic donation divided up among several anti-trafficking organizations.

Work Across the Company—This is not work that can be done behind closed doors or in silos. It requires input from across the company and horizontal implementation across the company, which goes against the grain. It typically includes a multidisciplinary team of CSR, supply chain, internal and external auditors, public relations, philanthropy, and corporate leadership. This is the approach used by the companies that want to be the leader in their industry on the issue.

Best practices in this area continue to develop, and there are resources available to point any company in the right direction. These resources include the United Nations Guiding Principles on Business and Human Rights,[4] the U.S. Department of Labor's Toolkit for Responsible Business,[5] and the ABA Model Business and Supplier Policies on Labor Trafficking and Child Labor which can be found at http://www.americanbar.org/content/dam/aba/administrative/house_of_delegates/resolutions/2014_hd_102b_REVISED.docx.

Damage Control

Reputation and profits suffer when devastating news of, for instance, faulty products, factory fires, or forced labor travel at the same lightning speed in today's age of instant communication. Consider these headlines:

- Victoria's Secret Cotton Being Supplied by Slave Labor?[6]
- Flextronics Accused of Using Slave Labor[7]
- Hershey Sued for Info on Use of Child Labor in Cocoa Supplies[8]
- Workers for Wal-Mart Supplier Forced into Slave Labor
- Zara Accused of Alleged "Slave Labor" in Brazil[9]
- Woman Finds Note from Chinese Labor Camp Prisoner in Kmart Decorations[10]

Corporate attorneys will be involved in litigation strategy as well as working with public relations personnel and outside firms on a coordinated media strategy.

Forced labor may also be uncovered more quietly, as part of a routine audit, an internal investigation, or an anonymous employee tip. Part of the process requires remediation, making reparations to the trafficked persons, and ensuring paid wages and transportation. The next step is an inquiry into how the incident arose and a reconsideration of the policies and practices in place. Alerting law enforcement may be required or if the victim has already reported the incident, an investigation may begin. The company will need to assure its stakeholders that the problem has been identified and rectified or there is an effort under way to strengthen policies and practices to prevent future occurrences.

Compliance and Risk Mitigation

In 2006, hundreds of companies signed on to the Athens Ethical Principles,[11] which consist of seven broad commitments to create policies and work toward prevention of human trafficking. In 2010, the Luxor Implementation Guidelines[12] expanded on these principles and provided a road map for the specific types of anti-trafficking activities companies could undertake. Then came the 2011 Ruggie Principles, not specific to trafficking, but inclusive of broader concepts about responsibility to "avoid infringing on the human rights of others," which also serves to prevent human trafficking.[13] Corporations are called to assess their actual and potential human rights impacts, including those of their suppliers and partners, integrate the response, respect human rights regardless of local enforcement, and treat the risk of human rights violations as a legal compliance matter. Specific industries have also signed on to voluntary codes of conduct, such as the Code of Conduct for the Protection of Children from Sexual Exploitation in Travel and Tourism,[14] which recognizes that child sex tourism and child trafficking can be identified and reported by hotel personnel. The Kimberley Process addresses conflict-free diamond-mining codes in the jewelry industry[15]; there are many other industry-specific codes and agreements.

Voluntary compliance has been the norm. However, in recent years there have been both federal and state government efforts to draft compliance or compliance-like laws. Some responsibility has been imparted for first-tier suppliers, but now there is a push for brands to know their entire supply chain.

California Transparency in Supply Chains Act

The California Transparency in Supply Chains Act (S.B. 657)[16] is one of those compliance-like efforts. It masquerades as compliance but is really a consumer information tool. Nevertheless, corporate attorneys and others are responsible for implementing their company's disclosure.

S.B. 657 affects any retailer or manufacturer doing business in California with annual worldwide revenue of more than $100 million. It requires a public statement on the corporate website's homepage describing the extent to which the retailer or manufacturer in question

1. verifies its supply chain to evaluate the risk of modern slavery,
2. conducts supplier audits to verify compliance with corporate anti-slavery policies,
3. requires supplier certification of compliance,
4. develops and maintains internal policy and standards, and
5. delivers human trafficking training to its employees.

These five requirements are among the same elements of the risk mitigation strategies presented earlier in this chapter. They form the core of anti-trafficking efforts in supply chains.

Consumer Tool

S.B. 657 is a small step in the direction of providing consumers with comparable information on corporate practices to eliminate forced labor in companies' supply chains. It suggests that retailers and manufacturers at the top of the supply chain assume responsibility for everything that goes into their products, including the harvested cotton later woven, dyed, and assembled into garments as well as the coltan mined, transformed into capacitors, and assembled into cell phones. The assumption is that consumers will hold corporations responsible for their inaction or insufficient action by withdrawing their business and, conversely, reward positive actions with their business.

SEC. 2. The Legislature finds and declares the following: . . .

(i) Absent publicly available disclosures, consumers are at a disadvantage in being able to distinguish companies on the merits of their efforts to supply products free from the taint of slavery and trafficking. Consumers are at a disadvantage in being able to force the eradication of slavery and trafficking by way of their purchasing decisions.

(j) It is the policy of this state to ensure large retailers and manufacturers provide consumers with information regarding their efforts to eradicate slavery and human trafficking from their supply chains, to educate consumers on how to purchase goods produced by companies that responsibly manage their supply chains, and, thereby, to improve the lives of victims of slavery and human trafficking.[17]

Risk and Marketplace Shame

Importantly, S.B. 657 is not a government regulation that sets out clear standards. The law is scant on the details that we as attorneys crave. It is silent on length, level of detail, and standards. There is no penalty for insufficient policies and procedures. As of the publication of this book, there is no enforcement of noncompliance.

As a result, not all companies comply with the California Act; some have no statement available. The disclosures available range from short, perfunctory statements, to confusing and vague references to existing policies that lead consumers on a scavenger hunt. Other companies have written moving descriptions of commitments. Without the availability of comparable information from all, there is not enough information for consumers to make an accurate comparison. NGOs creating smartphone consumer applications only have the data of companies' publicly disclosed information. A company may have all of the policies and training in place, yet with a poor statement their rating or score in these apps will be dismal, destroying brand loyalty and turning away other potential customers. Essentially, consumers can spend elsewhere because who wants to support a company that does not at least say it is against slavery?

Conversely, competitors can distinguish themselves as being more committed, being socially responsible, and standing behind their products. They recognize S.B. 657's intrinsic public relations value and the opportunity to bolster the brand's reputation. Competitors' disclosures then also create risk and shame for a company either without a disclosure statement or with a minimally compliant one.

To reduce the risk and likelihood of shame, any retailer or manufacturer subject to S.B. 657 can comply by releasing both a positive statement that each of the five elements is occurring and a satisfactory description of the extent to which each is occurring. To successfully build on this disclosure, the company should weave practices related to these five anti-trafficking measures into the company's existing structure of supply chain verification, supplier audits and certifications, corporate policies, and employee training. The response requires coordination and cooperation among public affairs, CSR, supply chain operations, compliance, and human resources.

Enforcement

S.B. 657's exclusive remedy is injunctive relief by the California Attorney General. NGOs are leading an effort to amend the legislation to provide stronger enforcement remedies. The Attorney General's office has indicated that they are contemplating other appropriate actions. Possibilities include the Truth in Labeling Act and the Fair Business Practices Act.

Industry associations have monitored and assisted their membership related to S.B. 657. For example, Nate Herman, General Counsel at the American Apparel and Footwear Association (AAFA), follows potential enforcement and legislative developments in order to keep the membership updated. He also issued guidance to AAFA membership regarding compliance. In-house counsel and law firms have also counseled corporations on the public disclosure statements and underlying activities. The majority of activity related to S.B. 657, however, occurred before the first compliance deadline of January 1, 2012, when the law was new and enforcement uncertain. Since then firms have noticed a decline in requests for assistance.

A Model for Future Laws

Other states are considering similar legislation using S.B. 657 as a model. A federal counterpart has been introduced, requiring any company submitting an annual report to the Securities and Exchange Commission (SEC) to provide a more detailed disclosure than the California Act requires. For example, the text of any policy must be included, as well as an assessment of the adequacy of suppliers' supply-chain management and procurement systems to identify risks, and details on suppliers' compliance to eliminate exploitative labor recruitment practices.

Thoughtful legislators and activists are considering how to multiply S.B. 657's impact across the country and to increase its scope.

Foreign Corrupt Practices Act

The Foreign Corrupt Practices Act (FCPA)[18] makes it illegal to bribe foreign officials in order to gain an improper business advantage. An offense consists of

1. a payment, offer, authorization, or promise to pay money or anything of value
2. to a foreign government official (including a party official or manager of a state-owned concern), or to any other person, knowing that the payment or promise will be passed on to a foreign official
3. with a corrupt motive
4. for the purpose of (a) influencing any act or decision of that person, (b) inducing such person to do or omit any action in violation of his lawful duty, (c) securing an improper advantage, or (d) inducing such person to use his influence to affect an official act or decision
5. in order to assist in obtaining or retaining business for or with, or directing any business to, any person.[19]

Parent companies can be liable for actions by companies acquired in mergers and acquisitions through successor liability as well as by their subsidiaries under traditional agency principles and *respondeat superior.* Enforced by the DOJ and the SEC, the FCPA subjects individuals—officers, directors, stockholders, and agents—as well as business entities in violation of the anti-bribery or recordkeeping provisions to substantial fines, imprisonment, debarment from the securities industry, disgorgement of resulting profits, ineligibility for export licenses, and related civil and criminal claims.

With this kind of risk and liability on the line, corporations often turn to law firms with FCPA expertise, primarily focused on developing a robust compliance program. According to the DOJ and the SEC,[20] effective compliance programs will include

- Commitment from senior management and a clearly articulated policy against corruption
- Code of conduct and compliance policies and procedures
- Oversight, autonomy, and resources

- Risk assessment
- Training and continuing advice
- Incentives and disciplinary measures
- Third-party due diligence and payments

Human Trafficking Linked to Corruption

Human trafficking, already a risk to corporations, is strongly correlated to corruption and should also be considered in FCPA compliance work. The U.S. Department of State's annual Trafficking in Persons Report has long connected its rankings of government action against human trafficking with the country's level of corruption as reported by Transparency International.[21] Governments that make the least amount of effort to address trafficking are also those reported to be the most corrupt.

The risk of corruption and human trafficking is most acute when corporations rely on other entities—labor brokers and third-party employment agencies—to secure labor, which necessitates working with foreign officials typically for immigration, labor, and law enforcement.[22] Trafficked persons have reported complicity of law enforcement, border control, and labor department government officials at all stages, including bribes to cross borders, facilitate visas and passports, and obtain work permits. The bribe is sometimes paid from inflated fees the worker is paid or is added to the workers' debts, another way in which traffickers create debt bondage. The risk is so high that some companies no longer outsource their recruiting but instead handle it all internally.

FCPA work is a great example of how attorneys can and should integrate anti-trafficking efforts into their clients' compliance programs. Doing so mitigates the risk not only of FCPA violations stemming from human trafficking but also the occurrence of human trafficking more generally. Michael Navarre, Special Counsel at Steptoe and Johnson, says the process is not static; just as the business landscape is always changing, there must be a corresponding continual reassessment of risk and responsive policies.

SEC Regulation on Conflict Minerals

The SEC Regulation on Conflict Minerals[23] requires certain publicly traded companies to annually disclose their use of conflict minerals from

the DRC and adjoining countries. Companies subject to the rule include
those that

1. use conflict minerals, which include
    *   columbite-tantalite, also known as coltan, the metal ore from
        which tantalum is extracted;
    *   cassiterite, the metal ore from which tin is extracted;
    *   gold;
    *   wolframite, the metal ore from which tungsten is extracted;
    *   or their derivatives;
    *   or any other mineral or its derivatives determined by the Secretary
        of State to be financing conflict in the DRC or an adjoining country
        (Angola, Burundi, Central African Republic, the Republic of the
        Congo, Rwanda, South Sudan, Tanzania, Uganda, and Zambia)
2. when the conflict minerals are necessary to the functionality or pro-
    duction of a product manufactured or contracted to be manufac-
    tured, and
3. when the company has influence over the product's manufacturing
    materials, parts, ingredients, or components.

If subject to the regulation, a company must make disclosure on Form
SD annually on May 31 beginning in 2014. Companies must conduct a
"reasonable country of origin inquiry" to determine whether the conflict
mineral originated in one of the covered countries and, if so or a company
believes so, must then exercise due diligence on the source and chain of
custody of the conflict minerals and may need to submit a conflict minerals report with their annual disclosure. The report would include whether
the company used any recognized standards or guidance or used a certified independent auditor and a description of the facilities, country of
origin, and efforts to determine the mine(s).

Purpose
The 2010 Dodd-Frank Wall Street Reform and Consumer Protection Act[24] mandated the regulation as a way to remove one method of

financing to the armed groups involved in violent conflict in the DRC. Congress's stated intent was also to increase consumer awareness about conflict minerals in products they purchase and to promote due diligence and corporate responsibility within conflict mineral supply chains. Not surprisingly, each of these conflict minerals is also confirmed by the U.S. Department of Labor to be mined by forced labor in the DRC. For companies eliminating minerals from the DRC in their products, they are also mitigating the risk of forced labor. The larger opportunity builds on the infrastructure established by these regulations.

Impact

Unlike any other law or regulation, the SEC Regulation on Conflict Minerals requires companies to trace the source of specific minerals within massively complex supply chains, when most often visibility only extends to first-tier suppliers. For an electronics brand, this means that the company primarily engages the suppliers assembling their products and perhaps a limited number of critical component manufacturers in the second tier. But the exercise required by the regulation requires that the company undertake the complicated task of tracing their raw mineral sources. During the rulemaking process, investors, corporations, and industry associations submitted lengthy comments about the expense and the challenge of obtaining accurate information from a multitude of suppliers.

The regulation affects approximately six thousand companies and their two hundred eighty thousand suppliers, rippling throughout entire supply chains. Consider that these minerals are most obviously used in the auto, aerospace, jewelry, and electronics industry but also in less obvious industries such as financial services because of the chips in credit and debit cards as well as apparel for adornments and fasteners.

Attorneys were involved throughout the rulemaking, advising the corporate clients on the regulation's developments and then implementation once the 356-page final rule was issued. They also manage compliance by working within multidisciplinary teams, including financial and accounting officers, supply chain personnel, information technology (IT) personnel, auditors, and communications personnel.

Federal Acquisition Regulation (FAR)

More than six hundred sixty thousand businesses hold contracts with the U.S. government (USG)—the largest purchaser of goods and products in the world. Federal contractors supply all manner of goods and services to the USG, including paper clips, tomatoes, and uniforms as well as IT services, construction, security, and fighter jets. Every federal contractor is subject to regulations mandating certain policies and actions, including anti-trafficking measures. Law firms with government contracting practice areas and in-house counsel to government contractors have been watching the development of a new federal regulation on human trafficking, awaiting the details of this new compliance measure, and putting into place the known pieces.

2006 FAR

Through the FAR, the USG has the leverage to shape corporate behavior and policy and is doing so quite purposefully with respect to human trafficking. The first effort began in 2006 with a new FAR stating the USG's zero-tolerance policy for human trafficking. FAR 22.17 requires contractors and subcontractors to notify government employees of trafficking violations and puts parties on notice that the government may impose remedies, including termination, for failure to comply with the requirements.[25] FAR 52.222-50 also requires federal contractors to put in place policies and procedures to identify and prevent forced labor, inform employees of the policy and consequences, and include the "Combating Trafficking in Persons" clause in any subcontracts.[26] The Department of Defense also has specific anti-trafficking regulations in its Defense Federal Acquisition Regulations.[27]

During the run-up to adoption of the 2006 FAR, occasionally allegations of human trafficking arose followed by congressional inquiries, which led to three years of congressionally mandated Inspector General reports on high-risk contracts at the U.S. Agency for International Development (USAID), the State Department, and the Defense Department. The reports highlighted subcontractor inspections that uncovered withheld passports, wage and hour violations, substandard housing conditions, and recruitment debts—all indicators of human trafficking. The report also disclosed that the required contract clause was not in place for subcontractors the majority of the time. Then came additional pressure as the Wartime Contracting Commission[28] identified human trafficking of third-country nationals in Iraq and Afghanistan, finding that prime contractors could have done more to supervise their labor brokers and subcontractors and thereby prevent forced labor.

At the same time, USG officials responsible for anti-trafficking policies saw the opportunity to create a robust tool to prevent forced labor. Since the regulation went into effect in 2006, no contract had been terminated, no contractor debarred, and no broader implementation or enforcement took effect. The USG recognized that this regulation was insufficient and wanted to ensure that its own house was in order, that it had a slavery-free supply chain.

Proposed Rule

Pressure from Congress, findings of the Wartime Contracting Commission, audit reports on high-risk government contracts, and the desire of senior government officials to lead by example culminated in a new Executive Order. In September 2012, President Obama announced the Executive Order,[29] "Strengthening Protections Against Trafficking in Persons in Federal Contracts," saying:

> [A]s one of the largest purchasers of goods and services in the world, the United States government will lead by example. We've already taken steps to make sure our contractors do not engage in forced labor. And today we're going to go further. I've signed a new executive order that raises the bar. It's specific about the prohibitions. It does more to protect workers. It ensures stronger compliance. In short, we're making clear that American tax dollars must never, ever be used to support the trafficking of human beings. We will have zero tolerance. We mean what we say. We will enforce it.

On January 2, 2013, President Obama signed the National Defense Authorization Act for Fiscal Year 2013 (NDAA), which included a section entitled "Ending Trafficking in Government Contracting."[30] It contains measures quite similar to the Executive Order in terms of prohibited behavior and compliance plan features; however, it also amended 18 U.S.C. § 1351, "Fraud in Foreign Labor Contracting," to include work outside of the United States:

> (a) FOR PURPOSES OF EMPLOYMENT IN THE UNITED STATES.— Whoever knowingly and with intent to defraud recruits, solicits, or hires a person outside the United States or causes another person to recruit, solicit, or hire a person outside the United States, or attempts to do so, for purposes of employment in the United States by means of materially false or fraudulent pretenses, representations or promises regarding that employment shall be fined under this title or imprisoned for not more than 5 years, or both.
>
> (b) FOR THE PURPOSES OF EMPLOYMENT PERFORMED ON A USG CONTRACT PERFORMED OUTSIDE THE UNITED STATES.—Whoever knowingly and with intent to defraud recruits, solicits, or hires a person outside the United States or causes another person to recruit, solicit, or hire a person outside the United States, or attempts to do so, for purposes of employment performed on a United States Government contract performed outside the United States, or on a United States military installation or mission outside the United States or other property or premises outside the United States owned or controlled by the United States Government, by means of materially false or fraudulent pretenses, representations, or promises regarding that employment, shall be fined under this title or imprisoned for not more than 5 years, or both.

In 2013, the FAR Council published a proposed rule[31] based on both the Executive Order and the NDAA (final rule had not been published yet as of the publication of this book). The proposed rule is now more specific and prescriptive than the 2006 rule, targeting the activity that is often overlooked yet contributes to labor exploitation and forced labor. Federal contractors, contractor employees, subcontractors, and subcontractor employees are expressly prohibited from

- engaging in fraudulent or misleading labor recruiting either by failing to disclose basic information or misrepresenting the terms of the job,

such as wage and benefits, location, housing, costs, and hazardous
nature of the work;

- charging recruitment fees; and
- destroying, concealing, confiscating, or denying employees access to
  their identity documents.

For all contracts $500,000 or greater or that are to be performed
abroad, contractors and subcontractors must maintain and post publicly
on their website a compliance plan that includes

- the process by which employees can report complaints and violations;
- recruitment by companies with trained employees and that does not
  charge fees;
- wages according to local law;
- housing that meets local housing and safety standards;
- an employee awareness program about the corporate policies and actions taken against employees for violations;
- procedures to prevent, monitor, detect, and terminate any subcontractors or subcontractor employees for engaging in human trafficking or related activities; and
- certification by each contractor and subcontractor that none have engaged in human trafficking or related activities and that there is a
  compliance plan in place.

Additionally, contractors and subcontractors are required to provide
reasonable access and comply with investigations and audits.

Alan Chvotkin is Executive Vice President and Counsel of the Professional Services Council, where he primarily engages in policy and advocacy on behalf of the association's membership of federal contractors. He
has followed the development of the rule quite closely, coordinating with
other trade associations, participating in public panel discussions, and
submitting comments to the FAR Council. He says (email communication
on April 21, 2014), "It is in our collective interest to have the FAR rule
crafted in a way that maximizes the reduction of incidents of trafficking
while minimizing the compliance burden on both government and industry." Chvotkin has also inquired among members to learn how many

of them are already acting to address human trafficking and plans to continue education efforts on human trafficking among the membership beyond the publication of the rule.

Law firms with substantial federal contractor practice areas have also been closely following the rule and have begun to bring clients into compliance.

Enforcement

The USG has already taken steps to augment enforcement. In 2012, the USG launched mandated training for federal contracting officers responsible for oversight of individual contracts. Contracting officers are now trained on human trafficking and contract requirements, how to assess compliance, how to conduct verification, and what to do in cases of violations, including terminating contracts and recommending contractors for suspension or debarment. Multiple agencies have issued official notices among their contracting officers emphasizing the heightened focus on human trafficking and desire for increased oversight.

Conclusion

In today's extended and complex supply chains, a forced-labor incident is inevitable. Even where the likelihood of an incident's occurring may appear low, the potential damage to a business is high. Ensuring due diligence today regarding compliance and developing broader risk mitigation strategies are efforts that protect the company from a known and certain risk while also enhancing the brand as a socially responsible company.

There is a growing cadre of attorneys involved in business and human rights and CSR, which we believe represents a shift in the degree to which corporations address any number of issues related to their operations. For the corporate law attorney, whether in-house or at a firm, anti-trafficking work is one of integration: integrating policies and practices that will prevent human trafficking into existing risk mitigation, ethics, and compliance programs.

CHAPTER 4

Labor and Employment Law Approaches to Human Trafficking

[W]e were promised the moon but given dirt.

—Dancy D'Souza

Legal professionals work in areas that touch employment and labor issues. Plaintiff attorneys, union organizers, corporate counsel, and worker rights attorneys all share one thing in common—they are likely in a position to address human trafficking through their work. These professionals are likely but unknowingly interfacing with trafficked persons, without the requisite understanding to identify trafficked persons and connect them with protections. They are also likely practicing in areas where expanding identification and protections for trafficked persons merely requires an expansion of their outreach strategies or the causes of action they plead. This chapter approaches solutions by developing opportunities for increased identification and expanding civil litigation opportunities on behalf of trafficked persons. It also provides context to employment defense attorneys who are strategizing to prevent human trafficking in the workplace.

Myths and Misconceptions in the Labor Context

By simply increasing capacity to identify and refer trafficked persons, the labor and employment law sectors will help labor trafficked persons overcome their primary obstacle—connecting their human trafficking experiences with the protections afforded to them. Labor trafficking is often misunderstood within the broader context of human trafficking. Media, and in turn the general public, often conflate sex trafficking and human trafficking, leaving people to believe that sex trafficking is the only manifestation of human trafficking.

Confusion about definitions also leads many to mistakenly characterize labor trafficking cases as sex trafficking. Traffickers use sexual violence as a method of coercion to compel individuals in labor. Yet when details of the sexual violence emerge, such cases are often publicly described as sex trafficking instead of labor trafficking cases. In other cases, trafficking in industries like dancing and modeling may be viewed through a sex lens and characterized as sex trafficking instead of labor trafficking. This perpetuates public confusion over what labor trafficking looks like and the indicators that may reveal trafficking.

Media also overemphasize the prevalence of sex trafficking over labor trafficking in the United States. There are no scientific studies of the prevalence of sex trafficking and labor trafficking in the United States. However, the International Labour Organization estimates that globally, 78 percent of human trafficking is in labor trafficking, with the remainder in sex trafficking.[1] Many noteworthy and indeed most of the largest human trafficking prosecutions have been labor trafficking cases. Still, labor trafficking remains largely overlooked by local criminal justice systems.[2]

Labor trafficking cases reflect common economic patterns involving the recruitment of the most economically vulnerable, those who will take risks to access a better employment opportunity. In the United States, labor trafficking largely targets overseas and undocumented immigrant communities. To a lesser degree, labor trafficking affects U.S. citizens. Those individuals typically have some characteristic of extreme vulnerability to exploitation, including drug addiction, homelessness, and mental disability. Overseas workers are defrauded into jobs with conditions different than promised. They are compelled through debt servitude, sexual assault, threats of deportation, and physical restraints.

The marginalization of labor trafficking within the human trafficking discourse has several important ramifications. First, it directly hinders the identification of labor trafficked persons. A public narrative dominated by sex trafficking as the predominant form of human trafficking means that we the public will not know what labor trafficking looks like, even when it is right in front of us. Labor trafficked persons, whether in our grocery stores, on a work site visited by union organizers, or in an attorney's office to pursue a wage and hour claim, are unlikely to be identified as a trafficked person. Instantly, their window for access to protections and resources has suddenly closed.

From an institutional perspective, the lack of dialogue on labor trafficking means that we dedicate fewer resources to identifying, investigating, and prosecuting all forms of trafficking. Programs are funded to conduct outreach campaigns only on sex trafficking. Communities invest in getting trained to identify sex trafficking alone. Movies and books promote sensationalized versions of sex trafficking, while a neighbor is engaged in labor trafficking of a domestic worker right under your nose.

Second, even for labor trafficked persons who are identified, the marginalization of labor trafficking affects their range of options. The criminal justice system in the United States has been slow to respond to labor trafficking. We discuss the reasons for this in Chapter 2. Because many more labor trafficking cases go uninvestigated, most labor trafficking victims do not have access to the criminal justice protections to which they are entitled: safety, restitution, and justice.

Attorneys and professionals working in the fields of labor law and employment law have not yet proactively engaged in mitigating these gaps in protection. Within the legal profession, many labor and employment law attorneys are situated to rectify some of the gaps. Many can create institution-wide programs to increase identification of trafficked persons. Plaintiff and labor union attorneys are likely already representing and interacting with trafficked people without realizing it. Union workers and others working in worker rights advocacy can build labor trafficking identification into their screening processes. Government agencies reviewing labor claims can improve their capacity to screen for trafficking and help those workers access the right resources.

Identification will also create an increased demand for civil litigators and government employment attorneys to begin or expand their practices on behalf of trafficked persons. Increased representation will help more labor trafficked persons receive the damages and justice to which they are entitled. In addition to plaintiff attorneys already positioned to expand their practice, there is already an increased demand for pro bono litigators to represent trafficked persons in civil litigation. Anti-trafficking legal services programs typically lack the capacity to take on civil litigation unless in partnership with pro bono law firms. Only with the expanded participation of plaintiff attorneys, pro bono law firms, and government labor agencies will trafficked persons fully avail themselves of civil remedies.

Beyond identification and protection, attorneys also play a critical role in prevention efforts. While most corporate attorneys rightly conclude that their clients are not likely engaged in human trafficking, this conclusion only reveals the hidden nature of labor trafficking. Labor trafficking occurs within sectors or companies where it is most easily hidden. Trafficking has been found in isolated settings in the United States, including agricultural fields and factories. Trafficking is also easily hidden by smaller contractors in service industries. Management and employers have opportunities to develop policies that mitigate risk of trafficking of employees, contractors, and others with whom they do business. Attorneys can take steps to prevent human trafficking, by reading Chapter 1 to understand what human trafficking looks like, studying the criminal implications set forth in Chapter 2, and understanding the civil implications that we discuss later in this chapter.

The Case for Proactive Identification

Throughout this book, we stress the importance of proactive identification efforts. Because trafficked persons rarely self-identify, the burden of identifying them shifts to others with whom they interact. The focus on identification as a starting point cannot be overstated in the context of labor trafficking.

Traffickers commonly use psychological coercion to compel trafficked persons. The tools of coercion are not visible and must be understood for their subjective impact on a trafficked person. A trafficked person might have the physical freedom to come and go, meet with an attorney, and even seek services regarding employment. Traffickers in some cases worry less about this physical movement and interaction because they believe their psychological coercion will prevent trafficked persons from revealing the exploitation to anyone. The coercion might involve debt bondage or threats. A trafficker could be holding a trafficked person's passport, knowing that the worker would not dare try to leave his or her employment without it. Guestworkers may fear speaking out for fear of blacklisting, which would prevent them from securing future work.

Other trafficked persons may have experienced trafficking in the past. They may have satisfied a debt, allowing them to move on. The job site might have been shut down. A worker may have run away, but rather than disclose the experience, the worker moved on and found a new job. In some cases, trafficked persons reached safety and were unaware of the protections available to them until years later.

Identification protocols will also reach larger groups of workers. Traffickers often use the same tactics on all of their employees. Therefore, identifying one potential trafficked person, or even conducting outreach to one worker in a worker community, may result in reaching a larger group of trafficked persons, who are otherwise unfamiliar with available protections. While most in the labor and employment fields have yet to embrace systematic training and implementation of identification protocols, those who do gain exposure to labor trafficking consistently report that they have likely overlooked victims with whom they have interacted.

Imagine the following scenario:

Jose worked on a strawberry farm in rural California. On the farm, there were two main groups of workers: one Latino group comprising low-wage workers who had been in the United States for a long time, and another group made up of workers who had been brought over from Mexico and Central America to work on the same farm. The latter group of workers were housed in a work camp and shuttled to the fields every day. Jose had heard that they owed debts, and he observed that the bosses tended to treat those workers poorly. Jose went to a farmworker legal clinic after getting fired for getting injured. When the attorney started probing, Jose told the attorney about this entire group of workers. Jose went to the work site and quietly passed on some information about their rights to these workers. A group of the workers decided to leave the site with Jose one day after work and were able to seek help from the attorney.

While there is a strong likelihood of trafficking in such work camps, there is a significant opportunity to increase outreach using safe methods to reach such workers, who are otherwise isolated and unfamiliar with human trafficking protections. Identification need not be limited to the individual who sits before us. Some of the individuals who come to us for help are the safest ambassadors of worker rights information.

Because so many labor trafficked persons are undocumented or have status tied to a trafficker, they are at risk of immigration enforcement, and they have few avenues to remain in the United States lawfully. Identification offers access to immigration protections primarily through the T or the U nonimmigrant visas,[3] options unfamiliar to most trafficked immigrants.[4] But these protections also shield undocumented workers openly pursuing civil litigation. These trafficking-specific forms of immigration relief are critical because they provide the visa holders with permission to accept employment, which allows them to seek higher-wage jobs.[5] They also trigger certain federal protections that offer access to social services that are necessary for a worker to avoid future exploitation. All of these services and protections not only help restore a trafficked person who has experienced exploitation but also provide economic means to remain in the United States while pursuing civil litigation, with the goal of better opportunities that provide financial security.

For those undocumented workers who have been unable to file T or U visas, or whose visa has expired or is invalidated, filing a civil lawsuit also provides protection from immigration enforcement in some specific cases. As part of the 2008 reauthorization of the Trafficking Victims Protection Act (TVPA), trafficking victims who file a civil suit under the TVPA are permitted to remain in the United States through the duration of civil litigation, even if their visa expires or is invalidated.[6] A-3 or G-5 visa holders, who are personal employees of certain overseas foreign government or organizational workers, may also remain in the United States while they seek civil relief for a violation of their contracts.[7]

The long-term goal of civil litigation for these trafficked persons is civil damages as a critical component in a trafficked person's economic empowerment. Trafficking is a crime of profit, with traffickers exploiting others for financial gain. Trafficked persons are often in an economically disadvantaged position, willing to trust and accept what seems to be a financially beneficial opportunity without being able to predict the force, fraud, or coercion to come. With fewer prosecutions, labor trafficked persons have less access to criminal restitution, leaving civil damages as their primary economic remedy.

Leaving a labor trafficking situation only to be put in an economically similar or marginally better position always puts a trafficked person at risk. Because labor trafficked persons are often recruited from low-income communities, they are often not equipped with job skills, especially without English proficiency, to find jobs outside the low-wage sector. Trafficked persons need access to enough financial stability that they will not be at risk of further exploitation. Although classification as a victim of trafficking triggers eligibility for victim compensation and public benefits, the amount available to each victim is far too inadequate to prevent an individual from being retrafficked. Civil damages can be used to offset previous debts unrelated to trafficking, pay for education, or provide long-term security. An award itself may not fully transition a trafficked person out of the low-wage workforce, but it might serve as a critical step in preventing further exploitation.

Beyond its being necessary for individual protection, identifying labor trafficking is important to data collection efforts. Currently, our main sources of federal data on human trafficking collect information by tracking victims involved in the criminal justice system or those working with victim service providers. Since so many labor trafficking cases do not proceed through the criminal justice system, they go unaccounted for in federal databases. This perpetuates the myth and narrative that emphasize the prevalence of sex trafficking. Nevertheless, this challenge can also easily be solved by increasing partnership between civil litigators and trafficking victim service providers, who contribute data to the national database.

Because this chapter targets attorneys working in the labor and employment law fields, we focus on labor trafficking here. We do note the instances in which sex trafficking remedies and strategies can equally be applied within the context of civil laws. Because damages are a core outcome of civil litigation, sex trafficking cases are not as easy to litigate. Some sex trafficked persons receive a significant amount of money from participation in commercial sex, offering them more financial stability and making them appear possibly less sympathetic. Sex trafficking also often involves those who participated in commercial sex outside the trafficking, which may be difficult for a jury to understand. Sex trafficking may be better addressed through the criminal justice system, which allows sex trafficking victims to protect their identity and avoid publicity.

Implementing a Screening Process

Given the case for increased identification, true impact requires not only adoption of the premise that human trafficking exists but also thoughtful deliberation to create effective screening policies and protocols. On a larger scale, we need a broad range of professionals to likewise implement screening practices if we are to reach beyond the sliver of trafficked persons who are identified every year. This burden of identifying trafficked persons falls even more on those in the fields of labor law and employment law because labor trafficking remains vastly under-identified.

Systematized screening efforts begin with wide-scale training so that all of an organization's employees and stakeholders understand exactly how to recognize human trafficking, where they are likely to come across trafficking, and how to respond. Building on that training, employees and stakeholders should be equipped with formal and tailored indicators, screening and intake forms, and interview questions to facilitate identification of trafficked persons. In anticipation of increased identification, institutions should develop protocols to foresee safety risks for the person reporting the trafficking and proper referral measures in order to facilitate immediate services to a potential trafficked person. After noticing a dearth of anti-trafficking experts working directly with non-traditional stakeholders to design and tailor such trainings and protocols, we founded the Global Freedom Center to meet these specific needs.

A number of people within the labor and employment law sectors are positioned to take action in these screening efforts. Civil litigators already representing workers are particularly suited to increase identification of labor trafficked persons. By accessing training designed for those in their field and then building trafficking screening questions into their client intake, attorneys can immediately have an impact and meaningfully address human trafficking. For example, labor trafficked persons are often housed by their employers, a fact that emerges during a wage calculation on any fair-wage case. Onsite housing is also an indicator of human trafficking, and an attorney trained to recognize that indicator would be able to probe further to ascertain trafficking-related claims.

Those conducting organizing and outreach efforts to worker groups might be able to increase identification using slightly different methods. Union and other organizers who receive human trafficking training can incorporate labor trafficking indicators into their workshops, presentations, and outreach materials. Finally, government labor agencies are perfectly positioned because of their infrastructure to receive staff training and then add human trafficking indicators into their forms.

Outreach and Collaboration

Currently, most trafficked persons are identified through law enforcement or anti-trafficking service providers, who refer civil litigation to the few civil litigation partners who already take on these cases. But a number of anti-trafficking programs do not have access to civil litigators. So while trafficked persons might be identified from a data perspective, they have not yet accessed all the important protections to assist them in their economic empowerment.

Other partners might work with communities where trafficking could exist, but the partners are less familiar with trafficking and unable to identify it. Civil litigators interested in taking on trafficking cases should explore partnerships that also include training and screening with the hopes that increased identification will lead to increased referrals. For example, immigrant rights and worker rights groups think broadly about workers' rights but may not yet be familiar with the indicators specific to trafficking. Attorneys interested in pursuing civil labor trafficking cases to fill the gap in labor trafficking representation can partner with these groups to increase capacity of both lawyers and these organizations to identify and refer labor trafficking cases.

Building Civil Litigation Cases and Practices[8]

A comprehensive response to human trafficking requires trafficked persons to have access to a range of protections that will not only restore them but also provide them meaningful alternatives to prevent repeated human trafficking or exploitation. For individuals who have experienced human trafficking, financial resources make it possible for them to gain stability and position themselves on a path out of poverty and toward economic opportunity. One of the most underutilized avenues for trafficked persons to get such financial resources is through an award of civil damages from their traffickers. Civil relief offers trafficked persons access to justice on their own terms as a plaintiff instead of as a third-party victim witness. Furthermore, the damages awarded to a trafficked person undercut a trafficker's profit margin, which is the main driver of human trafficking. Because of misconceptions about human trafficking, many of those eligible for civil relief go unidentified and unconnected to legal resources.

Too few of those victims who have been identified have proceeded with civil trafficking claims due to a number of barriers. As discussed previously, trafficked persons are typically identified by law enforcement or nonprofits providing victim services, few of whom have professional connections to local civil litigators. As an emerging field, the anti-trafficking movement has seen a proliferation of anti-trafficking programs that are not yet established enough to have a developed civil litigation referral network. Anti-trafficking advocates may not always have relationships with large firms willing to take on pro bono cases and likely even less connection with plaintiffs' attorneys who might take a case pro bono or on a contingency basis.

> **Tip**
> Identify the human trafficking and worker rights organizations in the area and offer to partner to represent trafficked persons in civil litigation. Work with the programs to develop a screening and referral protocol that easily fits in to the firm's preexisting intake, screening, and conflicts process. Firms seeking pro bono cases can design something that fits into existing pro bono screening processes.

Some pro bono law firms may be more reluctant to take on pro bono civil trafficking cases because in their regular practice, these firms represent the employer against the employee. Most trafficking cases involve individual and small employers, not large corporate entities, so it is unlikely that a pro bono law firm already represents an alleged trafficker. Conducting proper conflicts checks should overcome any hesitation to take on these cases. Some law firm leadership views pro bono civil trafficking cases as a conflict of issues, a term describing arguing both sides of a law on different cases. A conflict of issue is not an actual bar, so this narrow concern of attorneys may prevent many trafficked persons from having access to the critical civil remedies to which they are entitled.

> The Human Trafficking Pro Bono Legal Center provides training and mentoring to pro bono attorneys taking on civil litigation. Founded in 2012, the Center seeks to encourage pro bono attorneys to take on civil litigation against traffickers and increase trafficked persons' use of civil litigation protections.

Civil Causes of Action

A number of causes of action are available at the federal and state levels. Familiarity with the range of laws will allow civil litigators to help trafficked persons using all possible remedies. All of these laws have been tested on a very limited basis. This section is designed to provide a simple overview of options and considerations in accessing these options.

Causes of Action Under the Trafficking Victims Protection Act

Although Congress passed the TVPA in 2000, it was not until the 2003 reauthorization of the Act that Congress created a private right of action for anyone who is a victim under 18 U.S.C. § 1589, 1590, or 1591.[9] Those specific crimes are (1) forced labor; (2) peonage, slavery, involuntary servitude, or forced labor; and (3) sex trafficking of children or by force, fraud, or coercion.

1. Forced labor[10]:
    (a) Whoever knowingly provides or obtains the labor or services of a person by any one of, or by any combination of, the following means—
        (1) by means of force, threats of force, physical restraint, or threats of physical restraint to that person or another person;
        (2) by means of serious harm or threats of serious harm to that person or another person;
        (3) by means of the abuse or threatened abuse of law or legal process; or
        (4) by means of any scheme, plan, or pattern intended to cause the person to believe that, if that person did not perform such labor or services, that person or another person would suffer serious harm or physical restraint.

Forced labor is a misleading term; it implies a requirement of physical force. But the crime definition extends far beyond actual force to anticipate the range of labor trafficking scenarios that are better described as coercion. Therefore, beyond those physically restrained by barbed wire and locks, forced labor applies to those compelled through psychological coercion, invisible to the naked eye.

For example, Devendra Shukla came to the United States on an R-1 religious worker visa to work for Sat Prakasha Sharma, the president of a Hindu temple, and his wife, Geeta Sharma. The Sharmas confiscated Shukla's passport and required him to work long hours and sleep on the floor. Shukla prevailed in a lawsuit that included claims of forced labor, with the jury awarding $2.3 million.[11]

2. Peonage, slavery, involuntary servitude, or forced labor: This provision covers a number of actions that are perceived to fall within

Asian American Legal Defense and Education Fund (AALDEF) has successfully litigated and continues to litigate civil human trafficking cases. It has collected more than $2 million in restitution and awards on behalf of trafficked persons, with their litigation focused primarily on domestic workers and other low-wage workers. AALDEF is one of very few programs in the United States that takes on civil anti-trafficking litigation.

the scope of human trafficking. Congress defined an action in this category as "knowingly recruits, harbors, transports, provides, or obtains by any means, any person for labor or services."[12]

3. Sex trafficking of children or by force, fraud, or coercion: The final provision allows for civil relief against a person who knowingly—

   (1) in or affecting interstate or foreign commerce, or within the special maritime and territorial jurisdiction of the United States, recruits, entices, harbors, transports, provides, obtains, or maintains by any means a person; or

   (2) benefits, financially or by receiving anything of value, from participation in a venture which has engaged in an act described in violation of paragraph (1),

   knowing, or in reckless disregard of the fact, that means of force, threats of force, fraud, coercion described in subsection (e)(2), or any combination of such means will be used to cause the person to engage in a commercial sex act, or that the person has not attained the age of 18 years and will be caused to engage in a commercial sex act, shall be punished as provided in subsection (b).[13]

While available to trafficked persons, this provision has not yet been widely used as a basis for a civil claim, likely because of some of the concerns we addressed earlier.

Since reauthorization of the TVPA in 2003, civil remedies have been subsequently expanded and clarified. The 2008 reauthorization of the TVPA expanded the availability of civil relief to all of the Chapter 77 trafficking crimes,[14] which are discussed in detail in Chapter 2. Those crimes include a separate crime for peonage,[15] involuntary servitude,[16] and document servitude.[17]

Because so few trafficked persons self-identify or are identified by others, it can take a number of years after their trafficking experiences for a trafficked persons to learn or understand that there are protections available to them. Congress anticipated this and created a ten-year statute of limitations for TVPA civil remedies.[18]

Fair Labor Standards Act

The Fair Labor Standards Act (FLSA) is much more familiar to labor and employment law attorneys than the TVPA and makes available to trafficked persons some of the same relief. The FLSA offers federal wage and hour protections to workers. In addition, the FLSA allows claims based on an employer's failure to pay minimum wage and overtime pay.[19] It also requires compensation for work performed without breaks required by law. Human trafficking is at one end of a range of exploitation, with potential for overlapping indicators. Those indicators may include low wages, poor work conditions, onsite work, long hours, and more. Because wage violations are common in labor trafficking cases, claims under the FLSA should be explored in all civil trafficking cases.

Recall labor traffickers' profit motives. They compel labor because it offers an easier avenue to profit as they pay trafficked persons less than individuals working in freely chosen employment or even pay them nothing. Because these traffickers seek out the most vulnerable to exploit, their workers are likely to be immigrants housed by the employer. This also provides easy opportunities to compel very long hours of work from people who have no knowledge of minimum wages and overtime rules. Because trafficked persons often live in trafficker-provided accommodations, often onsite in a work camp or in a house where working as a domestic worker, there is less of a distinction between work and non-work hours.

Regardless of trafficking, the FLSA protects low-wage workers, who may also not understand their rights to a fair wage. Immigrant workers often receive wages better than what they could make in their home countries. Therefore, the FLSA must be considered independent of labor trafficking protections with similar expectations: that a worker may not realize his or her rights and present as FLSA-eligible.

Many traffickers also expect that their workers will not proceed with civil remedies because the workers lack immigration status and have not received permission to work. Protections against immigration enforcement previously discussed only apply to those seeking civil relief under the TVPA causes of action or after filing a T visa or a U visa. Those trafficked persons who do not meet the burden of proof or are for some reason unable to plead TVPA claims or file for T or U visas will not be able to access those shields against immigration enforcement. This is an important consideration where knowledge of local immigration enforcement and court practices is essential. However, courts are allowing undocumented plaintiffs to proceed with FLSA cases.[20] FLSA cases have a two-year statute of limitations after a violation occurs and three years for willful violations.[21]

Discrimination Laws

Although human trafficking is not often perceived through a lens of discrimination, many cases meet discriminatory elements, lending themselves to a Title VII action. Title VII prohibits discrimination in employment based on any of the five protected classes: race, color, religion, sex, and national origin.[22] Because traffickers are able to exploit the economic vulnerabilities of migrant workers, they are likely to discriminate in the treatment of employees, believing they have more leverage with migrants. This treatment may satisfy a claim for discriminatory treatment or disparate impact based on national origin, which is one category likely to be the basis for a discrimination claim.

Case Study[23]

The John D. Pickle Company recruited workers from India to come to the United States. The workers were promised lawful wages and proper working conditions. Upon arrival, the workers were housed in a cramped warehouse and paid between $1.00 and $3.17 an hour as compared to non-Indian workers, who made $14 per hour for the same type of work. The workers lived gated off until they ultimately escaped in 2002. Based on a suit filed by the Equal Employment Opportunity Commission (EEOC), the court found the John D. Pickle Company in violation of Title VII for discriminatory treatment of the workers based on their national origin and awarded the workers $1.24 million.

The scenario exemplified in the John D. Pickle case is common in labor trafficking cases. In farmworker communities, traffickers use irregular immigration status, threats of deportation, and workers' lack of familiarity with wage laws to further exploit migrant and seasonal workers over other workers. Often traffickers require the labor not only of those they compel but also that of other workers who may work in less exploitative conditions.

Title VII cases could also be based on sex discrimination. Recent reports have brought to light the sexual exploitation of female farmworkers.[24] Human trafficking has not been identified in many of those instances of sexual assault. However, implementation of screening indicators could reveal much more extensive human trafficking of female farmworkers. A number of labor trafficking cases have involved sexual assault as a method of coercion in labor trafficking. For example, in 2012, the Botsvynyuk brothers were convicted of human trafficking–related charges after trafficking a group of workers to perform custodial duties in big box stores in the Philadelphia area. Two women workers testified that they had been brutally raped by their traffickers.[25]

A number of other employment discrimination laws may be available to trafficked persons. Several cases of human trafficking have involved workers who were disabled. Although not specifically named as a human trafficking case, in 2013 the EEOC was awarded a historic $240 million verdict on behalf of workers who were exploited because of their mental disabilities.[26]

The EEOC, which has jurisdiction over employment discrimination suits, has led efforts to utilize Title VII as a tool and cause of action in labor trafficking cases. EEOC has continued to successfully file lawsuits alleging human trafficking using Title VII as a cause of action, including the following:

- *EEOC v. Trans Bay Steel, Inc.*—alleging trafficking of Thai welders whose passports were confiscated and movement restricted, forced to work on a Bay Bridge retrofit without pay and some living in terrible living conditions.[27]
- *EEOC v. Global Horizons, Inc.*—alleging trafficking of Thai farmworkers, who were held in debt bondage, assaulted and abused on the farm, monitored, and threatened with deportation.[28]

Trafficked persons seeking to assert a Title VII claim must first exhaust administrative remedies by filing a claim with the EEOC within 180 days of a discriminatory act.[29] This deadline may be extended to three hundred days in particular states.[30] Preserving state claims requires the exhaustion of state administrative remedies, but the EEOC coordinates with each state agency so a complaint can be filed with the EEOC or the state agency and not both. Attorneys can help coordinate among the interested agencies, which may include criminal prosecutors. The lack of familiarity with rights associated with being trafficked causes inevitable delays in identification, posing challenges in these cases, including Title VII causes of action. The EEOC attorneys who litigated the trafficking cases discussed here may help facilitate a prompt and strategic response.

Attorneys should also note that EEOC and state employment agency supervisors and designated representatives can sign a U visa certification. Chapter 5 has an in-depth discussion about immigration remedies for trafficked persons, including U visa requirements. Attorneys pursuing civil litigation should ensure that their clients have access to an attorney to assist them with obtaining immigration relief.

Although the EEOC has proactively sought trafficking cases and instituted internal protocols and training to identify cases, the same is not yet true of state fair employment agencies. Fully engaged state agencies could help not only to identify additional trafficking cases but also to seek justice for trafficked persons.

Racketeer Influenced and Corrupt Organizations Act

The Racketeer Influenced and Corrupt Organizations Act (RICO), an anti-racketeering statute, also overlaps with human trafficking fact patterns. Under federal law, racketeering encompasses a number of different crimes, several of which may emerge within the context of human trafficking. Those crimes include the following[31]:

- Kidnapping
- Extortion
- Fraud in connection with identification documents
- Fraud in foreign labor contracting
- Obstruction of justice and witness tampering

- False statements and use of immigration documents
- Peonage, slavery, and trafficking in persons
- Sexual exploitation of children
- Bringing, harboring, and employing aliens unlawfully

RICO primarily distinguishes itself from these crimes by requiring a "pattern of racketeering activity" of at least two acts, the most recent of which occurred within ten years of the first.[32]

A plaintiff can establish a RICO civil claim against a person who has

1. received any income from or collected unlawful debt as a principal participating in a racketeering activity and used income or proceeds in an operation affecting interstate or foreign commerce[33]; or
2. acquired or maintained interest or control in an enterprise engaged in interstate or foreign commerce through racketeering or collection of unlawful debt[34]; or
3. been employed or associated with an enterprise, affecting interstate or foreign commerce, in conducting affairs of the enterprise through racketeering or collection of unlawful debt[35]; or
4. conspiracy of any of the above.[36]

RICO requirements feature many similarities to human trafficking cases. First, human trafficking cases often involve interstate or foreign activities, from recruitment to transportation to labor and services. RICO also focuses on economic benefits, which as discussed serve as the primary motivation for traffickers. Finally, the cyclical nature of human trafficking is aligned with the pattern requirement of RICO. RICO should be considered and assessed in any multiple-victim or multiple-trafficker case, which typically features these factors. As prescribed by the Supreme Court, civil RICO cases have a four-year statute of limitations.[37]

RICO has not yet been fully utilized on human trafficking cases. However, in 2009, workers of the Grant Family Farms obtained a $7.8 million judgment, based on liability under a number of causes of action, including RICO.[38] Workers were transported across the United States–Mexico border to work on farms in Colorado. The workers lived and worked in terrible conditions for long hours, with wages deducted for various costs. They were held in debt bondage and made to believe that if they left, other workers would assume their debts.

Alien Tort Claims Act

The Alien Tort Claims Act (ATCA) is another cause of action thought to be available to trafficked persons, although it has been significantly limited recently. The ATCA was created to give federal courts jurisdiction over certain torts that are "in violation of the law of nations or a treaty with the United States."[39] It has been used to sue for human rights violations that occur at least in part outside the United States. The ATCA has only been revived as a cause of action in recent years and the scope of such claims remains uncertain at this point.

Thus far, our discussion has focused on human trafficking that occurs primarily in the United States, but the ATCA would likely be considered only for human trafficking occurring overseas. The ATCA has been pled in actions against corporate entities for acts that occur overseas. Given the complex nature of liability within a complex global supply chain, there are very few remedies available beyond ATCA against corporate entities for forced labor within their supply chain. However, a 2013 Supreme Court case limited the presumption of extraterritorial jurisdiction.[40]

State Civil Laws

A number of states have civil remedies available to victims of human trafficking under state law.[41] Some states only have civil causes of action related to sex trafficking and have none available to labor trafficked persons. State civil causes of action are new and remain untested. Still, state remedies should be properly evaluated as a course of action in civil litigation and pled when appropriate.

In addition to specific human trafficking causes of action, a number of tort claims may be available, including the following:

- Assault
- Battery
- False imprisonment

- Intentional infliction of emotional distress
- Fraud

These torts, too, should be pled in addition to trafficking claims when appropriate.

In some circumstances, traffickers may also be sued for breach of contract. Many trafficking victims are recruited with an oral expectation regarding their work in the United States, which poses obvious evidentiary challenges to a contract case. In some cases, however, traffickers sign written contracts with trafficked persons. Written contracts are particularly prevalent among workers whose employers are required to sign a contract as a condition for obtaining a visa for the worker. Workers arriving in the United States with contracts include domestic workers hired to work for diplomats, international organization workers, and those performing seasonal or temporary work, typically in agriculture or other low-wage jobs. The federal government is charged with oversight of these contracts. Yet, without adequate enforcement, traffickers may operate with impunity, violating the terms of these contracts. Traffickers in fact have more opportunity to exploit workers in these cases, leveraging the fact that the workers are tied to the trafficking employer through a visa.

The Practice of Civil Anti-Trafficking Litigation
Building Trust with Trafficked Persons

Throughout this book, we discuss trust building as an important component of providing effective legal services to trafficked persons. Trafficked persons are often taught to distrust any authorities and may even perceive lawyers as representatives of the government. Trafficked immigrants are likely to be unfamiliar with the U.S. legal process. They will not necessarily understand the difference between a criminal and civil court system. They are not likely to be familiar with American legal ethics, including the duty of confidentiality. Likewise, they are not likely to understand conflict of interest rules and may be worried about but not share concerns about the adverse interests of other victims or witnesses. Therefore, they may not immediately be as forthcoming as other clients.

Although there are important reasons why a trafficked person may not trust a civil litigator, this should not deter an attorney from attempting to provide representation. Instead, a litigator might anticipate this distrust from the outset. For example, a litigator might take some time before filing the complaint. While less ideal if up against a statute of limitations filing deadline, an attorney might plan to file an amended and far more detailed complaint later, knowing that the original facts may not be completely accurate and may be provided without the trafficked person's full trust in the process.

Time alone does not develop trust, however. A litigator may even have to depart from his or her traditional style of representation. Many attorneys who take on representation of trafficked persons report acting in part as an advocate or case manager. Trafficked persons require allies, and the attorneys who are most successful at building trust go far beyond legal representation of these victims. A civil litigator will likely have to embrace an advocate or case manager role and invest in developing a less traditional relationship with a client who has experienced human trafficking.

Even plaintiff employment attorneys who are accustomed to representing workers and employees may initially lack an understanding of the complexities of labor trafficking. Because labor trafficking involves a unique aspect of control, a trafficked person may have different needs than other clients. Developing client-centered services to respond to trafficked persons' experiences will only increase attorneys' ability to recognize and more effectively represent a greater number of trafficked persons over time.

Safety Planning

Though pursuing civil litigation is a critical step in the empowerment of trafficked people, human trafficking is first and foremost a crime. All trafficking cases should be approached, therefore, with the appropriate measure of caution, considering the criminal nature of the activity. Safety planning is critical whether a trafficked person expresses fear or whether a criminal investigation is pending. Even traffickers who appear to be operating as individuals acting alone could have contacts both in the United States and in a home country posing a risk to a trafficked person, his or her family members, and even attorneys and case managers. Although not a responsibility traditionally associated with civil litigation, attorneys may perhaps be the most appropriate to make an immediate safety assessment and plan. Attorneys may be more objective and able to consider safety risks than trafficked persons themselves.

Civil litigators should guarantee client safety by ensuring that traffickers are not given any information regarding the client's location or facts that will allow traffickers to deduce a likely location. Litigators should ensure that discovery and pleadings do not inadvertently disclose the trafficked person's residence, place of work, or place of school, and that other locations frequented by the victim are not easily identifiable. For example, naming a small city or town of residence may facilitate a traffickers discovering a trafficked person's new residence.

Civil litigators should also coordinate with both victim attorneys and law enforcement for additional protection and safety planning. In addition, litigators should anticipate the risk of witness tampering. At a minimum, litigators should seek judicial admonitions to traffickers. It is also important to anticipate the unique circumstances of human trafficking when making court appearances. Courts typically have safety protocols in place for criminal cases and civil domestic violence calendars but may not always anticipate the safety risks posed by civil trafficking court hearings. Attorneys may have to affirmatively request those protections. Some policies include asking a civil trafficking defendant to wait before exiting the court building to allow the trafficked person enough time to safely leave without being followed. Attorneys can also alert court personnel to particular safety issues.

Criminal cases typically include a stay-away order that provides additional protection for victims. When there is no criminal prosecution, an attorney may consider seeking a civil stay-away protective order for the trafficked person. In either case, a court order may not stop the most dangerous trafficker, but it does send a notice to a trafficker that the courts are aware of the danger, which can serve as a deterrent.

Coordination with a Criminal Case

Timing of a civil suit requires coordination with a possible criminal case. In enacting a civil cause of action in the 2003 TVPA reauthorization,

Congress also created a provision that automatically stays a civil case until the federal criminal case has concluded.[42] Trafficked persons often report crimes without a response from law enforcement. Therefore, it may be necessary to communicate with the appropriate law enforcement agency. Even for cases prosecuted under state laws without an automatic stay of civil litigation, prosecutors may still move to stay a civil case.

Informally, litigators can benefit from coordinating with prosecutors. Both prosecutions and civil litigation rely heavily on victim testimony. Litigators and prosecutors should take care to coordinate and anticipate statements that may have conflicting facts or messages. Civil litigators may find trailing a prosecution advantageous because the evidence introduced in the prosecution will be available in the civil litigation. Because the criminal burden of proof is higher than in a civil case, this evidence will be very beneficial to a civil case.

Still, delays in a civil case can have negative consequences for trafficked persons. Both criminal and civil cases can take a number of years before resolution. A stay in civil litigation will delay a trafficked person's access to the damages to which he or she is entitled. Attorneys should also anticipate difficulties related to preserving witness testimony over the years.

Financial Implications of a Civil Judgment

In most cases, damages are the primary motivation for trafficking victims to pursue civil litigation. There may be some possibility of obtaining injunctive relief or litigating a case of first impression, but those motivations for filing a civil suit are likely outweighed by an opportunity to receive damages. Enforcing a judgment will depend in part on the type of trafficker. The trafficker may be an individual, a small group, a clandestine criminal ring, or even a corporate enterprise. Enforcing a judgment requires a defendant to have some assets. Traffickers are criminals, and some are very savvy about transferring assets. Others flee the country. Therefore, it is important to ensure that a judgment is enforceable, preferably before filing.

For the trafficked persons who are able to enforce judgments, they will need counsel on the tax implications of their judgments. In addition to tax liability, many trafficked persons access a range of government services. Some of those services are designated for low-income individuals.

Assets and income received when a judgment is enforced could prevent trafficked persons from eligibility for particular programs. For example, depending on how the judgment is enforced, a trafficked person may not meet the financial aid eligibility criteria and therefore may not be able to access post secondary education loans. Attorneys should advise on these implications before proceeding with a civil suit.

Diplomatic Immunity

As discussed in Chapter 5, domestic workers of diplomats are particularly vulnerable because their work and visa are tied to the employing diplomat. However, in accordance with international law, the United States offers diplomatic immunity, which extends to civil lawsuits. Many diplomats have successfully asserted a diplomatic immunity defense. However, the State Department has an internal working group that works to resolve trafficking cases involving diplomats. Therefore, any attorneys pursuing civil cases on behalf of domestic workers employed by diplomats should contact the State Department's Office of Protocol. Attorneys will also benefit from working with organizations that can assist in coordinating advocacy.[43]

Immigration Exposure

Because most labor trafficked persons are undocumented or have status tied to a trafficker, civil litigation may also expose a trafficked person to risk of immigration enforcement. As we discuss in Chapter 5, traffickers control people by threatening deportation. This control can continue long after the trafficking experience has ended. When trafficked persons take any action against a trafficker, including filing a civil suit, traffickers may retaliate by acting on their threats of deportation by directly contacting Immigration and Customs Enforcement (ICE).

Congress anticipated this when they took protections originally created to prevent such retaliation by perpetrators of domestic violence and expanded them to traffickers.[44] Known as the "VAWA Confidentiality" protections, these three specific laws create shields against immigration enforcement for those at risk of retaliation. The protections are premised on eligibility based on the filing of a VAWA self-petition, a T visa application, or a U visa application. Therefore, litigators should ensure that clients have immediate referrals to and counsel of anti-trafficking immigration attorneys who can begin to file the appropriate application.

First, all information filed with a VAWA, T visa, or U visa application, including the fact of its existence, is confidential and cannot be disclosed by the Department of Homeland Security (DHS) or Department of Justice (DOJ) in a court of law or elsewhere.[45] This law can be used as a litigation tool when traffickers seek to discover T visa or other immigration filings. The best way to avoid having to defend against this discovery is not to disclose to the court anything regarding the immigration applications.

The second provision is less applicable to civil litigation but important to anticipate as a protection nevertheless. United States Citizenship and Immigration Services (USCIS) is precluded from relying on information from a perpetrator in adjudicating the underlying application.[46] Civil attorneys anticipating retaliation should coordinate with immigration attorneys in order to be prepared to advocate on behalf of trafficked persons. Finally, immigration officials are precluded from conducting enforcement actions at certain locations, including shelters and courthouses.[47] This provision is designed to anticipate that ICE agents may show up at a courtroom where a trafficking victim is offering testimony, after receiving a lead likely from a trafficker. ICE representatives are rarely aware of these less-invoked protections. Therefore, civil attorneys should be prepared with proof of eligibility for these protections, including receipts of immigration filings, and applicable law during any court proceedings.

Mitigating Against Human Trafficking and Resulting Lawsuits

Attorneys representing employers are beginning to take steps to mitigate the risk of human trafficking. As discussed, corporations are not typically at risk of being sued as traffickers. But employment defense attorneys can counsel clients about where there is risk exposure. For example, corporations can implement training and protocols regarding procurement practices to reduce the risk of trafficking by a contractor. Other companies that operate isolated worksites, such as in agriculture, or those with a majority immigrant workforce or reliance on labor brokers, might work with their clients to implement training policies through human resources.

Management will benefit from receiving training on human trafficking in order to understand the exact nature and how it might enter their workforce. From that training, employers will be better prepared to develop human resources and procurement policies that expressly prohibit trafficking but also take steps that will mitigate that risk. In California, a 2012 law now requires specific categories of employers to post a notice informing trafficking victims and the public of human trafficking hotline numbers and services available.[48] More such laws are likely to emerge to enhance employer obligations.

Best Practices for Employers

☑ Train all managers on prohibited behavior related to human trafficking.
☑ Prohibit confiscation of or denying access to passports and identity documents.
☑ Prohibit misleading and fraudulent recruiting practices.
☑ Prohibit charging worker recruitment fees.
☑ Provide accommodations for workers that meet safety and housing standards.
☑ Require timecards and other monitoring of hours.
☑ Ensure migrant workers are receiving minimum wages.
☑ Review the labor practices and policies of any contracted service agencies.
☑ Post information about human trafficking victim rights and phone numbers for services.
☑ Use independent third-party human trafficking expert auditors, including offsite interviews.

Beyond the Lawsuit
Coordination with Legal and Social Service Providers

Litigating a human trafficking case is very different from litigating most of the other cases civil litigators will take on. While a lawsuit is an important avenue for trafficked persons to access damages and hold traffickers accountable, it is only one of the myriad protections a trafficked person requires in order to rebuild a life free from future exploitation.

Beyond civil litigation, a trafficked person typically has a host of other legal needs. As discussed, labor trafficked persons often require immediate access to immigration relief. Litigators should identify anti-trafficking immigration experts in advance, as they will be required for most labor trafficked persons. Some trafficked persons have been arrested in the course of victimization and will need access to a criminal defense attorney. In other cases, litigators will closely coordinate with prosecutors investigating human trafficking. It is not uncommon for a litigator to expect to coordinate with multiple attorneys.

In the immediate aftermath, a trafficked person will need access to services that respond to the trauma experienced. These services include physical and mental health services, and social worker advocacy. These services will put trafficked persons on a path that will improve their effectiveness as plaintiffs or as witnesses. Other important services include emergency and long-term housing and access to public benefits.

Trafficked persons will not be able to rely on the possibility of a civil judgment that may only be available years down the line. As such, even a civil litigation attorney should coordinate with other anti-trafficking advocates to ensure that each trafficked person can access job training, English language classes, education, and an immigration work permit. Trafficked people are typically unaware that such services exist, so civil attorneys can play an important role in connecting trafficked persons with these services.

Conclusion

There are a number of civil legal remedies available to trafficked persons and a great need for civil attorneys to take up their cause. Labor and employment law attorneys in legal aid organizations, solo practitioner offices, law firms, state labor agencies, the U.S. Department of Labor, state fair employment agencies, and the EEOC are all desperately needed to increase identification and representation of labor trafficked persons. As demonstrated, the need for labor and employment law attorneys to expand their role in the anti-trafficking arena cannot be overstated. Human trafficking frequently touches attorneys working in these fields, and with that exposure labor and employment law attorneys hold the key to dramatically shift the anti-trafficking landscape. Whether their efforts lead to increased identification of trafficked persons, improved representation for them, or mitigation of human trafficking, such outcomes are readily attainable through their work in these critical endeavors.

CHAPTER 5

Access to Immigration Protections

> Wherever you have immigrants, you have potential for human trafficking.
>
> —U.S. Secretary of Labor, Tom Perez

Migration is inextricably linked with human trafficking, both globally and within the United States. The International Labour Organization estimates that globally, 29 percent of trafficked persons are cross-border migrants.[1] Despite limited U.S. data, one report estimated that nearly one-third of undocumented workers in the study had experienced human trafficking.[2] By extrapolation, up to three million undocumented people in the United States could be vulnerable to human trafficking.[3] These figures, coupled with fifteen years of successful federal prosecutions involving foreign-born victims, make it evident that immigration solutions are a critical component in any anti-trafficking framework.

Though most trafficked persons are unlikely to self-identify, trafficked immigrants experience an additional barrier to identification. If trafficked persons are undocumented or if their status is tied to their employer, fear of deportation will often take precedence over other issues. Identifying trafficked immigrants therefore requires additional strategies to inform them of immigration options less familiar to them. Awareness of such options will help immigrants feel safe revealing facts that would characterize them as trafficked. Attorneys interacting with immigrants are best positioned to overcome this fear by recognizing the trafficking experience and representing trafficked persons to access trafficking-specific immigration relief.

The United States immigration system is complicated for even the most informed citizen to understand. Within that complex system, trafficking-specific immigration remedies are even less known and understood. Current anti-trafficking immigration efforts rely on the small pool of expert human trafficking immigration attorneys. At a minimum, many other legal professionals are positioned to develop policies to improve identification of trafficked immigrants for the purpose of connecting them with those who can seek immigration relief and other protections for them. Among those who can identify trafficked persons are nonprofit, private-sector, and government attorneys, and in particular, those working with immigrant and migrant communities, those working on labor and employment issues, and even those providing counsel on health care issues. Even government attorneys, including immigration judges and Immigration and Customs Enforcement (ICE) trial counsel, are positioned to identify respondents in an immigration removal case.

This chapter provides an overview of the intersection between immigration and human trafficking. It serves as a tool to assist attorneys in understanding the gaps and challenges in responding to trafficked immigrants and what can be done to address them. Finally, it guides pro bono, nonprofit, and private immigration attorneys seeking to expand identification of noncitizen-trafficked persons and provide immigration representation.

The Nexus Between Immigration and Human Trafficking

Human trafficking is a crime of economics; the recruitment and exploitation of immigrants is often hidden within complex supply chains, in small businesses with little oversight, and among individuals with low-wage jobs, where traffickers exploit the economic vulnerability of their victims for their own financial gain.

Human traffickers use a variety of mechanisms to compel individuals into labor or commercial sex. Traffickers have used immigration laws to control trafficked persons and instill fear in them. In the labor trafficking context, foreign workers are recruited to perform a host of typically lower-wage jobs in the United States. Some of those jobs are exploitative in nature but do not rise to the level of human trafficking. But in many sectors, traffickers use a worker's lack of permanent immigration status as a tool to compel work. Human trafficking of immigrants occurs in almost every low-wage industry in the United States. Immigrants are trafficked in agriculture, caregiving, commercial sex, construction, custodial services, factories, fishing, retail, restaurants, teaching, and as domestic workers in homes. Typically the work and services exacted create economic gain for the trafficker.

For some trafficked immigrants, recruitment begins overseas. Traffickers recruit individuals who are often willing to take a risk or do not realize the risk, all for access to a better economic opportunity. Traffickers then facilitate these individuals' entry into the United States. For example, some traffickers have extensive networks where they bring people to Canada or Mexico or recruit directly in Mexico and then arrange for their travel into the United States through an unlawful border crossing. Before the work or service begins, the immigrant is already fearful that

---

Recruitment

Su Jin[4] was living with her parents in Seoul, Korea. Her older sister ran into some problems with her clothing store and borrowed money from loan sharks. Su Jin began looking for ways to help and protect her family. A friend told her she could easily make that money by going to the United States and working in bars or massage parlors. Her friend connected her with a recruiter. The recruiter secured a passport and ticket to Vancouver and a colleague transported her and some others to the United States. Upon arrival, she was told she would not be able to make good money and pay off her debt unless she provided commercial sex. She was also informed that additional costs for clothing, housing, food, and transportation would be added to her debt. Su Jin knew that only the pay she would make in commercial sex would be enough to pay off the debt.

the circumstances of entry into the United States will be disclosed. This fear offers traffickers the first point of leverage over trafficked persons.

Other traffickers recruit workers through formal U.S. visa programs, most of which tie a worker to a specific employer. Those on work visas are typically only permitted to work for a sponsoring employer. This facilitates a unique level of coercion because an employee has very little autonomy to raise issues or complain about the work without risk of being returned to the home country.

Visas tied to employers include those for some domestic workers, temporary migrant agriculture and manufacturing workers, and touring groups. Being tied to an employer means that for those workers, leaving that employment in most cases violates the terms of their visa and requires them to depart from the United States. Another category of trafficked immigrants includes undocumented workers who are recruited and trafficked once they are already in the United States, typically by traffickers willing to exploit that undocumented status.

Very few immigrants are familiar with specialized immigration relief available to them as trafficked persons. They assume there are no immigration options available and fear deportation. Traffickers manipulate this fear. They take advantage of this confusion, using the threat of deportation as a tool of coercion, creating a chasm between the victim and law enforcement charged with protecting victims. They may also hold immigrants' passports and documents as a further tool of control. Immigration protections are the fundamental step for trafficked immigrants to overcome this control from traffickers. It also positions them so that they will be less vulnerable to future exploitation.

The State of Play for Trafficked Immigrants

Recognizing the need to address the unique needs of trafficked immigrants, in 2000 Congress created specialized immigration relief through the Trafficking Victims Protection Act (TVPA).[5] In subsequent reauthorizations, Congress expanded these immigration protections[6] by addressing barriers that had prevented some trafficked immigrants from accessing the relief intended for them.

Between 2002 when T visas were first granted and 2013, U.S. Citizenship and Immigration Services (USCIS) granted 3,309 visas to trafficking victims and 2,921 T family members visas.[7] Despite a lack of clear data estimating the number of trafficked immigrants in the United States, data extrapolation suggests that the T visa remains far underutilized. This also suggests that many trafficked immigrants do not know how to access the protections that allow them to live and work free from trafficking.

Trafficked immigrants are overlooked for a number of reasons. In addition to barriers to identification, the public narrative on human trafficking focuses primarily on sex trafficked U.S. citizens. Local law enforcement agencies have an infrastructure to investigate vice cases and that has allowed some to adapt and respond more to U.S. citizen sex trafficking cases.[8] Local law enforcement enforcing federal immigration laws will have a limited capacity to simultaneously protect trafficked immigrants who are undocumented without clear strategies in place. Many attorneys can respond to these challenges by increasing identification.

Identifying Trafficked Immigrants

Filling the identification gap begins by expanding stakeholders. In addition to nonprofit anti-trafficking attorneys, many other professionals are unknowingly well positioned to bridge the identification gap. A number of other private-sector attorneys, including labor and employment law attorneys and private immigration attorneys, might be interacting with a trafficked immigrant without realizing it. Nonprofit and pro bono attorneys likewise take on other cases, with legal issues peripherally related to trafficking, without realizing that their clients have experienced human trafficking.

Government attorneys and other professionals also likely interact with trafficked immigrants without always being able to identify them. Among such professionals are those working through the immigration process, including State Department Consular Officers and Diplomatic Security personnel, Department of Homeland Security (DHS) Customs and Border Patrol Officers, monitors for foreign workers both at the Department of Labor and the State Department, other federal and state agencies that oversee labor issues, and local agencies that monitor labor and building safety issues. Immigration judges, ICE trial attorneys, and other court personnel are all positioned to identify trafficked immigrants among the respondents in immigration court. In immigration detention centers, the detained population is also likely to include trafficked persons who have not been identified. All personnel at detention centers, as well as contracted facilities, would benefit from an increased understanding of how to identify trafficked persons.

Screening in Detention Centers: American Gateways

American Gateways is a nonprofit immigration services organization based in Austin, Texas. Having long worked with trafficked immigrants, American Gateways has expanded their anti-trafficking practice to ensure that staff and partners working in immigration detention centers are screening for human trafficking. As partners of the National Legal Orientation Program, staff of American Gateways present workshops weekly at the South Texas Detention Center where they inform the detainee population about their rights and immigration options, including those based on human trafficking.

Finally, a number of legal professionals, including those working in immigrant communities informally and formally within labor unions, interact with trafficked immigrants without recognizing them. They, too, would benefit from an increased understanding of exactly what trafficking looks like and how to best connect trafficked immigrants with resources and protections.

Throughout this book, we address an underlying theme of distrust that contributes to the reluctance of trafficked persons to self-identify. Human trafficking identification begins with building trust. Even in the most comfortable setting, trafficked immigrants will be reluctant to discuss their situation. Shame, trauma, and fear of the unknown all inform this distrust. Legal professionals should anticipate that trafficked immigrants will not have any expectation of attorney-client privilege and any notion of confidentiality may be unfamiliar to them. In some countries, attorneys are often officers of the government, so nongovernment attorneys may have to initially clarify their role in order to build that trust.

Though a trafficked immigrant's story typically emerges as trust builds, attorneys who are able to recognize and apply trafficking indicators can serve as a primary and critical conduit by helping trafficked immigrants understand their rights and available protections. In addition to knowing general screening questions and trafficking indicators, there are particular screening questions that will assist attorneys in identifying a trafficked immigrant. As with other indicators, these should not be treated as requirements or dispositive of trafficking. These facts may, however, suggest the need to unpack a deeper and more detailed story that will slowly emerge.

Indicators of Trafficked Immigrants

1. Unlawful entry connected with employment/commercial sex in the United States
2. Accompanied into the United States by someone associated with the employer
3. Employer/recruiter assistance in facilitating travel documents
4. In debt related to travel and recruiter costs while employed or engaged in commercial sex
5. On a visa tied to a United States employer
6. Given scripted answers for immigration authorities in preparation for entry into the United States
7. Told to lie about actual work and living circumstances when asked
8. Employment or commercial sex conditions different from those initially described
9. Not always in possession of identity or travel documents
10. Living and other costs deducted from wages
11. Escorted between living quarters and worksite
12. Made fearful about immigration status or immigration enforcement entities
13. Made fearful about law enforcement
14. Concerned for safety of family members overseas
15. Prevented from communicating with family members or others

---

As evident in the supplementary indicators, it is important to understand how trafficked immigrants entered the United States. Some were recruited abroad and may enter unlawfully but facilitated by the trafficker. Or they may enter lawfully on one of a number of visas that may be available. Some of the visas are directly applicable to the service being provided and some are fraudulently obtained visas, typically facilitated by the trafficker. In either case, it is important to understand on which visa, if any, the individual entered. If the unlawful entry or fraudulent visa is facilitated by the trafficker and even otherwise, that does not foreclose a victim's eligibility to apply for immigration relief. Those exceptions are detailed later in the chapter.

Alphabet Soup: Nonimmigrant Visas

A-3 visa: Personal employees of foreign government officials (diplomatic and consular employees). Foreign officials are permitted to bring personal employees to the United States, typically to perform domestic work. An A-3 nonimmigrant is only permitted to work for the official who sponsored the worker. The Government Accountability Office (GAO) documented forty-two cases of abuse by diplomats and suggested the number was much greater.[9]

B1/B2 visa: Temporary business or pleasure. B1/B2 visas are valid for up to six months. Any employment during that duration is in violation of the terms of the visa. Traffickers have facilitated entry of trafficked persons on lawful B1/B2 visas under the guise of personal travel and training and compelled them in work, which violates the terms of the visa.[10]

G-5 visa: Personal employees of international organization workers. Like the A-3 visa holders, G-5 visa holders also accompany and are tied to an employer, which puts them at risk of exploitation.[11]

H1-B visa: Specialty occupation visa. Also tied to employers, H1-B visas are typically issued to engineers. But traffickers have compelled H1-B visa holders to remain in the job for which the visa was obtained or by creating fraudulent entities or work within the entity.[12]

P visa: Athlete and entertainer visitor visa. These visas are typically provided to individuals who participate in touring troupes. On occasion, these troupes are covers for trafficking operations.

H2-A visa: Temporary or seasonal agricultural work. Without effective oversight of the H2-A visa system, seasonal farmworkers are tied to employers and are exposed to exploitative conditions, including human trafficking.[13]

H2-B visa: Temporary or seasonal non agricultural work. These visas allow companies to recruit overseas workers for particular temporary, typically manual labor jobs. Like their counterpart, these visa holders work in situations rife with exploitation and trafficking.[14]

J-1 visa: Exchange cultural visitor visas. Exchange visas give the appearance of offering a cultural experience, but they have been used to recruit young workers to work low-wage jobs facilitated by United States government–approved recruiting agencies. The lack of oversight, however, has exposed the visa program to risk of slavery.[15]

The other major category of trafficked immigrants is undocumented persons. In some cases, traffickers facilitate unlawful entry through an unauthorized border crossing or facilitate entry on a visa that expires. Others are already undocumented and in the United States when they are recruited into trafficking. Though most undocumented immigrants are reluctant to disclose their history of migration, understanding an individual pattern will provide insight into the likelihood of human trafficking.

Several other factors are unique to the experience of trafficked immigrants. Debt bondage is a common method that traffickers use to compel immigrants. When immigrants are recruited from other countries, they typically incur a significant cost to travel to the United States. Recruiters justify this cost as travel expenses and sometimes arrange for travel papers such as a passport and a visa, building these into the debt. As a way to assuage potential recruits, traffickers sometimes suggest that the debt will be easy to pay off. Trafficked immigrants may also owe additional debts to separate informal lenders needed to sometimes pay up-front costs. Their family members may also carry debts, which in some countries may attach to all family members. While these debts are unlawful, trafficked immigrants may view these debts as legal obligations. Those subjective impressions can very much influence their willingness to escape or report the trafficking unless they understand that the debts are not enforceable. It is critical to offer this counsel at the identification stage.

Another unique concern of trafficked immigrants is the safety of their overseas family members. Trafficked immigrants may not want to come forward and cooperate because traffickers have threatened their family overseas. While reporting trafficking to law enforcement does not trigger law enforcement protections overseas, a number of immigration options allow for family reunification. Presenting this information may also overcome a trafficked immigrant's reluctance to disclose the trafficking details.

With identification comes an immediate need for accompanying services. Agencies expanding identification efforts will want to develop referral lists and protocols. Trafficked immigrants will have particular needs that should be anticipated in developing referrals. Particularly for those with limited capacity for immigration representation, those identifying trafficked persons should ensure immediate access to immigration attorneys with human trafficking specialization. Understanding immigration relief options is a great value for trafficked immigrants trying to ascertain their next steps. Trafficked immigrants will also have certain limitations. They will not likely have permission to work and will need alternative financial support from the outset. Even in states where driver's licenses are available to undocumented immigrants, trafficked immigrants may or may not have a driver's license, so their mobility may be limited. For all of these immediate service needs, those screening for trafficking will be well served to identify service providers with particular trafficked immigrant expertise. This will also help secure language access to support all of these services.

Immigration Relief and Protections

Increased identification will also create an increased need for attorneys to expand their practice to representing trafficked immigrants.

Immediate Access to Continued Presence

Continued presence is a type of temporary immigration relief, which offers potential trafficking victims an opportunity to have permissible continued presence in the United States.[16] Continued presence is designed to offer victims of human trafficking permission to remain in the United States during the course of an investigation or prosecution[17] and bridges the gap in protections while more long-term immigration applications are pending. The DHS authorizes continued presence for one year, but the status is renewable.

A trafficked person or that person's counsel cannot directly apply for continued presence. Only federal law enforcement can request continued presence.[18] Typically, an attorney seeking continued presence will work with a point of contact on the investigation or prosecution. When a case is being investigated or prosecuted by local authorities, an attorney will have to advocate to encourage cooperation between multiple entities to encourage a federal law enforcement officer to make a continued presence request. Strategies for making the most effective referrals are discussed in detail later in the chapter.

Once there is willingness from the appropriate criminal justice contact, attorneys can assist their clients by advocating for continued presence and facilitating the process by providing needed information for the federal law enforcement application.

Continued presence offers victims two very specific protections:

1. Eligibility for permission to accept employment authorization from USCIS.[19] This authorization also serves as an identity document, so it should be secured for trafficked minors as well.

2. U.S. Department of Health and Human Services (HHS) certification as a victim of a severe form of trafficking in persons.[20]

Outside continued presence, trafficked immigrants may alternatively obtain HHS certification by applying for a T visa, which is discussed below. USCIS issues a notice that the applicant has established a bona fide T visa application, which should precede the final T visa determination but is typically sent contemporaneously with the T visa approval.

This notice automatically triggers HHS certification. Certification offers victims eligibility for public benefits, health care, ESL classes, job training, and more. Specialized social service case managers are often available to coordinate these benefits upon receipt of certification.

T Nonimmigrant Status (T Visa) for Victims of Trafficking

A T status is the primary relief used to assist trafficked immigrants. It offers lawful status as a *T Nonimmigrant*,[21] which prevents deportation, gives victims a long-term path to permanent residence in the United States as they seek services to rebuild a life free from trafficking, and provides the security that allows victims to cooperate with a criminal investigation. Trafficking-specific immigration relief was designed to overcome the barriers, characterized as "inadmissibility criteria," which would make trafficked immigrants ineligible for more common immigration applications. The T visa has generous waivers available to applicants triggering grounds of inadmissibility for acts connected with trafficking.[22]

The T nonimmigrant visa offers victims of a severe form of trafficking a four-year nonimmigrant visa.[23] The T visa offers many critical immigration benefits to victims of human trafficking:

- Permission to accept lawful employment
- Family reunification: visa for eligible family members both in the United States and overseas, with accompanying work authorization[24]
- A path to lawful permanent residence

There is a misconception that T visas are rarely granted, despite an approval rate of 90 percent in fiscal year 2013.[25] In fact, the process has been streamlined to accommodate the unique circumstances of crime victims. For example, applicants for T visas are not estopped from reapplying, unlike some other immigration applicants. While this process may suggest an opportunity for fraudulent applications, this perspective has been successfully mitigated through specialized training of adjudicators to understand the unique circumstances of trafficking that are extremely difficult to fabricate. Adjudicators have also become well acquainted with the leading anti-trafficking experts who are providing services to T visa applicants and trust their expertise to screen for true trafficking cases.

As a policy, the USCIS service center that processes these applications does not make affirmative referrals to initiate removal proceedings on applicants who are denied a T visa. In other words, undocumented eligible victims face less risk in applying for a T visa than with some non-victim–based applications.

To obtain a T visa, an applicant must prove that he or she

1. is a victim of a severe form of a trafficking,
2. is physically present on account of trafficking,
3. has complied with reasonable requests with an investigation or prosecution or meets an exception, and
4. faces extreme hardship.[26]

A Severe Form of Trafficking in Persons

An applicant must demonstrate that he or she is a victim of a severe form of trafficking in persons. Specifically, the TVPA defines this as "(A) sex trafficking in which a commercial sex act is induced by force, fraud, or coercion, or in which the person induced to perform such act has not attained 18 years of age; or (B) the recruitment, harboring, transportation, provision, or obtaining of a person for labor or services, through the use of force, fraud, or coercion for the purpose of subjection to involuntary servitude, peonage, debt bondage, or slavery."[27]

To meet this element, a victim must offer evidence of the means (use of force, fraud, or coercion unless under age eighteen) and of the purpose (commercial sex act, labor, or services). Evidence of trafficking may include the following:

- A victim's declaration
- Criminal complaint or other criminal investigation material
- Media reports
- Personal witness declarations
- Expert witness declarations
- Photographs
- Medical records
- Civil complaint
- Restraining order
- Declaration of law enforcement officer
- HHS certification
- Identity documents to demonstrate age under eighteen
- Contracts or correspondence with or about the recruiter or trafficker

Because of the nature of trafficking, in most cases, victims will have little documentation or evidence beyond their own statement. This should not deter an attorney if the victim, through his or her statement, is able to demonstrate victimization and explain the lack of additional evidence.

Physically Present on Account of Trafficking

An applicant must also demonstrate that he or she "is physically present in the United States" on account of trafficking.[28] This requirement might facially suggest that eligible victims must have entered the United States on account of the trafficking, excluding those who were trafficked subsequent to arriving in the United States. However, USCIS explicitly allows applicants to demonstrate that they are physically present and have been unable to depart the United States after being freed from trafficking, regardless of whether their entry was facilitated by a trafficker or connected with a trafficking scheme.[29] An applicant who left the United States but returned because of continuing victimization can also meet this requirement.[30] Many trafficked immigrants are returned home by their traffickers or return home voluntarily, but later return to the United States to participate in an investigation or because they require protections in the United States.

Evidence of physical presence may include the following:

- A victim's declaration
- Proof of participation in a criminal investigation or prosecution
- Proof of accessing services available to victims of trafficking in the United States
- Service provider declarations
- Medical records
- Civil complaint
- Law enforcement endorsement
- HHS certification

Case Study

Maria[31] was recruited and transported to the United States from the Philippines to perform services in a brothel. A law enforcement raid freed her from the brothel, but Maria elected to return to the Philippines unsure of what else to do. When federal authorities brought Maria back to cooperate with the investigation of her traffickers, Maria was able to successfully apply for a T visa and meet the physical presence requirement.

Law Enforcement Cooperation

The T visa application requires evidence that the applicant "has complied with reasonable requests for assistance from those investigating or prosecuting the trafficking" or meets an exception.[32] Excepted are minors under the age of eighteen[33] and applicants who demonstrate an inability to cooperate because of "physical or psychological trauma."[34] This exception requires applicants to submit evidence to substantiate such trauma. Attorneys can help secure evidence from law enforcement and obtain medical documentation. They should also work with a mental health provider or social worker to develop an extensive assessment of the trauma.

This requirement to cooperate with law enforcement often prevents trafficked immigrants from applying. Cooperating with law enforcement is not always a simple decision. Although there are many victims who want to see that their traffickers are punished by the criminal justice system, attorneys should not make the mistake of expecting this cooperation as a foregone conclusion for a client. Some trafficked persons do not see themselves as victims and do not want to endure another traumatic experience. Some trafficked persons have relationships with their traffickers and may not want to see them convicted. Others do not feel comfortable participating and revealing sensitive and possibly shameful information. Some fear for the safety of themselves or their family members. From a practical standpoint, the cooperation process can be time-intensive and require sacrifice. Others may seek services, and only much later feel comfortable cooperating. Trafficked immigrants will have to weigh these considerations when deciding to apply for a T visa. They will require counsel as to what it requires of them to participate as a victim-witness in the criminal justice system.

For those who decide to cooperate, regulations state that the cooperation requests must be reasonable. In evaluating the reasonableness of the law enforcement requests, USCIS considers the totality of the circumstances, which includes law enforcement practices, the victimization, the victim's circumstances, the victim's age, and the victim's maturity.[35] A fully investigated and prosecuted trafficking case typically requires a victim to participate in law enforcement interviews and testify before a grand jury and/or at a trial. In some cases, law enforcement has requested a victim to wear a wire or travel overseas to help identify people and locations. These requests may extend beyond a reasonable request, depending on all the other circumstances.

Even cooperating victims typically provide inconsistent statements as they develop trust with law enforcement. Some law enforcement new to trafficking cases may not understand this and deem a victim uncooperative when the victim provides conflicting statements. Attorneys can work with law enforcement to educate them about this frequently occurring issue. In several circumstances, particularly working with law enforcement new to trafficking cases, law enforcement found our clients to be uncooperative, but the clients were still successful in meeting the T visa cooperation requirement.

T visa applicants have an ongoing obligation to cooperate. Law enforcement may contact USCIS and provide evidence of non cooperation. USCIS will consider this evidence in evaluating an application and also has the authority to revoke visas upon its receipt of evidence after granting T visa status.[36]

Evidence of cooperation may include the following:

- A victim's declaration
- Criminal complaint or other criminal investigation material
- Media reports
- Personal witness declarations
- Expert witness declarations
- Restraining order
- Law enforcement endorsement
- HHS certification
- Identity documents to demonstrate age under eighteen (to demonstrate an exception)
- Mental health provider statements (to demonstrate an exception)

Unlike the U visa eligibility discussed below, a T visa applicant is not required to submit a law enforcement endorsement.[37] Because of limited resources and backlogs, law enforcement may not even respond to a referral for many months. Instead, attorneys can expedite protections for victims by immediately making a referral to law enforcement and submitting that documentation with a T visa application, regardless of the response. T visa applicants can always later supplement the application with a law enforcement endorsement. In our practice, we were able to successfully obtain T visas for many clients who had never received certification.

When attorneys initially refer cases to law enforcement, the referrals should be carefully drafted in writing to anticipate multiple issues. First, that referral will be used as evidence in the T visa application and could potentially be discoverable in a civil lawsuit or criminal prosecution. Second, because trust building can take time, an immediate but detailed referral might risk being used as an inconsistent statement in a subsequent criminal or civil case. Brevity will mitigate both of these concerns.

Attorneys can make referrals to a number of law enforcement agencies. Local anti-trafficking service providers will be most familiar with the immediate point of contact for trafficked-immigrant referrals. The following agencies receive human trafficking referrals:

1. Human Smuggling and Trafficking Unit of Immigration and Customs Enforcement, Homeland Security Investigations (ICE HSI)
2. Federal Bureau of Investigation
3. Human Trafficking Prosecution Unit (HTPU) of the Department of Justice (DOJ) Civil Rights Division
4. Local law enforcement
5. Representatives of Department of Justice funded Human Trafficking Taskforce

Extreme Hardship

Applicants must also prove that it would be an extreme hardship involving severe and unusual harm if they were removed from the United States.[38] This requirement is less burdensome than the others as trafficked immigrants are almost always safer in the United States than in their home countries, and the United States provides a range of resources and protections not typically available in their home countries.

USCIS considers several factors regarding extreme hardship, including but not limited to[39]

1. age and personal circumstances of the applicant;
2. serious physical or mental health attention needed, not reasonably available overseas;
3. physical and psychological consequences of the trafficking;
4. loss of access to the U.S. courts;
5. penalizing nature of home country laws, social practices, or customs;
6. likelihood of re-victimization;
7. harm from the trafficker or the trafficker's agents; and
8. safety threatened by civil unrest or conflict.

The T Visa Application Process

The T visa application process is designed to accommodate the unique needs of trafficked persons in a number of ways. A specialized unit of the

Vermont Service Center (VSC) at USCIS adjudicates the T visa as well as the U visa and the Violence Against Women Act (VAWA) self-petition and trains adjudicators about the unique challenges faced by the applicants.

U.S. immigration laws and regulations accommodate the evidentiary challenges these applicants might face. USCIS applies the "any credible evidence" evidentiary standard to T visas.[40] Trafficked immigrants often leave their trafficking situation with no possessions and have little evidence from the period when they were trafficked. Traffickers use isolation as a technique of coercion, leaving very few witnesses privy to a victim's circumstances.

Therefore, the lack of evidence should not deter an eligible victim or a victim's representative from proceeding to file a T visa application. T visa applicants can often mitigate any lack of evidence of trafficking through a detailed declaration that establishes the facts required for eligibility and explains the lack of evidence.

This process also accommodates attorneys new to T visa cases, who may feel reticent when initially filing a T visa. Adjudicators send Requests for Evidence (RFE) where evidence is insufficient, giving attorneys and their clients opportunity to respond with clarifying and supplementary evidence. VSC responds to attorney inquiries through a special telephone line or designated email account.

When applying for a client's T visa, first-time attorneys should note that many immigrants do not anticipate the availability of immigration relief for family members, particularly those who are overseas. Yet T visas are in fact available to qualifying family members of trafficking victims. Attorneys should expect that many clients will not proactively disclose information about family members. Attorneys should make sure to advise clients on the possibility of bringing family members to the United States. Although there may be future opportunities to be reunited with family members, procedurally, it is best to include all eligible family members in the initial application. Successful primary applicants receive T-1 nonimmigrant status, and derivative family members receive a T nonimmigrant status numerically characterized by the eligible family relationship (e.g., T-2 nonimmigrant for a spouse of a T-1 nonimmigrant).

Attorney-Client Discussion Topics: Preparing a T Visa

☑ Explanation of the criminal justice process and a victim's role
☑ Expectations of cooperation with an investigation
☑ Expectations of ongoing cooperation after the T visa is filed
☑ Safety issues in cooperating
☑ Service plan that allows a victim meaningful alternatives to trafficking
☑ Reunification for eligible family members
☑ Risks associated with traveling home
☑ Comprehensive victim services options
☑ Alternative immigration options
☑ Timeline and process for a T visa–based adjustment of status
☑ Good moral character requirements

T Visa Adjustment of Status

Among the most critical benefits available to trafficked immigrants is a long-term path to permanent residence and citizenship. T visa holders are eligible to adjust their status,[41] an immigration term of art referencing the process of obtaining legal permanent residence, commonly called a green card. In order for a T nonimmigrant to adjust status and gain lawful permanent residence, he or she must meet several requirements that follow.

Continuous Physical Presence[42]

T-1 nonimmigrants must demonstrate continuous presence either for a period of at least three years after receiving T-1 status or for the period of investigation or prosecution of trafficking, whichever is less. Evidence to support continuous presence includes college transcripts, employment records, tax returns, rent receipts, and utility bills, but applicants need not submit evidence already submitted in the T visa application.[43] USCIS requires an applicant to submit a copy of his or her passport, documenting U.S. departures and reentries.[44] However, attorneys should note that reentry into the United States on a T visa is not guaranteed, and T visa holders are generally counseled to avoid leaving the United States during the duration of the visa. For those seeking to meet a requirement of a lesser period based on the completion of an investigation or prosecution,

USCIS requires documentation signed by an Attorney General designee stating that the investigation or prosecution is complete.[45]

Admissibility[46]

Applicants must either be admissible or seek a waiver of any inadmissibility grounds that were not waived in the earlier T visa approval. As with T visas, USCIS has very generous waivers of admissibility to respond to the trafficking circumstances that often trigger inadmissibility.

Good Moral Character

T nonimmigrants must also demonstrate good moral character for at least three years since either the T visa grant or during the investigation period, whichever is less. The good moral character requirement can be a barrier for sex trafficking victims, who may not always find meaningful alternatives to commercial sex. Attorneys should advise their clients who have been involved in commercial sex that continuing to participate in commercial sex may serve as a barrier to proving good moral character under USCIS regulations. An applicant can meet the good moral character requirement with an applicant affidavit and either a police clearance letter or a state criminal background check, unless the applicant is under age fourteen, in which case good moral character is presumed.[47]

Assistance in the Investigation or Prosecution, Extreme Hardship, or Age Under Eighteen When Victimized

An applicant seeking to demonstrate compliance with an investigation or prosecution requires a letter from the Department of Justice.[48] Even when a T nonimmigrant holder has continued to assist, it may still be difficult to obtain this letter. USCIS will alternatively accept evidence of extreme hardship.[49] Because T nonimmigrants would have already submitted extreme hardship evidence with their T visa applications, supplementing this initial evidence may prove easier than obtaining documentation of cooperation from the Department of Justice.

T-1 nonimmigrants can apply for adjustment of status either upon expiration of the visa or before, if the investigation is complete.[50] T-1 nonimmigrants can seek proof of completion of the investigation from the Department of Justice. In cases where the investigation was complete when an applicant initially applied for a T visa and this is indicated in the law enforcement certification, this form should satisfy the requirement for those adjusting status. Alternatively, T-1 nonimmigrants may renew their visa if they receive another law enforcement certification stating that their presence is necessary to assist in an investigation or prosecution.[51] T visa derivative family members can also adjust their status when the principal T-1 nonimmigrant applies to adjust status.[52]

U Visa for Victims of Crime

The original TVPA was passed as part of the Victims of Trafficking and Violence Protection Act of 2000, which also reauthorized VAWA.[53] In 2000, the VAWA expansions included a companion visa called the U visa, a three-year nonimmigrant status which is available to victims of trafficking but also other qualifying crimes.[54] The U visa provides a useful alternative to the T visa in cases in which physical presence or one of the other elements cannot be met or in cases in which it is easier to prove another qualifying crime, whether related or unrelated to the trafficking. For example, an individual may be too fearful to report trafficking because the traffickers pose a risk to a victim's family in the home country but subsequently experienced domestic violence, which he or she is willing to report. The U visa, therefore, provides a suitable alternative avenue of relief for trafficking victims.

The U visa still offers many critical benefits to victims of human trafficking:

- Ability to apply for employment authorization
- Family reunification: visa for eligible family members both in the United States and overseas, with accompanying work authorization[55]
- A path to lawful permanent residence

The specialized unit at USCIS's VSC also adjudicates the U visa. The U visa adjudication process likewise responds to the difficulties crime victims might encounter in securing evidence, applying the "any credible evidence" standard.[56] Also as in the T visa application process, USCIS does not make affirmative referrals to initiate removal proceedings on applicants who are denied a U visa. Finally, the U visa also offers generous waivers for certain acts, including crimes and immigration violations.[57]

There are, however, drawbacks to choosing the U visa. Since fiscal year 2010, USCIS has reached the statutory annual cap of 10,000 U visas granted before the fiscal year was complete, leaving applicants to wait until the new fiscal year begins.

To obtain a U visa, an applicant must prove that he or she

1. has suffered substantial physical or mental abuse related to the criminal activity;
2. has information about the criminal activity;
3. has been, is being, or is likely to be helpful in the investigation or prosecution of the criminal activity; and
4. can prove that the criminal activity violated the laws of or occurred in the United States.[58]

Case Study

Ana Rosa Diaz was a guestworker in Louisiana, peeling crawfish for a CJ's Seafood, then a crawfish supplier to Wal-Mart.[59] A supervisor threatened to send Diaz back to Mexico if she refused to work the long arduous hours. He also subtly mentioned that he knew where the workers' families lived. Diaz contacted the National Guestworkers Alliance and ultimately the Department of Labor. Diaz and another whistleblower alleged forced labor and received U visa certification and ultimately a U visa.

Substantial Physical or Mental Abuse

U visa applicants must demonstrate that they have experienced substantial physical or mental abuse.[60] USCIS will consider the following factors in determining the abuse: the nature of the injury, the severity of the perpetrator's conduct, the duration of harm, and the extent to which the harm affected mental and physical soundness.[61]

Trafficked persons are often compelled by psychological coercion, which may not result in direct physical abuse as a result of trafficking. More often, trafficked persons suffer substantial mental abuse, which can be more difficult to document. Because adjudicators receive training to understand the nuances of victimization, applicants may rely primarily on their own declaration describing the abuse.

Evidence of substantial physical or mental abuse may include the following:

- A victim's declaration
- Psychological evaluation
- Caseworker declaration
- Criminal complaint or other criminal investigation material
- Personal witness declarations
- Expert witness declarations
- Medical records
- Civil complaint

Possesses Information

The U visa is intended as a law enforcement tool, encouraging noncitizen victims to feel protected reporting crimes to the police. However, the "possesses information" requirement does not pass on the obligation of a law enforcement investigation to a victim. In other words, a victim is limited to his or her own direct knowledge of the victimization and cannot be required to investigate and demonstrate evidence of an investigation.

Evidence of possessing information may include what follows:

- A victim's declaration
- Criminal complaint or other criminal investigation material

Law Enforcement Cooperation

A U visa applicant must demonstrate that he or she "has been, is being, or is likely to be helpful" in the investigation or prosecution of the criminal activity.[62] Unlike the T visa statute, the U visa statute requires a certification (Form I-918 Supplement B) in order to demonstrate helpfulness.[63] Therefore, part of immigration representation includes advocacy with law enforcement to facilitate obtaining a certification.

U visa applicants can seek a certification from a number of different agencies authorized to investigate or prosecute the qualifying criminal activity, including a number of agencies characterized within USCIS regulations.[64] Signatories must be the agency head or his or her designee to certify.[65]

Possible U Visa Certifying Agencies

- Local law enforcement agencies
- Local and state prosecutors' offices
- Federal Bureau of Investigation
- DHS
- ICE/HSI
- U.S. Attorney's Offices
- U.S. Department of State, Diplomatic Security
- Department of Justice (multiple divisions housing investigators, prosecutors, and judges)
- Federal or state courts (judges as signatories)
- Equal Employment Opportunity Commission
- Department of Labor
- State labor agencies
- Child Protective Services

Applicants under age sixteen are required to have someone demonstrate helpfulness on their behalf, whether it be a family member, a guardian, or a next friend.[66] Because many trafficked juveniles do not have family members or guardians, it might be more difficult for a trafficked juvenile to meet the helpfulness requirement than the T visa cooperation requirement.

Qualifying Criminal Activity Violated Laws

The U visa is available to victims of enumerated crimes.[67] Trafficking, peonage, involuntary servitude, and slave trade are all U visa–enumerated crimes.[68]

Among the crimes that might overlap with human trafficking are as follows:

- Rape
- Torture
- Incest

- Domestic violence
- Sexual assault
- Abusive sexual contact
- Prostitution
- Sexual exploitation
- Stalking
- Female genital mutilation
- Being held hostage
- Kidnapping
- Abduction
- Unlawful criminal restraint
- False imprisonment
- Blackmail
- Extortion
- Felonious assault
- Witness tampering
- Obstruction of justice
- Perjury
- Fraud in foreign labor contracting

As discussed earlier, someone who has experienced human trafficking may have also experienced another U visa–enumerated crime and may find it easier to instead apply as a victim of that crime. It may be that there is only adequate evidence for a related crime, making it easier to secure the law enforcement certification using a different qualifying crime. That other crime need not have occurred in conjunction with the trafficking.

For example, imagine the scenario of a Maria who is repeatedly sexually assaulted in the fields where she works. She cannot leave the work because she still owes a debt related to her entry into the United States. A friend connects her with an advocacy group, which works with a police investigator. He does not see a way to investigate the trafficking unless he can connect her boss with those who brought her to the United States; he wants to prosecute the sexual assault case and is willing to sign a U visa certification with sexual assault as the qualifying crime.

Attorney-Client Discussion Topics: Preparing a U Visa

☑ Explanation of the criminal justice process
☑ Expectations of helpfulness with an investigation
☑ Expectations of ongoing helpfulness
☑ Safety issues in cooperating
☑ Service plan that allows a victim meaningful alternatives to trafficking
☑ Reunification for eligible family members
☑ Risk that a trip home has on extreme hardship and continuous presence requirements
☑ Comprehensive victim services
☑ Timeline and process to apply for a U visa–based adjustment of status
☑ Good moral character requirements
☑ U visa caps

Adjustment of Status

Like the T visa, the U visa also offers trafficked immigrants a long-term path to permanent residence and citizenship. A U nonimmigrant must submit evidence of being admitted as a U nonimmigrant[69] and meet several requirements:

Assistance in the Investigation or Prosecution

Unlike the T visa adjustment requirement, U nonimmigrants need only prove that they have not unreasonably refused to assist in an investigation or prosecution.[70] This rule anticipates the many cases where law enforcement will not conduct any further investigations. Therefore, applicants can show that they never received such a request.[71]

Continuous Physical Presence

Like T nonimmigrants, U nonimmigrants must also demonstrate continuous physical presence and cannot be absent from the United States for more than 90 days or an aggregate of more than 180 days.[72] All applicants must include an affidavit, and passport showing departures and reentries, and can supplement this with college transcripts, employment records, tax returns, rent receipts, and utility bills.[73]

Admissibility and Discretion

While U nonimmigrants technically need not prove admissibility again, as with other applications, USCIS always retains discretion to make favorable decisions. Therefore, USCIS will assess adverse factors, often related to inadmissibility. Applicants can attempt to mitigate any of these adverse factors with evidence of favorable factors, which may include family ties, hardship, and length of residence in the United States.[74]

VAWA Self-Petition and Cancellation

Trafficked immigrants typically seek relief through the T and U visa programs. However, attorneys representing trafficked immigrants must be familiar with the range of immigration relief available to someone without lawful status. Attorneys should familiarize themselves with the basic elements and how each type of relief might become available to a trafficked immigrant. However, as with the T and U visa discussions, this information provides just a glimpse into the options available so that attorneys may investigate further as the circumstances arise.

Primarily designed for immigrant domestic violence survivors who likely would have received status through a sponsoring family member, the VAWA self-petition is available to those who meet the following criteria[75]:

- Experienced battery or extreme cruelty from a U.S. citizen spouse, parent, or adult child or lawful permanent resident spouse or parent.
- Entered into good-faith marriage (when the qualifying family member is a spouse).
- Jointly resided (when the qualifying family member is a spouse).
- Have good moral character.

While these requirements do not typically align with the facts of most trafficking cases, there are scenarios in which a trafficker has been the qualifying relative. In such cases, though battery or extreme cruelty is typically used to qualify as domestic violence, trafficking may also constitute battery or extreme cruelty, depending on the facts of the case.

For those who are eligible, the VAWA self-petition is likely preferable to a T or U visa. The benefits include the following:

- Faster path to work authorization and to lawful permanent residence for those trafficked by certain family members
- No requirement of law enforcement cooperation

VAWA also enacted another form of immigration relief called VAWA Cancellation. Unlike the VAWA self-petition, VAWA Cancellation is only available to those already in immigration proceedings. The eligibility criteria vary slightly from the self-petition requirements. An applicant can receive cancellation and automatically receive lawful permanent resident status if he or she meets the following criteria[76]:

- Has experienced battery or extreme cruelty from a U.S. citizen or lawful permanent resident parent, spouse, former spouse, or intended spouse or is the non-abusive parent of a child who experienced battery or extreme cruelty by the U.S. citizen or lawful permanent resident.
- Has been physically present in the United States for three years.
- Has good moral character.
- Would experience or the applicant's child or parent would experience extreme hardship.

As with other immigration applications, VAWA Cancellation also includes a number of requirements for inadmissibility. Like the VAWA self-petition, there may be circumstances in which VAWA Cancellation is a better option for a trafficked immigrant applying for immigration relief. The most likely scenarios would be those in which the trafficker is also a qualifying family member. VAWA Cancellation is also an option for a trafficked immigrant who also and separately experienced domestic violence and is eligible for VAWA Cancellation based on the domestic violence experience.

Special Immigrant Juvenile Status

Unlike the other applications discussed in this chapter, Special Immigrant Juvenile (SIJ) Status does not evaluate victimization. SIJ is a status available to juveniles up to age twenty-one who are declared a dependent of juvenile court, legally committed to a juvenile court, or placed under custody of the State Department or a state- or court-appointed individual or entity.[77] It is designed to provide status to unaccompanied juveniles. SIJ is only an option for juveniles for whom parental reunification with one or both parents is not viable because of abuse, neglect, or abandonment.[78] This requirement is critical because SIJ also forecloses the opportunity for the juvenile to ever petition for immigration relief for those parents.[79]

SIJ requires a judicial determination that it would not be in the best interests of the child to return to the home country or country of habitual residence.[80] Attorneys assisting trafficking victims with SIJ applications will also have to ensure their representation in the juvenile court system. SIJ can be very beneficial, however, for trafficked youth, who may not be able to demonstrate proof of trafficking victimization. Those representing trafficked juveniles can coordinate with service providers specializing in services for immigrant youth.

Asylum

Before the passage of the TVPA, trafficked immigrants were primarily limited to seeking immigration relief through asylum, despite its limited application to trafficking specifically. Asylum continues to be available, but with the proliferation of other trafficking-specific protections, asylum may not be the best option. Nevertheless, it should be considered an alternative to the previously discussed applications, particularly when trafficking occurred outside the United States.

Asylum is available to those who have a reasonable fear of persecution based on their membership in one of five protected classes: national origin, race, religion, social group, and political opinion.[81] Though gender is not a protected class, many gender asylum cases have been argued as a social group. Attorneys might be able to make other social group arguments related to trafficking.

Though these criteria do not necessarily fit the facts of most human trafficking scenarios, trafficked immigrants have been successful at obtaining asylum based on trafficking that occurred inside and outside the United States. In either case, unless there are particular circumstances triggering eligibility in the other protected classes, attorneys would be left arguing that the applicant has a particular social group that puts that person at risk. The social group characterization has been refined by courts over the years, and could potentially include a particular group at risk of being recruited by traffickers, although this area of law continues to evolve. Asylum is most useful, however, to those who experienced trafficking outside the United States, since in most cases, T and U visas would not be available since the trafficking did not occur in the United States.

Still, asylum applications have risks associated with them. Denial of asylum application claims results in a referral into removal proceedings. Furthermore, unlike at the VSC, asylum officers do not typically receive specialized training on human trafficking and may be less inclined to understand a lack of evidence or unbelievable facts. Finally, unlike the adjudication of T and U visas, which is conducted based on a paper application, asylum interviews are conducted in person, which can further revictimize a trafficked immigrant.

Considerations in Representing Trafficked Immigrants

Language Considerations

Trafficked immigrants are often limited English proficient (LEP). Traffickers sometimes use language as a tool of coercion to isolate LEP persons and prevent them from learning about resources and protections. From the outset, language services are critical to any service plan. Only with those language services will trafficked immigrants be able to share enough of their experience for stakeholders to effectively identify, connect to, and provide services as well as provide legal representation.

LEP is a term of art used to identify persons who should be afforded meaningful language access under the law. An LEP individual has a limited ability to read, write, speak, or understand English. LEP individuals typically are unfamiliar with the laws that require meaningful language access. Many LEP individuals struggle and speak in broken English to navigate services. Therefore, service providers will have to proactively provide language services and inform LEP individuals of their rights to meaningful language access.

In some circumstances, providing meaningful language access is required by law. But even without legal obligations, providing language services is an opportunity to build trust and build the most effective response to serving trafficked immigrants. At a time when a person is transitioning from a place of exploitation to a place of autonomy, language services give trafficked immigrants the voice they need for autonomy in decision making as they rebuild their lives free of exploitation.

Agencies receiving federal financial assistance are subject to Title VI of the Civil Rights Act of 1964[82] and must provide meaningful language access. Many local government agencies and even nonprofit agencies receive federal financial assistance and are therefore subject to Title VI. Despite long-standing laws, there remain many gaps in the implementation of meaningful language access.

Many agencies subject to Title VI are just beginning to develop language access policies to proactively offer language services to LEP individuals. Institutional language access begins with identifying and recording an LEP individual's primary spoken and written language. Critical errors occur when individuals make assumptions without conducting a proper assessment. For example, many immigrants from Mexico and Central America speak an indigenous language as a primary language but are often presumed based on nationality to be Spanish speakers. They will use Spanish language services but may lack the Spanish proficiency to fully communicate and comprehend information. "I Speak" cards and posters are just some of the tools that assist in identifying a primary language. Using those tools, agencies providing services should record the individual's primary language in a database, to ensure consistent access to language services for the LEP individual.

Even after a language is identified, high-quality language services remain elusive in many communities. Whether obligated under the law, a trafficked person's attorney or advocate should ensure that language services are available for every system with which the individual interacts. There are special considerations with regard to law enforcement and court communications where conflicts of interest or bias may arise. For example, if law enforcement relied on an interview using a bilingual case manager, that might raise questions of credibility regarding the victim's testimony. However, assessing interpreter skill is an ongoing challenge, and use of court-certified interpreters or county-funded interpreter lines does not guarantee quality or neutrality. Where available, a victim's attorney can best assess this by bringing a separate interpreter for communications with outside systems.

Culturally Appropriate Services

Culture is a commonly misunderstood concept, often conflated with ethnicity. Assumptions about culture can create unnecessary trust barriers with trafficked immigrants. Instead, viewing culture as a set of shared practices and values allows practitioners not to stereotype a victim but instead to recognize that each has a unique cultural experience. There are, however, certain themes prevalent among trafficked persons that are important to view through a cultural lens.

1. Shame is often generalized as a moralistic objective value within the trafficking context. But there are other cultural contexts for shame. Shame can also be viewed in terms of economic success and its practical impact on debt and economically reliant family members. Shame might also be framed in terms of migration and the implications of returning home after risking travel to the United States.

2. Threats have cultural implications beyond an objective perception of harm. Traffickers might use veiled or coded threats that in an American context would not constitute a threat. However, in other communities, these same threats could be code for death. Trafficked immigrants may not always have the ability to independently explain or interpret the threats within an American paradigm, leaving attorneys to carefully probe.

3. Ethnicity as a surrogate for culture poses particular challenges. Those working with a trafficked immigrant may instinctually design "culturally appropriate services" that assume a particular food, clothing, or religious preference based on ethnicity. Service providers

may provide services through a member of the victim's ethnic community, when in fact the victim wants to distance himself or herself from that community or has more dominant identities, such as a particular sexual orientation, religion, language spoken, and more.

Those designing programs can successfully accommodate cultural values and identities by accessing training on culturally appropriate service design. But generally, ensuring that trafficked immigrants define their own cultural identity will allow service providers to provide the most effective services.

Immigration Enforcement Victims Protections

Although trafficked immigrants often fear immigration enforcement, DHS enforces measures to protect undocumented crime victims from being subject to enforcement. These measures include VAWA Confidentiality and prosecutorial discretion.

Congress created VAWA Confidentiality protections to specifically protect undocumented crime victims and applies these three provisions to those eligible for T and U visas as well as VAWA-related petitions. First, all information filed with a VAWA, T visa, or U visa application—including the fact of its existence—is confidential and cannot be disclosed by DHS or DOJ in a court of law or elsewhere.[83] The provision is critical to preserve the privacy and confidentiality of those who are undocumented and do not want their undocumented status disclosed. Because traffickers and other crime perpetrators have come to use this tool as an attempt to undermine victim testimony, this issue continues to be litigated, but a growing number of opinions are interpreting this provision favorably and protecting the confidentiality of the applications.

Second, USCIS is precluded from relying on information from a perpetrator in adjudicating the underlying application.[84] Because traffickers and others who perpetrate crimes against immigrant victims use immigration enforcement as a threat, Congress anticipated that perpetrators would carry out such threats. This provision protects victims against their perpetrators who do so and try to contact immigration authorities.

Finally, immigration officials are precluded from conducting enforcement actions at certain locations, including shelters and courthouses.[85] Without such protection, ICE agents might unknowingly rely on leads from traffickers providing likely false information and show up at a courtroom where a trafficking victim is offering testimony.

In addition to VAWA Confidentiality provisions, A second mechanism available to ICE officers is *prosecutorial discretion*, a tool that is available to ICE personnel involved at various stages of immigration enforcement. This tool is not actually a criminal prosecution tool, despite the terminology. ICE personnel have been instructed to use prosecutorial discretion and not detain or take enforcement measures against a trafficking victim.[86]

While directed at ICE, these tools are most utilized by immigration attorneys advocating for the rights of eligible immigrants. They can access written guidance for the purposes of providing notice to ICE and law enforcement agencies that may not yet be trained on how to respond to trafficked immigrants.

Coordinating with Law Enforcement

A fundamental challenge in assisting trafficked immigrants involves navigation of two law enforcement systems, which are often at odds. Federal laws allow those defined as trafficking victims to access immigration protections if they cooperate with a criminal investigation or prosecution. Since the passage of the TVPA, which enacted the first such trafficking victims' protections,[87] immigration enforcement has increased dramatically.[88] Partnerships between the federal government and local law enforcement, such as Secure Communities, allow local law enforcement coming into contact with immigrants to investigate their immigration status. This creates a chilling effect, preventing immigrant crime victims from seeking the protection of law enforcement. This compounds preexisting distrust that immigrant crime victims harbor based on corruption and lack of response in their home countries.

Meanwhile, Congress created a shield of protection from deportation with a path to permanent residence for trafficking victims. While immigrants and the American public are well aware of immigration enforcement risks, trafficking-specific immigration protections remain unfamiliar to most victims, law enforcement agencies, immigration attorneys, and the general public. And because law enforcement expertise in human trafficking remains specialized, untrained law enforcement may respond by first enforcing immigration laws. Even specialized local law enforcement units focus on sex trafficking cases.[89] Investigating labor trafficking, which predominantly affects immigrants, requires law enforcement to navigate complex immigration systems.

Law enforcement cooperation begins either by a referral to law enforcement or because a potential victim has been identified through a law enforcement action, such as a raid. In the former circumstance, attorneys will have to navigate referrals and coordinate in partnership with social service providers. Because of overlapping state and federal anti-trafficking laws, a law enforcement referral could be directed at a number of different law enforcement agencies, including local police departments, FBI, ICE, or U.S. Attorney's Offices. Established local anti-trafficking experts are typically familiar with the most appropriate points of contact and specific methods to protect the identity of trafficked immigrants at risk of deportation. Experts are also better positioned to predict the risk of immigration enforcement based on the facts presented.

Alternatively, a trafficking victim may already be identified to law enforcement and require immigration representation. Depending on the law enforcement agency, a victim electing not to cooperate might be subjected to immigration enforcement or foreclose methods of immigration relief. A victim always has that option of whether to cooperate but is exposed to consequences of noncooperation once law enforcement is involved. The cooperation requirement does not have a time requirement and in some cases, a victim may only feel comfortable cooperating over time. That victim may still be able to access some forms of immigration relief, although meeting the requirements may be more challenging.

Investigation and Prosecution

Because of the cooperation requirement, an immigration attorney's obligations in trafficking cases extend beyond the typical scope of immigration representation. Cooperation might include participating in law enforcement interviews, assisting with the collection of additional evidence, preparing for testimony, testifying, and filing witness impact statements. A victim's attorney will have to represent a victim's interests in cooperation, which may in some instances be adverse to the interests of a victim-witness. Chapter 4 includes a deeper discussion of victim representation.

Conclusion

Traffickers have long economically profited from and perpetuated crimes by taking advantage of their victims' immigration status. Increasing identification and protection of trafficked immigrants is an incredibly worthwhile endeavor. Attorneys taking on these cases must navigate complex interacting systems and overcome significant trust barriers. But the benefits of engaging in these efforts and developing this expertise will contribute to filling a vast identification and protection gap.

CHAPTER 6

International Law

Effective action to prevent and combat trafficking in persons, especially women and children, requires a comprehensive international approach in the countries of origin, transit and destination that includes measures to prevent such trafficking, to punish the traffickers and to protect the victims of such trafficking, including by protecting their internationally recognized human rights.

—Preamble of the Palermo Protocol

The seminal moment for human trafficking in international law was the adoption of the Protocol to Prevent, Suppress and Punish Trafficking in Persons, Especially Women and Children (Palermo Protocol) supplementing the United Nations Convention Against Transnational Organized Crime.[1] It provided the first definition of human trafficking:

The recruitment, transportation, transfer, harbouring or receipt of persons, by means of the threat or use of force or other forms of coercion, of abduction, of fraud, of deception, of the abuse of power or of a position of vulnerability, or of the giving or receiving of payments or benefits to achieve the consent of a person having control over another person, for the purpose of exploitation. Exploitation shall include, at a minimum, the exploitation of the prostitution of others or other forms of sexual exploitation, forced labour or services, slavery or practices similar to slavery, servitude or the removal of organs.

Before the creation of the Palermo Protocol, there were various legal instruments related to forced labor, slavery, and trafficking, but none were adequate to either encapsulate the forms of exploitation that make up human trafficking or spur sufficient international action to address it. Although human rights advocates originally decried human trafficking's inclusion in a transnational crime convention rather than a human rights instrument, the subsequent years of its rapid implementation worldwide proved the convention to be an extraordinarily valuable mechanism. No longer was trafficking a marginalized human rights issue. Today, as a result of the Palermo Protocol, more than 140 countries have criminalized human trafficking and provide some sort of remedial actions for victims.

This chapter seeks to highlight where trafficking obligations arise in international law and, as a result, where and how attorneys have been able to work on the issue in a very practical sense. The aftermath of the Palermo Protocol has been a fascinating time for lawyering as the Protocol's impact ripples through multiple areas of the law. Attorneys in transnational criminal law, refugee law, human rights law, and labor and employment law all have an opportunity to integrate anti-trafficking into their work, contribute their skills in a meaningful way, and further develop this area of the law.

A Brief History

The international community struggled for more than one hundred years to address the evolution of what we today term human trafficking. At the turn of the last century, international human rights law was focused on the "traffic" in women and children for prostitution with a limited number of primarily European State Parties. Other efforts focused on the continued abolition of slavery, the slave trade, and then slavery-like practices, which were to be criminalized. At the same time, the International Labour Organization (ILO) developed instruments regarding forced labor. All of these efforts were separate and distinct. The trafficking-specific instruments are as follows:

1904—International Agreement for the Suppression of the White Slave Traffic[2]—At the turn of the century, a "white slave panic" broke out over European women abducted and forced into prostitution in South America, Africa, and Asia. As a result, this Agreement focused on protecting women and girls who had been abducted for "immoral purposes abroad,"[3] ensuring their safe repatriation, and supervising employment agencies finding work for women abroad. Interestingly, the "white slave panic" coincided with women's migrating for work for the first time; very few cases of actual "white slavery" occurred.[4]

1910—International Convention for the Suppression of White Slave Traffic[5]—Following the 1904 Agreement, this Convention substantially broadened punishment for the crime of trafficking by covering not only abduction as in the 1904 Agreement but also procurement, enticement, leading away even with a woman's or girl's consent, and the use of fraud or violence.

1921—Convention on the Suppression of Traffic in Women and Children[6]—This Convention was the first instrument to recognize human trafficking of both girls and boys, but did not include men. It included supervising employment agencies and making regulations governing the safety of women and children traveling abroad, particularly on ships and in railroad stations and ports. There were no provisions for victim protections.

1933—The International Convention for the Suppression of the Traffic in Women of Full Age[7]—This Convention created punishment for the same offense described in the 1910 Convention for the enticement, procurement, or leading away "of a woman or girl of full age for immoral purposes to be carried out in another country. . . ."[8] The differentiating factor was the first mandate for international law enforcement cooperation regarding convictions and investigations to combat trafficking.[9] It included no provisions regarding the victims.

1949—Convention for the Suppression of the Traffic in Persons and of the Exploitation of the Prostitution of Others[10]—This Convention merged the former agreements. Although no definition of trafficking had yet been provided in any agreement through 1950, the Preamble indicated that prostitution was distinguished from trafficking, and that trafficking might refer to the acts of procurement and enticement: "Whereas prostitution and the accompanying evil of the traffic in persons for the purpose of prostitution . . . "[11] It expanded criminal acts to be punished to include exploiting the prostitution of another person, presumably man or woman, managing or financing a brothel, and renting or leasing a building for the prostitution of others.[12] Additional law enforcement provisions included punishing offenders, facilitating extradition, and collecting investigative information. Regarding victims, there is one provision that encouraged Parties to the Convention to help rehabilitate victims of prostitution. Another provision asked the Parties to the Convention to undertake "so far as possible" the temporary care of victims and required victims to pay for transportation back to their country of origin. Another provision addressed protecting immigrants and emigrants while en route and warning the public about trafficking.

International Criminal Law
The Palermo Protocol
Although trafficking had primarily been within the realm of international human rights law for a century, a renewal of interest led to an international criminal law response. Several circumstances gave rise to the United Nations Convention Against Transnational Organized Crime (Convention) and its protocols on smuggling, trafficking in persons,[13] and trafficking in firearms. Governments increasingly faced crimes that extended beyond their borders without adequate mechanisms for cross-border law enforcement cooperation; the most elusive perpetrators were organized-crime networks involving forgers, smugglers, recruiters, bankers, and corrupt government officials throughout multiple countries. Work-related migration was also at an all-time high, estimated at 150 million people each year, fueled by mobility, opportunity, discrimination, and escaping

armed conflict; all mired with exploitation.[14] Cases increasingly involved deception, coercion, fraud, and force for sexual exploitation as well as labor exploitation, and the laws were inadequate to address the phenomenon. Additionally, prosecutors were losing their witnesses to deportation and thereby losing cases. The few nations that had ratified the early trafficking agreements incorporated into their domestic law a narrow concept of trafficking by today's standards; their scope was limited to enticing or abducting women for prostitution abroad, not for labor purposes or within borders, or for men in addition to women and children.

The Palermo Protocol has three major successes: (1) the Convention as the first instrument to use international law against transnational organized crime; (2) international consensus on the first ever definition of human trafficking; and (3) a mandate for State Parties to criminalize trafficking through domestic legislation, meaning many countries would create their first criminal law against trafficking in persons.

More specifically, the Palermo Protocol requires State Parties to criminalize trafficking, attempted trafficking, participating as an accomplice, and organizing and directing trafficking. This opened the door to prosecution of the entire criminal enterprise, rather than select actors. Law enforcement and immigration officials must exchange information regarding transportation routes, fraudulent documents, and potential traffickers. They must strengthen border control and anti-fraud measures. Additionally, the Palermo Protocol mandates law enforcement training to identify trafficking victims and organized-crime methods.

The Palermo Protocol also mandates certain victim assistance measures. For example, State Parties must include provisions within their domestic legal frameworks regarding victim compensation and information on legal proceedings. They must facilitate the repatriation of citizens or nationals with due regard for the safety of the victim by providing necessary travel documentation and a return without unreasonable delay. They must also provide for confidentiality of legal proceedings and the victims' right to information regarding legal proceedings.

The victim protection and assistance provisions, while discretionary,[15] are defined in unprecedented detail, offering guidance on the types of assistance that national legislation should include—medical care, housing, language-appropriate mental health counseling, job training, language-appropriate legal assistance, and physical safety for victims' physical and psychological recovery. Temporary or permanent residence for victims is also considered.

Today's Lawyering

The Palermo Protocol was just the beginning. It initiated a wave of government implementation as more than 140 countries have signed on to the Palermo Protocol and passed domestic legislation criminalizing human trafficking. To varying degrees, legislation also included victim protection and prevention measures and the corresponding government infrastructure to implement the legislation and address human trafficking. There have been and continue to be many efforts to create and strengthen legislation and its implementation.

Most notably is the work of the Office to Monitor and Combat Trafficking in Persons (J/TIP) within the U.S. Department of State known for publishing the annual *Trafficking in Persons Report (TIP Report)*. Congress requires the annual publication of the *TIP Report*, which ranks the progress of governments in their efforts to address human trafficking, according to specific minimum standards related to prosecution, prevention, and protection. Ambassador-at-Large Luis CdeBaca, a former U.S. Department of Justice human trafficking prosecutor, led J/TIP from 2009 to 2014 and its efforts to encourage foreign governments to augment their efforts, providing financial and technical assistance to do so. That assistance may be legal experts deployed to work with legislative drafters or funding to do so through J/TIP's international grant program. For example, a few recent projects specific to legislation and infrastructure include the following[16]:

- In Kenya, "United Nations Office on Drugs and Crime (UNODC) will conduct multidisciplinary trainings on victim identification and on the investigation and prosecution of traffickers; develop a national referral mechanism to identify, assist, and protect victims of trafficking; and establish and institutionalize a trafficking in persons data collection and reporting mechanism."

- "In partnership with the Government of Mauritania and other relevant stakeholders, UNICEF [United Nations Children's Fund] will scale-up and reinforce the country's child protection system and its overall capacity to prevent and combat child trafficking. It will support the development and improvement of anti-trafficking legal and policy frameworks. It will train and enhance the capacity of anti-trafficking agencies and service providers."
- In Laos, UNODC will "provide support, training, and assistance to the Government of Laos in implementing its 2014 Trafficking in Persons Action Plan, including providing training on and assistance with drafting a more comprehensive anti-trafficking law."
- "UNODC will provide technical assistance to the Royal Government of Bhutan in assessing gaps in the legal framework and drafting appropriate legislation in line with international standards."

These examples illustrate the range of other organizations and actors involved in this work. In particular, UNODC is known as the "guardian" of the Palermo Protocol and, as such, helps State Parties to implement it, including drafting laws, creating national anti-trafficking strategies, conducting trainings, and encouraging cross-border cooperation to investigate and prosecute trafficking. This work is ongoing because "translating [the Palermo Protocol] into reality remains problematic. Very few criminals are convicted and most victims are probably never identified or assisted."[17] UNODC is the only UN entity focused on the criminal justice elements of trafficking.

Others have worked at the regional level. At the President's Interagency Council on Women in the late 1990s, Stephen Warnath held the first U.S. government position dedicated solely to the creation and development of U.S. and international law and policy of human trafficking. In this role, he served as the senior administration policy official for the development of both the Trafficking and Victims Protection Act (TVPA) and the Palermo Protocol. Then he became Deputy Director and Chief of Staff of the Stability Pact Task Force on Trafficking in Human Beings, working under the auspices of the Organization for Security and Cooperation in Europe. The Task Force's work focused on trafficking in the post-conflict countries of South Eastern Europe, creating a regional action plan as well as national action plans that were comprehensive frameworks, including legislative reform, law enforcement cooperation, public awareness, training, victim protection, return and reintegration, and prevention.

Al Moskowitz led the Criminal Section of the U.S. Department of Justice's Civil Rights Division pre-TVPA, overseeing the efforts of federal prosecutors using involuntary servitude statutes and a broader interagency Worker Exploitation Task Force. He grappled with the United States' criminal justice response and then participated in devising new legislation to address the existing legal limitations. He worked closely on the TVPA's development and then led the Criminal Section to prosecute human trafficking cases under the TVPA's new and revised statutes. This experience was invaluable when he joined the Asia Regional Trafficking in Persons (ARTIP) Project. The goal was to "contribute to the prevention of trafficking in persons in Asia by facilitating a more effective and coordinated approach to trafficking by the criminal justice systems of participating national governments," which included Cambodia, Indonesia, Lao PDR, Myanmar, the Philippines, Thailand, and Vietnam. More specifically, in the wake of the Palermo Protocol, ARTIP worked to strengthen national law enforcement, and judicial and prosecutorial functions; encourage bilateral and regional cooperation particularly through the Association of Southeast Asian Nations and the Coordinated Mekong Ministerial Initiative Against Trafficking; and enhance regional and national legal policy.

The ABA Rule of Law Initiative (ROLI) also actively engages experienced attorneys to provide technical legal assistance that strengthens institutions, processes, and access in developing and transitioning countries worldwide. There is a direct correlation between how effectively a government is addressing human trafficking and the extent of rule of law in the country. Consider how much progress can be made if, for example, the judicial system is corrupt, judges have no experience adjudicating these cases, law enforcement is not held accountable for extortion in trafficking investigations, or legal aid is unavailable to victims. The broader work of ABA ROLI in these core areas of access to justice, anti-corruption, criminal justice reform, judicial reform, and legal education therefore underpins any anti-trafficking efforts. Its anti-trafficking work has been focused in three priority areas:

- <u>Legal and Policy Reform</u>—As expected, this includes drafting or assessing comprehensive legislation, national action plans, and criminal codes. It also includes making recommendations for legal reform to better address and reduce human trafficking, such as establishing corporate accountability for forced labor in global supply chains, drafting asset forfeiture procedures, or increasing oversight of key industries.
- <u>Access to Justice</u>—ABA ROLI strengthens criminal justice responses to trafficking primarily through training and resources specific to investigating and prosecuting organized and transitional crimes. It also works with local attorneys, bar associations, and law students to support state prosecutions, seek civil remedies for victims, obtain pro bono assistance and compensation for victims, and create legal aid and holistic services for trafficking victims.
- <u>Multisectoral Collaboration and Regional Collaboration</u>—This work promotes cross-border and regional cooperation through task forces, mutual legal assistance procedures, and regional conferences.

Attorneys can participate either through short-term paid consultancies or short- or long-term pro bono projects through the legal specialist program. For example, Doug Kramer is a former prosecutor, civil litigator, and head of law reform for a large urban poverty law program who has participated in multiple ABA ROLI anti-trafficking projects. In Uganda, Mongolia, Solomon Islands, and elsewhere, Kramer has assisted nongovernmental organization (NGO) attorneys as well as investigators and prosecutors to creatively work with new trafficking laws. Sometimes this has required sensitization to the issue, working with government officials to remove obstacles to prosecution, or training on how to effectively present a case to prosecutors.

International Human Rights and Humanitarian Law

In 1948, the UN General Assembly first adopted the Universal Declaration of Human Rights known as the foundation of the human rights framework and then the binding global treaties of the International

Covenants on Civil and Political Rights and on Economic, Social and Cultural Rights. The treaties that followed protected specific rights of women, children, migrant workers, and people with disabilities, and provided for freedom from genocide, torture, and racial discrimination. Human trafficking arose in several instruments and, of course, as the brief history of trafficking instruments before the Palermo Protocol illustrates, trafficking originally developed within this human rights framework. Today, anti-trafficking is reflected in the work of a multitude of organizations working on these many issues.

Women

Women and girls constitute 55 percent of all trafficking victims, 98 percent of sex trafficking victims, and 42 percent of labor trafficking victims. Trafficking is considered to be a form of gender-based violence along with child marriage, rape as a tool of war, honor killings, domestic violence, female genital mutilation, sexual violence, and more. The link has been made through the Vienna Declaration[18] and Beijing Platform for Action[19] as well as the Convention to End Discrimination Against Women (CEDAW) Committee.[20] With the CEDAW Committee's identifying trafficking as a form of gender-based violence, it links trafficking to unlawful discrimination, thereby giving rise to specific international legal obligations.

Worldwide, attorneys are providing legal services, advocating for legal reform to end discrimination and violence against women, changing societal attitudes that perpetuate violence, and strengthening law enforcement responses to gender-based violence. Organizations that have long worked on gender-based violence issues are including trafficking within their work as well. For example, Vital Voices is a nonprofit organization founded to implement the Beijing Platform for Action. The organization supports emerging women leaders, many of whom are seeking elective office, advocating for legal protections and community change, creating economic opportunities for other women, and addressing gender-based violence. Vital Voices has long supported anti-trafficking champions. Within the United States, the Tahirih Justice Center provides legal services to immigrant women fleeing violence, including trafficking, and works on public policy initiatives affecting these women, such as initiatives on forced marriage.

And in another example, the Women's Learning Partnership is a nonprofit collaborative of twenty organizations working in seventeen different countries across Africa, the Americas, Asia, and the Middle East. Their training programs for women who face violence include refugee women, victims of trafficking and domestic violence, women affected by HIV/AIDS, and women living in conflict and post-conflict situations.

Children

There are of course many organizations that have long worked to ensure the rights of children worldwide, such as UNICEF, Save the Children, Covenant House, and World Vision. Today their work also includes antitrafficking; the types of protection and services they offer in addition to the prevention work they perform put them in the position to protect trafficked children as well.

Other organizations work on specific types of human trafficking; for example, the forcible recruitment of children into armed conflict is one type of trafficking that is the subject of a specific international instrument. The Optional Protocol on the Involvement of Children in Armed Conflict[21] bans compulsory recruitment of children under age eighteen into armed services and requires Parties to take measures to ensure children under eighteen years of age do not take part in hostilities. Many organizations such as the International Rescue Committee, Mercy Corps, and Child Soldiers International work to prevent the recruitment of child soldiers and to rehabilitate and reintegrate child soldiers post-conflict.

Another example of human trafficking is the narrower issue of child sex trafficking, part of the broader issue of child sexual exploitation. The Optional Protocol to the Convention on the Rights of the Child on the Sale of Children, Child Prostitution and Child Pornography[22] requires signatories to undertake efforts in criminalization, public awareness, and international cooperation regarding child sex trafficking. It covers not only sexual exploitation and abuse of children but also the sale of children for forced labor and illegal adoption. The Optional Protocol also protects the rights of child victims, requiring victim services to support the child victims' rehabilitation and considering the best interests of the child when interacting with the criminal justice system. ECPAT International is "a global network of organisations working together for the elimination of child prostitution, child pornography and the trafficking of children for sexual purposes."[23]

Business and Human Rights

In Chapter 3, we highlighted this growing field of business and human rights from the viewpoint of corporate attorneys looking at risk mitigation and compliance. However, NGOs and advocates worldwide are also monitoring corporate conduct, reporting on human rights violations, seeking accountability, and pushing for binding international standards beyond the UN Guiding Principles on Business and Human Rights (UNGPs), also known Ruggie Principles.

Human Rights Watch[24] devotes researchers to monitoring and reporting on business and human rights. Numerous reports have covered the corporate impact on the social, environmental, and labor health of communities in which they operate. On the issue of forced labor, these reports have included gold mining and construction for the World Cup in Qatar. Amnesty International engages in similar work, reporting not only about human rights abuses but also governments' failure to prevent abuses and hold companies accountable. Amnesty International has also advocated for an international legal instrument beyond the voluntary UNGPs.

Civil society groups also work in conjunction with companies on specific initiatives. The Electronics Industry Citizenship Coalition (EICC) membership comprises brand and first-tier suppliers that are held accountable to a common Code of Conduct, which includes a section specific to labor and forced labor. The EICC works with external stakeholders on its code, training, and assessment tools. The Fair Labor Association consists of companies, universities, and civil society organizations creating solutions to abusive labor practices through training for factory workers and managers, conducting assessments, and creating tools that for instance increase accountability and transparency. In another example, governments, the World Diamond Council representing the diamond industry, and civil society organizations work together through the Kimberley Process to stem the flow of conflict diamonds often mined through forced labor. Together, they created and implemented the Kimberley Process

Certification Scheme, which sets forth the requirements for controlling rough diamond production and trade.

Migrants

The International Convention on the Protection of the Rights of All Migrant Workers and Members of Their Families[25] seeks to protect the human rights of migrants recognizing inherent risks and, most relevant to trafficking, establishing that no migrant worker "shall be held in slavery or servitude" or "required to perform forced or compulsory labour." The migrant source countries rather than the employing countries are ratifying and acceding to the Migrant Worker Convention.

Globally, 56 percent of trafficked persons are enslaved in a country other than their own and 15 percent are enslaved elsewhere within their country. Organizations that have long been devoted to assisting and protecting migrants, such as the International Organization for Migration, have therefore engaged in anti-trafficking activities as well. Other trafficking-specific organizations formed, such as the Global Alliance Against Traffic in Women (GAATW), which consists of more than one hundred NGOs worldwide that believe in the intrinsic connection between trafficking and migration. GAATW members work in alliance to promote and defend the human rights and safety of migrant workers in the formal and informal sectors. And other organizations have formed specifically to provide legal services to wronged migrants. Cathleen Caron founded the Global Workers Justice Alliance to combat worker exploitation by promoting portable justice for transnational migrants through a cross-border network of worker advocates and resources. In other words, Global Workers helps transnational migrant workers to access justice in the countries of employment even after they have departed for their home countries. Valid legal claims are pursued for lost wages, work-related injuries, and human trafficking.

International Refugee Law

International refugee law is established under the 1951 United Nations Convention Relating to the Status of Refugees[26] and the 1967 Protocol Relating to the Status of Refugees.[27] Any country acceding to the 1967

Protocol is mandated under Article 33 from expelling or returning "a refugee in any manner whatsoever to the frontiers or territories where his life or freedom would be threatened." Practically, this means that anyone arriving, for instance, in the United States seeking protection must not be returned to the country from which he or she came; this immigration relief is called withholding of removal.[28] The 1967 Protocol's Article 34 encourages signatories to "facilitate the assimilation and naturalization of refugees," which in the United States is the discretionary immigration relief of asylum.[29]

Asylum

The Trafficking Protocol is explicit that trafficked persons have access to asylum as a potential remedy:

> Nothing in this Protocol shall affect the rights, obligations and responsibilities of States and individuals under international law, including international humanitarian law and international human rights law and, in particular, where applicable, the 1951 Convention and the 1967 Protocol relating to the Status of Refugees and the principle of non-refoulement as contained therein.[30]

Human trafficking does not automatically qualify a trafficked person for refugee status; the refugee definition must be met. A *refugee* is defined as any person "outside the country of their nationality who is unable or unwilling to return and unable or unwilling to avail himself or herself of the protection of that country because of persecution or a well-founded fear of persecution on account of race, religion, nationality, membership in a particular social group, or political opinion."[31] But there are some circumstances in which a trafficked person meets the refugee definition.

Well-Founded Fear of Persecution

Traffickers commit heinous acts that generally rise to the level of persecution, including physical and sexual abuse, forced prostitution, forced labor, starvation, and withholding medical treatment. The United Nations

High Commissioner for Refugees (UNHCR) Guidelines[32] shed some light on the types of cases that may warrant refugee status:

- Trafficking—When the applicant fears human trafficking will occur in the future.
- Previous persecution continues psychologically—When the applicant has already suffered human trafficking and there is no fear of future persecution, but the persecution was particularly egregious and there are lingering psychological effects that make return unbearable.
- Retribution—When fear of future persecution is based on the possibility of the trafficker's reprisals for the victim's escape or assistance to law enforcement.
- Retrafficking—When fear of future persecution stems from the possibility of retrafficking either from retribution for escape or increased vulnerability due to ostracism and discrimination.

Traffickers as Agents of Persecution

Perpetrators can be agents of the State or private actors. In many cases but not all, traffickers are indeed private actors. In these cases, potential victims must therefore demonstrate that the government is unwilling or unable to provide protection. There may be inadequate laws or implementation, corruption, or a failure of law enforcement to act. Trafficked persons must demonstrate that upon their return they would not be protected, which can have a broader meaning given the Trafficking Protocol's provisions related to privacy, identity, recovery, and overall safety.

Place of Persecution

Refugee status is based on a well-founded fear of persecution that occurred or may occur in the applicant's country of origin. Therefore, when human trafficking occurs in the country where the applicant is seeking asylum, the assessment turns on the relationship between the trafficking and the country of origin. Without a connection, there can be no claim. If, however, there were recruiters, labor brokers, or others that facilitated the trafficking in the country of origin, then retrafficking and retaliation is a possibility.

The Causal Link to the Grounds

Despite traffickers' primary motivation of profit from exploitation, they sometimes target their victims, the reasons for which can be protected under the Refugee Convention. This is the necessary link for refugee eligibility. The Trafficking Guidelines provide specific examples: that traffickers may target their victims based on their ethnicity, nationality, or religious or political views, particularly targeting marginalized and discriminated-against populations. The two most common grounds in trafficking cases have been political opinion and membership in a particular social group.

Karen Musalo is a former Board of Immigration Appeals judge as well as founder of the Center for Gender and Refugee Studies (CGRS) at the University of California Hastings School of Law. She has tracked the development of this case law in the United States since the passage of the TVPA in 2000. In those earliest years and still to some degree, courts were resistant to asylum claims based on human trafficking, believing that it is a crime inflicted for personal or random reasons and not based on one of the five grounds for asylum. Now the difficulty lies in what constitutes membership in a particular social group in human trafficking cases.

CGRS has argued and helped other attorneys argue that human trafficking can be a gender-based human rights violation and the result of government failures to protect women and girls. In 2013, the United States Court of Appeals for the Seventh Circuit determined that women fleeing sex trafficking may establish eligibility for asylum based on their membership in a particular social group defined by their gender. In that case,[33] a young woman fled Albania in fear of being sex trafficked because a gang leader known to force women into prostitution began stalking and harassing her; despite her repeated requests for protection, the police would not help.

Other cases have been successful with narrow, well-defined constructs of the social group. For example, in one case,[34] a woman fled China in fear of being sex trafficked in a salon run by the government. Her asylum was granted based on membership in a particular social group of women in China who oppose coerced involvement in government-sanctioned prostitution. The UNHCR Guidelines provide several other scenarios where certain vulnerable groups—ones that traffickers target for recruitment—may constitute a social group, including unaccompanied children, orphans or street children, widows, and single, divorced, or illiterate women. Additionally, the Guidelines suggest that former victims of trafficking may also constitute a social group when the shared quality is not only the persecution but also the fear of ostracism, discrimination, retribution, and retrafficking.

Lisa Frydman, Managing Attorney at CGRS, says that there are so many areas of asylum law ripe for development and creative arguments, particularly around gender. However, the single biggest hurdle for trafficking cases is simply that attorneys just do not see the trafficking angle in their clients. There still is not a high volume of these cases because of this identification issue. There are a number of U.S. organizations providing legal services to assist asylum applicants in the United States, including Lutheran Immigration and Refugee Services, Catholic Legal Immigration Network, Human Rights First, numerous law school clinics, and many others.

UNHCR Role

The UNHCR's mandate for refugee protection stems from the 1951 Convention Relating to the Status of Refugees and its 1967 Protocol. As relates to human trafficking, UNHCR recognizes that it has a responsibility to (1) "ensure that refugees, asylum-seekers and internally displaced persons, stateless persons and other persons of concern do not fall victim to trafficking" and (2) "ensure that individuals who have been trafficked and who fear being subjected to persecution upon a return to their country of origin, or individuals who fear being trafficked, whose claim to international protection falls within the refugee definition . . . are recognized as refugees and afforded the corresponding international protection."[35]

In later years, UNHCR further articulated this intersection of protection between refugee law and trafficking to include addressing the needs of trafficking victims, to ensure international protection needs for trafficking victims and identify those at risk, to protect stateless victims of trafficking, and to ensure that trafficking victims without identity documents are able to establish their identity and nationality status so they do not become stateless.[36] Practically, this means UNHCR engages in numerous activities worldwide to encourage State Parties to identify, assist, and protect trafficked persons. Attorneys are at the forefront of much of this continuously developing work:

- Drafting, issuing, and training on the UNHCR Guidelines related to human trafficking, which advises on the legal interpretation of the refugee definition in cases of trafficking[37]
- Submitting advisory opinions in individual cases
- Conducting border-monitoring missions and detention center visits to help identify potential trafficking victims
- Performing risk assessments for trafficking among certain refugee populations
- Raising awareness among refugees about the risk of human trafficking
- Advocating for national legislation to ensure the right of trafficked persons to seek asylum
- Using resettlement to protect refugee victims of trafficking

IOs and NGOs

Multiple international nongovernmental organizations (INGOs) are advancing the protection of trafficked persons or those at risk of trafficking within refugee contexts by working alongside many in-country implementing partners. The International Organization for Migration (IOM) carries out many anti-trafficking activities worldwide, including awareness raising to identify and prevent trafficking of refugees. In early 2014, the IOM worked in conjunction with the Jordanian Anti-Human Trafficking Department to inform Syrian refugees and host communities about types of trafficking, how to identify it, and how to report it. In Sudan, IOM is working with the government and UNHCR to increase security between the border and refugee camps to help ensure safe passage and create programs for unaccompanied children.

The International Rescue Committee (IRC) provides post-disaster assistance in more than forty countries, providing emergency relief, relocating refugees, and rebuilding lives. IRC also provides refugee resettlement assistance in the United States and operates trafficking programs through many of its resettlement offices.

International Labor Law

The ILO was created in 1919 and became a specialized agency under the United Nations in 1946. It has 185 member states. It seeks to govern globalization, eradicate poverty, promote sustainable development, and ensure that people can work in dignity and safety. These goals are reflected in international legal standards created through conventions and recommendations (nonbinding guidelines) agreed to by a tripartite consensus of governments, employers, and workers. Over the years, the ILO conventions have covered all manner of topics related to work, including wages, freedom of association, the right to organize and collective bargaining, discrimination, and minimum age. The practical impact is that governments and corporations alike adopt these standards into their policies and day-to-day operations. The ILO reports that the majority of the top five hundred corporations in the United States and United Kingdom have adopted supplier codes of conduct based on ILO conventions and recommendations.[38]

There are four conventions most relevant to human trafficking efforts:

- *Convention Concerning Forced or Compulsory Labour ILO No. 29*[39]—Ratifying States must prohibit all forms of forced or compulsory labor, defined as "all work or service which is extracted from any person under the menace of any penalty and for which the said person has not offered himself voluntarily." The exceptions include military service, conviction in court where a public authority supervises the labor, emergency cases, and minor services in a community.
- *Abolition of Forced Labour Convention ILO No. 105*[40]—This Convention prohibits forced or compulsory labor in additional situations, including as a means of coercion, education, or punishment for holding or expressing political views opposed to those established; for economic development; as punishment for participating in strikes; or as racial, social, national, or religious discrimination. In an effort to

update this 1930 Convention, the ILO adopted in 2014 a new legally binding Protocol on Forced Labour to advance prevention, protection, and compensation measures, as well as to intensify efforts to eliminate modern slavery.

- *Worst Forms of Child Labour Convention ILO No. 182*[41]—Ratifying States must eliminate the worst forms of child labor, which include all forms of slavery or slavery-like practices, including human trafficking, debt bondage, serfdom, forced or compulsory labor, child prostitution and pornography, forced or compulsory recruitment into armed conflict, use in illegal activities, and other work likely harmful to the health, safety, and morals of children.

- *Convention Concerning Decent Work for Domestic Workers ILO No. 189*[42]—This Convention establishes the first global standards for domestic workers, entitling them to the same rights available to other workers, including time off, limited work hours, minimum wage, minimum age, and overtime. Ratifying States must also put measures in place that protect migrant domestic workers, including regulating private employment and recruitment agencies and ensuring that fees are not deducted from workers' wages.

In Practice

The organizations and lawyers that put these standards into practice are quite varied. Of course, general counsel and firms incorporate the international labor standards into their policies and supplier codes of conduct, as discussed in Chapter 3. The ILO standards are certainly relied upon within the growing field of business and human rights.

In government, the U.S. Department of Labor's Bureau of International Labor Affairs (ILAB) works to "improve working conditions, raise living standards, protect workers' ability to exercise their rights, and address the workplace exploitation of children and other vulnerable populations." Related to forced and child labor, the office's responsibilities include worldwide research and reports, policy, and funding for multi-year projects to eliminate forced and child labor in particular industries and countries. ILAB has long focused on the elimination of child labor and forced child labor in West African cocoa production. The office issues the *List of Goods Produced with Forced and Child Labor*[43] and created a practical guide for corporate use, *Reducing Child Labor and Forced Labor: A Toolkit for Responsible Businesses.*[44] Examples of its funded forced-labor projects include Catholic Relief Services in Brazil for labor law compliance, Hagar International in Cambodia for expanding economic activity, and Winrock International in Sierra Leone for education innovations.

Also within government, the U.S. Department of State's Bureau of Democracy, Human Rights and Labor (DRL), also has a focus on international labor affairs, coordinating the work of foreign service labor officers staffing U.S. embassies worldwide. Labor officers are the diplomatic agents promoting and reporting on ILO standards. DRL also funds international projects that support unions, improve labor rights in supply chains, and promote dialogue among governments, employers, and workers.

The International Trade Union Confederation (ITUC)[45] promotes and defends workers' rights and interests through international cooperation between trade unions, global campaigns, and advocacy within major global institutions, including the ILO- and UN-specialized agencies. One of their many issue areas is child labor and forced labor, where they report on the application of core ILO labor standards and exploitation in specific industries as well as advocate for improved anti-trafficking responses. ITUC also launched a campaign in partnership with the International Domestic Workers Network to seek ratification of ILO Convention No. 189.

On the nongovernmental side, a number of organizations work on global human trafficking issues. For example, the Solidarity Center's mission is to help build a global labor movement by strengthening the economic and political power of workers around the world through effective, independent, and democratic unions. With programs in sixty countries operated through twenty-three offices, the Solidarity Center focuses on worker health and safety, human rights including child labor, organizing, and bargaining, raising living standards for workers in the informal economy, gender equality, and migration and human trafficking. Neha Misra has developed the Solidarity Center's human trafficking work for more than fifteen years, ensuring that unions worldwide are engaged in grassroots anti-trafficking strategies, whether that includes union-run legal aid, educating migrant workers about labor laws and workplace rights in their own and foreign countries, and drafting and passing strengthened anti-trafficking and safe migration legislation.

The International Labor Rights Forum (ILRF) is an advocacy organization whose core work is to (1) hold global corporations accountable for labor rights violations in their supply chains, (2) advance policies and laws that protect workers, and (3) strengthen workers' ability to advocate for their rights. ILRF also focuses on child labor and forced labor but stresses that the policy solutions can be found in essentially the ILO core standards, with rights to organize and bargain collectively, decent wages, and safe migration. The ILRF has worked to bring attention to forced child labor in Uzbekistan cotton and West African cocoa fields as well as forced labor in palm oil and Vietnam's state-run detention centers.

Conclusion

The Palermo Protocol set off a wave of development around human trafficking in international law. There are exciting opportunities for attorneys to contribute their skills in transnational criminal law, refugee law, human rights law, and international labor law because anti-trafficking overlaps with each of these areas. Within each there are a plethora of organizations through which to engage—UN agencies, multilateral organizations, regional organizations, NGOs, the U.S. government, pro bono firms, rule of law initiatives—as well as capacity in diplomacy, advocacy, academia, reports, program implementation, organizing, and legal representation. The examples in this chapter just scratch the surface of what is possible and where anti-trafficking efforts can be integrated within international law.

CHAPTER 7

A Call to Public Interest Advocates and Attorneys

Since 2000, a narrow sector of the public interest industry has led formal anti-trafficking efforts. Public interest law encompasses a wide range of practice and policy areas benefitting a larger public community, comprising primarily nonprofit organizations and pro bono attorneys. Anti-trafficking advocacy extends through the range of public interest functions, including direct representation of trafficked persons, class action or targeted litigation for the purposes of developing case law to benefit trafficked persons, and public policy advocacy to expand protections for trafficked persons.

While anti-trafficking efforts cover varied public interest approaches, the anti-trafficking field remains very specialized even within the public interest legal community. For the most part, nonprofit public interest attorneys and advocates have not yet incorporated anti-trafficking efforts into their work, even when it closely intersects. For public interest attorneys with practices that significantly overlap with human trafficking, this chapter offers a solution. The existing infrastructure of public interest agencies makes public interest attorneys a logical sector of anti-trafficking stakeholders. In this chapter, we discuss methods for public interest attorneys to incorporate anti-trafficking efforts into their work without dramatically altering the current scope of work.

Understanding the Intersections with Human Trafficking

Like other attorneys, those in public interest are critical to furthering anti-trafficking efforts. Although many public interest attorneys work very closely with low-income communities, the novelty of human trafficking means that these attorneys are similarly unexposed to the realities of human trafficking. Gaining a depth of knowledge about the nature of human trafficking and anti-trafficking efforts will provide attorneys with the foundation to expand their outreach, advocacy, and practice.

Overcoming Misconceptions

Public interest attorneys rely on the same misinformation that hinders our global community from taking action. But there are also some specific misconceptions that impact the program development of many nonprofit agencies. In many cases, these misconceptions explain the gaps and resulting opportunities for collaboration between public interest and anti-trafficking advocates and attorneys.

Anti-trafficking cases are time and resource intensive. Services for trafficked persons can sometimes take years and require hundreds of hours of representation. Because public interest attorneys work for nonprofit organizations with limited budgets and defined missions, collaborating on anti-trafficking cases can appear daunting and may put other funding streams at risk.

As the anti-trafficking field evolves, the required resources are likely to change as a result of advocacy and structural changes. Current representation focuses on those who are victims in a criminal investigation or prosecution. Victim advocacy work increases significantly in those cases. But as capacity increases to identify and provide services to trafficked persons, law enforcement will have to prioritize the cases they prosecute, similar to the way that only the more egregious domestic violence and sexual assault cases are prosecuted. Therefore, the next wave of advocacy will likely extend beyond criminal justice interventions, and individual cases will require fewer resources.

Anti-trafficking efforts have thus far been relatively siloed, with expertise and intervention resting in a narrow group of legal service providers across the United States. But human trafficking touches upon so many different areas that nonprofit organizations can easily expand their interventions without risking mission drift. Public interest attorneys are already representing individuals on legal issues related to housing and employment access, public benefits access, immigration, labor and employment, and violence against women—all issues that touch on human trafficking. With very little attention focused on these other legal needs, many public interest attorneys do not realize the value to trafficked persons of their practice and expertise. Anyone working in those areas can continue to provide the same representation without altering their legal practice, by merely including trafficked persons among their clients.

The increase resulting from public interest practitioners' expanding their practice to include trafficked persons leads to two positive outcomes. First, trafficked persons will benefit from a diverse set of legal protections beyond traditional trafficking remedies to assist them in rebuilding their lives after trafficking. Second, the expanded capacity of public interest attorneys and improved coordination will decrease the overall burden of representation and the resources required.

In addition to hesitance based on resources and mission, a number of public interest attorneys mistakenly believe that they are not authorized to represent trafficked persons. Through the Legal Services Corporation (LSC), the federal government funds nonprofit organizations to provide free legal services to indigent clients. LSC has strict guidelines that prohibit LSC-funded organizations from representing undocumented immigrants and those who are defendants in the criminal justice system. However, these are not absolute bars, and some exceptions open the door to LSC organizations' representing trafficked persons.

While LSC attorneys may not generally represent undocumented individuals, Congress exempted undocumented trafficking victims[1] from this LSC requirement and expanded this exemption to victims' family members as well.[2] Specifically, an undocumented person who would otherwise be ineligible for LSC services is eligible if the LSC attorney deems the client eligible and assists with federal certification of the individual as a "victim of a severe form of trafficking in persons" or the client is already certified.[3] In Chapter 5, we discuss the process for obtaining federal certification, which in most cases involves cooperating as a victim-witness in an investigation or prosecution.

A limited LSC exception also exists for some defendants, when trafficked persons are arrested for crimes. Sex trafficked persons are often arrested for commercial sex crimes before they are identified as trafficked persons. Labor trafficked persons are not necessarily compelled into committing labor-related crimes, but they may be forced to commit any number of other crimes as part of the coercion. A trafficked person who is arrested will still, however, require legal representation beyond criminal defense. Federal regulations, therefore, have created an exception, which allows criminal defense representation of defendants on misdemeanor or lesser offenses in Indian Tribal court and in other civil matters beyond the criminal defense.[4]

Public interest attorneys may also be deterred from anti-trafficking advocacy because human trafficking is framed as a criminal justice issue. Individual representation of victim-witnesses requires the navigation of complex competing interests. Victims' attorneys walk a fine line, developing collegial relationships with prosecutors while advocating for their clients' individual interests. For example, a victim's attorney is ethically bound to advocate for the client's interests and wishes. A client may wish not to cooperate or cooperate entirely with a criminal investigation. While ultimately the decision of the individual client, there are some benefits associated with cooperation. Because of these benefits, specialized anti-trafficking attorneys succeed by developing strong relationships with criminal justice personnel, in order to support any of their clients who seek to cooperate. Other agencies receive funding as a result of their coordination with law enforcement. Therefore, attorneys for victims may inadvertently encourage a perception that they have a shared mission with the criminal justice system, though their individual advocacy may contradict that. Chapter 2 includes details about the role of attorneys in providing victim-witness representation and navigating these competing interests.

Human trafficking is an abhorrent violation of a person's rights, and traffickers should not be able to repeatedly act with impunity. The early years of the anti-trafficking movement saw a number of traffickers receive lenient sentences. Advocates responded to these instances by seeking increased penalties. However, contrary to misconceptions that anti-trafficking advocates focus only on increased criminal penalties, the vast majority focus on broader policy advocacy that expands protection for trafficked persons and expands efforts to prevent human trafficking.

Because anti-trafficking attorneys are often viewed as victim services attorneys instead of human rights attorneys, this artificial chasm deters many public interest attorneys from engaging in anti-trafficking efforts. Public interest attorneys, who often work on poverty alleviation, human rights, and civil rights, cannot always reconcile the collaborative nature of victim services attorneys and the criminal justice system.

Throughout this book, however, we highlight the need to go beyond the criminal justice system to effectively address human trafficking. That need reflects a critical view among anti-trafficking practitioners that they must advocate for the human rights of trafficked persons, rather than characterize them as victims alone. Public interest attorneys will find a number of anti-trafficking partners with human rights–based practices, who do not work solely within the criminal justice context.

Identification: The First Steps in Taking Action
The Benefits of Expanded Identification

Public interest attorneys are deeply rooted in the communities they serve and with appropriate training and tools are well positioned to expand their capacity to identify and in some cases represent trafficked persons. Unfamiliar with their rights and available protections and deeply distrustful, trafficked persons do not typically self-identify. But they also typically do not present as trafficked persons. Therefore, even community-rooted public interest attorneys require training to identify human trafficking from among the community who are clients or potential clients.

Many trafficked persons do not present as victims at all. They may present as low-wage workers. Some will be stigmatized for their participation in commercial sex. Without adequate training and engagement of a sector likely to interact with trafficked persons, human trafficking continues to go largely unidentified. This leaves many trafficked persons continuing to be exploited by traffickers. Others who experienced human trafficking in the past but who were never identified are unable to access the critical protections that position them to reduce risk of retrafficking in the future.

Trafficked persons are entitled to certain protections under federal and state law if they are identified. These protections may extend beyond those available to other public interest clients and justify public interest attorneys' increasing their capacity to identify human trafficking. The protections include the following:

1. *Public benefits for victims of a severe form of trafficking in persons*[5]: Foreign-born victims of trafficking who are either under the age of eighteen years or willing to assist in an investigation or prosecution overcome restrictions that preclude public benefits eligibility of some nonimmigrants.

2. *Immigration relief for victims of trafficking*[6]: Congress enacted the T and U visa knowing that undocumented trafficked persons had limited options for immigration relief. Trafficked undocumented immigrants who go unidentified are therefore likely to remain undocumented. Immigration relief will allow a trafficked person to lawfully accept employment, access services like banking and driver's licenses not always available to undocumented immigrants, and avoid living in fear of deportation.

3. *Leverage to drop charges, dismiss a case, or apply for post-conviction relief*: Trafficked persons may commit crimes in the course of their trafficking. If they are arrested, being identified as victims and not perpetrators or offenders can bolster efforts to mitigate any criminal justice implications.

4. *Availability of civil remedies*: As detailed in Chapter 4, trafficked persons have access to a number of civil remedies giving them additional opportunities for access to justice and monetary relief.

5. *Networked service providers*: While funding remains somewhat limited, most major metropolitan areas have an existing infrastructure for anti-trafficking social services. Identifying a person as trafficked will direct the person into a comprehensive network of critical services designed specifically for a trafficked person's needs.

6. *Crime victim compensation*: Identification will give trafficked persons access to funds for relocation and other costs as determined by states.

7. *State benefits*: Some states offer additional benefits to victims of human trafficking. For example, identification in New York State triggers a number of New York State–specific resources, including shelter, food, medical care, and more.[7]

Leveraging the Public Interest Expertise

Through regular community outreach, the public interest sector is well integrated into the very communities where trafficked persons may be found. Although one misconception falsely conflates human trafficking with the abduction of girls, trafficked persons are typically recruited. That recruitment occurs because traffickers seek out characteristics and circumstances that are easy to exploit. Traffickers successfully recruit vulnerable individuals looking for ways out of their current circumstances. Many are low-income individuals. Others lack education or other paths to access economic opportunities. Trafficked persons also come from situations of instability, be it a personal family situation, environmental impact, or political instability. These are the very same populations typically served by public interest attorneys.

Public interest law agencies typically participate in networks and coalitions, which include social service providers and local government agencies. Public interest attorneys work in a range of substantive areas, so their partners could include nonprofit social service providers, community-organizing groups, educational institutions, local government services, and more. These partners are the very same stakeholders that are also in a position to identify human trafficking.

Unlike pro bono attorneys and other government agencies, public interest attorneys are set up to regularly conduct intake. Public interest agencies either specifically partner with or maintain their own hotlines, helplines, and clinics that facilitate this intake and even more entry points for trafficked persons. These intake practices could expand to include human trafficking indicators.

Finally, public interest attorneys in communities with immigrant populations also provide language services in intake and representation to assist limited English proficient (LEP) clients. Because traffickers use language as a method to isolate and compel trafficked persons, an LEP trafficked person may have few opportunities to call and access protections, and they should not be further isolated when they try to access assistance. Meaningful language access is critical not only in identification but also in full-scope representation. Chapter 5 has a more extensive discussion about language access.

Traditional Public Interest Lawyering

In addition to identification, there are a number of services already being provided by public interest attorneys that should be made available to trafficked persons. Representing a trafficked person requires far more than just victim-witness or immigration representation. The exploitation experienced by trafficked persons results in a number of other legal needs. Rather than stretch the very few anti-trafficking resources that are available, public interest attorneys can collaborate with anti-trafficking experts and offer their expertise.

Housing Most trafficked persons will require short-term, temporary housing after emerging from human trafficking and eventually transition to long-term housing. A person emerging from trafficking will likely be establishing a housing history for the first time.

But even after they have accessed freedom, trafficked persons continue to be in economically vulnerable positions. They may encounter challenges upon attempting to rent housing or subsequently as tenants. Housing is also a critical issue in the long term as often it is the most costly expense. Providing trafficked persons with housing stability significantly reduces the risk of retrafficking. Housing attorneys can assist trafficked persons in eviction defense, housing discrimination, and other legal issues.

Public Benefits Trafficked persons are also often initially without education and job skills and may rely on public benefits for immediate support. U.S. citizens and lawful permanent residents (LPRs) are eligible for public benefits, including cash assistance, food stamps, and medical coverage based on income and other eligibility. Noncitizens who would otherwise not be able to access public benefits are eligible by receiving certification from the Office of Refugee Resettlement and the U.S. Department of Health and Human Services if the applicant[8]

1. is a victim of a severe form of trafficking in persons,
2. cooperates with an investigation or prosecution of human trafficking or is under the age of eighteen, or
3. has received a bona fide T visa notification or continued presence.

Once certified, trafficking victims are eligible to receive refugee benefits for six to eight months as administered by their state of residence.

As with housing, access to public benefits is critical for a trafficked person to find meaningful alternatives to being retrafficked. A trafficked person emerging from trafficking often needs to seek services to address the trauma and seek education and job skills first before seeking permanent employment. Anti-trafficking advocates organize access to services such as English as a Second Language (ESL) classes and job training. Public benefits, including food stamps, help to bridge that immediate gap.

Government benefits workers are still largely unfamiliar with human trafficking eligibility. Untrained on the evidentiary requirements for eligibility and barriers to evidence for victims, benefits workers might deny benefits to eligible applicants. These denials or other barriers encountered in receiving those benefits may require a trafficked person to access a public benefits attorney. In these circumstances, attorneys can collaborate with anti-trafficking service providers for the purposes of cross-training and referrals.

Domestic Violence and Sexual Assault Attorneys

An extensive network of public interest attorneys across the United States work in programs for survivors of domestic violence and sexual assault. These services continue to be underfunded and in most cases are not positioned to significantly expand their capacity to representation of trafficked persons. Yet the existing expertise and infrastructure of these attorneys can strengthen anti-trafficking efforts.

Domestic violence and sexual assault attorneys are ideally suited to increase identification of trafficked women and girls. Public interest attorneys working in the violence against women field conduct regular outreach to women and girls. Most cities also have local hotlines and long-standing relationships with law enforcement that result in regular referrals. With a lack of familiarity to self-identify as a trafficked person, a trafficked woman or girl may first seek help for sexual assault. This allows her to enter the network of domestic violence and sexual assault service providers.

For domestic violence and sexual assault attorneys to more deeply engage in anti-trafficking efforts, it will be important to overcome several myths perpetuated in the domestic violence and sexual assault community. In Chapter 1, we discussed these myths but revisit them here for their application in particular to domestic violence and sexual assault service providers.

Myth #1: *Women are trafficked in sex; men are trafficked in labor.* Globally, women constitute the vast majority of those who experience sex trafficking.[9] But women also comprise approximately half of the labor trafficked persons.[10] In the United States, women have been trafficked in domestic work, agriculture, custodial work, teaching, begging, manufacturing, restaurants, and more. Many labor trafficked women and girls may seek domestic violence and sexual assault programs for services because they identify with the communities served. But without screening to help program staff understand how labor trafficking intersects with the clients they serve, trafficked persons are likely to go unidentified.

Myth #2: *Sexual assault only happens in sex trafficking.* Sexual assault is a powerful tool that traffickers use to control women and girls but also men and boys. In the United States, labor traffickers have sexually assaulted women in a range of industries.[11] The myth that sexual assault

happens only in sex trafficking has also been perpetuated by a misla-
beling of labor trafficking with sexual assault as sex trafficking, which
requires an element of commercial sex.[12] Without the right training,
those screening for sexual assault may not always recognize the connection between sexual assault in the workplace and labor trafficking.
Myth #3: *Sex trafficking of minors typically begins with abduction.* In
the context of U.S. citizen minors, traffickers entice and lure girls with
money or affection, as trusted family members, friends, or posing as
boyfriends.[13] They exploit the economic vulnerability and home instability of girls. These minors may be homeless, runaways, or in foster
care.[14] Narrowing screening to look specifically for minors who have
been abducted and more likely to come from privileged backgrounds
will overlook those most at risk of trafficking. In particular, domestic
violence and sexual assault services providers increasing anti-trafficking
engagement are best served by partnering with organizations serving
at-risk and foster girls.

Attorneys who understand these myths have the opportunity to develop the most expansive identification methods. Public interest attorneys
working in domestic violence and sexual assault organizations can expand identification by ensuring staff and partners are trained. They can
also integrate additional preliminary screening questions into their intake
forms that may trigger a longer human trafficking screening.

Some domestic violence and sexual assault preliminary screening indicators are the following:

1. Ever sexually assaulted by an employer
2. Ever physically assaulted by an employer
3. Minor who lives or lived with a non-parent or non-guardian
4. Ever involved in commercial sex

Once identified, domestic violence and sexual assault attorneys may provide legal services in their areas of expertise to complement the services
provided by anti-trafficking advocates. Trafficked persons are sometimes
in need of a restraining or protective order. These orders are not necessarily

designed for human trafficking cases; but in some instances, a trafficker has a qualifying relationship with the trafficked person, required for a restraining order. Traffickers can be parents and stepparents, other relatives, boyfriends and girlfriends, and former boyfriends and girlfriends. Particularly when there is no criminal prosecution of traffickers, a civil order may be the only legal protection available to a trafficked person. Domestic violence attorneys have extensive expertise in obtaining protective orders.

Trafficked persons may also benefit from other related family law representation, which is also often available through domestic violence programs. Because traffickers can also be family members, trafficked persons may require assistance with divorce, custody, and support orders. Trafficked minors in many cases will need assistance with matters regarding guardianship.

Immigration Attorneys

Nonprofit organizations serving immigrant communities often include public interest immigration attorneys. These attorneys are ideally situated to expand identification of trafficked immigrants. Although to date there are no accurate estimates of foreign-born versus U.S. citizen trafficking in the United States, one study estimated that nearly one-third of undocumented workers studied had experienced human trafficking.[15] Extrapolating from this data, there could be more than three million undocumented people in the United States who are vulnerable to human trafficking,[16] most of whom go unidentified. Public interest immigration attorneys interact with trafficked immigrants without recognizing the trafficking experience and therefore overlook presenting trafficking-specific options for immigration relief.

Human trafficking of immigrants occurs in almost every low-wage industry in the United States. Immigrants are trafficked in agriculture, caregiving, commercial sex, construction, custodial services, factories, fishing, retail, restaurants, teaching, and as domestic workers in homes. Typically the work and services exacted create economic gain for the trafficker. Traffickers use immigration laws and threats of deportation to compel service, creating a chasm between victims and the law enforcement charged with protecting victims. They hold victims' passports, making victims feel they will be arrested if they escape without their passports.

In 2000, Congress enacted specialized immigration relief and processes to respond to this exploitation,[17] but these protections go underutilized. U.S. Citizenship and Immigration Services began granting T visas in 2002, and by 2013, only 3,309 primary victim and family member T visas had been granted.[18] This gap is only reinforced by a dominant discourse that focuses on trafficking of U.S. citizens. Local law enforcement focusing on human trafficking favors citizen-trafficking cases that involve the commercial sexual exploitation of minors and is more reticent to take on trafficked-immigrant cases.[19]

The best way to overcome the underutilization of protections is to engage public interest immigration attorneys who are already in regular contact with immigrants. Although a trafficked immigrant's story typically emerges as trust builds, attorneys who are able to recognize and apply trafficking indicators can serve as a primary and critical conduit by helping trafficked immigrants understand their rights and available protections. In addition to knowing general screening questions and indicators, there are particular screening questions that will assist attorneys in identifying a trafficked immigrant, which are discussed further in Chapter 5.

With immigration attorneys, too, misconceptions prevent attorneys from expanding their identification efforts.

Myth #1: *All human trafficking involves sex trafficking.* While we do not have good estimates of the breakdown in the United States, globally 78 percent of all human trafficking is labor trafficking, with the remainder in sex trafficking.[20] Immigration attorneys who think of human trafficking only in terms of sex trafficking will overlook the vast numbers of undocumented labor trafficked persons. Those who work in and with undocumented communities who fail to understand how labor trafficking affects undocumented workers will likely overlook the vast majority of labor trafficked persons.

Myth #2: *T visas are too difficult to obtain.* The T visa process is actually designed to anticipate the many evidentiary barriers experienced by a trafficking victim. For example, unlike the U visa, the T visa application does not require a certification of cooperation from law enforcement.[21] Because many law enforcement agencies are too under-resourced to respond to a referral and others do not yet have the training to understand human trafficking cases, they are sometimes less responsive to certification requests from even the most cooperative victims.

Likewise, public interest attorneys working with immigrant communities can expand identification by ensuring that staff and partners are trained. Particularly because of their expertise, public interest immigration attorneys can best reach community organizers and other immigrant service providers who have less understanding about immigration remedies available. Public interest immigration attorneys and advocates also conduct "know your rights" trainings and screening in immigration detention centers. An attorney or advocate who successfully identifies a detained immigrant as trafficked will be able to provide that immigrant with likely their only option to be released from detention and remain in the United States.

The following preliminary screening issues will also alert them to potential human trafficking and a longer human trafficking screening:

1. Entered unlawfully connected with employment/commercial sex in the United States
2. Had employer/recruiter assistance in facilitating travel documents
3. Owed a debt to pay for travel to the United States
4. Lived or lives in housing provided by an employer
5. Was or is escorted between living quarters and the worksite
6. Is not always in possession of identity or travel documents
7. Is on a visa tied to one U.S. employer
8. Found employment or commercial sex conditions different than initially described
9. Paid large recruitment fee for the employment or commercial sex opportunity
10. Had living and other costs had been deducted from wages

Public interest immigration attorneys with the capacity can contribute their expertise further by representing trafficked immigrants. Their expertise is also critical in partnering and providing pro bono law firms with the technical assistance required to respond to the growing interest of those firms in representing trafficked immigrants. Chapter 5 provides a more extensive discussion of trafficked immigrants in the United States for public interest attorneys seeking to represent trafficked persons.

Juvenile Justice Attorneys

As the dominant discourse on human trafficking emphasizes U.S. minors who are in sex trafficking, an oversimplified discussion has isolated anti-trafficking experts from those who are best positioned to identify and assist trafficked minors: advocates and attorneys working within the juvenile justice system. Juvenile justice attorneys work for nonprofit organizations advocating for and representing youth involved in the system. Other attorneys positioned to identify and respond to human trafficking work within juvenile justice as local government personnel. These professionals regularly interact with minors in the juvenile justice system without recognizing their trafficking experience and the benefits that would accompany the minors' being identified as having been trafficked.

Sex trafficking is acting or benefitting financially from the recruitment, enticement, harboring, transport, providing, obtaining, or maintaining of a person—by means of force, threats of force, fraud, or coercion unless the person is not eighteen years of age—to engage the person in a commercial sex act.[22] Therefore, minors involved in commercial sex through the act or benefit of third parties are likely to be victims of human trafficking. And yet minors involved in commercial sex continue to present as offenders, not victims, and enter the juvenile justice system.[23]

Public interest juvenile justice attorneys and legal practitioners coming into contact with youth who are or have been in the juvenile detention system will be able to identify and connect minors with protections first by understanding the prevailing misconceptions in their field.

<u>Myth #1</u>: *The anti-trafficking movement is driven by efforts to criminalize and punish traffickers.* Without any human trafficking criminal laws, traffickers would violate human rights with impunity. However, many well-experienced anti-trafficking advocates espouse a harm reduction, human rights model, which recognizes some of the ways in

which a criminalization-only approach overlooks necessary efforts to increase protections for trafficked persons and prevent human trafficking in the future. Juvenile justice attorneys who, based on their missions, question the efficacy of criminalization efforts will still find anti-trafficking practitioners with whom they can partner.

<u>Myth #2</u>: *Sex trafficking of minors typically begins with abduction.* In the context of trafficked minors, this myth directs stakeholders to overlook those most at risk: homeless, runaways, or those in foster care and in low-income communities of color.[24] These minors are likely to interact with juvenile justice and defense attorneys more than any others outside the system. Arrests of sex trafficked minors on prostitution-related charges exemplify this misconception about the crime of human trafficking.

Like adults, trafficked minors are also unlikely to self-identify, not seeing themselves as victims and not understanding the associated protections. The barriers to identifying minors are considerable. First, traffickers recruit minors who are already cynical about receiving services and protection; many come from the foster care system, which they may reject and escape for financial motive or affection or both.[25] Trafficked minors may view traffickers in a positive light, as persons who help them access more money, affection, and community. Minors may not always characterize commercial sex as negative or harmful. Those who are trafficked may not be interested in leaving commercial sex or an associated community. Identification is further complicated by the stigmas associated with commercial sex, making it unlikely that a minor would immediately disclose those acts.

Therefore, identification requires much more than an initial assessment of facts. Instead, identification is an iterative process, occurring as advocates and other justice personnel develop trusting relationships over time. Resources that provide a meaningful alternative to commercial sex, acknowledging the economic position of these minors, may lead a minor to self-identify as a victim. Juvenile justice attorneys can begin by developing training and policies, including screening, to help staff and other key stakeholders learn how to build this trust and increase identification.

Identification also positions trafficked minors to overcome criminal issues that occur in the course of trafficking. At the earliest, identification can and should prevent wrongful arrest on prostitution-related grounds. For victims who are already in the juvenile justice system as offenders, an attorney can successfully advocate for their charges to be dropped. Until criminal justice systems are able to respond by identifying and not arresting trafficked minors, those minors rely on others to identify them and help them access services instead of criminalization.

Some law enforcement agencies knowingly arrest identified sex-trafficked minors and mandate services for them as a condition for release or a specific disposition of charges. Some criminal justice personnel believe that mandated services provided through the system will best assist a trafficked minor. The Uniform Act on Prevention of and Remedies for Human Trafficking (Uniform Act) creates immunity from liability for commercial sex and other nonviolent crimes related to trafficking,[26] signaling state protections likely to follow.

Finally, a number of states have enacted provisions allowing for post-conviction relief such as motions to vacate convictions. In 2010, New York State enacted the first statute in the United States that specifically allows trafficking victims to vacate prostitution-related convictions resulting from sex trafficking.[27] This statute allows defense attorneys to file motions to vacate convictions even after sentencing, giving victims of trafficking an opportunity for relief in case the defense attorney did not learn that the client is a trafficking victim until after plea or conviction.[28] The Uniform Act also includes a post-conviction relief provision,[29] thereby encouraging states to include this provision in future anti-trafficking legislation.

National Center for Youth Law is one of the first organizations to successfully bridge the gap between juvenile justice and anti-trafficking advocacy. As an Equal Justice Works fellow, Kate Walker provides representation, advocacy, and research on behalf of trafficked minors involved with the juvenile justice system. Working within a juvenile justice organization, such projects are critical to increase collaboration between these two sectors.

While gaining the trust of a trafficked person may be difficult, juvenile justice public interest attorneys may use the following screening indicators to make a preliminary identification of human trafficking. As with other indicators, these are never dispositive of human trafficking—but especially for those who have already entered the system, these initial indicators should signal the need for further questions and deeper trust building:

1. Engaged in commercial sex while a minor
2. Was recruited by a third party into commercial sex
3. Is or was homeless, a runaway, or in foster care
4. Has significant changes in school attendance
5. Associates with a noticeably older social circle
6. Is in controlling relationships

Because of their unique relationships within the community and long-standing expertise with youth communities at risk, juvenile justice attorneys have the potential to inform the anti-trafficking discourse with their engagement and leadership by engaging in anti-trafficking efforts. Juvenile justice attorneys seeking to extend their advocacy beyond identification can familiarize themselves with trafficking victim advocacy outlined in Chapter 2.

Labor and Employment Law Attorneys

Despite the prevalence of labor trafficking, public interest attorneys working in the worker and union rights space remain on the periphery of anti-trafficking efforts. Human trafficking lies at the end of the spectrum of labor exploitation, but lack of familiarity with the issue allows these attorneys to interact with trafficked persons without even knowing it. Federal laws offer labor trafficked persons a number of critical protections, including access to immigration status and civil remedies. But trafficked persons are unlikely to be familiar with these protections and their general rights as victims of human trafficking, thereby relying on labor and employment law attorneys to identify and connect them with available protections.

In the labor and employment law fields, misconceptions hinder these efforts.

Myth #1: *Human trafficking is not about labor.* As noted above, despite the global prevalence of labor trafficking, conflation of the term *human trafficking* with the term *sex trafficking* marginalizes labor trafficked persons by causing those interacting with workers to overlook the possibility of trafficking.

Myth #2: *Human trafficking only affects women and girls.* This myth directs people to overlook the many men and boys who are trafficked, primarily in labor. Globally, 45 percent of all trafficking involves men and boys.[30]

Myth #3: *Human trafficking identification, separate and distinct from other labor and exploitation, is not necessary.* Human trafficking falls at one end of the labor exploitation spectrum, which is itself a violation of human rights. While the experience of human trafficking should not make those individuals more deserving of protections, human trafficking protections were created to respond specifically to those working against their free will, possibly in addition to facing many other exploitative conditions.

Like juvenile justice attorneys, labor and employment law attorneys and their partners are often the only professionals regularly interacting with those who might have been trafficked. Labor trafficked persons seek general services most easily available to them. These services might include clinics for workers and immigrants, whereby overcoming this misconception among these service providers could increase identification.

The following preliminary indicators can assist labor and employment law attorneys to incorporate into their practices more developed screening tools. In particular, these indicators can assist in distinguishing a human trafficking case from a labor exploitation case. These indicators include whether the worker

1. entered the United States unlawfully, in connection with employment,
2. obtained travel documents facilitated by an employer/recruiter,

3. incurred a debt to pay for travel to the United States,
4. lived or lives in housing provided by an employer,
5. was always accompanied when leaving work or living site,
6. is or was not always in possession of identity or travel documents,
7. arrived on a visa tied to a U.S. employer,
8. worked in employment different than initially described,
9. had living and other costs had been deducted from wages, or
10. was physically or sexually assaulted by an employer.

Labor and employment law public interest attorneys are uniquely positioned to conduct outreach and training with regular collaborators, including union representatives; worker rights groups, including domestic work, agricultural work, and other informal work sectors; immigrant service providers; and others. Labor and employment law attorneys seeking to engage in full-scale anti-trafficking representation can find more detailed in other chapters: Chapter 2 for victim-witness advocacy and criminal defense, Chapter 4 for civil litigation, and Chapter 5 for immigration representation.

Designing Legal Programs
Providing Legal Representation
Throughout this book, we argue for implementation of practices that will increase identification of trafficked persons. But increased identification naturally leads to an increase in demand for services to be provided to trafficked persons. This creates an inevitable strain on existing anti-trafficking service programs.

In order to meet this increased demand, an expanded sector of public interest and pro bono attorneys is necessary to increase capacity to provide anti-trafficking legal services. Earlier in this chapter, we discussed the ancillary legal services that domestic violence, housing, and public benefit attorneys can provide, without changing the scope of their work but merely expanding to different client populations.

Other public interest attorneys are suited to expand their programs and provide specific anti-trafficking legal services to these newly identified populations. As we discuss, public interest immigration attorneys are desperately needed to increase capacity to handle the number of trafficked immigrants seeking immigration relief. Labor or employment law attorneys can expand their practices and provide access to a number of additional civil protections to populations already within the mission of their organizations. Similarly, juvenile justice advocates can add another tool to their efforts to extract youth from the system.

Funding for Primary Services

Organizations considering expanding their services will require additional funding. There are several funding streams available to nonprofit agencies seeking to expand into anti-trafficking representation. Federal funding sources available through a competitive grant process include the Office for Victims of Crime and the Office on Violence Against Women at the Department of Justice, and the Department of Health and Human Services. Some agencies have succeeded in securing state and local funding for anti-trafficking services. Finally, some private foundations are beginning to fund anti-trafficking efforts.

Agencies applying for initial anti-trafficking funding will have to demonstrate their capacity and expertise. Many organizations interested in pursuing funding are already providing services to trafficked persons. For example, a worker's rights organization has probably already provided services to trafficked persons. Before seeking out funding, the organization should begin to identify and track trafficked persons within their larger client population and develop certain structures to help implement an anti-trafficking program. Agencies can address this oversight with some simple organizational steps.

Protocol Checklist for Emerging Programs

☑ Develop appropriate screening indicators
☑ Train all staff on human trafficking and identification strategies
☑ Add human trafficking questionnaire to the intake form
☑ Add a human trafficking box to the client database

Ancillary Legal Services

Organizations providing ancillary services can also access existing funding streams while highlighting their new anti-trafficking efforts. Ancillary legal services do not emerge in every case. Therefore, each ancillary service may not independently merit a separate and sustainable funding stream. But these services and expertise are critical to a larger collaborative effort to ensure that a trafficked person's diverse legal services are provided and needs are met. Collaboration between these sectors will expand capacity through increased coordination and resulting funding, and also provide an opportunity to share expertise to better support each trafficked person served.

Collaboration

There are a number of established anti-trafficking programs in each metropolitan area. The nonprofit service providers typically include a small number of legal service providers. Agencies seeking to leverage their expertise on behalf of trafficked persons should work in collaboration with existing networks of service providers. Chapter 2 discusses the various stakeholders needed to build the most comprehensive task forces and how those task forces best offer protection to trafficked persons. Public interest attorneys in the diverse practice areas discussed should play a role in these task forces. In addition, public interest attorneys expanding into anti-trafficking services should partner with the few anti-trafficking attorneys in their community to expand legal capacity. Effective collaboration requires cross-training and the development of a simple referral protocol.

The Role of the Pro Bono Attorney

Particularly in response to a call to action from the American Bar Association, pro bono attorneys are increasingly seeking opportunities to provide anti-trafficking representation. Local bar associations, which typically run a lawyer referral resource line, are engaging and developing programs to expand legal services to trafficked persons. Public interest firms have recruited and should continue to recruit pro bono firms to provide legal representation in the areas of victim advocacy within the criminal justice system, immigration representation, civil litigation, post-conviction relief, and juvenile defense work. Attorneys can find deeper discussions throughout this book organized by legal practice areas.

With such a specialized issue and practice areas, pro bono attorneys should initially develop strong partnerships with local anti-trafficking attorneys. Public interest attorneys can provide training and technical assistance. This training should not only include substantive law and procedure but also client sensitivities. Because public interest attorneys work specifically with low-income and otherwise disenfranchised communities, they have a specialized understanding of the client needs that will emerge. In particular, pro bono attorneys should access training on trust building, culturally appropriate services, language services, and the complexities of human trafficking.

Pro bono attorneys may anticipate a case that matches the public narrative about human trafficking, which continues to be rife with misconceptions. They may be less familiar with clients who are less interested in cooperating with law enforcement, or who have loyalty to their traffickers. Certainly, anti-trafficking attorneys can offer pro bono attorneys additional expertise to navigate some of the deeper complexities, including navigating adverse views among victims in large, multiple-victim cases.

Beyond their role in increasing the number of trafficked people identified and referred, pro bono attorneys are uniquely suited to participate in expanded anti-trafficking efforts. Civil litigation can be very resource intensive. Very few nonprofit organizations have the financial capacity to litigate civil suits without at least the participation of pro bono co-counsel. Pro bono attorneys play a pivotal role in increasing trafficked persons' access to civil litigation.

Pro bono attorneys can also play an important role in large cases. Sometimes a human trafficking case involves hundreds of trafficked persons. No single agency will have the capacity to provide the legal services needed to every person. Some of those services are urgent, particularly in the context of a criminal prosecution with a high level of interaction between victims and law enforcement. For trafficked migrants, immigration services are also very urgent because only at a certain point in an immigration case will the trafficked person have permission to accept employment. Therefore, it is critical to begin the immigration process immediately.

Public interest attorneys working in partnership with pro bono attorneys should design a partnership that takes certain processes into consideration. First, the conflicts check undertaken by pro bono firms looks different from a typical public interest conflicts check. Pro bono law firms represent a large number of corporations. When alleged traffickers are corporations or corporate employees, there is a slightly greater risk of a conflict of interest.

The nature of human trafficking investigations sometimes results in anti-trafficking service providers and attorneys immediately responding to law enforcement engaged in a law enforcement raid. Any delays mean more time that a potentially trafficked person could be detained, which creates trust barriers. An attorney who quickly responds is better positioned to overcome that barrier and identify a person as a trafficked person, and will be able to explain to that person his or her rights and begin to provide the protections and resources available to him or her. A delayed response may result in losing the trafficked person back to the trafficker. Pro bono attorneys may not always be positioned to respond so quickly to a potential pro bono case. Public interest and pro bono attorneys will want to design a process to ensure that someone reaches a potentially trafficked person as soon as possible.

Conclusion

There are multiple ways for public interest attorneys to expand their anti-trafficking efforts. That expansion may require minimal time but have dramatic impact, as in the case of identification and screening. It could also serve as a force multiplier, capitalizing on existing expertise and resources within a particular practice. Taking myths and barriers head on, this chapter now provides public interest attorneys with the understanding and arguments to delve deeper into other chapters appropriate to their practice.

Epilogue

On an issue of this magnitude and complexity, solutions are neither easy nor quick. The challenges are enormous—misidentification, under-identification, misconceptions, insufficient laws, an invisible crime, great rhetoric but little funding, a narrow criminal justice approach, and victim arrests and deportations. The enormity can become paralyzing for some, not knowing what can be done or where to contribute. But attorneys have skills and hold positions that allow them to make tangible inroads toward solutions. Throughout this book we have described the nascent efforts to address each of these issues by attorneys across the country. To make real progress we need *more*: more attorneys building on and replicating these efforts; more attorneys adopting anti-trafficking efforts into their own work where possible; more attorneys seeking new solutions.

Within criminal law alone, existing federal and state laws remain underutilized. The entire pipeline must be ready—trained judges equipped with jury instructions, state prosecutors adept at using their new state laws to encourage more investigations, and all law enforcement prepared to identify and investigate labor *and* sex trafficking cases. Simply put, the participation of more criminal justice system actors engaged in proactive rather than reactive efforts will bring the biggest change. At the same time, defense attorneys and victim service attorneys are breaking new ground, taking on duties beyond the typical scope of representation to ensure holistic representation.

We also need more corporate attorneys integrating into existing risk mitigation, ethics, and compliance programs new policies and practices that will prevent human trafficking. Ensuring due diligence today regarding compliance and developing broader risk mitigation strategies protect a company from a known and certain risk while also enhancing the brand as a socially responsible company. The expansion of corporate social responsibility, ethical sourcing, sustainability, and business and human rights along with regulations and laws related to forced labor represents a key strategy in the prevention and mitigation of human trafficking, touching the livelihoods and freedom of millions of trafficked persons worldwide.

The labor and employment law sectors, and civil litigators in particular, have tremendous potential to dramatically affect the number of trafficked persons identified and assisted. These attorneys unknowingly encounter trafficked persons with greater frequency. Moreover, the prevalence but under-identification of labor trafficking compared to sex trafficking summons up proactive efforts by these attorneys to shift the anti-trafficking landscape. Plaintiff labor and employment law attorneys in legal aid organizations and private firm offices, pro bono attorneys in law firms, and state and federal labor and fair employment agencies are well positioned to increase identification and representation of labor trafficked persons.

Even more difficult to identify are trafficked immigrants, who often harbor deep fear of law enforcement and resulting deportation. Traffickers use culture and language in addition to physical isolation to further control trafficked immigrants. The immigration remedies designed to alleviate the fears of these trafficked immigrants are extremely underutilized. Attorneys taking on these cases must navigate complex interacting systems and overcome significant trust barriers. But the benefits of engaging in these efforts and developing this expertise will contribute to filling a vast identification and protection gap.

Within international law, attorneys working within United Nation agencies, multilateral organizations, regional organizations, international nongovernmental organizations (INGOs), the U.S. government, pro bono firms, and rule of law initiatives, as well as those with capacity in diplomacy, advocacy, academia, reports, program implementation, organizing, and legal representation can all contribute to anti-trafficking efforts. The Palermo Protocol specifically offers tremendous opportunities for attorneys to contribute their skills in transnational criminal law, refugee law, human rights law, and international labor law.

Finally, public interest attorneys are also expanding their anti-trafficking efforts, whether in health, services, labor, housing, child welfare, education, or another field. Some are expanding their identification and direct services capacity while others are engaging in public policy. Often already serving or working on behalf of low-income and other vulnerable communities who are frequently targeted by traffickers, public interest attorneys are poised to leverage their skills to partner on anti-trafficking advocacy.

Our changing anti-trafficking landscape reflects the number of concerned citizens and professionals wanting to devote their time and talents to anti-trafficking efforts. Growing international, national, and state human trafficking laws and policies make attorneys critical to the success of these efforts. There have been and will continue to be substantial, important anti-trafficking contributions made by attorneys in multiple areas of the law. Recalling our early years when we were among very few attorneys engaged in anti-trafficking efforts, we are excited about the rising interest and the prospect of many more attorneys embracing this opportunity. And we know, from the countless trafficked persons we represented and the many more that remain unidentified and unprotected, there is an urgency to scale the integration of a diverse set of attorneys into these efforts. Trafficked persons desperately need attorneys to be involved. They need you to be part of the solution.

Resources for Attorneys

U.S. Government

- U.S. Department of State, Office to Monitor and Combat Trafficking in Persons—leads diplomatic efforts to address anti-trafficking worldwide and annually publishes the *Trafficking in Persons Report*: http://www.state.gov/j/tip/
- U.S. Department of Defense, Combating Trafficking in Persons—works to ensure that contracting, procurement, law enforcement, and personnel have the tools required to prevent trafficking: http://ctip.defense.gov
- U.S. Department of Justice, Civil Rights Division, Human Trafficking Prosecution Unit—works with U.S. Attorneys and law enforcement to streamline and ensure consistent application of anti-trafficking statutes, provide victim resources, provide legal guidance, and coordinate in multijurisdictional cases: http://www.justice.gov/crt/about/crm/htpu.php

1-888-428-7581—U.S. Department of Justice Trafficking in Persons and Worker Exploitation Task Force Complaint Line, from 9:00 A.M. to 5:00 P.M. (EST), to report incidents to federal prosecutors

- U.S. Department of Justice, Office for Victims of Crime, Training and Technical Assistance Center (OVCTTAC)—provides training and technical assistance to those serving crime victims: https://www.ovcttac.gov/views/HowWeCanHelp/dspHumanTrafficking.cfm
- U.S. Department of Labor, Bureau of International Labor Affairs (ILAB)—publishes resources and advances policy and cooperation to address human trafficking and forced labor: http://www.dol.gov/ilab/

    1-866-4USWAGE—U.S. Department of Labor, Wage and Hour Division—a 24/7 hotline to report labor exploitation cases that may not rise to the level of trafficking

    1-800-347-3756—U.S. Department of Labor Office of Inspector General Hotline—to report allegations of trafficking committed through fraud in DOL programs such as the H-1B, H-2A, H-2B, and PERM

- U.S. Department of Homeland Security Blue Campaign—coordinates efforts of multiple DHS agencies to address human trafficking and provides outreach materials to the general public: http://www.dhs.gov/end-human-trafficking
- U.S. Department of Health and Human Services—through the Administration for Children and Families provides outreach materials, training, and technical assistance: http://www.acf.hhs.gov/programs/endtrafficking

    1-88-373-7888—A 24/7 hotline funded by HHS for referrals to local law enforcement and service providers

- U.S. Department of Health and Human Services, Office of Refugee Resettlement, Anti-Trafficking in Persons (ATIP) program—funds programs to serve trafficked persons, provides eligibility for victims to receive public benefits, and raises awareness about human trafficking: http://www.acf.hhs.gov/programs/orr/programs/anti-trafficking
- U.S. Department of Transportation—works with transportation stakeholders nationwide to raise awareness about human trafficking: http://www.dot.gov/stophumantrafficking

- U.S. Department of Education—provides resources to help schools identify trafficked children: http://www2.ed.gov/about/offices/list/oese/oshs/factsheet.html
- U.S. Agency for International Development—invests in anti-trafficking programs, particularly in countries with significant trafficking problems and conflict- and crisis-affected areas: http://www.usaid.gov/trafficking
- U.S. Equal Employment Opportunity Commission—enforces anti-discrimination laws on the bases of race, color, religion, national origin, age, disability, genetic information, and sex, including sexual harassment: http://www.eeoc.gov/eeoc/interagency/trafficking.cfm

  1-800-669-4000—Equal Employment Opportunity Commission—from 7:00 A.M. to 8:00 P.M. (EST)—for information about how trafficking victims can file a charge of employment discrimination

Local Resources

- Victim service organizations funded by the Department of Justice, Office for Victims of Crime: http://ojp.gov/ovc/grants/traffickingmatrix.html
- Victim service organizations funded by the Department of Health and Human Services, Office of Refugee Resettlement (ORR): http://www.acf.hhs.gov/programs/orr/resource/anti-trafficking-in-persons-grants
- Alliance to End Slavery and Trafficking (ATEST)—a coalition of anti-trafficking organizations advocating for legislative and administrative policy changes: http://www.endslaveryandtrafficking.org/coalition-partners
- Freedom Network (USA) Members—an alliance of service-providing organizations nationwide working with survivors of human trafficking: http://freedomnetworkusa.org/membership/current-members/
- Department of Justice, Bureau of Justice Assistance/Office for Victims of Crime, Human Trafficking Task Forces: http://www.justice.gov/usao/briefing_room/crt/task_forces.html

Other Resources

- American Bar Association, Human Trafficking Task Force: http://www.americanbar.org/groups/human_rights/projects/task_force_human_trafficking/resources.html

Appendix

Texts of relevant laws

- Palermo Protocol
- TVPA and Reauthorizations
- The Athens Ethical Principals
- Luxor Implementation Guidelines to the Athens Ethical Principles
- SB 657 California Transparency in Supply Chains Act

PROTOCOL TO PREVENT, SUPPRESS AND PUNISH TRAFFICKING IN PERSONS, ESPECIALLY WOMEN AND CHILDREN, SUPPLEMENTING THE UNITED NATIONS CONVENTION AGAINST TRANSNATIONAL ORGANIZED CRIME

> Advance copy of the authentic text. The copy certified by the Secretary-General will be issued at a later time.

UNITED NATIONS
2000

PROTOCOL TO PREVENT, SUPPRESS AND PUNISH TRAFFICKING IN PERSONS, ESPECIALLY WOMEN AND CHILDREN, SUPPLEMENTING THE UNITED NATIONS CONVENTION AGAINST TRANSNATIONAL ORGANIZED CRIME

Preamble

The States Parties to this Protocol,

Declaring that effective action to prevent and combat trafficking in persons, especially women and children, requires a comprehensive international approach in the countries of origin, transit and destination that includes measures to prevent such trafficking, to punish the traffickers and to protect the victims of such trafficking, including by protecting their internationally recognized human rights,

Taking into account the fact that, despite the existence of a variety of international instruments containing rules and practical measures to combat the exploitation of persons, especially women and children, there is no universal instrument that addresses all aspects of trafficking in persons,

Concerned that, in the absence of such an instrument, persons who are vulnerable to trafficking will not be sufficiently protected,

Recalling General Assembly resolution 53/111 of 9 December 1998, in which the Assembly decided to establish an open-ended intergovernmental ad hoc committee for the purpose of elaborating a comprehensive international convention against transnational organized crime and of discussing the elaboration of, inter alia, an international instrument addressing trafficking in women and children,

Convinced that supplementing the United Nations Convention against Transnational Organized Crime with an international instrument for the prevention, suppression and punishment of trafficking in persons, especially women and children, will be useful in preventing and combating that crime,

Have agreed as follows:

I. General provisions

Article 1

Relation with the United Nations Convention against Transnational Organized Crime

1.   This Protocol supplements the United Nations Convention against Transnational Organized Crime. It shall be interpreted together with the Convention.

2.   The provisions of the Convention shall apply, mutatis mutandis, to this Protocol unless otherwise provided herein.

3.   The offences established in accordance with article 5 of this Protocol shall be regarded as offences established in accordance with the Convention.

Article 2
Statement of purpose

The purposes of this Protocol are:

(a)   To prevent and combat trafficking in persons, paying particular attention to women and children;

(b)   To protect and assist the victims of such trafficking, with full respect for their human rights; and

(c)   To promote cooperation among States Parties in order to meet those objectives.

Article 3
Use of terms

For the purposes of this Protocol:

(a)   "Trafficking in persons" shall mean the recruitment, transportation, transfer, harbouring or receipt of persons, by means of the threat or use of force or other forms of coercion, of abduction, of fraud, of deception, of the abuse of power or of a position of vulnerability or of the giving or receiving of payments or benefits to achieve the consent of a person having control over another person, for the purpose of exploitation. Exploitation shall include, at a minimum, the exploitation of the prostitution of others or other forms of sexual exploitation, forced labour or services, slavery or practices similar to slavery, servitude or the removal of organs;

(b)   The consent of a victim of trafficking in persons to the intended exploitation set forth in subparagraph (a) of this article shall be irrelevant where any of the means set forth in subparagraph (a) have been used;

(c)   The recruitment, transportation, transfer, harbouring or receipt of a child for the purpose of exploitation shall be considered "trafficking in persons" even if this does not involve any of the means set forth in subparagraph (a) of this article;

(d)   "Child" shall mean any person under eighteen years of age.

Article 4
Scope of application

This Protocol shall apply, except as otherwise stated herein, to the prevention, investigation and prosecution of the offences established in accordance with article 5 of this Protocol, where those offences are transnational in nature and involve an organized criminal group, as well as to the protection of victims of such offences.

Article 5
Criminalization

1.   Each State Party shall adopt such legislative and other measures as may be necessary to establish as criminal offences the conduct set forth in article 3 of this Protocol, when committed intentionally.

2.   Each State Party shall also adopt such legislative and other measures as may be necessary to establish as criminal offences:

(a)   Subject to the basic concepts of its legal system, attempting to commit an offence established in accordance with paragraph 1 of this article;

(b)   Participating as an accomplice in an offence established in accordance with paragraph 1 of this article; and

(c)   Organizing or directing other persons to commit an offence established in accordance with paragraph 1 of this article.

II. Protection of victims of trafficking in persons

Article 6
Assistance to and protection of victims of
trafficking in persons

1.   In appropriate cases and to the extent possible under its domestic law, each State Party shall protect the privacy and identity of victims of trafficking in persons, including, inter alia, by making legal proceedings relating to such trafficking confidential.

2.   Each State Party shall ensure that its domestic legal or administrative system contains measures that provide to victims of trafficking in persons, in appropriate cases:

(a)   Information on relevant court and administrative proceedings;

(b)   Assistance to enable their views and concerns to be presented and considered at appropriate stages of criminal proceedings against offenders, in a manner not prejudicial to the rights of the defence.

3.   Each State Party shall consider implementing measures to provide for the physical, psychological and social recovery of victims of

trafficking in persons, including, in appropriate cases, in cooperation with non-governmental organizations, other relevant organizations and other elements of civil society, and, in particular, the provision of:

(a)   Appropriate housing;

(b)   Counselling and information, in particular as regards their legal rights, in a language that the victims of trafficking in persons can understand;

(c)   Medical, psychological and material assistance; and

(d)   Employment, educational and training opportunities.

4.   Each State Party shall take into account, in applying the provisions of this article, the age, gender and special needs of victims of trafficking in persons, in particular the special needs of children, including appropriate housing, education and care.

5.   Each State Party shall endeavour to provide for the physical safety of victims of trafficking in persons while they are within its territory.

6.   Each State Party shall ensure that its domestic legal system contains measures that offer victims of trafficking in persons the possibility of obtaining compensation for damage suffered.

Article 7
Status of victims of trafficking in persons in receiving States

1.   In addition to taking measures pursuant to article 6 of this Protocol, each State Party shall consider adopting legislative or other appropriate measures that permit victims of trafficking in persons to remain in its territory, temporarily or permanently, in appropriate cases.

2.   In implementing the provision contained in paragraph 1 of this article, each State Party shall give appropriate consideration to humanitarian and compassionate factors.

Article 8
Repatriation of victims of trafficking in persons

1.   The State Party of which a victim of trafficking in persons is a national or in which the person had the right of permanent residence at the time of entry into the territory of the receiving State Party shall facilitate and accept, with due regard for the safety of that person, the return of that person without undue or unreasonable delay.

2.   When a State Party returns a victim of trafficking in persons to a State Party of which that person is a national or in which he or she had, at the time of entry into the territory of the receiving State Party, the right of permanent residence, such return shall be with due regard for the safety of

that person and for the status of any legal proceedings related to the fact that the person is a victim of trafficking and shall preferably be voluntary.

3. At the request of a receiving State Party, a requested State Party shall, without undue or unreasonable delay, verify whether a person who is a victim of trafficking in persons is its national or had the right of permanent residence in its territory at the time of entry into the territory of the receiving State Party.

4. In order to facilitate the return of a victim of trafficking in persons who is without proper documentation, the State Party of which that person is a national or in which he or she had the right of permanent residence at the time of entry into the territory of the receiving State Party shall agree to issue, at the request of the receiving State Party, such travel documents or other authorization as may be necessary to enable the person to travel to and re-enter its territory.

5. This article shall be without prejudice to any right afforded to victims of trafficking in persons by any domestic law of the receiving State Party.

6. This article shall be without prejudice to any applicable bilateral or multilateral agreement or arrangement that governs, in whole or in part, the return of victims of trafficking in persons.

III. Prevention, cooperation and other measures

Article 9
Prevention of trafficking in persons

1. States Parties shall establish comprehensive policies, programmes and other measures:

(a) To prevent and combat trafficking in persons; and

(b) To protect victims of trafficking in persons, especially women and children, from revictimization.

2. States Parties shall endeavour to undertake measures such as research, information and mass media campaigns and social and economic initiatives to prevent and combat trafficking in persons.

3. Policies, programmes and other measures established in accordance with this article shall, as appropriate, include cooperation with non-governmental organizations, other relevant organizations and other elements of civil society.

4. States Parties shall take or strengthen measures, including through bilateral or multilateral cooperation, to alleviate the factors that make persons, especially women and children, vulnerable to trafficking, such as poverty, underdevelopment and lack of equal opportunity.

5.   States Parties shall adopt or strengthen legislative or other measures, such as educational, social or cultural measures, including through bilateral and multilateral cooperation, to discourage the demand that fosters all forms of exploitation of persons, especially women and children, that leads to trafficking.

Article 10
Information exchange and training

1.   Law enforcement, immigration or other relevant authorities of States Parties shall, as appropriate, cooperate with one another by exchanging information, in accordance with their domestic law, to enable them to determine:

(a)   Whether individuals crossing or attempting to cross an international border with travel documents belonging to other persons or without travel documents are perpetrators or victims of trafficking in persons;

(b)   The types of travel document that individuals have used or attempted to use to cross an international border for the purpose of trafficking in persons; and

(c)   The means and methods used by organized criminal groups for the purpose of trafficking in persons, including the recruitment and transportation of victims, routes and links between and among individuals and groups engaged in such trafficking, and possible measures for detecting them.

2.   States Parties shall provide or strengthen training for law enforcement, immigration and other relevant officials in the prevention of trafficking in persons. The training should focus on methods used in preventing such trafficking, prosecuting the traffickers and protecting the rights of the victims, including protecting the victims from the traffickers. The training should also take into account the need to consider human rights and child- and gender-sensitive issues and it should encourage cooperation with non-governmental organizations, other relevant organizations and other elements of civil society.

3.   A State Party that receives information shall comply with any request by the State Party that transmitted the information that places restrictions on its use.

Article 11
Border measures

1.   Without prejudice to international commitments in relation to the free movement of people, States Parties shall strengthen, to the extent

possible, such border controls as may be necessary to prevent and detect trafficking in persons.

2.   Each State Party shall adopt legislative or other appropriate measures to prevent, to the extent possible, means of transport operated by commercial carriers from being used in the commission of offences established in accordance with article 5 of this Protocol.

3.   Where appropriate, and without prejudice to applicable international conventions, such measures shall include establishing the obligation of commercial carriers, including any transportation company or the owner or operator of any means of transport, to ascertain that all passengers are in possession of the travel documents required for entry into the receiving State.

4.   Each State Party shall take the necessary measures, in accordance with its domestic law, to provide for sanctions in cases of violation of the obligation set forth in paragraph 3 of this article.

5.   Each State Party shall consider taking measures that permit, in accordance with its domestic law, the denial of entry or revocation of visas of persons implicated in the commission of offences established in accordance with this Protocol.

6.   Without prejudice to article 27 of the Convention, States Parties shall consider strengthening cooperation among border control agencies by, inter alia, establishing and maintaining direct channels of communication.

Article 12
Security and control of documents

Each State Party shall take such measures as may be necessary, within available means:

(a)   To ensure that travel or identity documents issued by it are of such quality that they cannot easily be misused and cannot readily be falsified or unlawfully altered, replicated or issued; and

(b)   To ensure the integrity and security of travel or identity documents issued by or on behalf of the State Party and to prevent their unlawful creation, issuance and use.

Article 13
Legitimacy and validity of documents

At the request of another State Party, a State Party shall, in accordance with its domestic law, verify within a reasonable time the legitimacy and validity of travel or identity documents issued or purported to have been issued in its name and suspected of being used for trafficking in persons.

IV. Final provisions

Article 14
Saving clause

1.   Nothing in this Protocol shall affect the rights, obligations and responsibilities of States and individuals under international law, including international humanitarian law and international human rights law and, in particular, where applicable, the 1951 Convention and the 1967 Protocol relating to the Status of Refugees and the principle of non-refoulement as contained therein.

2.   The measures set forth in this Protocol shall be interpreted and applied in a way that is not discriminatory to persons on the ground that they are victims of trafficking in persons. The interpretation and application of those measures shall be consistent with internationally recognized principles of non-discrimination.

Article 15
Settlement of disputes

1.   States Parties shall endeavour to settle disputes concerning the interpretation or application of this Protocol through negotiation.

2.   Any dispute between two or more States Parties concerning the interpretation or application of this Protocol that cannot be settled through negotiation within a reasonable time shall, at the request of one of those States Parties, be submitted to arbitration. If, six months after the date of the request for arbitration, those States Parties are unable to agree on the organization of the arbitration, any one of those States Parties may refer the dispute to the International Court of Justice by request in accordance with the Statute of the Court.

3.   Each State Party may, at the time of signature, ratification, acceptance or approval of or accession to this Protocol, declare that it does not consider itself bound by paragraph 2 of this article. The other States Parties shall not be bound by paragraph 2 of this article with respect to any State Party that has made such a reservation.

4.   Any State Party that has made a reservation in accordance with paragraph 3 of this article may at any time withdraw that reservation by notification to the Secretary-General of the United Nations.

Article 16
Signature, ratification, acceptance,
approval and accession

1.   This Protocol shall be open to all States for signature from 12 to 15 December 2000 in Palermo, Italy, and thereafter at United Nations Headquarters in New York until 12 December 2002.

2.   This Protocol shall also be open for signature by regional economic integration organizations provided that at least one member State of such organization has signed this Protocol in accordance with paragraph 1 of this article.

3.   This Protocol is subject to ratification, acceptance or approval. Instruments of ratification, acceptance or approval shall be deposited with the Secretary-General of the United Nations. A regional economic integration organization may deposit its instrument of ratification, acceptance or approval if at least one of its member States has done likewise. In that instrument of ratification, acceptance or approval, such organization shall declare the extent of its competence with respect to the matters governed by this Protocol. Such organization shall also inform the depositary of any relevant modification in the extent of its competence.

4.   This Protocol is open for accession by any State or any regional economic integration organization of which at least one member State is a Party to this Protocol. Instruments of accession shall be deposited with the Secretary-General of the United Nations. At the time of its accession, a regional economic integration organization shall declare the extent of its competence with respect to matters governed by this Protocol. Such organization shall also inform the depositary of any relevant modification in the extent of its competence.

Article 17
Entry into force

1.   This Protocol shall enter into force on the ninetieth day after the date of deposit of the fortieth instrument of ratification, acceptance, approval or accession, except that it shall not enter into force before the entry into force of the Convention. For the purpose of this paragraph, any instrument deposited by a regional economic integration organization shall not be counted as additional to those deposited by member States of such organization.

2.   For each State or regional economic integration organization ratifying, accepting, approving or acceding to this Protocol after the deposit of the fortieth instrument of such action, this Protocol shall enter into force on the thirtieth day after the date of deposit by such State or organization of

the relevant instrument or on the date this Protocol enters into force pursuant to paragraph 1 of this article, whichever is the later.

Article 18
Amendment

1.   After the expiry of five years from the entry into force of this Protocol, a State Party to the Protocol may propose an amendment and file it with the Secretary-General of the United Nations, who shall thereupon communicate the proposed amendment to the States Parties and to the Conference of the Parties to the Convention for the purpose of considering and deciding on the proposal. The States Parties to this Protocol meeting at the Conference of the Parties shall make every effort to achieve consensus on each amendment. If all efforts at consensus have been exhausted and no agreement has been reached, the amendment shall, as a last resort, require for its adoption a two-thirds majority vote of the States Parties to this Protocol present and voting at the meeting of the Conference of the Parties.

2.   Regional economic integration organizations, in matters within their competence, shall exercise their right to vote under this article with a number of votes equal to the number of their member States that are Parties to this Protocol. Such organizations shall not exercise their right to vote if their member States exercise theirs and vice versa.

3.   An amendment adopted in accordance with paragraph 1 of this article is subject to ratification, acceptance or approval by States Parties.

4.   An amendment adopted in accordance with paragraph 1 of this article shall enter into force in respect of a State Party ninety days after the date of the deposit with the Secretary-General of the United Nations of an instrument of ratification, acceptance or approval of such amendment.

5.   When an amendment enters into force, it shall be binding on those States Parties which have expressed their consent to be bound by it. Other States Parties shall still be bound by the provisions of this Protocol and any earlier amendments that they have ratified, accepted or approved.

Article 19
Denunciation

1.   A State Party may denounce this Protocol by written notification to the Secretary-General of the United Nations. Such denunciation shall become effective one year after the date of receipt of the notification by the Secretary-General.

2.   A regional economic integration organization shall cease to be a Party to this Protocol when all of its member States have denounced it.

Article 20
Depositary and languages

1.   The Secretary-General of the United Nations is designated depositary of this Protocol.

2.   The original of this Protocol, of which the Arabic, Chinese, English, French, Russian and Spanish texts are equally authentic, shall be deposited with the Secretary-General of the United Nations.

IN WITNESS WHEREOF, the undersigned plenipotentiaries, being duly authorized thereto by their respective Governments, have signed this Protocol.

VICTIMS OF TRAFFICKING AND VIOLENCE PROTECTION ACT OF 2000

Public Law 106–386
106th Congress

An Act

Oct. 28, 2000
[H.R. 3244]

To combat trafficking in persons, especially into the sex trade, slavery, and involuntary servitude, to reauthorize certain Federal programs to prevent violence against
women, and for other purposes.

Victims of
Trafficking and
Violence
Protection Act of
2000.
22 USC 7101
note.

*Be it enacted by the Senate and House of Representatives of
the United States of America in Congress assembled,*

SECTION 1. SHORT TITLE.

This Act may be cited as the "Victims of Trafficking and
Violence Protection Act of 2000".

SEC. 2. ORGANIZATION OF ACT INTO DIVISIONS; TABLE OF CONTENTS.

(a) DIVISIONS.—This Act is organized into three divisions, as
follows:

(1) DIVISION A.—Trafficking Victims Protection Act of 2000.
(2) DIVISION B.—Violence Against Women Act of 2000.
(3) DIVISION C.—Miscellaneous Provisions.

(b) TABLE OF CONTENTS.—The table of contents for this Act
is as follows:

Sec. 1. Short title.
Sec. 2. Organization of Act into divisions; table of contents.

DIVISION A—TRAFFICKING VICTIMS PROTECTION ACT OF 2000

Sec. 101. Short title.
Sec. 102. Purposes and findings.
Sec. 103. Definitions.
Sec. 104. Annual Country Reports on Human Rights Practices.
Sec. 105. Interagency Task Force To Monitor and Combat Trafficking.
Sec. 106. Prevention of trafficking.
Sec. 107. Protection and assistance for victims of trafficking.
Sec. 108. Minimum standards for the elimination of trafficking.
Sec. 109. Assistance to foreign countries to meet minimum standards.
Sec. 110. Actions against governments failing to meet minimum standards.
Sec. 111. Actions against significant traffickers in persons.
Sec. 112. Strengthening prosecution and punishment of traffickers.
Sec. 113. Authorizations of appropriations.

DIVISION B—VIOLENCE AGAINST WOMEN ACT OF 2000

Sec. 1001. Short title.
Sec. 1002. Definitions.
Sec. 1003. Accountability and oversight.

TITLE I—STRENGTHENING LAW ENFORCEMENT TO REDUCE VIOLENCE
AGAINST WOMEN

Sec. 1101. Full faith and credit enforcement of protection orders.
Sec. 1102. Role of courts.
Sec. 1103. Reauthorization of STOP grants.
Sec. 1104. Reauthorization of grants to encourage arrest policies.
Sec. 1105. Reauthorization of rural domestic violence and child abuse enforcement
        grants.
Sec. 1106. National stalker and domestic violence reduction.

PUBLIC LAW 106–386—OCT. 28, 2000   114 STAT. 1465

Sec. 1107. Amendments to domestic violence and stalking offenses.
Sec. 1108. School and campus security.
Sec. 1109. Dating violence.

TITLE II—STRENGTHENING SERVICES TO VICTIMS OF VIOLENCE

Sec. 1201. Legal assistance for victims.
Sec. 1202. Shelter services for battered women and children.
Sec. 1203. Transitional housing assistance for victims of domestic violence.
Sec. 1204. National domestic violence hotline.
Sec. 1205. Federal victims counselors.
Sec. 1206. Study of State laws regarding insurance discrimination against victims of violence against women.
Sec. 1207. Study of workplace effects from violence against women.
Sec. 1208. Study of unemployment compensation for victims of violence against women.
Sec. 1209. Enhancing protections for older and disabled women from domestic violence and sexual assault.

TITLE III—LIMITING THE EFFECTS OF VIOLENCE ON CHILDREN

Sec. 1301. Safe havens for children pilot program.
Sec. 1302. Reauthorization of victims of child abuse programs.
Sec. 1303. Report on effects of parental kidnapping laws in domestic violence cases.

TITLE IV—STRENGTHENING EDUCATION AND TRAINING TO COMBAT VIOLENCE AGAINST WOMEN

Sec. 1401. Rape prevention and education.
Sec. 1402. Education and training to end violence against and abuse of women with disabilities.
Sec. 1403. Community initiatives.
Sec. 1404. Development of research agenda identified by the Violence Against Women Act of 1994.
Sec. 1405. Standards, practice, and training for sexual assault forensic examinations.
Sec. 1406. Education and training for judges and court personnel.
Sec. 1407. Domestic Violence Task Force.

TITLE V—BATTERED IMMIGRANT WOMEN

Sec. 1501. Short title.
Sec. 1502. Findings and purposes.
Sec. 1503. Improved access to immigration protections of the Violence Against Women Act of 1994 for battered immigrant women.
Sec. 1504. Improved access to cancellation of removal and suspension of deportation under the Violence Against Women Act of 1994.
Sec. 1505. Offering equal access to immigration protections of the Violence Against Women Act of 1994 for all qualified battered immigrant self-petitioners.
Sec. 1506. Restoring immigration protections under the Violence Against Women Act of 1994.
Sec. 1507. Remedying problems with implementation of the immigration provisions of the Violence Against Women Act of 1994.
Sec. 1508. Technical correction to qualified alien definition for battered immigrants.
Sec. 1509. Access to Cuban Adjustment Act for battered immigrant spouses and children.
Sec. 1510. Access to the Nicaraguan Adjustment and Central American Relief Act for battered spouses and children.
Sec. 1511. Access to the Haitian Refugee Fairness Act of 1998 for battered spouses and children.
Sec. 1512. Access to services and legal representation for battered immigrants.
Sec. 1513. Protection for certain crime victims including victims of crimes against women.

TITLE VI—MISCELLANEOUS

Sec. 1601. Notice requirements for sexually violent offenders.
Sec. 1602. Teen suicide prevention study.
Sec. 1603. Decade of pain control and research.

DIVISION C—MISCELLANEOUS PROVISIONS

Sec. 2001. Aimee's law.
Sec. 2002. Payment of anti-terrorism judgments.
Sec. 2003. Aid to victims of terrorism.
Sec. 2004. Twenty-first amendment enforcement.

114 STAT. 1466   PUBLIC LAW 106–386—OCT. 28, 2000

Trafficking
Victims
Protection Act of
2000.

DIVISION A—TRAFFICKING VICTIMS PROTECTION ACT OF 2000

22 USC 7101
note.

SEC. 101. SHORT TITLE.

This division may be cited as the "Trafficking Victims Protection Act of 2000".

22 USC 7101.

SEC. 102. PURPOSES AND FINDINGS.

(a) PURPOSES.—The purposes of this division are to combat trafficking in persons, a contemporary manifestation of slavery whose victims are predominantly women and children, to ensure just and effective punishment of traffickers, and to protect their victims.

(b) FINDINGS.—Congress finds that:

(1) As the 21st century begins, the degrading institution of slavery continues throughout the world. Trafficking in persons is a modern form of slavery, and it is the largest manifestation of slavery today. At least 700,000 persons annually, primarily women and children, are trafficked within or across international borders. Approximately 50,000 women and children are trafficked into the United States each year.

(2) Many of these persons are trafficked into the international sex trade, often by force, fraud, or coercion. The sex industry has rapidly expanded over the past several decades. It involves sexual exploitation of persons, predominantly women and girls, involving activities related to prostitution, pornography, sex tourism, and other commercial sexual services. The low status of women in many parts of the world has contributed to a burgeoning of the trafficking industry.

(3) Trafficking in persons is not limited to the sex industry. This growing transnational crime also includes forced labor and involves significant violations of labor, public health, and human rights standards worldwide.

(4) Traffickers primarily target women and girls, who are disproportionately affected by poverty, the lack of access to education, chronic unemployment, discrimination, and the lack of economic opportunities in countries of origin. Traffickers lure women and girls into their networks through false promises of decent working conditions at relatively good pay as nannies, maids, dancers, factory workers, restaurant workers, sales clerks, or models. Traffickers also buy children from poor families and sell them into prostitution or into various types of forced or bonded labor.

(5) Traffickers often transport victims from their home communities to unfamiliar destinations, including foreign countries away from family and friends, religious institutions, and other sources of protection and support, leaving the victims defenseless and vulnerable.

(6) Victims are often forced through physical violence to engage in sex acts or perform slavery-like labor. Such force includes rape and other forms of sexual abuse, torture, starvation, imprisonment, threats, psychological abuse, and coercion.

(7) Traffickers often make representations to their victims that physical harm may occur to them or others should the victim escape or attempt to escape. Such representations can

PUBLIC LAW 106–386—OCT. 28, 2000   114 STAT. 1467

have the same coercive effects on victims as direct threats to inflict such harm.

(8) Trafficking in persons is increasingly perpetrated by organized, sophisticated criminal enterprises. Such trafficking is the fastest growing source of profits for organized criminal enterprises worldwide. Profits from the trafficking industry contribute to the expansion of organized crime in the United States and worldwide. Trafficking in persons is often aided by official corruption in countries of origin, transit, and destination, thereby threatening the rule of law.

(9) Trafficking includes all the elements of the crime of forcible rape when it involves the involuntary participation of another person in sex acts by means of fraud, force, or coercion.

(10) Trafficking also involves violations of other laws, including labor and immigration codes and laws against kidnapping, slavery, false imprisonment, assault, battery, pandering, fraud, and extortion.

(11) Trafficking exposes victims to serious health risks. Women and children trafficked in the sex industry are exposed to deadly diseases, including HIV and AIDS. Trafficking victims are sometimes worked or physically brutalized to death.

(12) Trafficking in persons substantially affects interstate and foreign commerce. Trafficking for such purposes as involuntary servitude, peonage, and other forms of forced labor has an impact on the nationwide employment network and labor market. Within the context of slavery, servitude, and labor or services which are obtained or maintained through coercive conduct that amounts to a condition of servitude, victims are subjected to a range of violations.

(13) Involuntary servitude statutes are intended to reach cases in which persons are held in a condition of servitude through nonviolent coercion. In United States v. Kozminski, 487 U.S. 931 (1988), the Supreme Court found that section 1584 of title 18, United States Code, should be narrowly interpreted, absent a definition of involuntary servitude by Congress. As a result, that section was interpreted to criminalize only servitude that is brought about through use or threatened use of physical or legal coercion, and to exclude other conduct that can have the same purpose and effect.

(14) Existing legislation and law enforcement in the United States and other countries are inadequate to deter trafficking and bring traffickers to justice, failing to reflect the gravity of the offenses involved. No comprehensive law exists in the United States that penalizes the range of offenses involved in the trafficking scheme. Instead, even the most brutal instances of trafficking in the sex industry are often punished under laws that also apply to lesser offenses, so that traffickers typically escape deserved punishment.

(15) In the United States, the seriousness of this crime and its components is not reflected in current sentencing guidelines, resulting in weak penalties for convicted traffickers.

(16) In some countries, enforcement against traffickers is also hindered by official indifference, by corruption, and sometimes even by official participation in trafficking.

(17) Existing laws often fail to protect victims of trafficking, and because victims are often illegal immigrants in the destination country, they are repeatedly punished more harshly than the traffickers themselves.

(18) Additionally, adequate services and facilities do not exist to meet victims' needs regarding health care, housing, education, and legal assistance, which safely reintegrate trafficking victims into their home countries.

(19) Victims of severe forms of trafficking should not be inappropriately incarcerated, fined, or otherwise penalized solely for unlawful acts committed as a direct result of being trafficked, such as using false documents, entering the country without documentation, or working without documentation.

(20) Because victims of trafficking are frequently unfamiliar with the laws, cultures, and languages of the countries into which they have been trafficked, because they are often subjected to coercion and intimidation including physical detention and debt bondage, and because they often fear retribution and forcible removal to countries in which they will face retribution or other hardship, these victims often find it difficult or impossible to report the crimes committed against them or to assist in the investigation and prosecution of such crimes.

(21) Trafficking of persons is an evil requiring concerted and vigorous action by countries of origin, transit or destination, and by international organizations.

(22) One of the founding documents of the United States, the Declaration of Independence, recognizes the inherent dignity and worth of all people. It states that all men are created equal and that they are endowed by their Creator with certain unalienable rights. The right to be free from slavery and involuntary servitude is among those unalienable rights. Acknowledging this fact, the United States outlawed slavery and involuntary servitude in 1865, recognizing them as evil institutions that must be abolished. Current practices of sexual slavery and trafficking of women and children are similarly abhorrent to the principles upon which the United States was founded.

(23) The United States and the international community agree that trafficking in persons involves grave violations of human rights and is a matter of pressing international concern. The international community has repeatedly condemned slavery and involuntary servitude, violence against women, and other elements of trafficking, through declarations, treaties, and United Nations resolutions and reports, including the Universal Declaration of Human Rights; the 1956 Supplementary Convention on the Abolition of Slavery, the Slave Trade, and Institutions and Practices Similar to Slavery; the 1948 American Declaration on the Rights and Duties of Man; the 1957 Abolition of Forced Labor Convention; the International Covenant on Civil and Political Rights; the Convention Against Torture and Other Cruel, Inhuman or Degrading Treatment or Punishment; United Nations General Assembly Resolutions 50/167, 51/66, and 52/98; the Final Report of the World Congress against Sexual Exploitation of Children (Stockholm, 1996); the Fourth World Conference on Women (Beijing, 1995); and the 1991 Moscow Document of the Organization for Security and Cooperation in Europe.

PUBLIC LAW 106–386—OCT. 28, 2000   114 STAT. 1469

(24) Trafficking in persons is a transnational crime with national implications. To deter international trafficking and bring its perpetrators to justice, nations including the United States must recognize that trafficking is a serious offense. This is done by prescribing appropriate punishment, giving priority to the prosecution of trafficking offenses, and protecting rather than punishing the victims of such offenses. The United States must work bilaterally and multilaterally to abolish the trafficking industry by taking steps to promote cooperation among countries linked together by international trafficking routes. The United States must also urge the international community to take strong action in multilateral fora to engage recalcitrant countries in serious and sustained efforts to eliminate trafficking and protect trafficking victims.

SEC. 103. DEFINITIONS.   22 USC 7102.

In this division:
(1) APPROPRIATE CONGRESSIONAL COMMITTEES.—The term "appropriate congressional committees" means the Committee on Foreign Relations and the Committee on the Judiciary of the Senate and the Committee on International Relations and the Committee on the Judiciary of the House of Representatives.
(2) COERCION.—The term "coercion" means—
(A) threats of serious harm to or physical restraint against any person;
(B) any scheme, plan, or pattern intended to cause a person to believe that failure to perform an act would result in serious harm to or physical restraint against any person; or
(C) the abuse or threatened abuse of the legal process.
(3) COMMERCIAL SEX ACT.—The term "commercial sex act" means any sex act on account of which anything of value is given to or received by any person.
(4) DEBT BONDAGE.—The term "debt bondage" means the status or condition of a debtor arising from a pledge by the debtor of his or her personal services or of those of a person under his or her control as a security for debt, if the value of those services as reasonably assessed is not applied toward the liquidation of the debt or the length and nature of those services are not respectively limited and defined.
(5) INVOLUNTARY SERVITUDE.—The term "involuntary servitude" includes a condition of servitude induced by means of—
(A) any scheme, plan, or pattern intended to cause a person to believe that, if the person did not enter into or continue in such condition, that person or another person would suffer serious harm or physical restraint; or
(B) the abuse or threatened abuse of the legal process.
(6) MINIMUM STANDARDS FOR THE ELIMINATION OF TRAFFICKING.—The term "minimum standards for the elimination of trafficking" means the standards set forth in section 108.
(7) NONHUMANITARIAN, NONTRADE-RELATED FOREIGN ASSISTANCE.—The term "nonhumanitarian, nontrade-related foreign assistance" means—
(A) any assistance under the Foreign Assistance Act of 1961, other than—

(i) assistance under chapter 4 of part II of that Act that is made available for any program, project, or activity eligible for assistance under chapter 1 of part I of that Act;

(ii) assistance under chapter 8 of part I of that Act;

(iii) any other narcotics-related assistance under part I of that Act or under chapter 4 or 5 part II of that Act, but any such assistance provided under this clause shall be subject to the prior notification procedures applicable to reprogrammings pursuant to section 634A of that Act;

(iv) disaster relief assistance, including any assistance under chapter 9 of part I of that Act;

(v) antiterrorism assistance under chapter 8 of part II of that Act;

(vi) assistance for refugees;

(vii) humanitarian and other development assistance in support of programs of nongovernmental organizations under chapters 1 and 10 of that Act;

(viii) programs under title IV of chapter 2 of part I of that Act, relating to the Overseas Private Investment Corporation; and

(ix) other programs involving trade-related or humanitarian assistance; and

(B) sales, or financing on any terms, under the Arms Export Control Act, other than sales or financing provided for narcotics-related purposes following notification in accordance with the prior notification procedures applicable to reprogrammings pursuant to section 634A of the Foreign Assistance Act of 1961.

(8) SEVERE FORMS OF TRAFFICKING IN PERSONS.—The term "severe forms of trafficking in persons" means—

(A) sex trafficking in which a commercial sex act is induced by force, fraud, or coercion, or in which the person induced to perform such act has not attained 18 years of age; or

(B) the recruitment, harboring, transportation, provision, or obtaining of a person for labor or services, through the use of force, fraud, or coercion for the purpose of subjection to involuntary servitude, peonage, debt bondage, or slavery.

(9) SEX TRAFFICKING.—The term "sex trafficking" means the recruitment, harboring, transportation, provision, or obtaining of a person for the purpose of a commercial sex act.

(10) STATE.—The term "State" means each of the several States of the United States, the District of Columbia, the Commonwealth of Puerto Rico, the United States Virgin Islands, Guam, American Samoa, the Commonwealth of the Northern Mariana Islands, and territories and possessions of the United States.

(11) TASK FORCE.—The term "Task Force" means the Interagency Task Force to Monitor and Combat Trafficking established under section 105.

(12) UNITED STATES.—The term "United States" means the fifty States of the United States, the District of Columbia,

the Commonwealth of Puerto Rico, the Virgin Islands, American Samoa, Guam, the Commonwealth of the Northern Mariana Islands, and the territories and possessions of the United States.

(13) VICTIM OF A SEVERE FORM OF TRAFFICKING.—The term "victim of a severe form of trafficking" means a person subject to an act or practice described in paragraph (8).

(14) VICTIM OF TRAFFICKING.—The term "victim of trafficking" means a person subjected to an act or practice described in paragraph (8) or (9).

SEC. 104. ANNUAL COUNTRY REPORTS ON HUMAN RIGHTS PRACTICES.   22 USC 2151n.

(a) COUNTRIES RECEIVING ECONOMIC ASSISTANCE.—Section 116(f) of the Foreign Assistance Act of 1961 (22 U.S.C. 2151(f)) is amended to read as follows:

"(f)(1) The report required by subsection (d) shall include the following:

"(A) A description of the nature and extent of severe forms of trafficking in persons, as defined in section 103 of the Trafficking Victims Protection Act of 2000, in each foreign country.

"(B) With respect to each country that is a country of origin, transit, or destination for victims of severe forms of trafficking in persons, an assessment of the efforts by the government of that country to combat such trafficking. The assessment shall address the following:

"(i) Whether government authorities in that country participate in, facilitate, or condone such trafficking.

"(ii) Which government authorities in that country are involved in activities to combat such trafficking.

"(iii) What steps the government of that country has taken to prohibit government officials from participating in, facilitating, or condoning such trafficking, including the investigation, prosecution, and conviction of such officials.

"(iv) What steps the government of that country has taken to prohibit other individuals from participating in such trafficking, including the investigation, prosecution, and conviction of individuals involved in severe forms of trafficking in persons, the criminal and civil penalties for such trafficking, and the efficacy of those penalties in eliminating or reducing such trafficking.

"(v) What steps the government of that country has taken to assist victims of such trafficking, including efforts to prevent victims from being further victimized by traffickers, government officials, or others, grants of relief from deportation, and provision of humanitarian relief, including provision of mental and physical health care and shelter.

"(vi) Whether the government of that country is cooperating with governments of other countries to extradite traffickers when requested, or, to the extent that such cooperation would be inconsistent with the laws of such country or with extradition treaties to which such country is a party, whether the government of that country is taking all appropriate measures to modify or replace such laws and treaties so as to permit such cooperation.

"(vii) Whether the government of that country is assisting in international investigations of transnational trafficking networks and in other cooperative efforts to combat severe forms of trafficking in persons.

"(viii) Whether the government of that country refrains from prosecuting victims of severe forms of trafficking in persons due to such victims having been trafficked, and refrains from other discriminatory treatment of such victims.

"(ix) Whether the government of that country recognizes the rights of victims of severe forms of trafficking in persons and ensures their access to justice.

"(C) Such other information relating to trafficking in persons as the Secretary of State considers appropriate.

"(2) In compiling data and making assessments for the purposes of paragraph (1), United States diplomatic mission personnel shall consult with human rights organizations and other appropriate nongovernmental organizations.".

(b) COUNTRIES RECEIVING SECURITY ASSISTANCE.—Section 502B of the Foreign Assistance Act of 1961 (22 U.S.C. 2304) is amended by adding at the end the following new subsection:

"(h)(1) The report required by subsection (b) shall include the following:

"(A) A description of the nature and extent of severe forms of trafficking in persons, as defined in section 103 of the Trafficking Victims Protection Act of 2000, in each foreign country.

"(B) With respect to each country that is a country of origin, transit, or destination for victims of severe forms of trafficking in persons, an assessment of the efforts by the government of that country to combat such trafficking. The assessment shall address the following:

"(i) Whether government authorities in that country participate in, facilitate, or condone such trafficking.

"(ii) Which government authorities in that country are involved in activities to combat such trafficking.

"(iii) What steps the government of that country has taken to prohibit government officials from participating in, facilitating, or condoning such trafficking, including the investigation, prosecution, and conviction of such officials.

"(iv) What steps the government of that country has taken to prohibit other individuals from participating in such trafficking, including the investigation, prosecution, and conviction of individuals involved in severe forms of trafficking in persons, the criminal and civil penalties for such trafficking, and the efficacy of those penalties in eliminating or reducing such trafficking.

"(v) What steps the government of that country has taken to assist victims of such trafficking, including efforts to prevent victims from being further victimized by traffickers, government officials, or others, grants of relief from deportation, and provision of humanitarian relief, including provision of mental and physical health care and shelter.

"(vi) Whether the government of that country is cooperating with governments of other countries to extradite traffickers when requested, or, to the extent that such cooperation would be inconsistent with the laws of such country or with extradition treaties to which such country is a party, whether the government of that country is taking

PUBLIC LAW 106–386—OCT. 28, 2000   114 STAT. 1473

all appropriate measures to modify or replace such laws and treaties so as to permit such cooperation.

"(vii) Whether the government of that country is assisting in international investigations of transnational trafficking networks and in other cooperative efforts to combat severe forms of trafficking in persons.

"(viii) Whether the government of that country refrains from prosecuting victims of severe forms of trafficking in persons due to such victims having been trafficked, and refrains from other discriminatory treatment of such victims.

"(ix) Whether the government of that country recognizes the rights of victims of severe forms of trafficking in persons and ensures their access to justice.

"(C) Such other information relating to trafficking in persons as the Secretary of State considers appropriate.

"(2) In compiling data and making assessments for the purposes of paragraph (1), United States diplomatic mission personnel shall consult with human rights organizations and other appropriate nongovernmental organizations.".

SEC. 105. INTERAGENCY TASK FORCE TO MONITOR AND COMBAT TRAFFICKING.

22 USC 7103.

(a) ESTABLISHMENT.—The President shall establish an Interagency Task Force to Monitor and Combat Trafficking.

President.

(b) APPOINTMENT.—The President shall appoint the members of the Task Force, which shall include the Secretary of State, the Administrator of the United States Agency for International Development, the Attorney General, the Secretary of Labor, the Secretary of Health and Human Services, the Director of Central Intelligence, and such other officials as may be designated by the President.

(c) CHAIRMAN.—The Task Force shall be chaired by the Secretary of State.

(d) ACTIVITIES OF THE TASK FORCE.—The Task Force shall carry out the following activities:

(1) Coordinate the implementation of this division.

(2) Measure and evaluate progress of the United States and other countries in the areas of trafficking prevention, protection, and assistance to victims of trafficking, and prosecution and enforcement against traffickers, including the role of public corruption in facilitating trafficking. The Task Force shall have primary responsibility for assisting the Secretary of State in the preparation of the reports described in section 110.

(3) Expand interagency procedures to collect and organize data, including significant research and resource information on domestic and international trafficking. Any data collection procedures established under this subsection shall respect the confidentiality of victims of trafficking.

(4) Engage in efforts to facilitate cooperation among countries of origin, transit, and destination. Such efforts shall aim to strengthen local and regional capacities to prevent trafficking, prosecute traffickers and assist trafficking victims, and shall include initiatives to enhance cooperative efforts between destination countries and countries of origin and assist in the appropriate reintegration of stateless victims of trafficking.

(5) Examine the role of the international "sex tourism" industry in the trafficking of persons and in the sexual exploitation of women and children around the world.

(6) Engage in consultation and advocacy with governmental and nongovernmental organizations, among other entities, to advance the purposes of this division.

(e) SUPPORT FOR THE TASK FORCE.—The Secretary of State is authorized to establish within the Department of State an Office to Monitor and Combat Trafficking, which shall provide assistance to the Task Force. Any such Office shall be headed by a Director. The Director shall have the primary responsibility for assisting the Secretary of State in carrying out the purposes of this division and may have additional responsibilities as determined by the Secretary. The Director shall consult with nongovernmental organizations and multilateral organizations, and with trafficking victims or other affected persons. The Director shall have the authority to take evidence in public hearings or by other means. The agencies represented on the Task Force are authorized to provide staff to the Office on a nonreimbursable basis.

22 USC 7104.

SEC. 106. PREVENTION OF TRAFFICKING.

(a) ECONOMIC ALTERNATIVES TO PREVENT AND DETER TRAFFICKING.—The President shall establish and carry out international initiatives to enhance economic opportunity for potential victims of trafficking as a method to deter trafficking. Such initiatives may include—

(1) microcredit lending programs, training in business development, skills training, and job counseling;

(2) programs to promote women's participation in economic decisionmaking;

(3) programs to keep children, especially girls, in elementary and secondary schools, and to educate persons who have been victims of trafficking;

(4) development of educational curricula regarding the dangers of trafficking; and

(5) grants to nongovernmental organizations to accelerate and advance the political, economic, social, and educational roles and capacities of women in their countries.

(b) PUBLIC AWARENESS AND INFORMATION.—The President, acting through the Secretary of Labor, the Secretary of Health and Human Services, the Attorney General, and the Secretary of State, shall establish and carry out programs to increase public awareness, particularly among potential victims of trafficking, of the dangers of trafficking and the protections that are available for victims of trafficking.

(c) CONSULTATION REQUIREMENT.—The President shall consult with appropriate nongovernmental organizations with respect to the establishment and conduct of initiatives described in subsections (a) and (b).

22 USC 7105.

SEC. 107. PROTECTION AND ASSISTANCE FOR VICTIMS OF TRAFFICKING.

(a) ASSISTANCE FOR VICTIMS IN OTHER COUNTRIES.—

(1) IN GENERAL.—The Secretary of State and the Administrator of the United States Agency for International Development, in consultation with appropriate nongovernmental organizations, shall establish and carry out programs and initiatives in foreign countries to assist in the safe integration,

reintegration, or resettlement, as appropriate, of victims of trafficking. Such programs and initiatives shall be designed to meet the appropriate assistance needs of such persons and their children, as identified by the Task Force.

(2) ADDITIONAL REQUIREMENT.—In establishing and conducting programs and initiatives described in paragraph (1), the Secretary of State and the Administrator of the United States Agency for International Development shall take all appropriate steps to enhance cooperative efforts among foreign countries, including countries of origin of victims of trafficking, to assist in the integration, reintegration, or resettlement, as appropriate, of victims of trafficking, including stateless victims.

(b) VICTIMS IN THE UNITED STATES.—

(1) ASSISTANCE.—

(A) ELIGIBILITY FOR BENEFITS AND SERVICES.—Notwithstanding title IV of the Personal Responsibility and Work Opportunity Reconciliation Act of 1996, an alien who is a victim of a severe form of trafficking in persons shall be eligible for benefits and services under any Federal or State program or activity funded or administered by any official or agency described in subparagraph (B) to the same extent as an alien who is admitted to the United States as a refugee under section 207 of the Immigration and Nationality Act.

(B) REQUIREMENT TO EXPAND BENEFITS AND SERVICES.—Subject to subparagraph (C) and, in the case of nonentitlement programs, to the availability of appropriations, the Secretary of Health and Human Services, the Secretary of Labor, the Board of Directors of the Legal Services Corporation, and the heads of other Federal agencies shall expand benefits and services to victims of severe forms of trafficking in persons in the United States, without regard to the immigration status of such victims.

(C) DEFINITION OF VICTIM OF A SEVERE FORM OF TRAFFICKING IN PERSONS.—For the purposes of this paragraph, the term "victim of a severe form of trafficking in persons" means only a person—

(i) who has been subjected to an act or practice described in section 103(8) as in effect on the date of the enactment of this Act; and

(ii)(I) who has not attained 18 years of age; or

(II) who is the subject of a certification under subparagraph (E).

(D) ANNUAL REPORT.—Not later than December 31 of each year, the Secretary of Health and Human Services, in consultation with the Secretary of Labor, the Board of Directors of the Legal Services Corporation, and the heads of other appropriate Federal agencies shall submit a report, which includes information on the number of persons who received benefits or other services under this paragraph in connection with programs or activities funded or administered by such agencies or officials during the preceding fiscal year, to the Committee on Ways and Means, the Committee on International Relations, and the Committee on the Judiciary of the House of Representatives and the Committee on Finance, the Committee on Foreign

Deadline.

Relations, and the Committee on the Judiciary of the Senate.

(E) CERTIFICATION.—

(i) IN GENERAL.—Subject to clause (ii), the certification referred to in subparagraph (C) is a certification by the Secretary of Health and Human Services, after consultation with the Attorney General, that the person referred to in subparagraph (C)(ii)(II)—

(I) is willing to assist in every reasonable way in the investigation and prosecution of severe forms of trafficking in persons; and

(II)(aa) has made a bona fide application for a visa under section 101(a)(15)(T) of the Immigration and Nationality Act, as added by subsection (e), that has not been denied; or

(bb) is a person whose continued presence in the United States the Attorney General is ensuring in order to effectuate prosecution of traffickers in persons.

(ii) PERIOD OF EFFECTIVENESS.—A certification referred to in subparagraph (C), with respect to a person described in clause (i)(II)(bb), shall be effective only for so long as the Attorney General determines that the continued presence of such person is necessary to effectuate prosecution of traffickers in persons.

(iii) INVESTIGATION AND PROSECUTION DEFINED.— For the purpose of a certification under this subparagraph, the term "investigation and prosecution" includes—

(I) identification of a person or persons who have committed severe forms of trafficking in persons;

(II) location and apprehension of such persons; and

(III) testimony at proceedings against such persons.

(2) GRANTS.—

(A) IN GENERAL.—Subject to the availability of appropriations, the Attorney General may make grants to States, Indian tribes, units of local government, and nonprofit, nongovernmental victims' service organizations to develop, expand, or strengthen victim service programs for victims of trafficking.

(B) ALLOCATION OF GRANT FUNDS.—Of amounts made available for grants under this paragraph, there shall be set aside—

(i) three percent for research, evaluation, and statistics;

(ii) two percent for training and technical assistance; and

(iii) one percent for management and administration.

(C) LIMITATION ON FEDERAL SHARE.—The Federal share of a grant made under this paragraph may not exceed 75 percent of the total costs of the projects described in the application submitted.

PUBLIC LAW 106–386—OCT. 28, 2000   114 STAT. 1477

(c) TRAFFICKING VICTIM REGULATIONS.—Not later than 180 days Deadline. after the date of the enactment of this Act, the Attorney General and the Secretary of State shall promulgate regulations for law enforcement personnel, immigration officials, and Department of State officials to implement the following:

(1) PROTECTIONS WHILE IN CUSTODY.—Victims of severe forms of trafficking, while in the custody of the Federal Government and to the extent practicable, shall—

(A) not be detained in facilities inappropriate to their status as crime victims;

(B) receive necessary medical care and other assistance; and

(C) be provided protection if a victim's safety is at risk or if there is danger of additional harm by recapture of the victim by a trafficker, including—

(i) taking measures to protect trafficked persons and their family members from intimidation and threats of reprisals and reprisals from traffickers and their associates; and

(ii) ensuring that the names and identifying information of trafficked persons and their family members are not disclosed to the public.

(2) ACCESS TO INFORMATION.—Victims of severe forms of trafficking shall have access to information about their rights and translation services.

(3) AUTHORITY TO PERMIT CONTINUED PRESENCE IN THE UNITED STATES.—Federal law enforcement officials may permit an alien individual's continued presence in the United States, if after an assessment, it is determined that such individual is a victim of a severe form of trafficking and a potential witness to such trafficking, in order to effectuate prosecution of those responsible, and such officials in investigating and prosecuting traffickers shall protect the safety of trafficking victims, including taking measures to protect trafficked persons and their family members from intimidation, threats of reprisals, and reprisals from traffickers and their associates.

(4) TRAINING OF GOVERNMENT PERSONNEL.—Appropriate personnel of the Department of State and the Department of Justice shall be trained in identifying victims of severe forms of trafficking and providing for the protection of such victims.

(d) CONSTRUCTION.—Nothing in subsection (c) shall be construed as creating any private cause of action against the United States or its officers or employees.

(e) PROTECTION FROM REMOVAL FOR CERTAIN CRIME VICTIMS.—

(1) IN GENERAL.—Section 101(a)(15) of the Immigration and Nationality Act (8 U.S.C. 1101(a)(15)) is amended—

(A) by striking "or" at the end of subparagraph (R);

(B) by striking the period at the end of subparagraph (S) and inserting "; or"; and

(C) by adding at the end the following new subparagraph:

"(T)(i) subject to section 214(n), an alien who the Attorney General determines—

"(I) is or has been a victim of a severe form of trafficking in persons, as defined in section 103 of the Trafficking Victims Protection Act of 2000,

"(II) is physically present in the United States, American Samoa, or the Commonwealth of the Northern Mariana Islands, or at a port of entry thereto, on account of such trafficking,
"(III)(aa) has complied with any reasonable request for assistance in the investigation or prosecution of acts of trafficking, or
"(bb) has not attained 15 years of age, and
"(IV) the alien would suffer extreme hardship involving unusual and severe harm upon removal; and
"(ii) if the Attorney General considers it necessary to avoid extreme hardship—
"(I) in the case of an alien described in clause (i) who is under 21 years of age, the spouse, children, and parents of such alien; and
"(II) in the case of an alien described in clause (i) who is 21 years of age or older, the spouse and children of such alien,
if accompanying, or following to join, the alien described in clause (i).".

(2) CONDITIONS OF NONIMMIGRANT STATUS.—Section 214 of the Immigration and Nationality Act (8 U.S.C. 1184) is amended—
(A) by redesignating the subsection (l) added by section 625(a) of the Illegal Immigration Reform and Immigrant Responsibility Act of 1996 (Public Law 104–208; 110 Stat. 3009–1820) as subsection (m); and
(B) by adding at the end the following:
"(n)(1) No alien shall be eligible for admission to the United States under section 101(a)(15)(T) if there is substantial reason to believe that the alien has committed an act of a severe form of trafficking in persons (as defined in section 103 of the Trafficking Victims Protection Act of 2000).
"(2) The total number of aliens who may be issued visas or otherwise provided nonimmigrant status during any fiscal year under section 101(a)(15)(T) may not exceed 5,000.
"(3) The numerical limitation of paragraph (2) shall only apply to principal aliens and not to the spouses, sons, daughters, or parents of such aliens.".

(3) WAIVER OF GROUNDS FOR INELIGIBILITY FOR ADMISSION.—Section 212(d) of the Immigration and Nationality Act (8 U.S.C. 1182(d)) is amended by adding at the end the following:
"(13)(A) The Attorney General shall determine whether a ground for inadmissibility exists with respect to a nonimmigrant described in section 101(a)(15)(T).
"(B) In addition to any other waiver that may be available under this section, in the case of a nonimmigrant described in section 101(a)(15)(T), if the Attorney General considers it to be in the national interest to do so, the Attorney General, in the Attorney General's discretion, may waive the application of—
"(i) paragraphs (1) and (4) of subsection (a); and
"(ii) any other provision of such subsection (excluding paragraphs (3), (10)(C), and (10(E)) if the activities rendering the alien inadmissible under the provision were caused by, or were incident to, the victimization described in section 101(a)(15)(T)(i)(I).".

(4) DUTIES OF THE ATTORNEY GENERAL WITH RESPECT TO "T" VISA NONIMMIGRANTS.—Section 101 of the Immigration and Nationality Act (8 U.S.C. 1101) is amended by adding at the end the following new subsection:

"(i) With respect to each nonimmigrant alien described in subsection (a)(15)(T)(i)—

"(1) the Attorney General and other Government officials, where appropriate, shall provide the alien with a referral to a nongovernmental organization that would advise the alien regarding the alien's options while in the United States and the resources available to the alien; and

"(2) the Attorney General shall, during the period the alien is in lawful temporary resident status under that subsection, grant the alien authorization to engage in employment in the United States and provide the alien with an 'employment authorized' endorsement or other appropriate work permit.".

(5) STATUTORY CONSTRUCTION.—Nothing in this section, or in the amendments made by this section, shall be construed as prohibiting the Attorney General from instituting removal proceedings under section 240 of the Immigration and Nationality Act (8 U.S.C. 1229a) against an alien admitted as a nonimmigrant under section 101(a)(15)(T)(i) of that Act, as added by subsection (e), for conduct committed after the alien's admission into the United States, or for conduct or a condition that was not disclosed to the Attorney General prior to the alien's admission as a nonimmigrant under such section 101(a)(15)(T)(i).

(f) ADJUSTMENT TO PERMANENT RESIDENT STATUS.—Section 245 of such Act (8 U.S.C 1255) is amended by adding at the end the following new subsection:

"(l)(1) If, in the opinion of the Attorney General, a nonimmigrant admitted into the United States under section 101(a)(15)(T)(i)—

"(A) has been physically present in the United States for a continuous period of at least 3 years since the date of admission as a nonimmigrant under section 101(a)(15)(T)(i),

"(B) has, throughout such period, been a person of good moral character, and

"(C)(i) has, during such period, complied with any reasonable request for assistance in the investigation or prosecution of acts of trafficking, or

"(ii) the alien would suffer extreme hardship involving unusual and severe harm upon removal from the United States, the Attorney General may adjust the status of the alien (and any person admitted under that section as the spouse, parent, or child of the alien) to that of an alien lawfully admitted for permanent residence.

"(2) Paragraph (1) shall not apply to an alien admitted under section 101(a)(15)(T) who is inadmissible to the United States by reason of a ground that has not been waived under section 212, except that, if the Attorney General considers it to be in the national interest to do so, the Attorney General, in the Attorney General's discretion, may waive the application of—

"(A) paragraphs (1) and (4) of section 212(a); and

"(B) any other provision of such section (excluding paragraphs (3), (10)(C), and (10(E)), if the activities rendering the alien inadmissible under the provision were caused by, or were incident to, the victimization described in section 101(a)(15)(T)(i)(I).

"(2) An alien shall be considered to have failed to maintain continuous physical presence in the United States under paragraph (1)(A) if the alien has departed from the United States for any period in excess of 90 days or for any periods in the aggregate exceeding 180 days.

"(3)(A) The total number of aliens whose status may be adjusted under paragraph (1) during any fiscal year may not exceed 5,000.

"(B) The numerical limitation of subparagraph (A) shall only apply to principal aliens and not to the spouses, sons, daughters, or parents of such aliens.

"(4) Upon the approval of adjustment of status under paragraph (1), the Attorney General shall record the alien's lawful admission for permanent residence as of the date of such approval.".

(g) ANNUAL REPORTS.—On or before October 31 of each year, the Attorney General shall submit a report to the appropriate congressional committees setting forth, with respect to the preceding fiscal year, the number, if any, of otherwise eligible applicants who did not receive visas under section 101(a)(15)(T) of the Immigration and Nationality Act, as added by subsection (e), or who were unable to adjust their status under section 245(l) of such Act, solely on account of the unavailability of visas due to a limitation imposed by section 214(n)(1) or 245(l)(4)(A) of such Act.

22 USC 7106.

SEC. 108. MINIMUM STANDARDS FOR THE ELIMINATION OF TRAFFICKING.

(a) MINIMUM STANDARDS.—For purposes of this division, the minimum standards for the elimination of trafficking applicable to the government of a country of origin, transit, or destination for a significant number of victims of severe forms of trafficking are the following:

(1) The government of the country should prohibit severe forms of trafficking in persons and punish acts of such trafficking.

(2) For the knowing commission of any act of sex trafficking involving force, fraud, coercion, or in which the victim of sex trafficking is a child incapable of giving meaningful consent, or of trafficking which includes rape or kidnapping or which causes a death, the government of the country should prescribe punishment commensurate with that for grave crimes, such as forcible sexual assault.

(3) For the knowing commission of any act of a severe form of trafficking in persons, the government of the country should prescribe punishment that is sufficiently stringent to deter and that adequately reflects the heinous nature of the offense.

(4) The government of the country should make serious and sustained efforts to eliminate severe forms of trafficking in persons.

(b) CRITERIA.—In determinations under subsection (a)(4), the following factors should be considered as indicia of serious and sustained efforts to eliminate severe forms of trafficking in persons:

(1) Whether the government of the country vigorously investigates and prosecutes acts of severe forms of trafficking

in persons that take place wholly or partly within the territory of the country.

(2) Whether the government of the country protects victims of severe forms of trafficking in persons and encourages their assistance in the investigation and prosecution of such trafficking, including provisions for legal alternatives to their removal to countries in which they would face retribution or hardship, and ensures that victims are not inappropriately incarcerated, fined, or otherwise penalized solely for unlawful acts as a direct result of being trafficked.

(3) Whether the government of the country has adopted measures to prevent severe forms of trafficking in persons, such as measures to inform and educate the public, including potential victims, about the causes and consequences of severe forms of trafficking in persons.

(4) Whether the government of the country cooperates with other governments in the investigation and prosecution of severe forms of trafficking in persons.

(5) Whether the government of the country extradites persons charged with acts of severe forms of trafficking in persons on substantially the same terms and to substantially the same extent as persons charged with other serious crimes (or, to the extent such extradition would be inconsistent with the laws of such country or with international agreements to which the country is a party, whether the government is taking all appropriate measures to modify or replace such laws and treaties so as to permit such extradition).

(6) Whether the government of the country monitors immigration and emigration patterns for evidence of severe forms of trafficking in persons and whether law enforcement agencies of the country respond to any such evidence in a manner that is consistent with the vigorous investigation and prosecution of acts of such trafficking, as well as with the protection of human rights of victims and the internationally recognized human right to leave any country, including one's own, and to return to one's own country.

(7) Whether the government of the country vigorously investigates and prosecutes public officials who participate in or facilitate severe forms of trafficking in persons, and takes all appropriate measures against officials who condone such trafficking.

SEC. 109. ASSISTANCE TO FOREIGN COUNTRIES TO MEET MINIMUM STANDARDS.

Chapter 1 of part I of the Foreign Assistance Act of 1961 (22 U.S.C. 2151 et seq.) is amended by adding at the end the following new section:

"SEC. 134. ASSISTANCE TO FOREIGN COUNTRIES TO MEET MINIMUM STANDARDS FOR THE ELIMINATION OF TRAFFICKING.   22 USC 2152d.

"(a) AUTHORIZATION.—The President is authorized to provide assistance to foreign countries directly, or through nongovernmental and multilateral organizations, for programs, projects, and activities designed to meet the minimum standards for the elimination of trafficking (as defined in section 103 of the Trafficking Victims Protection Act of 2000), including—

"(1) the drafting of laws to prohibit and punish acts of trafficking;

"(2) the investigation and prosecution of traffickers;

"(3) the creation and maintenance of facilities, programs, projects, and activities for the protection of victims; and

"(4) the expansion of exchange programs and international visitor programs for governmental and nongovernmental personnel to combat trafficking.

"(b) FUNDING.—Amounts made available to carry out the other provisions of this part (including chapter 4 of part II of this Act) and the Support for East European Democracy (SEED) Act of 1989 shall be made available to carry out this section.".

22 USC 7107.

SEC. 110. ACTIONS AGAINST GOVERNMENTS FAILING TO MEET MINIMUM STANDARDS.

(a) STATEMENT OF POLICY.—It is the policy of the United States not to provide nonhumanitarian, nontrade-related foreign assistance to any government that—

(1) does not comply with minimum standards for the elimination of trafficking; and

(2) is not making significant efforts to bring itself into compliance with such standards.

(b) REPORTS TO CONGRESS.—

Deadline.

(1) ANNUAL REPORT.—Not later than June 1 of each year, the Secretary of State shall submit to the appropriate congressional committees a report with respect to the status of severe forms of trafficking in persons that shall include—

(A) a list of those countries, if any, to which the minimum standards for the elimination of trafficking are applicable and whose governments fully comply with such standards;

(B) a list of those countries, if any, to which the minimum standards for the elimination of trafficking are applicable and whose governments do not yet fully comply with such standards but are making significant efforts to bring themselves into compliance; and

(C) a list of those countries, if any, to which the minimum standards for the elimination of trafficking are applicable and whose governments do not fully comply with such standards and are not making significant efforts to bring themselves into compliance.

(2) INTERIM REPORTS.—In addition to the annual report under paragraph (1), the Secretary of State may submit to the appropriate congressional committees at any time one or more interim reports with respect to the status of severe forms of trafficking in persons, including information about countries whose governments—

(A) have come into or out of compliance with the minimum standards for the elimination of trafficking; or

(B) have begun or ceased to make significant efforts to bring themselves into compliance,

since the transmission of the last annual report.

(3) SIGNIFICANT EFFORTS.—In determinations under paragraph (1) or (2) as to whether the government of a country is making significant efforts to bring itself into compliance with the minimum standards for the elimination of trafficking, the Secretary of State shall consider—

(A) the extent to which the country is a country of origin, transit, or destination for severe forms of trafficking;

PUBLIC LAW 106–386—OCT. 28, 2000   114 STAT. 1483

(B) the extent of noncompliance with the minimum standards by the government and, particularly, the extent to which officials or employees of the government have participated in, facilitated, condoned, or are otherwise complicit in severe forms of trafficking; and

(C) what measures are reasonable to bring the government into compliance with the minimum standards in light of the resources and capabilities of the government.

(c) NOTIFICATION.—Not less than 45 days or more than 90 days after the submission, on or after January 1, 2003, of an annual report under subsection (b)(1), or an interim report under subsection (b)(2), the President shall submit to the appropriate congressional committees a notification of one of the determinations listed in subsection (d) with respect to each foreign country whose government, according to such report— *Deadline.*

(A) does not comply with the minimum standards for the elimination of trafficking; and

(B) is not making significant efforts to bring itself into compliance, as described in subsection (b)(1)(C).

(d) PRESIDENTIAL DETERMINATIONS.—The determinations referred to in subsection (c) are the following:

(1) WITHHOLDING OF NONHUMANITARIAN, NONTRADE-RELATED ASSISTANCE.—The President has determined that— *President.*

(A)(i) the United States will not provide nonhumanitarian, nontrade-related foreign assistance to the government of the country for the subsequent fiscal year until such government complies with the minimum standards or makes significant efforts to bring itself into compliance; or

(ii) in the case of a country whose government received no nonhumanitarian, nontrade-related foreign assistance from the United States during the previous fiscal year, the United States will not provide funding for participation by officials or employees of such governments in educational and cultural exchange programs for the subsequent fiscal year until such government complies with the minimum standards or makes significant efforts to bring itself into compliance; and

(B) the President will instruct the United States Executive Director of each multilateral development bank and of the International Monetary Fund to vote against, and to use the Executive Director's best efforts to deny, any loan or other utilization of the funds of the respective institution (other than for humanitarian assistance, for trade-related assistance, or for development assistance which directly addresses basic human needs, is not administered by the government of the sanctioned country, and confers no benefit to that government) for the subsequent fiscal year until such government complies with the minimum standards or makes significant efforts to bring itself into compliance.

(2) ONGOING, MULTIPLE, BROAD-BASED RESTRICTIONS ON ASSISTANCE IN RESPONSE TO HUMAN RIGHTS VIOLATIONS.—The President has determined that such country is already subject to multiple, broad-based restrictions on assistance imposed in significant part in response to human rights abuses and such restrictions are ongoing and are comparable to the restrictions

provided in paragraph (1). Such determination shall be accompanied by a description of the specific restriction or restrictions that were the basis for making such determination.

(3) SUBSEQUENT COMPLIANCE.—The Secretary of State has determined that the government of the country has come into compliance with the minimum standards or is making significant efforts to bring itself into compliance.

(4) CONTINUATION OF ASSISTANCE IN THE NATIONAL INTEREST.—Notwithstanding the failure of the government of the country to comply with minimum standards for the elimination of trafficking and to make significant efforts to bring itself into compliance, the President has determined that the provision to the country of nonhumanitarian, nontrade-related foreign assistance, or the multilateral assistance described in paragraph (1)(B), or both, would promote the purposes of this division or is otherwise in the national interest of the United States.

(5) EXERCISE OF WAIVER AUTHORITY.—

(A) IN GENERAL.—The President may exercise the authority under paragraph (4) with respect to—

(i) all nonhumanitarian, nontrade-related foreign assistance to a country;

(ii) all multilateral assistance described in paragraph (1)(B) to a country; or

(iii) one or more programs, projects, or activities of such assistance.

(B) AVOIDANCE OF SIGNIFICANT ADVERSE EFFECTS.—

President. The President shall exercise the authority under paragraph (4) when necessary to avoid significant adverse effects on vulnerable populations, including women and children.

(6) DEFINITION OF MULTILATERAL DEVELOPMENT BANK.—In this subsection, the term "multilateral development bank" refers to any of the following institutions: the International Bank for Reconstruction and Development, the International Development Association, the International Finance Corporation, the Inter-American Development Bank, the Asian Development Bank, the Inter-American Investment Corporation, the African Development Bank, the African Development Fund, the European Bank for Reconstruction and Development, and the Multilateral Investment Guaranty Agency.

President. (e) CERTIFICATION.—Together with any notification under subsection (c), the President shall provide a certification by the Secretary of State that, with respect to any assistance described in clause (ii), (iii), or (v) of section 103(7)(A), or with respect to any assistance described in section 103(7)(B), no assistance is intended to be received or used by any agency or official who has participated in, facilitated, or condoned a severe form of trafficking in persons.

22 USC 7108. **SEC. 111. ACTIONS AGAINST SIGNIFICANT TRAFFICKERS IN PERSONS.**

(a) AUTHORITY TO SANCTION SIGNIFICANT TRAFFICKERS IN PERSONS.—

(1) IN GENERAL.—The President may exercise the authorities set forth in section 203 of the International Emergency Economic Powers Act (50 U.S.C. 1701) without regard to section 202 of that Act (50 U.S.C. 1701) in the case of any of the following persons:

PUBLIC LAW 106–386—OCT. 28, 2000   114 STAT. 1485

(A) Any foreign person that plays a significant role in a severe form of trafficking in persons, directly or indirectly in the United States.

(B) Foreign persons that materially assist in, or provide financial or technological support for or to, or provide goods or services in support of, activities of a significant foreign trafficker in persons identified pursuant to subparagraph (A).

(C) Foreign persons that are owned, controlled, or directed by, or acting for or on behalf of, a significant foreign trafficker identified pursuant to subparagraph (A).

(2) PENALTIES.—The penalties set forth in section 206 of the International Emergency Economic Powers Act (50 U.S.C. 1705) apply to violations of any license, order, or regulation issued under this section.

(b) REPORT TO CONGRESS ON IDENTIFICATION AND SANCTIONING OF SIGNIFICANT TRAFFICKERS IN PERSONS.—

(1) IN GENERAL.—Upon exercising the authority of subsection (a), the President shall report to the appropriate congressional committees— President.

(A) identifying publicly the foreign persons that the President determines are appropriate for sanctions pursuant to this section and the basis for such determination; and

(B) detailing publicly the sanctions imposed pursuant to this section.

(2) REMOVAL OF SANCTIONS.—Upon suspending or terminating any action imposed under the authority of subsection (a), the President shall report to the committees described in paragraph (1) on such suspension or termination. President.

(3) SUBMISSION OF CLASSIFIED INFORMATION.—Reports submitted under this subsection may include an annex with classified information regarding the basis for the determination made by the President under paragraph (1)(A).

(c) LAW ENFORCEMENT AND INTELLIGENCE ACTIVITIES NOT AFFECTED.—Nothing in this section prohibits or otherwise limits the authorized law enforcement or intelligence activities of the United States, or the law enforcement activities of any State or subdivision thereof.

(d) EXCLUSION OF PERSONS WHO HAVE BENEFITED FROM ILLICIT ACTIVITIES OF TRAFFICKERS IN PERSONS.—Section 212(a)(2) of the Immigration and Nationality Act (8 U.S.C. 1182(a)(2)) is amended by inserting at the end the following new subparagraph:

"(H) SIGNIFICANT TRAFFICKERS IN PERSONS.—

"(i) IN GENERAL.—Any alien who is listed in a report submitted pursuant to section 111(b) of the Trafficking Victims Protection Act of 2000, or who the consular officer or the Attorney General knows or has reason to believe is or has been a knowing aider, abettor, assister, conspirator, or colluder with such a trafficker in severe forms of trafficking in persons, as defined in the section 103 of such Act, is inadmissible.

"(ii) BENEFICIARIES OF TRAFFICKING.—Except as provided in clause (iii), any alien who the consular officer or the Attorney General knows or has reason to believe is the spouse, son, or daughter of an alien

114 STAT. 1486   PUBLIC LAW 106–386—OCT. 28, 2000

inadmissible under clause (i), has, within the previous 5 years, obtained any financial or other benefit from the illicit activity of that alien, and knew or reasonably should have known that the financial or other benefit was the product of such illicit activity, is inadmissible.

"(iii) EXCEPTION FOR CERTAIN SONS AND DAUGHTERS.—Clause (ii) shall not apply to a son or daughter who was a child at the time he or she received the benefit described in such clause.".

(e) IMPLEMENTATION.—

(1) DELEGATION OF AUTHORITY.—The President may delegate any authority granted by this section, including the authority to designate foreign persons under paragraphs (1)(B) and (1)(C) of subsection (a).

(2) PROMULGATION OF RULES AND REGULATIONS.—The head of any agency, including the Secretary of Treasury, is authorized to take such actions as may be necessary to carry out any authority delegated by the President pursuant to paragraph (1), including promulgating rules and regulations.

(3) OPPORTUNITY FOR REVIEW.—Such rules and regulations shall include procedures affording an opportunity for a person to be heard in an expeditious manner, either in person or through a representative, for the purpose of seeking changes to or termination of any determination, order, designation or other action associated with the exercise of the authority in subsection (a).

(f) DEFINITION OF FOREIGN PERSONS.—In this section, the term "foreign person" means any citizen or national of a foreign state or any entity not organized under the laws of the United States, including a foreign government official, but does not include a foreign state.

(g) CONSTRUCTION.—Nothing in this section shall be construed as precluding judicial review of the exercise of the authority described in subsection (a).

22 USC 7109.   **SEC. 112. STRENGTHENING PROSECUTION AND PUNISHMENT OF TRAFFICKERS.**

(a) TITLE 18 AMENDMENTS.—Chapter 77 of title 18, United States Code, is amended—

(1) in each of sections 1581(a), 1583, and 1584—

(A) by striking "10 years" and inserting "20 years"; and

(B) by adding at the end the following: "If death results from the violation of this section, or if the violation includes kidnapping or an attempt to kidnap, aggravated sexual abuse or the attempt to commit aggravated sexual abuse, or an attempt to kill, the defendant shall be fined under this title or imprisoned for any term of years or life, or both.";

(2) by inserting at the end the following:

"§ 1589. Forced labor

"Whoever knowingly provides or obtains the labor or services of a person—

"(1) by threats of serious harm to, or physical restraint against, that person or another person;

"(2) by means of any scheme, plan, or pattern intended to cause the person to believe that, if the person did not perform such labor or services, that person or another person would suffer serious harm or physical restraint; or

"(3) by means of the abuse or threatened abuse of law or the legal process,

shall be fined under this title or imprisoned not more than 20 years, or both. If death results from the violation of this section, or if the violation includes kidnapping or an attempt to kidnap, aggravated sexual abuse or the attempt to commit aggravated sexual abuse, or an attempt to kill, the defendant shall be fined under this title or imprisoned for any term of years or life, or both.

"§ 1590. Trafficking with respect to peonage, slavery, involuntary servitude, or forced labor

"Whoever knowingly recruits, harbors, transports, provides, or obtains by any means, any person for labor or services in violation of this chapter shall be fined under this title or imprisoned not more than 20 years, or both. If death results from the violation of this section, or if the violation includes kidnapping or an attempt to kidnap, aggravated sexual abuse, or the attempt to commit aggravated sexual abuse, or an attempt to kill, the defendant shall be fined under this title or imprisoned for any term of years or life, or both.

"§ 1591. Sex trafficking of children or by force, fraud or coercion

"(a) Whoever knowingly—

"(1) in or affecting interstate commerce, recruits, entices, harbors, transports, provides, or obtains by any means a person; or

"(2) benefits, financially or by receiving anything of value, from participation in a venture which has engaged in an act described in violation of paragraph (1),

knowing that force, fraud, or coercion described in subsection (c)(2) will be used to cause the person to engage in a commercial sex act, or that the person has not attained the age of 18 years and will be caused to engage in a commercial sex act, shall be punished as provided in subsection (b).

"(b) The punishment for an offense under subsection (a) is—

"(1) if the offense was effected by force, fraud, or coercion or if the person transported had not attained the age of 14 years at the time of such offense, by a fine under this title or imprisonment for any term of years or for life, or both; or

"(2) if the offense was not so effected, and the person transported had attained the age of 14 years but had not attained the age of 18 years at the time of such offense, by a fine under this title or imprisonment for not more than 20 years, or both.

"(c) In this section:

"(1) The term 'commercial sex act' means any sex act, on account of which anything of value is given to or received by any person.

"(2) The term 'coercion' means—

"(A) threats of serious harm to or physical restraint against any person;

"(B) any scheme, plan, or pattern intended to cause a person to believe that failure to perform an act would result in serious harm to or physical restraint against any person; or

"(C) the abuse or threatened abuse of law or the legal process.

"(3) The term 'venture' means any group of two or more individuals associated in fact, whether or not a legal entity.

"§ 1592. Unlawful conduct with respect to documents in furtherance of trafficking, peonage, slavery, involuntary servitude, or forced labor

"(a) Whoever knowingly destroys, conceals, removes, confiscates, or possesses any actual or purported passport or other immigration document, or any other actual or purported government identification document, of another person—

"(1) in the course of a violation of section 1581, 1583, 1584, 1589, 1590, 1591, or 1594(a);

"(2) with intent to violate section 1581, 1583, 1584, 1589, 1590, or 1591; or

"(3) to prevent or restrict or to attempt to prevent or restrict, without lawful authority, the person's liberty to move or travel, in order to maintain the labor or services of that person, when the person is or has been a victim of a severe form of trafficking in persons, as defined in section 103 of the Trafficking Victims Protection Act of 2000,

shall be fined under this title or imprisoned for not more than 5 years, or both.

"(b) Subsection (a) does not apply to the conduct of a person who is or has been a victim of a severe form of trafficking in persons, as defined in section 103 of the Trafficking Victims Protection Act of 2000, if that conduct is caused by, or incident to, that trafficking.

"§ 1593. Mandatory restitution

"(a) Notwithstanding section 3663 or 3663A, and in addition to any other civil or criminal penalties authorized by law, the court shall order restitution for any offense under this chapter.

"(b)(1) The order of restitution under this section shall direct the defendant to pay the victim (through the appropriate court mechanism) the full amount of the victim's losses, as determined by the court under paragraph (3) of this subsection.

"(2) An order of restitution under this section shall be issued and enforced in accordance with section 3664 in the same manner as an order under section 3663A.

"(3) As used in this subsection, the term 'full amount of the victim's losses' has the same meaning as provided in section 2259(b)(3) and shall in addition include the greater of the gross income or value to the defendant of the victim's services or labor or the value of the victim's labor as guaranteed under the minimum wage and overtime guarantees of the Fair Labor Standards Act (29 U.S.C. 201 et seq.).

"(c) As used in this section, the term 'victim' means the individual harmed as a result of a crime under this chapter, including, in the case of a victim who is under 18 years of age, incompetent, incapacitated, or deceased, the legal guardian of the victim or a representative of the victim's estate, or another family member, or any other person appointed as suitable by the court, but in no event shall the defendant be named such representative or guardian.

"§ 1594. General provisions

"(a) Whoever attempts to violate section 1581, 1583, 1584, 1589, 1590, or 1591 shall be punishable in the same manner as a completed violation of that section.

"(b) The court, in imposing sentence on any person convicted of a violation of this chapter, shall order, in addition to any other sentence imposed and irrespective of any provision of State law, that such person shall forfeit to the United States—

"(1) such person's interest in any property, real or personal, that was used or intended to be used to commit or to facilitate the commission of such violation; and

"(2) any property, real or personal, constituting or derived from, any proceeds that such person obtained, directly or indirectly, as a result of such violation.

"(c)(1) The following shall be subject to forfeiture to the United States and no property right shall exist in them:

"(A) Any property, real or personal, used or intended to be used to commit or to facilitate the commission of any violation of this chapter.

"(B) Any property, real or personal, which constitutes or is derived from proceeds traceable to any violation of this chapter.

"(2) The provisions of chapter 46 of this title relating to civil forfeitures shall extend to any seizure or civil forfeiture under this subsection.

"(d) WITNESS PROTECTION.—Any violation of this chapter shall be considered an organized criminal activity or other serious offense for the purposes of application of chapter 224 (relating to witness protection)."; and

(3) by amending the table of sections at the beginning of chapter 77 by adding at the end the following new items:

"1589. Forced labor.
"1590. Trafficking with respect to peonage, slavery, involuntary servitude, or forced labor.
"1591. Sex trafficking of children or by force, fraud, or coercion.
"1592. Unlawful conduct with respect to documents in furtherance of trafficking, peonage, slavery, involuntary servitude, or forced labor.
"1593. Mandatory restitution.
"1594. General provisions.".

(b) AMENDMENT TO THE SENTENCING GUIDELINES.—

(1) Pursuant to its authority under section 994 of title 28, United States Code, and in accordance with this section, the United States Sentencing Commission shall review and, if appropriate, amend the sentencing guidelines and policy statements applicable to persons convicted of offenses involving the trafficking of persons including component or related crimes of peonage, involuntary servitude, slave trade offenses, and possession, transfer or sale of false immigration documents in furtherance of trafficking, and the Fair Labor Standards Act and the Migrant and Seasonal Agricultural Worker Protection Act.

(2) In carrying out this subsection, the Sentencing Commission shall—

(A) take all appropriate measures to ensure that these sentencing guidelines and policy statements applicable to the offenses described in paragraph (1) of this subsection are sufficiently stringent to deter and adequately reflect the heinous nature of such offenses;

(B) consider conforming the sentencing guidelines applicable to offenses involving trafficking in persons to the guidelines applicable to peonage, involuntary servitude, and slave trade offenses; and

(C) consider providing sentencing enhancements for those convicted of the offenses described in paragraph (1) of this subsection that—

(i) involve a large number of victims;

(ii) involve a pattern of continued and flagrant violations;

(iii) involve the use or threatened use of a dangerous weapon; or

(iv) result in the death or bodily injury of any person.

(3) The Commission may promulgate the guidelines or amendments under this subsection in accordance with the procedures set forth in section 21(a) of the Sentencing Act of 1987, as though the authority under that Act had not expired.

22 USC 7110.

SEC. 113. AUTHORIZATIONS OF APPROPRIATIONS.

(a) AUTHORIZATION OF APPROPRIATIONS IN SUPPORT OF THE TASK FORCE.—To carry out the purposes of sections 104, 105, and 110, there are authorized to be appropriated to the Secretary of State $1,500,000 for fiscal year 2001 and $3,000,000 for fiscal year 2002.

(b) AUTHORIZATION OF APPROPRIATIONS TO THE SECRETARY OF HEALTH AND HUMAN SERVICES.—To carry out the purposes of section 107(b), there are authorized to be appropriated to the Secretary of Health and Human Services $5,000,000 for fiscal year 2001 and $10,000,000 for fiscal year 2002.

(c) AUTHORIZATION OF APPROPRIATIONS TO THE SECRETARY OF STATE.—

(1) ASSISTANCE FOR VICTIMS IN OTHER COUNTRIES.—To carry out the purposes of section 107(a), there are authorized to be appropriated to the Secretary of State $5,000,000 for fiscal year 2001 and $10,000,000 for fiscal year 2002.

(2) VOLUNTARY CONTRIBUTIONS TO OSCE.—To carry out the purposes of section 109, there are authorized to be appropriated to the Secretary of State $300,000 for voluntary contributions to advance projects aimed at preventing trafficking, promoting respect for human rights of trafficking victims, and assisting the Organization for Security and Cooperation in Europe participating states in related legal reform for fiscal year 2001.

(3) PREPARATION OF ANNUAL COUNTRY REPORTS ON HUMAN RIGHTS.—To carry out the purposes of section 104, there are authorized to be appropriated to the Secretary of State such sums as may be necessary to include the additional information required by that section in the annual Country Reports on Human Rights Practices, including the preparation and publication of the list described in subsection (a)(1) of that section.

PUBLIC LAW 106–386—OCT. 28, 2000   114 STAT. 1491

(d) AUTHORIZATION OF APPROPRIATIONS TO ATTORNEY GEN-
ERAL.—To carry out the purposes of section 107(b), there are authorized to be appropriated to the Attorney General $5,000,000 for
fiscal year 2001 and $10,000,000 for fiscal year 2002.
(e) AUTHORIZATION OF APPROPRIATIONS TO PRESIDENT.—
(1) FOREIGN VICTIM ASSISTANCE.—To carry out the purposes
of section 106, there are authorized to be appropriated to the
President $5,000,000 for fiscal year 2001 and $10,000,000 for
fiscal year 2002.
(2) ASSISTANCE TO FOREIGN COUNTRIES TO MEET MINIMUM
STANDARDS.—To carry out the purposes of section 109, there
are authorized to be appropriated to the President $5,000,000
for fiscal year 2001 and $10,000,000 for fiscal year 2002.
(f) AUTHORIZATION OF APPROPRIATIONS TO THE SECRETARY OF
LABOR.—To carry out the purposes of section 107(b), there are
authorized to be appropriated to the Secretary of Labor $5,000,000
for fiscal year 2001 and $10,000,000 for fiscal year 2002.

DIVISION B—VIOLENCE AGAINST WOMEN ACT OF 2000

Violence Against
Women Act of
2000.

SEC. 1001. SHORT TITLE.

42 USC 13701
note.

This division may be cited as the "Violence Against Women
Act of 2000".

SEC. 1002. DEFINITIONS.

42 USC 3796gg–
2 note.

In this division—
(1) the term "domestic violence" has the meaning given
the term in section 2003 of title I of the Omnibus Crime
Control and Safe Streets Act of 1968 (42 U.S.C. 3796gg–2);
and
(2) the term "sexual assault" has the meaning given the
term in section 2003 of title I of the Omnibus Crime Control
and Safe Streets Act of 1968 (42 U.S.C. 3796gg–2).

SEC. 1003. ACCOUNTABILITY AND OVERSIGHT.

42 USC 3789p.

(a) REPORT BY GRANT RECIPIENTS.—The Attorney General or
Secretary of Health and Human Services, as applicable, shall
require grantees under any program authorized or reauthorized
by this division or an amendment made by this division to report
on the effectiveness of the activities carried out with amounts
made available to carry out that program, including number of
persons served, if applicable, numbers of persons seeking services
who could not be served and such other information as the Attorney
General or Secretary may prescribe.
(b) REPORT TO CONGRESS.—The Attorney General or Secretary
of Health and Human Services, as applicable, shall report biennially
to the Committees on the Judiciary of the House of Representatives
and the Senate on the grant programs described in subsection
(a), including the information contained in any report under that
subsection.

114 STAT. 1492   PUBLIC LAW 106–386—OCT. 28, 2000

TITLE I—STRENGTHENING LAW EN-FORCEMENT TO REDUCE VIOLENCE AGAINST WOMEN

SEC. 1101. FULL FAITH AND CREDIT ENFORCEMENT OF PROTECTION ORDERS.

(a) IN GENERAL.—Part U of title I of the Omnibus Crime Control and Safe Streets Act of 1968 (42 U.S.C. 3796hh et seq.) is amended—

    (1) in the heading, by adding "**AND ENFORCEMENT OF PROTECTION ORDERS**" at the end;

    (2) in section 2101(b)—

        (A) in paragraph (6), by inserting "(including juvenile courts)" after "courts"; and

        (B) by adding at the end the following:

"(7) To provide technical assistance and computer and other equipment to police departments, prosecutors, courts, and tribal jurisdictions to facilitate the widespread enforcement of protection orders, including interstate enforcement, enforcement between States and tribal jurisdictions, and enforcement between tribal jurisdictions."; and

    (3) in section 2102—

        (A) in subsection (b)—

            (i) in paragraph (1), by striking "and" at the end;

            (ii) in paragraph (2), by striking the period at the end and inserting ", including the enforcement of protection orders from other States and jurisdictions (including tribal jurisdictions);"; and

            (iii) by adding at the end the following:

"(3) have established cooperative agreements or can demonstrate effective ongoing collaborative arrangements with neighboring jurisdictions to facilitate the enforcement of protection orders from other States and jurisdictions (including tribal jurisdictions); and

"(4) in applications describing plans to further the purposes stated in paragraph (4) or (7) of section 2101(b), will give priority to using the grant to develop and install data collection and communication systems, including computerized systems, and training on how to use these systems effectively to link police, prosecutors, courts, and tribal jurisdictions for the purpose of identifying and tracking protection orders and violations of protection orders, in those jurisdictions where such systems do not exist or are not fully effective."; and

        (B) by adding at the end the following:

"(c) DISSEMINATION OF INFORMATION.—The Attorney General shall annually compile and broadly disseminate (including through electronic publication) information about successful data collection and communication systems that meet the purposes described in this section. Such dissemination shall target States, State and local courts, Indian tribal governments, and units of local government.".

(b) PROTECTION ORDERS.—

    (1) FILING COSTS.—Section 2006 of part T of title I of the Omnibus Crime Control and Safe Streets Act of 1968 (42 U.S.C. 3796gg–5) is amended—

42 USC 3796hh.

42 USC 3796hh–1.

(A) in the heading, by striking "FILING" and inserting "AND PROTECTION ORDERS" after "CHARGES";

(B) in subsection (a)—

(i) by striking paragraph (1) and inserting the following:

"(1) certifies that its laws, policies, and practices do not require, in connection with the prosecution of any misdemeanor or felony domestic violence offense, or in connection with the filing, issuance, registration, or service of a protection order, or a petition for a protection order, to protect a victim of domestic violence, stalking, or sexual assault, that the victim bear the costs associated with the filing of criminal charges against the offender, or the costs associated with the filing, issuance, registration, or service of a warrant, protection order, petition for a protection order, or witness subpoena, whether issued inside or outside the State, tribal, or local jurisdiction; or"; and

(ii) in paragraph (2)(B), by striking "2 years" and inserting "2 years after the date of the enactment of the Violence Against Women Act of 2000"; and

(C) by adding at the end the following:

"(c) DEFINITION.—In this section, the term 'protection order' has the meaning given the term in section 2266 of title 18, United States Code.".

(2) ELIGIBILITY FOR GRANTS TO ENCOURAGE ARREST POLICIES.—Section 2101 of part U of title I of the Omnibus Crime Control and Safe Streets Act of 1968 (42 U.S.C. 3796hh) is amended—

(A) in subsection (c), by striking paragraph (4) and inserting the following:

"(4) certify that their laws, policies, and practices do not require, in connection with the prosecution of any misdemeanor or felony domestic violence offense, or in connection with the filing, issuance, registration, or service of a protection order, or a petition for a protection order, to protect a victim of domestic violence, stalking, or sexual assault, that the victim bear the costs associated with the filing of criminal charges against the offender, or the costs associated with the filing, issuance, registration, or service of a warrant, protection order, petition for a protection order, or witness subpoena, whether issued inside or outside the State, tribal, or local jurisdiction."; and

(B) by adding at the end the following:

"(d) DEFINITION.—In this section, the term 'protection order' has the meaning given the term in section 2266 of title 18, United States Code.".

(3) APPLICATION FOR GRANTS TO ENCOURAGE ARREST POLICIES.—Section 2102(a)(1)(B) of part U of title I of the Omnibus Crime Control and Safe Streets Act of 1968 (42 U.S.C. 3796hh–1(a)(1)(B)) is amended by inserting before the semicolon the following: "or, in the case of the condition set forth in subsection 2101(c)(4), the expiration of the 2-year period beginning on the date the of the enactment of the Violence Against Women Act of 2000".

(4) REGISTRATION FOR PROTECTION ORDERS.—Section 2265 of title 18, United States Code, is amended by adding at the end the following:

"(d) NOTIFICATION AND REGISTRATION.—

"(1) NOTIFICATION.—A State or Indian tribe according full faith and credit to an order by a court of another State or Indian tribe shall not notify or require notification of the party against whom a protection order has been issued that the protection order has been registered or filed in that enforcing State or tribal jurisdiction unless requested to do so by the party protected under such order.

"(2) NO PRIOR REGISTRATION OR FILING AS PREREQUISITE FOR ENFORCEMENT.—Any protection order that is otherwise consistent with this section shall be accorded full faith and credit, notwithstanding failure to comply with any requirement that the order be registered or filed in the enforcing State or tribal jurisdiction.

"(e) TRIBAL COURT JURISDICTION.—For purposes of this section, a tribal court shall have full civil jurisdiction to enforce protection orders, including authority to enforce any orders through civil contempt proceedings, exclusion of violators from Indian lands, and other appropriate mechanisms, in matters arising within the authority of the tribe.".

(c) TECHNICAL AMENDMENT.—The table of contents for title I of the Omnibus Crime Control and Safe Streets Act of 1968 (42 U.S.C. 3711 et seq.) is amended in the item relating to part U, by adding "AND ENFORCEMENT OF PROTECTION ORDERS" at the end.

SEC. 1102. ROLE OF COURTS.

(a) COURTS AS ELIGIBLE STOP SUBGRANTEES.—Part T of title I of the Omnibus Crime Control and Safe Streets Act of 1968 (42 U.S.C. 3796gg et seq.) is amended—

42 USC 3796gg.

(1) in section 2001—

(A) in subsection (a), by striking "Indian tribal governments," and inserting "State and local courts (including juvenile courts), Indian tribal governments, tribal courts,"; and

(B) in subsection (b)—

(i) in paragraph (1), by inserting ", judges, other court personnel," after "law enforcement officers";

(ii) in paragraph (2), by inserting ", judges, other court personnel," after "law enforcement officers"; and

(iii) in paragraph (3), by inserting ", court," after "police"; and

42 USC 3796gg–1.

(2) in section 2002—

(A) in subsection (a), by inserting "State and local courts (including juvenile courts)," after "States," the second place it appears;

(B) in subsection (c), by striking paragraph (3) and inserting the following:

"(3) of the amount granted—

"(A) not less than 25 percent shall be allocated to police and not less than 25 percent shall be allocated to prosecutors;

"(B) not less than 30 percent shall be allocated to victim services; and

"(C) not less than 5 percent shall be allocated for State and local courts (including juvenile courts); and"; and

PUBLIC LAW 106–386—OCT. 28, 2000   114 STAT. 1495

(C) in subsection (d)(1), by inserting "court," after "law enforcement,".

(b) ELIGIBLE GRANTEES; USE OF GRANTS FOR EDUCATION.— Section 2101 of part U of title I of the Omnibus Crime Control and Safe Streets Act of 1968 (42 U.S.C. 3796hh) is amended—

(1) in subsection (a), by inserting "State and local courts (including juvenile courts), tribal courts," after "Indian tribal governments,";

(2) in subsection (b)—

(A) by inserting "State and local courts (including juvenile courts)," after "Indian tribal governments";

(B) in paragraph (2), by striking "policies and" and inserting "policies, educational programs, and";

(C) in paragraph (3), by inserting "parole and probation officers," after "prosecutors,"; and

(D) in paragraph (4), by inserting "parole and probation officers," after "prosecutors,";

(3) in subsection (c), by inserting "State and local courts (including juvenile courts)," after "Indian tribal governments"; and

(4) by adding at the end the following:

"(e) ALLOTMENT FOR INDIAN TRIBES.—Not less than 5 percent of the total amount made available for grants under this section for each fiscal year shall be available for grants to Indian tribal governments.".

SEC. 1103. REAUTHORIZATION OF STOP GRANTS.

(a) REAUTHORIZATION.—Section 1001(a) of title I of the Omnibus Crime Control and Safe Streets Act of 1968 (42 U.S.C. 3793(a)) is amended by striking paragraph (18) and inserting the following:

"(18) There is authorized to be appropriated to carry out part T $185,000,000 for each of fiscal years 2001 through 2005.".

(b) GRANT PURPOSES.—Part T of title I of the Omnibus Crime Control and Safe Streets Act of 1968 (42 U.S.C. 3796gg et seq.) is amended—

(1) in section 2001—   42 USC 3796gg.

(A) in subsection (b)—

(i) in paragraph (5), by striking "racial, cultural, ethnic, and language minorities" and inserting "underserved populations";

(ii) in paragraph (6), by striking "and" at the end;

(iii) in paragraph (7), by striking the period at the end and inserting a semicolon; and

(iv) by adding at the end the following:

"(8) supporting formal and informal statewide, multidisciplinary efforts, to the extent not supported by State funds, to coordinate the response of State law enforcement agencies, prosecutors, courts, victim services agencies, and other State agencies and departments, to violent crimes against women, including the crimes of sexual assault, domestic violence, and dating violence;

"(9) training of sexual assault forensic medical personnel examiners in the collection and preservation of evidence, analysis, prevention, and providing expert testimony and treatment of trauma related to sexual assault;"; and

(B) by adding at the end the following:

"(c) STATE COALITION GRANTS.—

"(1) PURPOSE.—The Attorney General shall award grants to each State domestic violence coalition and sexual assault coalition for the purposes of coordinating State victim services activities, and collaborating and coordinating with Federal, State, and local entities engaged in violence against women activities.

"(2) GRANTS TO STATE COALITIONS.—The Attorney General shall award grants to—

"(A) each State domestic violence coalition, as determined by the Secretary of Health and Human Services through the Family Violence Prevention and Services Act (42 U.S.C. 10410 et seq.); and

"(B) each State sexual assault coalition, as determined by the Center for Injury Prevention and Control of the Centers for Disease Control and Prevention under the Public Health Service Act (42 U.S.C. 280b et seq.).

"(3) ELIGIBILITY FOR OTHER GRANTS.—Receipt of an award under this subsection by each State domestic violence and sexual assault coalition shall not preclude the coalition from receiving additional grants under this part to carry out the purposes described in subsection (b).";

42 USC 3796gg–1.

(2) in section 2002(b)—

(A) by redesignating paragraphs (2) and (3) as paragraphs (5) and (6), respectively;

(B) in paragraph (1), by striking "4 percent" and inserting "5 percent";

(C) in paragraph (5), as redesignated, by striking "$500,000" and inserting "$600,000"; and

(D) by inserting after paragraph (1) the following:

"(2) 2.5 percent shall be available for grants for State domestic violence coalitions under section 2001(c), with the coalition for each State, the coalition for the District of Columbia, the coalition for the Commonwealth of Puerto Rico, and the coalition for the combined Territories of the United States, each receiving an amount equal to 1/54 of the total amount made available under this paragraph for each fiscal year;

"(3) 2.5 percent shall be available for grants for State sexual assault coalitions under section 2001(c), with the coalition for each State, the coalition for the District of Columbia, the coalition for the Commonwealth of Puerto Rico, and the coalition for the combined Territories of the United States, each receiving an amount equal to 1/54 of the total amount made available under this paragraph for each fiscal year;

"(4) 1/54 shall be available for the development and operation of nonprofit tribal domestic violence and sexual assault coalitions in Indian country;";

42 USC 3796gg–2.

(3) in section 2003, by striking paragraph (7) and inserting the following:

"(7) the term 'underserved populations' includes populations underserved because of geographic location (such as rural isolation), underserved racial and ethnic populations, populations underserved because of special needs (such as language barriers, disabilities, alienage status, or age), and any other population determined to be underserved by the State planning process in consultation with the Attorney General;"; and

PUBLIC LAW 106–386—OCT. 28, 2000   114 STAT. 1497

(4) in section 2004(b)(3), by inserting ", and the membership of persons served in any underserved population" before the semicolon.

42 USC 3796gg–3.

SEC. 1104. REAUTHORIZATION OF GRANTS TO ENCOURAGE ARREST POLICIES.

Section 1001(a) of title I of the Omnibus Crime Control and Safe Streets Act of 1968 (42 U.S.C. 3793(a)) is amended by striking paragraph (19) and inserting the following:

"(19) There is authorized to be appropriated to carry out part U $65,000,000 for each of fiscal years 2001 through 2005.".

SEC. 1105. REAUTHORIZATION OF RURAL DOMESTIC VIOLENCE AND CHILD ABUSE ENFORCEMENT GRANTS.

Section 40295(c) of the Violence Against Women Act of 1994 (42 U.S.C. 13971(c)) is amended—

(1) by striking paragraph (1) and inserting the following:

"(1) IN GENERAL.—There is authorized to be appropriated to carry out this section $40,000,000 for each of fiscal years 2001 through 2005."; and

(2) by adding at the end the following:

"(3) ALLOTMENT FOR INDIAN TRIBES.—Not less than 5 percent of the total amount made available to carry out this section for each fiscal year shall be available for grants to Indian tribal governments.".

SEC. 1106. NATIONAL STALKER AND DOMESTIC VIOLENCE REDUCTION.

(a) REAUTHORIZATION.—Section 40603 of the Violence Against Women Act of 1994 (42 U.S.C. 14032) is amended to read as follows:

"SEC. 40603. AUTHORIZATION OF APPROPRIATIONS.

"There is authorized to be appropriated to carry out this subtitle $3,000,000 for each of fiscal years 2001 through 2005.".

(b) TECHNICAL AMENDMENT.—Section 40602(a) of the Violence Against Women Act of 1994 (42 U.S.C. 14031 note) is amended by inserting "and implement" after "improve".

42 USC 14031.

SEC. 1107. AMENDMENTS TO DOMESTIC VIOLENCE AND STALKING OFFENSES.

(a) INTERSTATE DOMESTIC VIOLENCE.—Section 2261 of title 18, United States Code, is amended by striking subsection (a) and inserting the following:

"(a) OFFENSES.—

"(1) TRAVEL OR CONDUCT OF OFFENDER.—A person who travels in interstate or foreign commerce or enters or leaves Indian country with the intent to kill, injure, harass, or intimidate a spouse or intimate partner, and who, in the course of or as a result of such travel, commits or attempts to commit a crime of violence against that spouse or intimate partner, shall be punished as provided in subsection (b).

"(2) CAUSING TRAVEL OF VICTIM.—A person who causes a spouse or intimate partner to travel in interstate or foreign commerce or to enter or leave Indian country by force, coercion, duress, or fraud, and who, in the course of, as a result of, or to facilitate such conduct or travel, commits or attempts to commit a crime of violence against that spouse or intimate partner, shall be punished as provided in subsection (b).".

(b) INTERSTATE STALKING.—

(1) IN GENERAL.—Section 2261A of title 18, United States Code, is amended to read as follows:

"§ 2261A. Interstate stalking

"Whoever—

"(1) travels in interstate or foreign commerce or within the special maritime and territorial jurisdiction of the United States, or enters or leaves Indian country, with the intent to kill, injure, harass, or intimidate another person, and in the course of, or as a result of, such travel places that person in reasonable fear of the death of, or serious bodily injury to, that person, a member of the immediate family (as defined in section 115) of that person, or the spouse or intimate partner of that person; or

"(2) with the intent—

"(A) to kill or injure a person in another State or tribal jurisdiction or within the special maritime and territorial jurisdiction of the United States; or

"(B) to place a person in another State or tribal jurisdiction, or within the special maritime and territorial jurisdiction of the United States, in reasonable fear of the death of, or serious bodily injury to—

"(i) that person;

"(ii) a member of the immediate family (as defined in section 115) of that person; or

"(iii) a spouse or intimate partner of that person,

uses the mail or any facility of interstate or foreign commerce to engage in a course of conduct that places that person in reasonable fear of the death of, or serious bodily injury to, any of the persons described in clauses (i) through (iii),

shall be punished as provided in section 2261(b).".

28 USC 994 note.

(2) AMENDMENT OF FEDERAL SENTENCING GUIDELINES.—

(A) IN GENERAL.—Pursuant to its authority under section 994 of title 28, United States Code, the United States Sentencing Commission shall amend the Federal Sentencing Guidelines to reflect the amendment made by this subsection.

(B) FACTORS FOR CONSIDERATION.—In carrying out subparagraph (A), the Commission shall consider—

(i) whether the Federal Sentencing Guidelines relating to stalking offenses should be modified in light of the amendment made by this subsection; and

(ii) whether any changes the Commission may make to the Federal Sentencing Guidelines pursuant to clause (i) should also be made with respect to offenses under chapter 110A of title 18, United States Code.

(c) INTERSTATE VIOLATION OF PROTECTION ORDER.—Section 2262 of title 18, United States Code, is amended by striking subsection (a) and inserting the following:

"(a) OFFENSES.—

"(1) TRAVEL OR CONDUCT OF OFFENDER.—A person who travels in interstate or foreign commerce, or enters or leaves Indian country, with the intent to engage in conduct that violates the portion of a protection order that prohibits or provides protection against violence, threats, or harassment against, contact or communication with, or physical proximity to, another person, or that would violate such a portion of a protection order in the jurisdiction in which the order was issued, and subsequently engages in such conduct, shall be punished as provided in subsection (b).

"(2) CAUSING TRAVEL OF VICTIM.—A person who causes another person to travel in interstate or foreign commerce or to enter or leave Indian country by force, coercion, duress, or fraud, and in the course of, as a result of, or to facilitate such conduct or travel engages in conduct that violates the portion of a protection order that prohibits or provides protection against violence, threats, or harassment against, contact or communication with, or physical proximity to, another person, or that would violate such a portion of a protection order in the jurisdiction in which the order was issued, shall be punished as provided in subsection (b).".

(d) DEFINITIONS.—Section 2266 of title 18, United States Code, is amended to read as follows:

"§ 2266. Definitions

"In this chapter:

"(1) BODILY INJURY.—The term 'bodily injury' means any act, except one done in self-defense, that results in physical injury or sexual abuse.

"(2) COURSE OF CONDUCT.—The term 'course of conduct' means a pattern of conduct composed of 2 or more acts, evidencing a continuity of purpose.

"(3) ENTER OR LEAVE INDIAN COUNTRY.—The term 'enter or leave Indian country' includes leaving the jurisdiction of 1 tribal government and entering the jurisdiction of another tribal government.

"(4) INDIAN COUNTRY.—The term 'Indian country' has the meaning stated in section 1151 of this title.

"(5) PROTECTION ORDER.—The term 'protection order' includes any injunction or other order issued for the purpose of preventing violent or threatening acts or harassment against, or contact or communication with or physical proximity to, another person, including any temporary or final order issued by a civil and criminal court (other than a support or child custody order issued pursuant to State divorce and child custody laws, except to the extent that such an order is entitled to full faith and credit under other Federal law) whether obtained by filing an independent action or as a pendente lite order in another proceeding so long as any civil order was issued in response to a complaint, petition, or motion filed by or on behalf of a person seeking protection.

"(6) SERIOUS BODILY INJURY.—The term 'serious bodily injury' has the meaning stated in section 2119(2).

"(7) SPOUSE OR INTIMATE PARTNER.—The term 'spouse or intimate partner' includes—

"(A) for purposes of—

"(i) sections other than 2261A, a spouse or former spouse of the abuser, a person who shares a child in common with the abuser, and a person who cohabits or has cohabited as a spouse with the abuser; and

"(ii) section 2261A, a spouse or former spouse of the target of the stalking, a person who shares a child in common with the target of the stalking, and a person who cohabits or has cohabited as a spouse with the target of the stalking; and

"(B) any other person similarly situated to a spouse who is protected by the domestic or family violence laws of the State or tribal jurisdiction in which the injury occurred or where the victim resides.

"(8) STATE.—The term 'State' includes a State of the United States, the District of Columbia, and a commonwealth, territory, or possession of the United States.

"(9) TRAVEL IN INTERSTATE OR FOREIGN COMMERCE.—The term 'travel in interstate or foreign commerce' does not include travel from 1 State to another by an individual who is a member of an Indian tribe and who remains at all times in the territory of the Indian tribe of which the individual is a member.".

SEC. 1108. SCHOOL AND CAMPUS SECURITY.

(a) GRANTS TO REDUCE VIOLENT CRIMES AGAINST WOMEN ON CAMPUS.—Section 826 of the Higher Education Amendments of 1998 (20 U.S.C. 1152) is amended—

(1) in paragraphs (2), (6), (7), and (9) of subsection (b), by striking "and domestic violence" and inserting "domestic violence, and dating violence";

(2) in subsection (c)(2)(B), by striking "and domestic violence" and inserting ", domestic violence and dating violence";

(3) in subsection (f)—

(A) by redesignating paragraphs (1), (2), and (3) as paragraphs (2), (3), and (4), respectively;

(B) by inserting before paragraph (2) (as redesignated by subparagraph (A)) the following:

"(1) the term 'dating violence' means violence committed by a person—

"(A) who is or has been in a social relationship of a romantic or intimate nature with the victim; and

"(B) where the existence of such a relationship shall be determined based on a consideration of the following factors:

"(i) the length of the relationship;
"(ii) the type of relationship; and
"(iii) the frequency of interaction between the persons involved in the relationship.";

(C) in paragraph (2) (as redesignated by subparagraph (A)), by inserting ", dating" after "domestic" each place the term appears; and

(D) in paragraph (4) (as redesignated by subparagraph (A))—

(i) by inserting "or a public, nonprofit organization acting in a nongovernmental capacity" after "organization";

(ii) by inserting ", dating violence" after "assists domestic violence";

(iii) by striking "or domestic violence" and inserting ", domestic violence or dating violence"; and

(iv) by inserting "dating violence," before "stalking,"; and

(4) in subsection (g), by striking "fiscal year 1999 and such sums as may be necessary for each of the 4 succeeding fiscal years" and inserting "each of fiscal years 2001 through 2005".

(b) MATCHING GRANT PROGRAM FOR SCHOOL SECURITY.—Title I of the Omnibus Crime Control and Safe Streets Act of 1968 is amended by inserting after part Z the following new part:

"PART AA—MATCHING GRANT PROGRAM FOR SCHOOL SECURITY

"SEC. 2701. PROGRAM AUTHORIZED.   42 USC 3797a.

"(a) IN GENERAL.—The Attorney General is authorized to make grants to States, units of local government, and Indian tribes to provide improved security, including the placement and use of metal detectors and other deterrent measures, at schools and on school grounds.

"(b) USES OF FUNDS.—Grants awarded under this section shall be distributed directly to the State, unit of local government, or Indian tribe, and shall be used to improve security at schools and on school grounds in the jurisdiction of the grantee through one or more of the following:

"(1) Placement and use of metal detectors, locks, lighting, and other deterrent measures.

"(2) Security assessments.

"(3) Security training of personnel and students.

"(4) Coordination with local law enforcement.

"(5) Any other measure that, in the determination of the Attorney General, may provide a significant improvement in security.

"(c) PREFERENTIAL CONSIDERATION.—In awarding grants under this part, the Attorney General shall give preferential consideration, if feasible, to an application from a jurisdiction that has a demonstrated need for improved security, has a demonstrated need for financial assistance, and has evidenced the ability to make the improvements for which the grant amounts are sought.

"(d) MATCHING FUNDS.—

"(1) The portion of the costs of a program provided by a grant under subsection (a) may not exceed 50 percent.

"(2) Any funds appropriated by Congress for the activities of any agency of an Indian tribal government or the Bureau of Indian Affairs performing law enforcement functions on any Indian lands may be used to provide the non-Federal share of a matching requirement funded under this subsection.

"(3) The Attorney General may provide, in the guidelines implementing this section, for the requirement of paragraph (1) to be waived or altered in the case of a recipient with a financial need for such a waiver or alteration.

"(e) EQUITABLE DISTRIBUTION.—In awarding grants under this part, the Attorney General shall ensure, to the extent practicable, an equitable geographic distribution among the regions of the United States and among urban, suburban, and rural areas.

"(f) ADMINISTRATIVE COSTS.—The Attorney General may reserve not more than 2 percent from amounts appropriated to carry out this part for administrative costs.

42 USC 3797b.

"SEC. 2702. APPLICATIONS.

"(a) IN GENERAL.—To request a grant under this part, the chief executive of a State, unit of local government, or Indian tribe shall submit an application to the Attorney General at such time, in such manner, and accompanied by such information as the Attorney General may require. Each application shall—

"(1) include a detailed explanation of—

"(A) the intended uses of funds provided under the grant; and

"(B) how the activities funded under the grant will meet the purpose of this part; and

"(2) be accompanied by an assurance that the application was prepared after consultation with individuals not limited to law enforcement officers (such as school violence researchers, child psychologists, social workers, teachers, principals, and other school personnel) to ensure that the improvements to be funded under the grant are—

"(A) consistent with a comprehensive approach to preventing school violence; and

"(B) individualized to the needs of each school at which those improvements are to be made.

Deadline.

"(b) GUIDELINES.—Not later than 90 days after the date of the enactment of this part, the Attorney General shall promulgate guidelines to implement this section (including the information that must be included and the requirements that the States, units of local government, and Indian tribes must meet) in submitting the applications required under this section.

42 USC 3797c.

"SEC. 2703. ANNUAL REPORT TO CONGRESS.

"Not later than November 30th of each year, the Attorney General shall submit a report to the Congress regarding the activities carried out under this part. Each such report shall include, for the preceding fiscal year, the number of grants funded under this part, the amount of funds provided under those grants, and the activities for which those funds were used.

42 USC 3797d.

"SEC. 2704. DEFINITIONS.

"For purposes of this part—

"(1) the term 'school' means a public elementary or secondary school;

"(2) the term 'unit of local government' means a county, municipality, town, township, village, parish, borough, or other unit of general government below the State level; and

"(3) the term 'Indian tribe' has the same meaning as in section 4(e) of the Indian Self-Determination and Education Assistance Act (25 U.S.C. 450b(e)).

42 USC 3797e.

"SEC. 2705. AUTHORIZATION OF APPROPRIATIONS.

"There are authorized to be appropriated to carry out this part $30,000,000 for each of fiscal years 2001 through 2003.".

SEC. 1109. DATING VIOLENCE.

(a) DEFINITIONS.—

(1) SECTION 2003.—Section 2003 of title I of the Omnibus Crime Control and Safe Streets Act of 1968 (42 U.S.C. 3996gg–2) is amended—

(A) in paragraph (8), by striking the period at the end and inserting "; and"; and

(B) by adding at the end the following:

"(9) the term 'dating violence' means violence committed by a person—

"(A) who is or has been in a social relationship of a romantic or intimate nature with the victim; and

"(B) where the existence of such a relationship shall be determined based on a consideration of the following factors:

"(i) the length of the relationship;

"(ii) the type of relationship; and

"(iii) the frequency of interaction between the persons involved in the relationship.".

(2) SECTION 2105.—Section 2105 of title I of the Omnibus Crime Control and Safe Streets Act of 1968 (42 U.S.C. 3796hh–4) is amended—

(A) in paragraph (1), by striking "and" at the end;

(B) in paragraph (2), by striking the period at the end and inserting "; and"; and

(C) by adding at the end the following:

"(3) the term 'dating violence' means violence committed by a person—

"(A) who is or has been in a social relationship of a romantic or intimate nature with the victim; and

"(B) where the existence of such a relationship shall be determined based on a consideration of the following factors:

"(i) the length of the relationship;

"(ii) the type of relationship; and

"(iii) the frequency of interaction between the persons involved in the relationship.".

(b) STOP GRANTS.—Section 2001(b) of title I of the Omnibus Crime Control and Safe Streets Act of 1968 (42 U.S.C. 3796gg(b)) is amended—

(1) in paragraph (1), by striking "sexual assault and domestic violence" and inserting "sexual assault, domestic violence, and dating violence"; and

(2) in paragraph (5), by striking "sexual assault and domestic violence" and inserting "sexual assault, domestic violence, and dating violence".

(c) GRANTS TO ENCOURAGE ARREST POLICIES.—Section 2101(b) of title I of the Omnibus Crime Control and Safe Streets Act of 1968 (42 U.S.C. 3796hh(b)) is amended—

(1) in paragraph (2), by inserting "and dating violence" after "domestic violence"; and

(2) in paragraph (5), by inserting "and dating violence" after "domestic violence".

(d) RURAL DOMESTIC VIOLENCE AND CHILD ABUSE ENFORCEMENT.—Section 40295(a) of the Safe Homes for Women Act of 1994 (42 U.S.C. 13971(a)) is amended—

(1) in paragraph (1), by inserting "and dating violence (as defined in section 2003 of title I of the Omnibus Crime Control and Safe Streets Act of 1968 (42 U.S.C. 3996gg–2))" after "domestic violence"; and

(2) in paragraph (2), by inserting "and dating violence (as defined in section 2003 of title I of the Omnibus Crime Control and Safe Streets Act of 1968 (42 U.S.C. 3996gg–2))" after "domestic violence".

114 STAT. 1504   PUBLIC LAW 106–386—OCT. 28, 2000

TITLE II—STRENGTHENING SERVICES TO VICTIMS OF VIOLENCE

42 USC 3796gg–
6.
SEC. 1201. LEGAL ASSISTANCE FOR VICTIMS.

(a) IN GENERAL.—The purpose of this section is to enable the Attorney General to award grants to increase the availability of legal assistance necessary to provide effective aid to victims of domestic violence, stalking, or sexual assault who are seeking relief in legal matters arising as a consequence of that abuse or violence, at minimal or no cost to the victims.

(b) DEFINITIONS.—In this section:

(1) DOMESTIC VIOLENCE.—The term "domestic violence" has the meaning given the term in section 2003 of title I of the Omnibus Crime Control and Safe Streets Act of 1968 (42 U.S.C. 3796gg–2).

(2) LEGAL ASSISTANCE FOR VICTIMS.—The term "legal assistance" includes assistance to victims of domestic violence, stalking, and sexual assault in family, immigration, administrative agency, or housing matters, protection or stay away order proceedings, and other similar matters. No funds made available under this section may be used to provide financial assistance in support of any litigation described in paragraph (14) of section 504 of Public Law 104–134.

(3) SEXUAL ASSAULT.—The term "sexual assault" has the meaning given the term in section 2003 of title I of the Omnibus Crime Control and Safe Streets Act of 1968 (42 U.S.C. 3796gg–2).

(c) LEGAL ASSISTANCE FOR VICTIMS GRANTS.—The Attorney General may award grants under this subsection to private non-profit entities, Indian tribal governments, and publicly funded organizations not acting in a governmental capacity such as law schools, and which shall be used—

(1) to implement, expand, and establish cooperative efforts and projects between domestic violence and sexual assault victim services organizations and legal assistance providers to provide legal assistance for victims of domestic violence, stalking, and sexual assault;

(2) to implement, expand, and establish efforts and projects to provide legal assistance for victims of domestic violence, stalking, and sexual assault by organizations with a demonstrated history of providing direct legal or advocacy services on behalf of these victims; and

(3) to provide training, technical assistance, and data collection to improve the capacity of grantees and other entities to offer legal assistance to victims of domestic violence, stalking, and sexual assault.

(d) ELIGIBILITY.—To be eligible for a grant under subsection (c), applicants shall certify in writing that—

(1) any person providing legal assistance through a program funded under subsection (c) has completed or will complete training in connection with domestic violence or sexual assault and related legal issues;

(2) any training program conducted in satisfaction of the requirement of paragraph (1) has been or will be developed with input from and in collaboration with a State, local, or

tribal domestic violence or sexual assault program or coalition, as well as appropriate State and local law enforcement officials;

(3) any person or organization providing legal assistance through a program funded under subsection (c) has informed and will continue to inform State, local, or tribal domestic violence or sexual assault programs and coalitions, as well as appropriate State and local law enforcement officials of their work; and

(4) the grantee's organizational policies do not require mediation or counseling involving offenders and victims physically together, in cases where sexual assault, domestic violence, or child sexual abuse is an issue.

(e) EVALUATION.—The Attorney General may evaluate the grants funded under this section through contracts or other arrangements with entities expert on domestic violence, stalking, and sexual assault, and on evaluation research.

(f) AUTHORIZATION OF APPROPRIATIONS.—

(1) IN GENERAL.—There is authorized to be appropriated to carry out this section $40,000,000 for each of fiscal years 2001 through 2005.

(2) ALLOCATION OF FUNDS.—

(A) TRIBAL PROGRAMS.—Of the amount made available under this subsection in each fiscal year, not less than 5 percent shall be used for grants for programs that assist victims of domestic violence, stalking, and sexual assault on lands within the jurisdiction of an Indian tribe.

(B) VICTIMS OF SEXUAL ASSAULT.—Of the amount made available under this subsection in each fiscal year, not less than 25 percent shall be used for direct services, training, and technical assistance to support projects focused solely or primarily on providing legal assistance to victims of sexual assault.

(3) NONSUPPLANTATION.—Amounts made available under this section shall be used to supplement and not supplant other Federal, State, and local funds expended to further the purpose of this section.

SEC. 1202. SHELTER SERVICES FOR BATTERED WOMEN AND CHILDREN.

(a) REAUTHORIZATION.—Section 310(a) of the Family Violence Prevention and Services Act (42 U.S.C. 10409(a)) is amended to read as follows:

"(a) IN GENERAL.—There are authorized to be appropriated to carry out this title $175,000,000 for each of fiscal years 2001 through 2005.".

(b) STATE MINIMUM; REALLOTMENT.—Section 304 of the Family Violence Prevention and Services Act (42 U.S.C. 10403) is amended—

(1) in subsection (a), by striking "for grants to States for any fiscal year" and all that follows and inserting the following: "and available for grants to States under this subsection for any fiscal year—

"(1) Guam, American Samoa, the United States Virgin Islands, and the Commonwealth of the Northern Mariana Islands shall each be allotted not less than ⅛ of 1 percent of the amounts available for grants under section 303(a) for the fiscal year for which the allotment is made; and

"(2) each State shall be allotted for payment in a grant authorized under section 303(a), $600,000, with the remaining funds to be allotted to each State in an amount that bears the same ratio to such remaining funds as the population of such State bears to the population of all States.";

(2) in subsection (c), in the first sentence, by inserting "and available" before "for grants"; and

(3) by adding at the end the following:

"(e) In subsection (a)(2), the term "State" does not include any jurisdiction specified in subsection (a)(1).".

SEC. 1203. TRANSITIONAL HOUSING ASSISTANCE FOR VICTIMS OF DOMESTIC VIOLENCE.

Title III of the Family Violence Prevention and Services Act (42 U.S.C. 10401 et seq.) is amended by adding at the end the following:

42 USC 10419.   **"SEC. 319. TRANSITIONAL HOUSING ASSISTANCE.**

"(a) IN GENERAL.—The Secretary shall award grants under this section to carry out programs to provide assistance to individuals, and their dependents—

"(1) who are homeless or in need of transitional housing or other housing assistance, as a result of fleeing a situation of domestic violence; and

"(2) for whom emergency shelter services are unavailable or insufficient.

"(b) ASSISTANCE DESCRIBED.—Assistance provided under this section may include—

"(1) short-term housing assistance, including rental or utilities payments assistance and assistance with related expenses, such as payment of security deposits and other costs incidental to relocation to transitional housing, in cases in which assistance described in this paragraph is necessary to prevent homelessness because an individual or dependent is fleeing a situation of domestic violence; and

"(2) support services designed to enable an individual or dependent who is fleeing a situation of domestic violence to locate and secure permanent housing, and to integrate the individual or dependent into a community, such as transportation, counseling, child care services, case management, employment counseling, and other assistance.

"(c) TERM OF ASSISTANCE.—

"(1) IN GENERAL.—Subject to paragraph (2), an individual or dependent assisted under this section may not receive assistance under this section for a total of more than 12 months.

"(2) WAIVER.—The recipient of a grant under this section may waive the restrictions of paragraph (1) for up to an additional 6-month period with respect to any individual (and dependents of the individual) who has made a good-faith effort to acquire permanent housing and has been unable to acquire the housing.

"(d) REPORTS.—

"(1) REPORT TO SECRETARY.—

"(A) IN GENERAL.—An entity that receives a grant under this section shall annually prepare and submit to the Secretary a report describing the number of individuals and dependents assisted, and the types of housing assistance and support services provided, under this section.

PUBLIC LAW 106–386—OCT. 28, 2000   114 STAT. 1507

"(B) CONTENTS.—Each report shall include information on—

"(i) the purpose and amount of housing assistance provided to each individual or dependent assisted under this section;

"(ii) the number of months each individual or dependent received the assistance;

"(iii) the number of individuals and dependents who were eligible to receive the assistance, and to whom the entity could not provide the assistance solely due to a lack of available housing; and

"(iv) the type of support services provided to each individual or dependent assisted under this section.

"(2) REPORT TO CONGRESS.—The Secretary shall annually prepare and submit to the Committee on the Judiciary of the House of Representatives and the Committee on the Judiciary of the Senate a report that contains a compilation of the information contained in reports submitted under paragraph (1).

"(e) EVALUATION, MONITORING, AND ADMINISTRATION.—Of the amount appropriated under subsection (f) for each fiscal year, not more than 1 percent shall be used by the Secretary for evaluation, monitoring, and administrative costs under this section.

"(f) AUTHORIZATION OF APPROPRIATIONS.—There are authorized to be appropriated to carry out this section $25,000,000 for fiscal year 2001.".

SEC. 1204. NATIONAL DOMESTIC VIOLENCE HOTLINE.

Section 316(f) of the Family Violence Prevention and Services Act (42 U.S.C. 10416(f)) is amended by striking paragraph (1) and inserting the following:

"(1) IN GENERAL.—There are authorized to be appropriated to carry out this section $2,000,000 for each of fiscal years 2001 through 2005.".

SEC. 1205. FEDERAL VICTIMS COUNSELORS.

Section 40114 of the Violent Crime Control and Law Enforcement Act of 1994 (Public Law 103–322; 108 Stat. 1910) is amended by striking "(such as District of Columbia)—" and all that follows and inserting "(such as District of Columbia), $1,000,000 for each of fiscal years 2001 through 2005.".

SEC. 1206. STUDY OF STATE LAWS REGARDING INSURANCE DISCRIMINATION AGAINST VICTIMS OF VIOLENCE AGAINST WOMEN.

42 USC 14042 note.

(a) IN GENERAL.—The Attorney General shall conduct a national study to identify State laws that address discrimination against victims of domestic violence and sexual assault related to issuance or administration of insurance policies.

(b) REPORT.—Not later than 1 year after the date of the enactment of this Act, the Attorney General shall submit to Congress a report on the findings and recommendations of the study required by subsection (a).

Deadline.

SEC. 1207. STUDY OF WORKPLACE EFFECTS FROM VIOLENCE AGAINST WOMEN.

42 USC 14042 note.

The Attorney General shall—

(1) conduct a national survey of plans, programs, and practices developed to assist employers and employees on appropriate responses in the workplace related to victims of domestic violence, stalking, or sexual assault; and

(2) not later than 18 months after the date of the enactment of this Act, submit to Congress a report describing the results of that survey, which report shall include the recommendations of the Attorney General to assist employers and employees affected in the workplace by incidents of domestic violence, stalking, and sexual assault.

42 USC 14042 note.

SEC. 1208. STUDY OF UNEMPLOYMENT COMPENSATION FOR VICTIMS OF VIOLENCE AGAINST WOMEN.

The Secretary of Labor, in consultation with the Attorney General, shall—

(1) conduct a national study to identify State laws that address the separation from employment of an employee due to circumstances directly resulting from the experience of domestic violence by the employee and circumstances governing that receipt (or nonreceipt) by the employee of unemployment compensation based on such separation; and

(2) not later than 1 year after the date of the enactment of this Act, submit to Congress a report describing the results of that study, together with any recommendations based on that study.

SEC. 1209. ENHANCING PROTECTIONS FOR OLDER AND DISABLED WOMEN FROM DOMESTIC VIOLENCE AND SEXUAL ASSAULT.

(a) ELDER ABUSE, NEGLECT, AND EXPLOITATION.—The Violence Against Women Act of 1994 (108 Stat. 1902 et seq.) is amended by adding at the end the following:

"Subtitle H—Elder Abuse, Neglect, and Exploitation, Including Domestic Violence and Sexual Assault Against Older or Disabled Individuals

42 USC 14041.

"**SEC. 40801. DEFINITIONS.**

"In this subtitle:

"(1) IN GENERAL.—The terms 'elder abuse, neglect, and exploitation', and 'older individual' have the meanings given the terms in section 102 of the Older Americans Act of 1965 (42 U.S.C. 3002).

"(2) DOMESTIC VIOLENCE.—The term 'domestic violence' has the meaning given such term by section 2003 of title I of the Omnibus Crime Control and Safe Streets Act of 1968 (42 U.S.C. 3796gg–2).

"(3) SEXUAL ASSAULT.—The term 'sexual assault' has the meaning given the term in section 2003 of title I of the Omnibus Crime Control and Safe Streets Act of 1968 (42 U.S.C. 3796gg–2).

"SEC. 40802. TRAINING PROGRAMS FOR LAW ENFORCEMENT OFFI-   42 USC 14041a.
CERS.

"The Attorney General may make grants for training programs
to assist law enforcement officers, prosecutors, and relevant officers
of Federal, State, tribal, and local courts in recognizing, addressing,
investigating, and prosecuting instances of elder abuse, neglect,
and exploitation and violence against individuals with disabilities,
including domestic violence and sexual assault, against older or
disabled individuals.

"SEC. 40803. AUTHORIZATION OF APPROPRIATIONS.   42 USC 14041b.

"There are authorized to be appropriated to carry out this
subtitle $5,000,000 for each of fiscal years 2001 through 2005.".

(b) PROTECTIONS FOR OLDER AND DISABLED INDIVIDUALS FROM
DOMESTIC VIOLENCE AND SEXUAL ASSAULT IN PRO-ARREST
GRANTS.—Section 2101(b) of part U of title I of the Omnibus Crime
Control and Safe Streets Act of 1968 (42 U.S.C. 3796hh et seq.)   42 USC 3796hh.
is amended by adding at the end the following:

"(8) To develop or strengthen policies and training for
police, prosecutors, and the judiciary in recognizing, investigating, and prosecuting instances of domestic violence and
sexual assault against older individuals (as defined in section
102 of the Older Americans Act of 1965 (42 U.S.C. 3002))
and individuals with disabilities (as defined in section 3(2)
of the Americans with Disabilities Act of 1990 (42 U.S.C.
12102(2))).".

(c) PROTECTIONS FOR OLDER AND DISABLED INDIVIDUALS FROM
DOMESTIC VIOLENCE AND SEXUAL ASSAULT IN STOP GRANTS.—
Section 2001(b) of title I of the Omnibus Crime Control and Safe
Streets Act of 1968 (42 U.S.C. 3796gg(b)) (as amended by section
1103(b) of this division) is amended by adding at the end the
following:

"(10) developing, enlarging, or strengthening programs to
assist law enforcement, prosecutors, courts, and others to
address the needs and circumstances of older and disabled
women who are victims of domestic violence or sexual assault,
including recognizing, investigating, and prosecuting instances
of such violence or assault and targeting outreach and support,
counseling, and other victim services to such older and disabled
individuals; and".

TITLE III—LIMITING THE EFFECTS OF VIOLENCE ON CHILDREN

SEC. 1301. SAFE HAVENS FOR CHILDREN PILOT PROGRAM.   42 USC 10420.

(a) IN GENERAL.—The Attorney General may award grants
to States, units of local government, and Indian tribal governments
that propose to enter into or expand the scope of existing contracts
and cooperative agreements with public or private nonprofit entities
to provide supervised visitation and safe visitation exchange of
children by and between parents in situations involving domestic
violence, child abuse, sexual assault, or stalking.

(b) CONSIDERATIONS.—In awarding grants under subsection (a),
the Attorney General shall take into account—

(1) the number of families to be served by the proposed
visitation programs and services;

(2) the extent to which the proposed supervised visitation programs and services serve underserved populations (as defined in section 2003 of title I of the Omnibus Crime Control and Safe Streets Act of 1968 (42 U.S.C. 3796gg–2));

(3) with respect to an applicant for a contract or cooperative agreement, the extent to which the applicant demonstrates cooperation and collaboration with nonprofit, nongovernmental entities in the local community served, including the State or tribal domestic violence coalition, State or tribal sexual assault coalition, local shelters, and programs for domestic violence and sexual assault victims; and

(4) the extent to which the applicant demonstrates coordination and collaboration with State and local court systems, including mechanisms for communication and referral.

(c) APPLICANT REQUIREMENTS.—The Attorney General shall award grants for contracts and cooperative agreements to applicants that—

(1) demonstrate expertise in the area of family violence, including the areas of domestic violence or sexual assault, as appropriate;

(2) ensure that any fees charged to individuals for use of programs and services are based on the income of those individuals, unless otherwise provided by court order;

(3) demonstrate that adequate security measures, including adequate facilities, procedures, and personnel capable of preventing violence, are in place for the operation of supervised visitation programs and services or safe visitation exchange; and

(4) prescribe standards by which the supervised visitation or safe visitation exchange will occur.

(d) REPORTING.—

Deadline.

(1) IN GENERAL.—Not later than 1 year after the last day of the first fiscal year commencing on or after the date of the enactment of this Act, and not later than 180 days after the last day of each fiscal year thereafter, the Attorney General shall submit to Congress a report that includes information concerning—

(A) the number of—

(i) individuals served and the number of individuals turned away from visitation programs and services and safe visitation exchange (categorized by State);

(ii) the number of individuals from underserved populations served and turned away from services; and

(iii) the type of problems that underlie the need for supervised visitation or safe visitation exchange, such as domestic violence, child abuse, sexual assault, other physical abuse, or a combination of such factors;

(B) the numbers of supervised visitations or safe visitation exchanges ordered under this section during custody determinations under a separation or divorce decree or protection order, through child protection services or other social services agencies, or by any other order of a civil, criminal, juvenile, or family court;

(C) the process by which children or abused partners are protected during visitations, temporary custody transfers, and other activities for which supervised visitation is established under this section;

(D) safety and security problems occurring during the reporting period during supervised visitation under this section, including the number of parental abduction cases; and

(E) the number of parental abduction cases in a judicial district using supervised visitation programs and services under this section, both as identified in criminal prosecution and custody violations.

(2) GUIDELINES.—The Attorney General shall establish guidelines for the collection and reporting of data under this subsection.

(e) AUTHORIZATION OF APPROPRIATIONS.—There is authorized to be appropriated to carry out this section $15,000,000 for each of fiscal years 2001 and 2002.

(f) ALLOTMENT FOR INDIAN TRIBES.—Not less than 5 percent of the total amount made available for each fiscal year to carry out this section shall be available for grants to Indian tribal governments.

SEC. 1302. REAUTHORIZATION OF VICTIMS OF CHILD ABUSE PROGRAMS.

(a) COURT-APPOINTED SPECIAL ADVOCATE PROGRAM.—Section 218 of the Victims of Child Abuse Act of 1990 (42 U.S.C. 13014) is amended by striking subsection (a) and inserting the following:

"(a) AUTHORIZATION.—There is authorized to be appropriated to carry out this subtitle $12,000,000 for each of fiscal years 2001 through 2005.".

(b) CHILD ABUSE TRAINING PROGRAMS FOR JUDICIAL PERSONNEL AND PRACTITIONERS.—Section 224 of the Victims of Child Abuse Act of 1990 (42 U.S.C. 13024) is amended by striking subsection (a) and inserting the following:

"(a) AUTHORIZATION.—There is authorized to be appropriated to carry out this subtitle $2,300,000 for each of fiscal years 2001 through 2005.".

(c) GRANTS FOR TELEVISED TESTIMONY.—Section 1001(a) of title I of the Omnibus Crime Control and Safe Streets Act of 1968 (42 U.S.C. 3793(a)) is amended by striking paragraph (7) and inserting the following:

"(7) There is authorized to be appropriated to carry out part N $1,000,000 for each of fiscal years 2001 through 2005.".

(d) DISSEMINATION OF INFORMATION.—The Attorney General shall—   42 USC 3793 note.

(1) annually compile and disseminate information (including through electronic publication) about the use of amounts expended and the projects funded under section 218(a) of the Victims of Child Abuse Act of 1990 (42 U.S.C. 13014(a)), section 224(a) of the Victims of Child Abuse Act of 1990 (42 U.S.C. 13024(a)), and section 1007(a)(7) of title I of the Omnibus Crime Control and Safe Streets Act of 1968 (42 U.S.C. 3793(a)(7)), including any evaluations of the projects and information to enable replication and adoption of the strategies identified in the projects; and

(2) focus dissemination of the information described in paragraph (1) toward community-based programs, including domestic violence and sexual assault programs.

114 STAT. 1512   PUBLIC LAW 106-386—OCT. 28, 2000

28 USC 1738A
note.

SEC. 1303. REPORT ON EFFECTS OF PARENTAL KIDNAPPING LAWS IN DOMESTIC VIOLENCE CASES.

(a) IN GENERAL.—The Attorney General shall—

(1) conduct a study of Federal and State laws relating to child custody, including custody provisions in protection orders, the Uniform Child Custody Jurisdiction and Enforcement Act adopted by the National Conference of Commissioners on Uniform State Laws in July 1997, the Parental Kidnaping Prevention Act of 1980 and the amendments made by that Act, and the effect of those laws on child custody cases in which domestic violence is a factor; and

(2) submit to Congress a report describing the results of that study, including the effects of implementing or applying model State laws, and the recommendations of the Attorney General to reduce the incidence or pattern of violence against women or of sexual assault of the child.

(b) SUFFICIENCY OF DEFENSES.—In carrying out subsection (a) with respect to the Parental Kidnaping Prevention Act of 1980 and the amendments made by that Act, the Attorney General shall examine the sufficiency of defenses to parental abduction charges available in cases involving domestic violence, and the burdens and risks encountered by victims of domestic violence arising from jurisdictional requirements of that Act and the amendments made by that Act.

(c) AUTHORIZATION OF APPROPRIATIONS.—There is authorized to be appropriated to carry out this section $200,000 for fiscal year 2001.

(d) CONDITION FOR CUSTODY DETERMINATION.—Section 1738A(c)(2)(C)(ii) of title 28, United States Code, is amended by striking "he" and inserting "the child, a sibling, or parent of the child".

TITLE IV—STRENGTHENING EDUCATION AND TRAINING TO COMBAT VIOLENCE AGAINST WOMEN

SEC. 1401. RAPE PREVENTION AND EDUCATION.

(a) IN GENERAL.—Part J of title III of the Public Health Service Act (42 U.S.C. 280b et seq.) is amended by inserting after section 393A the following:

42 USC 280b–1c.

"SEC. 393B. USE OF ALLOTMENTS FOR RAPE PREVENTION EDUCATION.

"(a) PERMITTED USE.—The Secretary, acting through the National Center for Injury Prevention and Control at the Centers for Disease Control and Prevention, shall award targeted grants to States to be used for rape prevention and education programs conducted by rape crisis centers, State sexual assault coalitions, and other public and private nonprofit entities for—

"(1) educational seminars;

"(2) the operation of hotlines;

"(3) training programs for professionals;

"(4) the preparation of informational material;

"(5) education and training programs for students and campus personnel designed to reduce the incidence of sexual assault at colleges and universities;

PUBLIC LAW 106–386—OCT. 28, 2000   114 STAT. 1513

"(6) education to increase awareness about drugs used to facilitate rapes or sexual assaults; and

"(7) other efforts to increase awareness of the facts about, or to help prevent, sexual assault, including efforts to increase awareness in underserved communities and awareness among individuals with disabilities (as defined in section 3 of the Americans with Disabilities Act of 1990 (42 U.S.C. 12102)).

"(b) COLLECTION AND DISSEMINATION OF INFORMATION ON SEXUAL ASSAULT.—The Secretary shall, through the National Resource Center on Sexual Assault established under the National Center for Injury Prevention and Control at the Centers for Disease Control and Prevention, provide resource information, policy, training, and technical assistance to Federal, State, local, and Indian tribal agencies, as well as to State sexual assault coalitions and local sexual assault programs and to other professionals and interested parties on issues relating to sexual assault, including maintenance of a central resource library in order to collect, prepare, analyze, and disseminate information and statistics and analyses thereof relating to the incidence and prevention of sexual assault.

"(c) AUTHORIZATION OF APPROPRIATIONS.—

"(1) IN GENERAL.—There is authorized to be appropriated to carry out this section $80,000,000 for each of fiscal years 2001 through 2005.

"(2) NATIONAL RESOURCE CENTER ALLOTMENT.—Of the total amount made available under this subsection in each fiscal year, not more than the greater of $1,000,000 or 2 percent of such amount shall be available for allotment under subsection (b).

"(d) LIMITATIONS.—

"(1) SUPPLEMENT NOT SUPPLANT.—Amounts provided to States under this section shall be used to supplement and not supplant other Federal, State, and local public funds expended to provide services of the type described in subsection (a).

"(2) STUDIES.—A State may not use more than 2 percent of the amount received by the State under this section for each fiscal year for surveillance studies or prevalence studies.

"(3) ADMINISTRATION.—A State may not use more than 5 percent of the amount received by the State under this section for each fiscal year for administrative expenses.".

(b) REPEAL.—Section 40151 of the Violence Against Women Act of 1994 (108 Stat. 1920), and the amendment made by such section, is repealed.

42 USC 300w–10.

SEC. 1402. EDUCATION AND TRAINING TO END VIOLENCE AGAINST AND ABUSE OF WOMEN WITH DISABILITIES.

42 USC 3796gg–7.

(a) IN GENERAL.—The Attorney General, in consultation with the Secretary of Health and Human Services, may award grants to States, units of local government, Indian tribal governments, and nongovernmental private entities to provide education and technical assistance for the purpose of providing training, consultation, and information on domestic violence, stalking, and sexual assault against women who are individuals with disabilities (as defined in section 3 of the Americans with Disabilities Act of 1990 (42 U.S.C. 12102)).

(b) PRIORITIES.—In awarding grants under this section, the Attorney General shall give priority to applications designed to provide education and technical assistance on—

(1) the nature, definition, and characteristics of domestic violence, stalking, and sexual assault experienced by women who are individuals with disabilities;

(2) outreach activities to ensure that women who are individuals with disabilities who are victims of domestic violence, stalking, and sexual assault receive appropriate assistance;

(3) the requirements of shelters and victim services organizations under Federal anti-discrimination laws, including the Americans with Disabilities Act of 1990 and section 504 of the Rehabilitation Act of 1973; and

(4) cost-effective ways that shelters and victim services may accommodate the needs of individuals with disabilities in accordance with the Americans with Disabilities Act of 1990.

(c) USES OF GRANTS.—Each recipient of a grant under this section shall provide information and training to organizations and programs that provide services to individuals with disabilities, including independent living centers, disability-related service organizations, and domestic violence programs providing shelter or related assistance.

(d) AUTHORIZATION OF APPROPRIATIONS.—There is authorized to be appropriated to carry out this section $7,500,000 for each of fiscal years 2001 through 2005.

SEC. 1403. COMMUNITY INITIATIVES.

Section 318 of the Family Violence Prevention and Services Act (42 U.S.C. 10418) is amended by striking subsection (h) and inserting the following:

"(h) AUTHORIZATION OF APPROPRIATIONS.—There are authorized to be appropriated to carry out this section $6,000,000 for each of fiscal years 2001 through 2005.".

42 USC 13961 note.

SEC. 1404. DEVELOPMENT OF RESEARCH AGENDA IDENTIFIED BY THE VIOLENCE AGAINST WOMEN ACT OF 1994.

(a) IN GENERAL.—The Attorney General shall—

(1) direct the National Institute of Justice, in consultation and coordination with the Bureau of Justice Statistics and the National Academy of Sciences, through its National Research Council, to develop a research agenda based on the recommendations contained in the report entitled "Understanding Violence Against Women" of the National Academy of Sciences; and

Deadline.

(2) not later than 1 year after the date of the enactment of this Act, in consultation with the Secretary of the Department of Health and Human Services, submit to Congress a report which shall include—

(A) a description of the research agenda developed under paragraph (1) and a plan to implement that agenda; and

(B) recommendations for priorities in carrying out that agenda to most effectively advance knowledge about and means by which to prevent or reduce violence against women.

PUBLIC LAW 106–386—OCT. 28, 2000   114 STAT. 1515

(b) AUTHORIZATION OF APPROPRIATIONS.—There are authorized
to be appropriated such sums as may be necessary to carry out
this section.

SEC. 1405. STANDARDS, PRACTICE, AND TRAINING FOR SEXUAL ASSAULT FORENSIC EXAMINATIONS.

42 USC 3796gg note.

(a) IN GENERAL.—The Attorney General shall—
(1) evaluate existing standards of training and practice
for licensed health care professionals performing sexual assault
forensic examinations and develop a national recommended
standard for training;
(2) recommend sexual assault forensic examination training
for all health care students to improve the recognition of
injuries suggestive of rape and sexual assault and baseline
knowledge of appropriate referrals in victim treatment and
evidence collection; and
(3) review existing national, State, tribal, and local protocols on sexual assault forensic examinations, and based on
this review, develop a recommended national protocol and
establish a mechanism for its nationwide dissemination.
(b) CONSULTATION.—The Attorney General shall consult with
national, State, tribal, and local experts in the area of rape and
sexual assault, including rape crisis centers, State and tribal sexual
assault and domestic violence coalitions and programs, and programs for criminal justice, forensic nursing, forensic science, emergency room medicine, law, social services, and sex crimes in underserved communities (as defined in section 2003(7) of title I of
the Omnibus Crime Control and Safe Streets Act of 1968 (42 U.S.C.
3796gg–2(7)), as amended by this division).
(c) REPORT.—The Attorney General shall ensure that not later
than 1 year after the date of the enactment of this Act, a report
of the actions taken pursuant to subsection (a) is submitted to
Congress.
(d) AUTHORIZATION OF APPROPRIATIONS.—There is authorized
to be appropriated to carry out this section $200,000 for fiscal
year 2001.

**SEC. 1406. EDUCATION AND TRAINING FOR JUDGES AND COURT PER-
SONNEL.**

(a) GRANTS FOR EDUCATION AND TRAINING FOR JUDGES AND
COURT PERSONNEL IN STATE COURTS.—
(1) SECTION 40412.—Section 40412 of the Equal Justice
for Women in the Courts Act of 1994 (42 U.S.C. 13992) is
amended—
(A) by striking "and" at the end of paragraph (18);
(B) by striking the period at the end of paragraph
(19) and inserting a semicolon; and
(C) by inserting after paragraph (19) the following:
"(20) the issues raised by domestic violence in determining
custody and visitation, including how to protect the safety
of the child and of a parent who is not a predominant aggressor
of domestic violence, the legitimate reasons parents may report
domestic violence, the ways domestic violence may relate to
an abuser's desire to seek custody, and evaluating expert testimony in custody and visitation determinations involving
domestic violence;
"(21) the issues raised by child sexual assault in determining custody and visitation, including how to protect the

safety of the child, the legitimate reasons parents may report child sexual assault, and evaluating expert testimony in custody and visitation determinations involving child sexual assault, including the current scientifically-accepted and empirically valid research on child sexual assault;

"(22) the extent to which addressing domestic violence and victim safety contributes to the efficient administration of justice;".

(2) SECTION 40414.—Section 40414(a) of the Equal Justice for Women in the Courts Act of 1994 (42 U.S.C. 13994(a)) is amended by inserting "and $1,500,000 for each of the fiscal years 2001 through 2005" after "1996".

(b) GRANTS FOR EDUCATION AND TRAINING FOR JUDGES AND COURT PERSONNEL IN FEDERAL COURTS.—

(1) SECTION 40421.—Section 40421(d) of the Equal Justice for Women in the Courts Act of 1994 (42 U.S.C. 14001(d)) is amended to read as follows:

"(d) CONTINUING EDUCATION AND TRAINING PROGRAMS.—The Federal Judicial Center, in carrying out section 620(b)(3) of title 28, United States Code, shall include in the educational programs it prepares, including the training programs for newly appointed judges, information on the aspects of the topics listed in section 40412 that pertain to issues within the jurisdiction of the Federal courts, and shall prepare materials necessary to implement this subsection.".

(2) SECTION 40422.—Section 40422(2) of the Equal Justice for Women in the Courts Act of 1994 (42 U.S.C. 14002(2)) is amended by inserting "and $500,000 for each of the fiscal years 2001 through 2005" after "1996".

(c) TECHNICAL AMENDMENTS TO THE EQUAL JUSTICE FOR WOMEN IN THE COURTS ACT OF 1994.—

(1) ENSURING COLLABORATION WITH DOMESTIC VIOLENCE AND SEXUAL ASSAULT PROGRAMS.—Section 40413 of the Equal Justice for Women in the Courts Act of 1994 (42 U.S.C. 13993) is amended by adding ", including national, State, tribal, and local domestic violence and sexual assault programs and coalitions" after "victim advocates".

(2) PARTICIPATION OF TRIBAL COURTS IN STATE TRAINING AND EDUCATION PROGRAMS.—Section 40411 of the Equal Justice for Women in the Courts Act of 1994 (42 U.S.C. 13991) is amended by adding at the end the following: "Nothing shall preclude the attendance of tribal judges and court personnel at programs funded under this section for States to train judges and court personnel on the laws of the States.".

(3) USE OF FUNDS FOR DISSEMINATION OF MODEL PROGRAMS.—Section 40414 of the Equal Justice for Women in the Courts Act of 1994 (42 U.S.C. 13994) is amended by adding at the end the following:

"(c) STATE JUSTICE INSTITUTE.—The State Justice Institute may use up to 5 percent of the funds appropriated under this section for annually compiling and broadly disseminating (including through electronic publication) information about the use of funds and about the projects funded under this section, including any evaluations of the projects and information to enable the replication and adoption of the projects.".

(d) DATING VIOLENCE.—

PUBLIC LAW 106–386—OCT. 28, 2000   114 STAT. 1517

(1) SECTION 40411.—Section 40411 of the Equal Justice for Women in Courts Act of 1994 (42 U.S.C 13991) is amended by inserting "dating violence," after "domestic violence,".

(2) SECTION 40412.—Section 40412 of such Act (42 U.S.C 13992) is amended—

(A) in paragraph (10), by inserting "and dating violence (as defined in section 2003 of title I of the Omnibus Crime Control and Safe Streets Act of 1968 (42 U.S.C. 3996gg–2))" before the semicolon;

(B) in paragraph (11), by inserting "and dating violence" after "domestic violence";

(C) in paragraph (13), by inserting "and dating violence" after "domestic violence" in both places that it appears;

(D) in paragraph (17), by inserting "or dating violence" after "domestic violence" in both places that it appears; and

(E) in paragraph (18), by inserting "and dating violence" after "domestic violence".

SEC. 1407. DOMESTIC VIOLENCE TASK FORCE

The Violence Against Women Act of 1994 (108 Stat. 1902 et seq.) (as amended by section 1209(a) of this division) is amended by adding at the end the following:

"Subtitle I—Domestic Violence Task Force

"SEC. 40901. TASK FORCE.

42 USC 14042.

"(a) ESTABLISH.—The Attorney General, in consultation with national nonprofit, nongovernmental organizations whose primary expertise is in domestic violence, shall establish a task force to coordinate research on domestic violence and to report to Congress on any overlapping or duplication of efforts on domestic violence issues. The task force shall be comprised of representatives from all Federal agencies that fund such research.

"(b) USES OF FUNDS.—Funds appropriated under this section shall be used to—

"(1) develop a coordinated strategy to strengthen research focused on domestic violence education, prevention, and intervention strategies;

"(2) track and report all Federal research and expenditures on domestic violence; and

"(3) identify gaps and duplication of efforts in domestic violence research and governmental expenditures on domestic violence issues.

"(c) REPORT.—The Task Force shall report to Congress annually on its work under subsection (b).

"(d) DEFINITION.—For purposes of this section, the term 'domestic violence' has the meaning given such term by section 2003 of title I of the Omnibus Crime Control and Safe Streets Act of 1968 (42 U.S.C. 3796gg–2(1)).

"(e) AUTHORIZATION OF APPROPRIATIONS.—There is authorized to be appropriated to carry out this section $500,000 for each of fiscal years 2001 through 2004.".

114 STAT. 1518   PUBLIC LAW 106–386—OCT. 28, 2000

Battered
Immigrant
Women
Protection Act of
2000.
8 USC 1101 note.
TITLE V—BATTERED IMMIGRANT WOMEN

SEC. 1501. SHORT TITLE.

This title may be cited as the "Battered Immigrant Women Protection Act of 2000".

8 USC 1101 note. **SEC. 1502. FINDINGS AND PURPOSES.**

(a) FINDINGS.—Congress finds that—

(1) the goal of the immigration protections for battered immigrants included in the Violence Against Women Act of 1994 was to remove immigration laws as a barrier that kept battered immigrant women and children locked in abusive relationships;

(2) providing battered immigrant women and children who were experiencing domestic violence at home with protection against deportation allows them to obtain protection orders against their abusers and frees them to cooperate with law enforcement and prosecutors in criminal cases brought against their abusers and the abusers of their children without fearing that the abuser will retaliate by withdrawing or threatening withdrawal of access to an immigration benefit under the abuser's control; and

(3) there are several groups of battered immigrant women and children who do not have access to the immigration protections of the Violence Against Women Act of 1994 which means that their abusers are virtually immune from prosecution because their victims can be deported as a result of action by their abusers and the Immigration and Naturalization Service cannot offer them protection no matter how compelling their case under existing law.

(b) PURPOSES.—The purposes of this title are—

(1) to remove barriers to criminal prosecutions of persons who commit acts of battery or extreme cruelty against immigrant women and children; and

(2) to offer protection against domestic violence occurring in family and intimate relationships that are covered in State and tribal protection orders, domestic violence, and family law statutes.

SEC. 1503. IMPROVED ACCESS TO IMMIGRATION PROTECTIONS OF THE VIOLENCE AGAINST WOMEN ACT OF 1994 FOR BATTERED IMMIGRANT WOMEN.

(a) INTENDED SPOUSE DEFINED.—Section 101(a) of the Immigration and Nationality Act (8 U.S.C. 1101(a)) is amended by adding at the end the following:

"(50) The term 'intended spouse' means any alien who meets the criteria set forth in section 204(a)(1)(A)(iii)(II)(aa)(BB), 204(a)(1)(B)(ii)(II)(aa)(BB), or 240A(b)(2)(A)(i)(III).".

(b) IMMEDIATE RELATIVE STATUS FOR SELF-PETITIONERS MARRIED TO U.S. CITIZENS.—

(1) SELF-PETITIONING SPOUSES.—

(A) BATTERY OR CRUELTY TO ALIEN OR ALIEN'S CHILD.—Section 204(a)(1)(A)(iii) of the Immigration and Nationality Act (8 U.S.C. 1154(a)(1)(A)(iii)) is amended to read as follows:

PUBLIC LAW 106–386—OCT. 28, 2000   114 STAT. 1519

"(iii)(I) An alien who is described in subclause (II) may file a petition with the Attorney General under this clause for classification of the alien (and any child of the alien) if the alien demonstrates to the Attorney General that—

"(aa) the marriage or the intent to marry the United States citizen was entered into in good faith by the alien; and

"(bb) during the marriage or relationship intended by the alien to be legally a marriage, the alien or a child of the alien has been battered or has been the subject of extreme cruelty perpetrated by the alien's spouse or intended spouse.

"(II) For purposes of subclause (I), an alien described in this subclause is an alien—

"(aa)(AA) who is the spouse of a citizen of the United States;

"(BB) who believed that he or she had married a citizen of the United States and with whom a marriage ceremony was actually performed and who otherwise meets any applicable requirements under this Act to establish the existence of and bona fides of a marriage, but whose marriage is not legitimate solely because of the bigamy of such citizen of the United States; or

"(CC) who was a bona fide spouse of a United States citizen within the past 2 years and—

"(aaa) whose spouse died within the past 2 years;

"(bbb) whose spouse lost or renounced citizenship status within the past 2 years related to an incident of domestic violence; or

"(ccc) who demonstrates a connection between the legal termination of the marriage within the past 2 years and battering or extreme cruelty by the United States citizen spouse;

"(bb) who is a person of good moral character;

"(cc) who is eligible to be classified as an immediate relative under section 201(b)(2)(A)(i) or who would have been so classified but for the bigamy of the citizen of the United States that the alien intended to marry; and

"(dd) who has resided with the alien's spouse or intended spouse.".

(2) SELF-PETITIONING CHILDREN.—Section 204(a)(1)(A)(iv) of the Immigration and Nationality Act (8 U.S.C. 1154(a)(1)(A)(iv)) is amended to read as follows:

"(iv) An alien who is the child of a citizen of the United States, or who was a child of a United States citizen parent who within the past 2 years lost or renounced citizenship status related to an incident of domestic violence, and who is a person of good moral character, who is eligible to be classified as an immediate relative under section 201(b)(2)(A)(i), and who resides, or has resided in the past, with the citizen parent may file a petition with the Attorney General under this subparagraph for classification of the alien (and any child of the alien) under such section if the alien demonstrates to the Attorney General that the alien has been battered by or has been the subject of extreme cruelty perpetrated by the alien's citizen parent. For purposes of this clause, residence includes any period of visitation.".

(3) FILING OF PETITIONS.—Section 204(a)(1)(A) of the Immigration and Nationality Act (8 U.S.C. 1154(a)(1)(A)) is amended by adding at the end the following:

"(v) An alien who—
"(I) is the spouse, intended spouse, or child living abroad of a citizen who—
"(aa) is an employee of the United States Government;
"(bb) is a member of the uniformed services (as defined in section 101(a) of title 10, United States Code); or
"(cc) has subjected the alien or the alien's child to battery or extreme cruelty in the United States; and
"(II) is eligible to file a petition under clause (iii) or (iv), shall file such petition with the Attorney General under the procedures that apply to self-petitioners under clause (iii) or (iv), as applicable.".

(c) SECOND PREFERENCE IMMIGRATION STATUS FOR SELF-PETITIONERS MARRIED TO LAWFUL PERMANENT RESIDENTS.—

(1) SELF-PETITIONING SPOUSES.—Section 204(a)(1)(B)(ii) of the Immigration and Nationality Act (8 U.S.C. 1154(a)(1)(B)(ii)) is amended to read as follows:

"(ii)(I) An alien who is described in subclause (II) may file a petition with the Attorney General under this clause for classification of the alien (and any child of the alien) if such a child has not been classified under clause (iii) of section 203(a)(2)(A) and if the alien demonstrates to the Attorney General that—

"(aa) the marriage or the intent to marry the lawful permanent resident was entered into in good faith by the alien; and

"(bb) during the marriage or relationship intended by the alien to be legally a marriage, the alien or a child of the alien has been battered or has been the subject of extreme cruelty perpetrated by the alien's spouse or intended spouse.

"(II) For purposes of subclause (I), an alien described in this paragraph is an alien—

"(aa)(AA) who is the spouse of a lawful permanent resident of the United States; or

"(BB) who believed that he or she had married a lawful permanent resident of the United States and with whom a marriage ceremony was actually performed and who otherwise meets any applicable requirements under this Act to establish the existence of and bona fides of a marriage, but whose marriage is not legitimate solely because of the bigamy of such lawful permanent resident of the United States; or

"(CC) who was a bona fide spouse of a lawful permanent resident within the past 2 years and—

"(aaa) whose spouse lost status within the past 2 years due to an incident of domestic violence; or

"(bbb) who demonstrates a connection between the legal termination of the marriage within the past 2 years and battering or extreme cruelty by the lawful permanent resident spouse;

"(bb) who is a person of good moral character;

"(cc) who is eligible to be classified as a spouse of an alien lawfully admitted for permanent residence under section 203(a)(2)(A) or who would have been so classified but for the bigamy of the lawful permanent resident of the United States that the alien intended to marry; and

"(dd) who has resided with the alien's spouse or intended spouse.".

(2) SELF-PETITIONING CHILDREN.—Section 204(a)(1)(B)(iii) of the Immigration and Nationality Act (8 U.S.C. 1154(a)(1)(B)(iii)) is amended to read as follows:

"(iii) An alien who is the child of an alien lawfully admitted for permanent residence, or who was the child of a lawful permanent resident who within the past 2 years lost lawful permanent resident status due to an incident of domestic violence, and who is a person of good moral character, who is eligible for classification under section 203(a)(2)(A), and who resides, or has resided in the past, with the alien's permanent resident alien parent may file a petition with the Attorney General under this subparagraph for classification of the alien (and any child of the alien) under such section if the alien demonstrates to the Attorney General that the alien has been battered by or has been the subject of extreme cruelty perpetrated by the alien's permanent resident parent.".

(3) FILING OF PETITIONS.—Section 204(a)(1)(B) of the Immigration and Nationality Act (8 U.S.C. 1154(a)(1)(B)) is amended by adding at the end the following:

"(iv) An alien who—

"(I) is the spouse, intended spouse, or child living abroad of a lawful permanent resident who—

"(aa) is an employee of the United States Government;

"(bb) is a member of the uniformed services (as defined in section 101(a) of title 10, United States Code); or

"(cc) has subjected the alien or the alien's child to battery or extreme cruelty in the United States; and

"(II) is eligible to file a petition under clause (ii) or (iii), shall file such petition with the Attorney General under the procedures that apply to self-petitioners under clause (ii) or (iii), as applicable.".

(d) GOOD MORAL CHARACTER DETERMINATIONS FOR SELF-PETITIONERS AND TREATMENT OF CHILD SELF-PETITIONERS AND PETITIONS INCLUDING DERIVATIVE CHILDREN ATTAINING 21 YEARS OF AGE.—Section 204(a)(1) of the Immigration and Nationality Act (8 U.S.C. 1154(a)(1)) is amended—

(1) by redesignating subparagraphs (C) through (H) as subparagraphs (E) through (J), respectively;

(2) by inserting after subparagraph (B) the following:

"(C) Notwithstanding section 101(f), an act or conviction that is waivable with respect to the petitioner for purposes of a determination of the petitioner's admissibility under section 212(a) or deportability under section 237(a) shall not bar the Attorney General from finding the petitioner to be of good moral character under subparagraph (A)(iii), (A)(iv), (B)(ii), or (B)(iii) if the Attorney General finds that the act or conviction was connected to the alien's having been battered or subjected to extreme cruelty.

"(D)(i)(I) Any child who attains 21 years of age who has filed a petition under clause (iv) of section 204(a)(1)(A) that was filed or approved before the date on which the child attained 21 years of age shall be considered (if the child has not been admitted or approved for lawful permanent residence by the date the child attained 21 years of age) a petitioner for preference status under paragraph (1), (2), or (3) of section 203(a), whichever paragraph is applicable, with the same priority date assigned to the self-petition filed under clause (iv) of section 204(a)(1)(A). No new petition shall be required to be filed.

"(II) Any individual described in subclause (I) is eligible for deferred action and work authorization.

"(III) Any derivative child who attains 21 years of age who is included in a petition described in clause (ii) that was filed or approved before the date on which the child attained 21 years of age shall be considered (if the child has not been admitted or approved for lawful permanent residence by the date the child attained 21 years of age) a petitioner for preference status under paragraph (1), (2), or (3) of section 203(a), whichever paragraph is applicable, with the same priority date as that assigned to the petitioner in any petition described in clause (ii). No new petition shall be required to be filed.

"(IV) Any individual described in subclause (III) and any derivative child of a petition described in clause (ii) is eligible for deferred action and work authorization.

"(ii) The petition referred to in clause (i)(III) is a petition filed by an alien under subparagraph (A)(iii), (A)(iv), (B)(ii) or (B)(iii) in which the child is included as a derivative beneficiary.";
and

(3) in subparagraph (J) (as so redesignated), by inserting "or in making determinations under subparagraphs (C) and (D)," after "subparagraph (B),".

(e) ACCESS TO NATURALIZATION FOR DIVORCED VICTIMS OF ABUSE.—Section 319(a) of the Immigration and Nationality Act (8 U.S.C. 1430(a)) is amended—

(1) by inserting ", or any person who obtained status as a lawful permanent resident by reason of his or her status as a spouse or child of a United States citizen who battered him or her or subjected him or her to extreme cruelty," after "United States" the first place such term appears; and

(2) by inserting "(except in the case of a person who has been battered or subjected to extreme cruelty by a United States citizen spouse or parent)" after "has been living in marital union with the citizen spouse".

SEC. 1504. IMPROVED ACCESS TO CANCELLATION OF REMOVAL AND SUSPENSION OF DEPORTATION UNDER THE VIOLENCE AGAINST WOMEN ACT OF 1994.

(a) CANCELLATION OF REMOVAL AND ADJUSTMENT OF STATUS FOR CERTAIN NONPERMANENT RESIDENTS.—Section 240A(b)(2) of the Immigration and Nationality Act (8 U.S.C. 1229b(b)(2)) is amended to read as follows:

"(2) SPECIAL RULE FOR BATTERED SPOUSE OR CHILD.—

"(A) AUTHORITY.—The Attorney General may cancel removal of, and adjust to the status of an alien lawfully admitted for permanent residence, an alien who is inadmissible or deportable from the United States if the alien demonstrates that—

"(i)(I) the alien has been battered or subjected to extreme cruelty by a spouse or parent who is or was a United States citizen (or is the parent of a child of a United States citizen and the child has been battered or subjected to extreme cruelty by such citizen parent);

"(II) the alien has been battered or subjected to extreme cruelty by a spouse or parent who is or was a lawful permanent resident (or is the parent of a

PUBLIC LAW 106–386—OCT. 28, 2000   114 STAT. 1523

child of an alien who is or was a lawful permanent resident and the child has been battered or subjected to extreme cruelty by such permanent resident parent); or

"(III) the alien has been battered or subjected to extreme cruelty by a United States citizen or lawful permanent resident whom the alien intended to marry, but whose marriage is not legitimate because of that United States citizen's or lawful permanent resident's bigamy;

"(ii) the alien has been physically present in the United States for a continuous period of not less than 3 years immediately preceding the date of such application, and the issuance of a charging document for removal proceedings shall not toll the 3-year period of continuous physical presence in the United States;

"(iii) the alien has been a person of good moral character during such period, subject to the provisions of subparagraph (C);

"(iv) the alien is not inadmissible under paragraph (2) or (3) of section 212(a), is not deportable under paragraphs (1)(G) or (2) through (4) of section 237(a) (except in a case described in section 237(a)(7) where the Attorney General exercises discretion to grant a waiver), and has not been convicted of an aggravated felony; and

"(v) the removal would result in extreme hardship to the alien, the alien's child, or the alien's parent.

"(B) PHYSICAL PRESENCE.—Notwithstanding subsection (d)(2), for purposes of subparagraph (A)(i)(II) or for purposes of section 244(a)(3) (as in effect before the title III–A effective date in section 309 of the Illegal Immigration Reform and Immigrant Responsibility Act of 1996), an alien shall not be considered to have failed to maintain continuous physical presence by reason of an absence if the alien demonstrates a connection between the absence and the battering or extreme cruelty perpetrated against the alien. No absence or portion of an absence connected to the battering or extreme cruelty shall count toward the 90-day or 180-day limits established in subsection (d)(2). If any absence or aggregate absences exceed 180 days, the absences or portions of the absences will not be considered to break the period of continuous presence. Any such period of time excluded from the 180-day limit shall be excluded in computing the time during which the alien has been physically present for purposes of the 3-year requirement set forth in section 240A(b)(2)(B) and section 244(a)(3) (as in effect before the title III–A effective date in section 309 of the Illegal Immigration Reform and Immigrant Responsibility Act of 1996).

"(C) GOOD MORAL CHARACTER.—Notwithstanding section 101(f), an act or conviction that does not bar the Attorney General from granting relief under this paragraph by reason of subparagraph (A)(iv) shall not bar the Attorney General from finding the alien to be of good moral character under subparagraph (A)(i)(III) or section 244(a)(3) (as in effect before the title III–A effective date in section 309 of the Illegal Immigration Reform and Immigrant Responsibility Act of 1996), if the Attorney General finds that the act or conviction was connected to the alien's having been battered or subjected to extreme cruelty and determines that a waiver is otherwise warranted.

"(D) CREDIBLE EVIDENCE CONSIDERED.—In acting on applications under this paragraph, the Attorney General shall consider any credible evidence relevant to the application. The determination of what evidence is credible and the weight to be given that evidence shall be within the sole discretion of the Attorney General.".

(b) CHILDREN OF BATTERED ALIENS AND PARENTS OF BATTERED ALIEN CHILDREN.—Section 240A(b) of the Immigration and Nationality Act (8 U.S.C. 1229b(b)) is amended by adding at the end the following:

"(4) CHILDREN OF BATTERED ALIENS AND PARENTS OF BATTERED ALIEN CHILDREN.—

"(A) IN GENERAL.—The Attorney General shall grant parole under section 212(d)(5) to any alien who is a—

"(i) child of an alien granted relief under section 240A(b)(2) or 244(a)(3) (as in effect before the title III–A effective date in section 309 of the Illegal Immigration Reform and Immigrant Responsibility Act of 1996); or

"(ii) parent of a child alien granted relief under section 240A(b)(2) or 244(a)(3) (as in effect before the title III–A effective date in section 309 of the Illegal Immigration Reform and Immigrant Responsibility Act of 1996).

"(B) DURATION OF PAROLE.—The grant of parole shall extend from the time of the grant of relief under section 240A(b)(2) or section 244(a)(3) (as in effect before the title III–A effective date in section 309 of the Illegal Immigration Reform and Immigrant Responsibility Act of 1996) to the time the application for adjustment of status filed by aliens covered under this paragraph has been finally adjudicated. Applications for adjustment of status filed by aliens covered under this paragraph shall be treated as if they were applications filed under section 204(a)(1) (A)(iii), (A)(iv), (B)(ii), or (B)(iii) for purposes of section 245 (a) and (c). Failure by the alien granted relief under section 240A(b)(2) or section 244(a)(3) (as in effect before the title III–A effective date in section 309 of the Illegal Immigration Reform and Immigrant Responsibility Act of 1996) to exercise due diligence in filing a visa petition on behalf of an alien described in clause (i) or (ii) may result in revocation of parole.".

8 USC 1229b note.

(c) EFFECTIVE DATE.—Any individual who becomes eligible for relief by reason of the enactment of the amendments made by subsections (a) and (b), shall be eligible to file a motion to reopen pursuant to section 240(c)(6)(C)(iv). The amendments made by subsections (a) and (b) shall take effect as if included in the enactment of section 304 of the Illegal Immigration Reform and Immigrant Responsibility Act of 1996 (Public Law 104–208; 110 Stat. 587). Such portions of the amendments made by subsection (b) that relate to section 244(a)(3) (as in effect before the title III–A effective date in section 309 of the Illegal Immigration Reform and

Immigrant Responsibility Act of 1996) shall take effect as if included in subtitle G of title IV of the Violent Crime Control and Law Enforcement Act of 1994 (Public Law 103–322; 108 Stat. 1953 et seq.).

SEC. 1505. OFFERING EQUAL ACCESS TO IMMIGRATION PROTECTIONS OF THE VIOLENCE AGAINST WOMEN ACT OF 1994 FOR ALL QUALIFIED BATTERED IMMIGRANT SELF-PETITIONERS.

(a) BATTERED IMMIGRANT WAIVER.—Section 212(a)(9)(C)(ii) of the Immigration and Nationality Act (8 U.S.C. 1182(a)(9)(C)(ii)) is amended by adding at the end the following: "The Attorney General in the Attorney General's discretion may waive the provisions of section 212(a)(9)(C)(i) in the case of an alien to whom the Attorney General has granted classification under clause (iii), (iv), or (v) of section 204(a)(1)(A), or classification under clause (ii), (iii), or (iv) of section 204(a)(1)(B), in any case in which there is a connection between—

"(1) the alien's having been battered or subjected to extreme cruelty; and

"(2) the alien's—

"(A) removal;

"(B) departure from the United States;

"(C) reentry or reentries into the United States; or

"(D) attempted reentry into the United States.".

(b) DOMESTIC VIOLENCE VICTIM WAIVER.—

(1) WAIVER FOR VICTIMS OF DOMESTIC VIOLENCE.—Section 237(a) of the Immigration and Nationality Act (8 U.S.C. 1227(a)) is amended by inserting at the end the following:

"(7) WAIVER FOR VICTIMS OF DOMESTIC VIOLENCE.—

"(A) IN GENERAL.—The Attorney General is not limited by the criminal court record and may waive the application of paragraph (2)(E)(i) (with respect to crimes of domestic violence and crimes of stalking) and (ii) in the case of an alien who has been battered or subjected to extreme cruelty and who is not and was not the primary perpetrator of violence in the relationship—

"(i) upon a determination that—

"(I) the alien was acting is self-defense;

"(II) the alien was found to have violated a protection order intended to protect the alien; or

"(III) the alien committed, was arrested for, was convicted of, or pled guilty to committing a crime—

"(aa) that did not result in serious bodily injury; and

"(bb) where there was a connection between the crime and the alien's having been battered or subjected to extreme cruelty.

"(B) CREDIBLE EVIDENCE CONSIDERED.—In acting on applications under this paragraph, the Attorney General shall consider any credible evidence relevant to the application. The determination of what evidence is credible and the weight to be given that evidence shall be within the sole discretion of the Attorney General.".

(2) CONFORMING AMENDMENT.—Section 240A(b)(1)(C) of the Immigration and Nationality Act (8 U.S.C. 1229b(b)(1)(C)) is

amended by inserting "(except in a case described in section 237(a)(7) where the Attorney General exercises discretion to grant a waiver)" after "237(a)(3)".

(c) MISREPRESENTATION WAIVERS FOR BATTERED SPOUSES OF UNITED STATES CITIZENS AND LAWFUL PERMANENT RESIDENTS.—

(1) WAIVER OF INADMISSIBILITY.—Section 212(i)(1) of the Immigration and Nationality Act (8 U.S.C. 1182(i)(1)) is amended by inserting before the period at the end the following: "or, in the case of an alien granted classification under clause (iii) or (iv) of section 204(a)(1)(A) or clause (ii) or (iii) of section 204(a)(1)(B), the alien demonstrates extreme hardship to the alien or the alien's United States citizen, lawful permanent resident, or qualified alien parent or child".

(2) WAIVER OF DEPORTABILITY.—Section 237(a)(1)(H) of the Immigration and Nationality Act (8 U.S.C. 1227(a)(1)(H)) is amended—

(A) in clause (i), by inserting "(I)" after "(i)";

(B) by redesignating clause (ii) as subclause (II); and

(C) by adding after clause (i) the following:

"(ii) is an alien who qualifies for classification under clause (iii) or (iv) of section 204(a)(1)(A) or clause (ii) or (iii) of section 204(a)(1)(B).".

(d) BATTERED IMMIGRANT WAIVER.—Section 212(g)(1) of the Immigration and Nationality Act (8 U.S.C. 1182(g)(1)) is amended—

(1) in subparagraph (A), by striking "or" at the end;

(2) in subparagraph (B), by adding "or" at the end; and

(3) by inserting after subparagraph (B) the following:

"(C) qualifies for classification under clause (iii) or (iv) of section 204(a)(1)(A) or classification under clause (ii) or (iii) of section 204(a)(1)(B);".

(e) WAIVERS FOR VAWA ELIGIBLE BATTERED IMMIGRANTS.— Section 212(h)(1) of the Immigration and Nationality Act (8 U.S.C. 1182(h)(1)) is amended—

(1) in subparagraph (B), by striking "and" and inserting "or"; and

(2) by adding at the end the following:

"(C) the alien qualifies for classification under clause (iii) or (iv) of section 204(a)(1)(A) or classification under clause (ii) or (iii) of section 204(a)(1)(B); and".

(f) PUBLIC CHARGE.—Section 212 of the Immigration and Nationality Act (8 U.S.C. 1182) is amended by adding at the end the following:

"(p) In determining whether an alien described in subsection (a)(4)(C)(i) is inadmissible under subsection (a)(4) or ineligible to receive an immigrant visa or otherwise to adjust to the status of permanent resident by reason of subsection (a)(4), the consular officer or the Attorney General shall not consider any benefits the alien may have received that were authorized under section 501 of the Illegal Immigration Reform and Immigrant Responsibility Act of 1996 (8 U.S.C. 1641(c)).".

Deadline.

(g) REPORT.—Not later than 6 months after the date of the enactment of this Act, the Attorney General shall submit a report to the Committees on the Judiciary of the Senate and the House of Representatives covering, with respect to fiscal year 1997 and each fiscal year thereafter—

(1) the policy and procedures of the Immigration and Naturalization Service under which an alien who has been battered

PUBLIC LAW 106–386—OCT. 28, 2000   114 STAT. 1527

or subjected to extreme cruelty who is eligible for suspension of deportation or cancellation of removal can request to be placed, and be placed, in deportation or removal proceedings so that such alien may apply for suspension of deportation or cancellation of removal;

(2) the number of requests filed at each district office under this policy;

(3) the number of these requests granted reported separately for each district; and

(4) the average length of time at each Immigration and Naturalization office between the date that an alien who has been subject to battering or extreme cruelty eligible for suspension of deportation or cancellation of removal requests to be placed in deportation or removal proceedings and the date that the immigrant appears before an immigration judge to file an application for suspension of deportation or cancellation of removal.

SEC. 1506. RESTORING IMMIGRATION PROTECTIONS UNDER THE VIOLENCE AGAINST WOMEN ACT OF 1994.

(a) REMOVING BARRIERS TO ADJUSTMENT OF STATUS FOR VICTIMS OF DOMESTIC VIOLENCE.—

(1) IMMIGRATION AMENDMENTS.—Section 245 of the Immigration and Nationality Act (8 U.S.C. 1255) is amended—

(A) in subsection (a), by inserting "or the status of any other alien having an approved petition for classification under subparagraph (A)(iii), (A)(iv), (B)(ii), or (B)(iii) of section 204(a)(1) or" after "into the United States."; and

(B) in subsection (c), by striking "Subsection (a) shall not be applicable to" and inserting the following: "Other than an alien having an approved petition for classification under subparagraph (A)(iii), (A)(iv), (A)(v), (A)(vi), (B)(ii), (B)(iii), or (B)(iv) of section 204(a)(1), subsection (a) shall not be applicable to".

(2) EFFECTIVE DATE.—The amendments made by paragraph (1) shall apply to applications for adjustment of status pending on or made on or after January 14, 1998.   8 USC 1255 note.

(b) REMOVING BARRIERS TO CANCELLATION OF REMOVAL AND SUSPENSION OF DEPORTATION FOR VICTIMS OF DOMESTIC VIOLENCE.—

(1) NOT TREATING SERVICE OF NOTICE AS TERMINATING CONTINUOUS PERIOD.—Section 240A(d)(1) of the Immigration and Nationality Act (8 U.S.C. 1229b(d)(1)) is amended by striking "when the alien is served a notice to appear under section 239(a) or" and inserting "(A) except in the case of an alien who applies for cancellation of removal under subsection (b)(2), when the alien is served a notice to appear under section 239(a), or (B)".

(2) EFFECTIVE DATE.—The amendment made by paragraph (1) shall take effect as if included in the enactment of section 304 of the Illegal Immigration Reform and Immigrant Responsibility Act of 1996 (Public Law 104–208; 110 Stat. 587).   8 USC 1229b note.

(3) MODIFICATION OF CERTAIN TRANSITION RULES FOR BATTERED SPOUSE OR CHILD.—Section 309(c)(5)(C) of the Illegal Immigration Reform and Immigrant Responsibility Act of 1996 (8 U.S.C. 1101 note) is amended—

(A) by striking the subparagraph heading and inserting the following:

"(C) SPECIAL RULE FOR CERTAIN ALIENS GRANTED TEMPORARY PROTECTION FROM DEPORTATION AND FOR BATTERED SPOUSES AND CHILDREN.—"; and

(B) in clause (i)—

(i) in subclause (IV), by striking "or" at the end;

(ii) in subclause (V), by striking the period at the end and inserting "; or"; and

(iii) by adding at the end the following:

"(VI) is an alien who was issued an order to show cause or was in deportation proceedings before April 1, 1997, and who applied for suspension of deportation under section 244(a)(3) of the Immigration and Nationality Act (as in effect before the date of the enactment of this Act).".

8 USC 1101 note.   (4) EFFECTIVE DATE.—The amendments made by paragraph (3) shall take effect as if included in the enactment of section 309 of the Illegal Immigration Reform and Immigrant Responsibility Act of 1996 (8 U.S.C. 1101 note).

(c) ELIMINATING TIME LIMITATIONS ON MOTIONS TO REOPEN REMOVAL AND DEPORTATION PROCEEDINGS FOR VICTIMS OF DOMESTIC VIOLENCE.—

(1) REMOVAL PROCEEDINGS.—

(A) IN GENERAL.—Section 240(c)(6)(C) of the Immigration and Nationality Act (8 U.S.C. 1229a(c)(6)(C)) is amended by adding at the end the following:

"(iv) SPECIAL RULE FOR BATTERED SPOUSES AND CHILDREN.—The deadline specified in subsection (b)(5)(C) for filing a motion to reopen does not apply—

"(I) if the basis for the motion is to apply for relief under clause (iii) or (iv) of section 204(a)(1)(A), clause (ii) or (iii) of section 204(a)(1)(B), or section 240A(b)(2);

"(II) if the motion is accompanied by a cancellation of removal application to be filed with the Attorney General or by a copy of the self-petition that has been or will be filed with the Immigration and Naturalization Service upon the granting of the motion to reopen; and

"(III) if the motion to reopen is filed within 1 year of the entry of the final order of removal, except that the Attorney General may, in the Attorney General's discretion, waive this time limitation in the case of an alien who demonstrates extraordinary circumstances or extreme hardship to the alien's child.".

8 USC 1229a note.   (B) EFFECTIVE DATE.—The amendment made by subparagraph (A) shall take effect as if included in the enactment of section 304 of the Illegal Immigration Reform and Immigrant Responsibility Act of 1996 (8 U.S.C. 1229–1229c).

8 USC 1229a note.   (2) DEPORTATION PROCEEDINGS.—

(A) IN GENERAL.—Notwithstanding any limitation imposed by law on motions to reopen or rescind deportation proceedings under the Immigration and Nationality Act (as in effect before the title III–A effective date in section

PUBLIC LAW 106–386—OCT. 28, 2000   114 STAT. 1529

309 of the Illegal Immigration Reform and Immigrant
Responsibility Act of 1996 (8 U.S.C. 1101 note)), there
is no time limit on the filing of a motion to reopen such
proceedings, and the deadline specified in section 242B(c)(3)
of the Immigration and Nationality Act (as so in effect)
(8 U.S.C. 1252b(c)(3)) does not apply—
        (i) if the basis of the motion is to apply for relief
    under clause (iii) or (iv) of section 204(a)(1)(A) of the
    Immigration   and   Nationality   Act   (8   U.S.C.
    1154(a)(1)(A)), clause (ii) or (iii) of section 204(a)(1)(B)
    of such Act (8 U.S.C. 1154(a)(1)(B)), or section 244(a)(3)
    of such Act (as so in effect) (8 U.S.C. 1254(a)(3)); and
        (ii) if the motion is accompanied by a suspension
    of deportation application to be filed with the Attorney
    General or by a copy of the self-petition that will
    be filed with the Immigration and Naturalization
    Service upon the granting of the motion to reopen.
    (B) APPLICABILITY.—Subparagraph (A) shall apply to
motions filed by aliens who—
        (i) are, or were, in deportation proceedings under
    the Immigration and Nationality Act (as in effect before
    the title III–A effective date in section 309 of the
    Illegal Immigration Reform and Immigrant Responsi-
    bility Act of 1996 (8 U.S.C. 1101 note)); and
        (ii) have become eligible to apply for relief under
    clause (iii) or (iv) of section 204(a)(1)(A) of the Immigra-
    tion and Nationality Act (8 U.S.C. 1154(a)(1)(A)), clause
    (ii) or (iii) of section 204(a)(1)(B) of such Act (8 U.S.C.
    1154(a)(1)(B)), or section 244(a)(3) of such Act (as in
    effect before the title III–A effective date in section
    309 of the Illegal Immigration Reform and Immigrant
    Responsibility Act of 1996 (8 U.S.C. 1101 note)) as
    a result of the amendments made by—
            (I) subtitle G of title IV of the Violent Crime
        Control and Law Enforcement Act of 1994 (Public
        Law 103–322; 108 Stat. 1953 et seq.); or
            (II) this title.

**SEC. 1507. REMEDYING PROBLEMS WITH IMPLEMENTATION OF THE
IMMIGRATION PROVISIONS OF THE VIOLENCE AGAINST
WOMEN ACT OF 1994.**

    (a) EFFECT OF CHANGES IN ABUSERS' CITIZENSHIP STATUS ON
SELF-PETITION.—
        (1) RECLASSIFICATION.—Section   204(a)(1)(A)   of   the
    Immigration and Nationality Act (8 U.S.C. 1154(a)(1)(A)) (as
    amended by section 1503(b)(3) of this title) is amended by
    adding at the end the following:
    "(vi) For the purposes of any petition filed under clause (iii)
or (iv), the denaturalization, loss or renunciation of citizenship,
death of the abuser, divorce, or changes to the abuser's citizenship
status after filing of the petition shall not adversely affect the
approval of the petition, and for approved petitions shall not preclude the classification of the eligible self-petitioning spouse or
child as an immediate relative or affect the alien's ability to adjust
status under subsections (a) and (c) of section 245 or obtain status
as a lawful permanent resident based on the approved self-petition
under such clauses.".

(2) LOSS OF STATUS.—Section 204(a)(1)(B) of the Immigration and Nationality Act (8 U.S.C. 1154(a)(1)(B)) (as amended by section 1503(c)(3) of this title) is amended by adding at the end the following:

"(v)(I) For the purposes of any petition filed or approved under clause (ii) or (iii), divorce, or the loss of lawful permanent resident status by a spouse or parent after the filing of a petition under that clause shall not adversely affect approval of the petition, and, for an approved petition, shall not affect the alien's ability to adjust status under subsections (a) and (c) of section 245 or obtain status as a lawful permanent resident based on an approved self-petition under clause (ii) or (iii).

"(II) Upon the lawful permanent resident spouse or parent becoming or establishing the existence of United States citizenship through naturalization, acquisition of citizenship, or other means, any petition filed with the Immigration and Naturalization Service and pending or approved under clause (ii) or (iii) on behalf of an alien who has been battered or subjected to extreme cruelty shall be deemed reclassified as a petition filed under subparagraph (A) even if the acquisition of citizenship occurs after divorce or termination of parental rights.".

8 USC 1151.   (3) DEFINITION OF IMMEDIATE RELATIVES.—Section 201(b)(2)(A)(i) of the Immigration and Nationality Act (8 U.S.C. 1154(b)(2)(A)(i)) is amended by adding at the end the following: "For purposes of this clause, an alien who has filed a petition under clause (iii) or (iv) of section 204(a)(1)(A) of this Act remains an immediate relative in the event that the United States citizen spouse or parent loses United States citizenship on account of the abuse.".

(b) ALLOWING REMARRIAGE OF BATTERED IMMIGRANTS.—Section 204(h) of the Immigration and Nationality Act (8 U.S.C. 1154(h)) is amended by adding at the end the following: "Remarriage of an alien whose petition was approved under section 204(a)(1)(B)(ii) or 204(a)(1)(A)(iii) or marriage of an alien described in clause (iv) or (vi) of section 204(a)(1)(A) or in section 204(a)(1)(B)(iii) shall not be the basis for revocation of a petition approval under section 205.".

SEC. 1508. TECHNICAL CORRECTION TO QUALIFIED ALIEN DEFINITION FOR BATTERED IMMIGRANTS.

Section 431(c)(1)(B)(iii) of the Personal Responsibility and Work Opportunity Reconciliation Act of 1996 (8 U.S.C. 1641(c)(1)(B)(iii)) is amended to read as follows:

"(iii) suspension of deportation under section 244(a)(3) of the Immigration and Nationality Act (as in effect before the title III–A effective date in section 309 of the Illegal Immigration Reform and Immigrant Responsibility Act of 1996).".

SEC. 1509. ACCESS TO CUBAN ADJUSTMENT ACT FOR BATTERED IMMIGRANT SPOUSES AND CHILDREN.

(a) IN GENERAL.—The last sentence of the first section of Public Law 89–732 (November 2, 1966; 8 U.S.C. 1255 note) is amended by striking the period at the end and inserting the following: ", except that such spouse or child who has been battered or subjected to extreme cruelty may adjust to permanent resident status under this Act without demonstrating that he or she is residing with the Cuban spouse or parent in the United States. In acting on applications under this section with respect to spouses or children who have been battered or subjected to extreme cruelty, the Attorney General shall apply the provisions of section 204(a)(1)(H).".

(b) EFFECTIVE DATE.—The amendment made by subsection (a) shall be effective as if included in subtitle G of title IV of the Violent Crime Control and Law Enforcement Act of 1994 (Public Law 103–322; 108 Stat. 1953 et seq.).

8 USC 1255 note.

SEC. 1510. ACCESS TO THE NICARAGUAN ADJUSTMENT AND CENTRAL AMERICAN RELIEF ACT FOR BATTERED SPOUSES AND CHILDREN.

(a) ADJUSTMENT OF STATUS OF CERTAIN NICARAGUAN AND CUBAN BATTERED SPOUSES.—Section 202(d) of the Nicaraguan Adjustment and Central American Relief Act (8 U.S.C. 1255 note; Public Law 105–100, as amended) is amended—

(1) in paragraph (1), by striking subparagraph (B) and inserting the following:

"(B) the alien—

"(i) is the spouse, child, or unmarried son or daughter of an alien whose status is adjusted to that of an alien lawfully admitted for permanent residence under subsection (a), except that in the case of such an unmarried son or daughter, the son or daughter shall be required to establish that the son or daughter has been physically present in the United States for a continuous period beginning not later than December 1, 1995, and ending not earlier than the date on which the application for adjustment under this subsection is filed; or

"(ii) was, at the time at which an alien filed for adjustment under subsection (a), the spouse or child of an alien whose status is adjusted to that of an alien lawfully admitted for permanent residence under subsection (a), and the spouse, child, or child of the spouse has been battered or subjected to extreme cruelty by the alien that filed for adjustment under subsection (a);"; and

(2) by adding at the end the following:

"(3) PROCEDURE.—In acting on an application under this section with respect to a spouse or child who has been battered or subjected to extreme cruelty, the Attorney General shall apply section 204(a)(1)(H).".

(b) CANCELLATION OF REMOVAL AND SUSPENSION OF DEPORTATION TRANSITION RULES FOR CERTAIN BATTERED SPOUSES.—Section 309(c)(5)(C) of the Illegal Immigration and Reform and Immigrant Responsibility Act of 1996 (division C of Public Law 104–208; 8 U.S.C. 1101 note) (as amended by section 1506(b)(3) of this title) is amended—

(1) in clause (i)—

(A) by striking the period at the end of subclause (VI) (as added by section 1506(b)(3) of this title) and inserting "; or"; and

(B) by adding at the end the following:

"(VII)(aa) was the spouse or child of an alien described in subclause (I), (II), or (V)—

"(AA) at the time at which a decision is rendered to suspend the deportation or cancel the removal of the alien;

"(BB) at the time at which the alien filed an application for suspension of deportation or cancellation of removal; or

"(CC) at the time at which the alien registered for benefits under the settlement agreement in American Baptist Churches, et. al. v. Thornburgh (ABC), applied for temporary protected status, or applied for asylum; and

"(bb) the spouse, child, or child of the spouse has been battered or subjected to extreme cruelty by the alien described in subclause (I), (II), or (V)."; and

(2) by adding at the end the following:

"(iii) CONSIDERATION OF PETITIONS.—In acting on a petition filed under subclause (VII) of clause (i) the provisions set forth in section 204(a)(1)(H) shall apply.

"(iv) RESIDENCE WITH SPOUSE OR PARENT NOT REQUIRED.—For purposes of the application of clause (i)(VII), a spouse or child shall not be required to demonstrate that he or she is residing with the spouse or parent in the United States.".

8 USC 1101 note.

(c) EFFECTIVE DATE.—The amendments made by subsections (a) and (b) shall be effective as if included in the Nicaraguan Adjustment and Central American Relief Act (8 U.S.C. 1255 note; Public Law 105–100, as amended).

8 USC 1255 note.

SEC. 1511. ACCESS TO THE HAITIAN REFUGEE FAIRNESS ACT OF 1998 FOR BATTERED SPOUSES AND CHILDREN.

(a) IN GENERAL.—Section 902(d)(1)(B) of the Haitian Refugee Immigration Fairness Act of 1998 (division A of section 101(h) of Public Law 105–277; 112 Stat. 2681–538) is amended to read as follows:

"(B)(i) the alien is the spouse, child, or unmarried son or daughter of an alien whose status is adjusted to that of an alien lawfully admitted for permanent residence under subsection (a), except that, in the case of such an unmarried son or daughter, the son or daughter shall be required to establish that the son or daughter has been physically present in the United States for a continuous period beginning not later than December 1, 1995, and ending not earlier than the date on which the application for such adjustment is filed;

"(ii) at the time of filing of the application for adjustment under subsection (a), the alien is the spouse or child of an alien whose status is adjusted to that of an alien lawfully admitted for permanent residence under subsection (a) and the spouse, child, or child of the spouse has been battered or subjected to extreme cruelty by the individual described in subsection (a); and

"(iii) in acting on applications under this section with respect to spouses or children who have been battered or subjected to extreme cruelty, the Attorney General shall apply the provisions of section 204(a)(1)(H).".

PUBLIC LAW 106–386—OCT. 28, 2000   114 STAT. 1533

(b) EFFECTIVE DATE.—The amendment made by subsection (a) shall be effective as if included in the Haitian Refugee Immigration Fairness Act of 1998 (division A of section 101(h) of Public Law 105–277; 112 Stat. 2681–538).

SEC. 1512. ACCESS TO SERVICES AND LEGAL REPRESENTATION FOR BATTERED IMMIGRANTS.

(a) LAW ENFORCEMENT AND PROSECUTION GRANTS.—Section 2001(b) of part T of title I of the Omnibus Crime Control and Safe Streets Act of 1968 (42 U.S.C. 3796gg(b)) (as amended by section 1209(c) of this division) is amended by adding at the end the following:

"(11) providing assistance to victims of domestic violence and sexual assault in immigration matters.".

(b) GRANTS TO ENCOURAGE ARRESTS.—Section 2101(b)(5) of part U of title I of the Omnibus Crime Control and Safe Streets Act of 1968 (42 U.S.C. 3796hh(b)(5)) is amended by inserting before the period the following: ", including strengthening assistance to such victims in immigration matters".

(c) RURAL DOMESTIC VIOLENCE AND CHILD ABUSE ENFORCEMENT GRANTS.—Section 40295(a)(2) of the Violent Crime Control and Law Enforcement Act of 1994 (Public Law 103–322; 108 Stat. 1953; 42 U.S.C. 13971(a)(2)) is amended to read as follows:

"(2) to provide treatment, counseling, and assistance to victims of domestic violence and child abuse, including in immigration matters; and".

(d) CAMPUS DOMESTIC VIOLENCE GRANTS.—Section 826(b)(5) of the Higher Education Amendments of 1998 (Public Law 105–244; 20 U.S.C. 1152) is amended by inserting before the period at the end the following: ", including assistance to victims in immigration matters".

SEC. 1513. PROTECTION FOR CERTAIN CRIME VICTIMS INCLUDING VICTIMS OF CRIMES AGAINST WOMEN.

(a) FINDINGS AND PURPOSE.—   8 USC 1101 note.

(1) FINDINGS.—Congress makes the following findings:

(A) Immigrant women and children are often targeted to be victims of crimes committed against them in the United States, including rape, torture, kidnaping, trafficking, incest, domestic violence, sexual assault, female genital mutilation, forced prostitution, involuntary servitude, being held hostage or being criminally restrained.

(B) All women and children who are victims of these crimes committed against them in the United States must be able to report these crimes to law enforcement and fully participate in the investigation of the crimes committed against them and the prosecution of the perpetrators of such crimes.

(2) PURPOSE.—

(A) The purpose of this section is to create a new nonimmigrant visa classification that will strengthen the ability of law enforcement agencies to detect, investigate, and prosecute cases of domestic violence, sexual assault, trafficking of aliens, and other crimes described in section 101(a)(15)(U)(iii) of the Immigration and Nationality Act committed against aliens, while offering protection to victims of such offenses in keeping with the humanitarian interests of the United States. This visa will encourage law enforcement officials to better serve immigrant crime victims and to prosecute crimes committed against aliens.

(B) Creating a new nonimmigrant visa classification will facilitate the reporting of crimes to law enforcement officials by trafficked, exploited, victimized, and abused aliens who are not in lawful immigration status. It also gives law enforcement officials a means to regularize the status of cooperating individuals during investigations or prosecutions. Providing temporary legal status to aliens who have been severely victimized by criminal activity also comports with the humanitarian interests of the United States.

(C) Finally, this section gives the Attorney General discretion to convert the status of such nonimmigrants to that of permanent residents when doing so is justified on humanitarian grounds, for family unity, or is otherwise in the public interest.

(b) ESTABLISHMENT OF HUMANITARIAN/MATERIAL WITNESS NON-IMMIGRANT CLASSIFICATION.—Section 101(a)(15) of the Immigration and Nationality Act (8 U.S.C. 1101(a)(15)) (as amended by section 107 of this Act) is amended—

(1) by striking "or" at the end of subparagraph (S);

(2) by striking the period at the end of subparagraph (T) and inserting "; or"; and

(3) by adding at the end the following new subparagraph:

"(U)(i) subject to section 214(o), an alien who files a petition for status under this subparagraph, if the Attorney General determines that—

"(I) the alien has suffered substantial physical or mental abuse as a result of having been a victim of criminal activity described in clause (iii);

"(II) the alien (or in the case of an alien child under the age of 16, the parent, guardian, or next friend of the alien) possesses information concerning criminal activity described in clause (iii);

"(III) the alien (or in the case of an alien child under the age of 16, the parent, guardian, or next friend of the alien) has been helpful, is being helpful, or is likely to be helpful to a Federal, State, or local law enforcement official, to a Federal, State, or local prosecutor, to a Federal or State judge, to the Service, or to other Federal, State, or local authorities investigating or prosecuting criminal activity described in clause (iii); and

"(IV) the criminal activity described in clause (iii) violated the laws of the United States or occurred in the United States (including in Indian country and military installations) or the territories and possessions of the United States;

"(ii) if the Attorney General considers it necessary to avoid extreme hardship to the spouse, the child, or, in the case of an alien child, the parent of the alien described in clause (i), the Attorney General may also grant status under this paragraph based upon certification of a government official listed in clause (i)(III) that an investigation or prosecution would be harmed without the assistance of the spouse, the child, or, in the case of an alien child, the parent of the alien; and

"(iii) the criminal activity referred to in this clause is that involving one or more of the following or any similar activity in violation of Federal, State, or local criminal law: rape; torture; trafficking; incest; domestic violence; sexual assault; abusive sexual contact; prostitution; sexual exploitation; female genital mutilation; being held hostage; peonage; involuntary servitude; slave trade; kidnapping; abduction; unlawful criminal restraint; false imprisonment; blackmail; extortion; manslaughter; murder; felonious assault; witness tampering; obstruction of justice; perjury; or attempt, conspiracy, or solicitation to commit any of the above mentioned crimes.".

(c) CONDITIONS FOR ADMISSION AND DUTIES OF THE ATTORNEY GENERAL.—Section 214 of such Act (8 U.S.C. 1184) (as amended by section 107 of this Act) is amended by adding at the end the following new subsection:

"(o) REQUIREMENTS APPLICABLE TO SECTION 101(a)(15)(U) VISAS.—

"(1) PETITIONING PROCEDURES FOR SECTION 101(a)(15)(U) VISAS.—The petition filed by an alien under section 101(a)(15)(U)(i) shall contain a certification from a Federal, State, or local law enforcement official, prosecutor, judge, or other Federal, State, or local authority investigating criminal activity described in section 101(a)(15)(U)(iii). This certification may also be provided by an official of the Service whose ability to provide such certification is not limited to information concerning immigration violations. This certification shall state that the alien "has been helpful, is being helpful, or is likely to be helpful" in the investigation or prosecution of criminal activity described in section 101(a)(15)(U)(iii).

"(2) NUMERICAL LIMITATIONS.—

"(A) The number of aliens who may be issued visas or otherwise provided status as nonimmigrants under section 101(a)(15)(U) in any fiscal year shall not exceed 10,000.

"(B) The numerical limitations in subparagraph (A) shall only apply to principal aliens described in section 101(a)(15)(U)(i), and not to spouses, children, or, in the case of alien children, the alien parents of such children.

"(3) DUTIES OF THE ATTORNEY GENERAL WITH RESPECT TO 'U' VISA NONIMMIGRANTS.—With respect to nonimmigrant aliens described in subsection (a)(15)(U)—

"(A) the Attorney General and other government officials, where appropriate, shall provide those aliens with referrals to nongovernmental organizations to advise the aliens regarding their options while in the United States and the resources available to them; and

"(B) the Attorney General shall, during the period those aliens are in lawful temporary resident status under that subsection, provide the aliens with employment authorization.

"(4) CREDIBLE EVIDENCE CONSIDERED.—In acting on any petition filed under this subsection, the consular officer or the Attorney General, as appropriate, shall consider any credible evidence relevant to the petition.

"(5) NONEXCLUSIVE RELIEF.—Nothing in this subsection limits the ability of aliens who qualify for status under section 101(a)(15)(U) to seek any other immigration benefit or status for which the alien may be eligible.".

8 USC 1367.

(d) PROHIBITION ON ADVERSE DETERMINATIONS OF ADMISSIBILITY OR DEPORTABILITY.—Section 384(a) of the Illegal Immigration Reform and Immigrant Responsibility Act of 1996 is amended—

(1) by striking "or" at the end of paragraph (1)(C);

(2) by striking the comma at the end of paragraph (1)(D) and inserting ", or"; and

(3) by inserting after paragraph (1)(D) the following new subparagraph:

"(E) in the case of an alien applying for status under section 101(a)(15)(U) of the Immigration and Nationality Act, the perpetrator of the substantial physical or mental abuse and the criminal activity,"; and

(4) in paragraph (2), by inserting "section 101(a)(15)(U)," after "section 216(c)(4)(C),".

(e) WAIVER OF GROUNDS OF INELIGIBILITY FOR ADMISSION.—Section 212(d) of the Immigration and Nationality Act (8 U.S.C. 1182(d)) is amended by adding at the end the following new paragraph:

"(13) The Attorney General shall determine whether a ground of inadmissibility exists with respect to a nonimmigrant described in section 101(a)(15)(U). The Attorney General, in the Attorney General's discretion, may waive the application of subsection (a) (other than paragraph (3)(E)) in the case of a nonimmigrant described in section 101(a)(15)(U), if the Attorney General considers it to be in the public or national interest to do so.".

(f) ADJUSTMENT TO PERMANENT RESIDENT STATUS.—Section 245 of such Act (8 U.S.C. 1255) is amended by adding at the end the following new subsection:

"(l)(1) The Attorney General may adjust the status of an alien admitted into the United States (or otherwise provided nonimmigrant status) under section 101(a)(15)(U) to that of an alien lawfully admitted for permanent residence if the alien is not described in section 212(a)(3)(E), unless the Attorney General determines based on affirmative evidence that the alien unreasonably refused to provide assistance in a criminal investigation or prosecution, if—

"(A) the alien has been physically present in the United States for a continuous period of at least 3 years since the date of admission as a nonimmigrant under clause (i) or (ii) of section 101(a)(15)(U); and

"(B) in the opinion of the Attorney General, the alien's continued presence in the United States is justified on humanitarian grounds, to ensure family unity, or is otherwise in the public interest.

"(2) An alien shall be considered to have failed to maintain continuous physical presence in the United States under paragraph (1)(A) if the alien has departed from the United States for any period in excess of 90 days or for any periods in the aggregate exceeding 180 days unless the absence is in order to assist in the investigation or prosecution or unless an official involved in the investigation or prosecution certifies that the absence was otherwise justified.

PUBLIC LAW 106–386—OCT. 28, 2000   114 STAT. 1537

"(3) Upon approval of adjustment of status under paragraph (1) of an alien described in section 101(a)(15)(U)(i) the Attorney General may adjust the status of or issue an immigrant visa to a spouse, a child, or, in the case of an alien child, a parent who did not receive a nonimmigrant visa under section 101(a)(15)(U)(ii) if the Attorney General considers the grant of such status or visa necessary to avoid extreme hardship.

"(4) Upon the approval of adjustment of status under paragraph (1) or (3), the Attorney General shall record the alien's lawful admission for permanent residence as of the date of such approval.".

TITLE VI—MISCELLANEOUS

SEC. 1601. NOTICE REQUIREMENTS FOR SEXUALLY VIOLENT OFFENDERS.

(a) SHORT TITLE.—This section may be cited as the "Campus Sex Crimes Prevention Act".

(b) NOTICE WITH RESPECT TO INSTITUTIONS OF HIGHER EDUCATION.—

(1) IN GENERAL.—Section 170101 of the Violent Crime Control and Law Enforcement Act of 1994 (42 U.S.C. 14071) is amended by adding at the end the following:

"(j) NOTICE OF ENROLLMENT AT OR EMPLOYMENT BY INSTITUTIONS OF HIGHER EDUCATION.—

"(1) NOTICE BY OFFENDERS.—

"(A) IN GENERAL.—In addition to any other requirements of this section, any person who is required to register in a State shall provide notice as required under State law—

"(i) of each institution of higher education in that State at which the person is employed, carries on a vocation, or is a student; and

"(ii) of each change in enrollment or employment status of such person at an institution of higher education in that State.

"(B) CHANGE IN STATUS.—A change in status under subparagraph (A)(ii) shall be reported by the person in the manner provided by State law. State procedures shall ensure that the updated information is promptly made available to a law enforcement agency having jurisdiction where such institution is located and entered into the appropriate State records or data system.

"(2) STATE REPORTING.—State procedures shall ensure that the registration information collected under paragraph (1)—

"(A) is promptly made available to a law enforcement agency having jurisdiction where such institution is located; and

"(B) entered into the appropriate State records or data system.

"(3) REQUEST.—Nothing in this subsection shall require an educational institution to request such information from any State.".

(2) EFFECTIVE DATE.—The amendment made by this subsection shall take effect 2 years after the date of the enactment of this Act.

(c) DISCLOSURES BY INSTITUTIONS OF HIGHER EDUCATION.—

Campus Sex Crimes Prevention Act. 20 USC 1001 note.

42 USC 14071 note.

(1) IN GENERAL.—Section 485(f)(1) of the Higher Education Act of 1965 (20 U.S.C. 1092(f)(1)) is amended by adding at the end the following:

"(I) A statement advising the campus community where law enforcement agency information provided by a State under section 170101(j) of the Violent Crime Control and Law Enforcement Act of 1994 (42 U.S.C. 14071(j)), concerning registered sex offenders may be obtained, such as the law enforcement office of the institution, a local law enforcement agency with jurisdiction for the campus, or a computer network address.".

20 USC 1092
note.

(2) EFFECTIVE DATE.—The amendment made by this subsection shall take effect 2 years after the date of the enactment of this Act.

(d) AMENDMENT TO FAMILY EDUCATIONAL RIGHTS AND PRIVACY ACT OF 1974.—Section 444(b) of the General Education Provisions Act (20 U.S.C. 1232g(b)), also known as the Family Educational Rights and Privacy Act of 1974, is amended by adding at the end the following:

"(7)(A) Nothing in this section may be construed to prohibit an educational institution from disclosing information provided to the institution under section 170101 of the Violent Crime Control and Law Enforcement Act of 1994 (42 U.S.C. 14071) concerning registered sex offenders who are required to register under such section.

"(B) The Secretary shall take appropriate steps to notify educational institutions that disclosure of information described in subparagraph (A) is permitted.".

Teen Suicide
Prevention Act of
2000.
42 USC 290bb–
36 note.

SEC. 1602. TEEN SUICIDE PREVENTION STUDY.

(a) SHORT TITLE.—This section may be cited as the "Teen Suicide Prevention Act of 2000".

(b) FINDINGS.—Congress finds that—

(1) measures that increase public awareness of suicide as a preventable public health problem, and target parents and youth so that suicide risks and warning signs can be recognized, will help to eliminate the ignorance and stigma of suicide as barriers to youth and families seeking preventive care;

(2) suicide prevention efforts in the year 2000 should—

(A) target at-risk youth, particularly youth with mental health problems, substance abuse problems, or contact with the juvenile justice system;

(B) involve—

(i) the identification of the characteristics of the at-risk youth and other youth who are contemplating suicide, and barriers to treatment of the youth; and

(ii) the development of model treatment programs for the youth;

(C) include a pilot study of the outcomes of treatment for juvenile delinquents with mental health or substance abuse problems;

(D) include a public education approach to combat the negative effects of the stigma of, and discrimination against individuals with, mental health and substance abuse problems; and

PUBLIC LAW 106–386—OCT. 28, 2000   114 STAT. 1539

(E) include a nationwide effort to develop, implement, and evaluate a mental health awareness program for schools, communities, and families;

(3) although numerous symptoms, diagnoses, traits, characteristics, and psychosocial stressors of suicide have been investigated, no single factor or set of factors has ever come close to predicting suicide with accuracy;

(4) research of United States youth, such as a 1994 study by Lewinsohn, Rohde, and Seeley, has shown predictors of suicide, such as a history of suicide attempts, current suicidal ideation and depression, a recent attempt or completed suicide by a friend, and low self-esteem; and

(5) epidemiological data illustrate—

(A) the trend of suicide at younger ages as well as increases in suicidal ideation among youth in the United States; and

(B) distinct differences in approaches to suicide by gender, with—

(i) 3 to 5 times as many females as males attempting suicide; and

(ii) 3 to 5 times as many males as females completing suicide.

(c) PURPOSE.—The purpose of this section is to provide for a study of predictors of suicide among at-risk and other youth, and barriers that prevent the youth from receiving treatment, to facilitate the development of model treatment programs and public education and awareness efforts.

(d) STUDY.—Not later than 1 year after the date of the enactment of this Act, the Secretary of Health and Human Services shall carry out, directly or by grant or contract, a study that is designed to identify—

(1) the characteristics of at-risk and other youth age 13 through 21 who are contemplating suicide;

(2) the characteristics of at-risk and other youth who are younger than age 13 and are contemplating suicide; and

(3) the barriers that prevent youth described in paragraphs (1) and (2) from receiving treatment.

(e) AUTHORIZATION OF APPROPRIATIONS.—There are authorized to be appropriated to carry out this section such sums as may be necessary.

SEC. 1603. DECADE OF PAIN CONTROL AND RESEARCH.

The calendar decade beginning January 1, 2001, is designated as the "Decade of Pain Control and Research".

DIVISION C—MISCELLANEOUS PROVISIONS

SEC. 2001. AIMEE'S LAW.

Aimee's Law.
42 USC 13713.

(a) SHORT TITLE.—This section may be cited as "Aimee's Law".

(b) DEFINITIONS.—In this section:

(1) DANGEROUS SEXUAL OFFENSE.—The term "dangerous sexual offense" means any offense under State law for conduct that would constitute an offense under chapter 109A of title 18, United States Code, had the conduct occurred in the special

maritime and territorial jurisdiction of the United States or in a Federal prison.

(2) MURDER.—The term "murder" has the meaning given the term in part I of the Uniform Crime Reports of the Federal Bureau of Investigation.

(3) RAPE.—The term "rape" has the meaning given the term in part I of the Uniform Crime Reports of the Federal Bureau of Investigation.

(c) PENALTY.—

(1) SINGLE STATE.—In any case in which a State convicts an individual of murder, rape, or a dangerous sexual offense, who has a prior conviction for any one of those offenses in a State described in paragraph (3), the Attorney General shall transfer an amount equal to the costs of incarceration, prosecution, and apprehension of that individual, from Federal law enforcement assistance funds that have been allocated to but not distributed to the State that convicted the individual of the prior offense, to the State account that collects Federal law enforcement assistance funds of the State that convicted that individual of the subsequent offense.

(2) MULTIPLE STATES.—In any case in which a State convicts an individual of murder, rape, or a dangerous sexual offense, who has a prior conviction for any one or more of those offenses in more than one other State described in paragraph (3), the Attorney General shall transfer an amount equal to the costs of incarceration, prosecution, and apprehension of that individual, from Federal law enforcement assistance funds that have been allocated to but not distributed to each State that convicted such individual of the prior offense, to the State account that collects Federal law enforcement assistance funds of the State that convicted that individual of the subsequent offense.

(3) STATE DESCRIBED.—A State is described in this paragraph if—

(A) the average term of imprisonment imposed by the State on individuals convicted of the offense for which the individual described in paragraph (1) or (2), as applicable, was convicted by the State is less than the average term of imprisonment imposed for that offense in all States; or

(B) with respect to the individual described in paragraph (1) or (2), as applicable, the individual had served less than 85 percent of the term of imprisonment to which that individual was sentenced for the prior offense.

For purposes of subparagraph (B), in a State that has indeterminate sentencing, the term of imprisonment to which that individual was sentenced for the prior offense shall be based on the lower of the range of sentences.

(d) STATE APPLICATIONS.—In order to receive an amount transferred under subsection (c), the chief executive of a State shall submit to the Attorney General an application, in such form and containing such information as the Attorney General may reasonably require, which shall include a certification that the State has convicted an individual of murder, rape, or a dangerous sexual offense, who has a prior conviction for one of those offenses in another State.

(e) SOURCE OF FUNDS.—

(1) IN GENERAL.—Any amount transferred under subsection (c) shall be derived by reducing the amount of Federal law enforcement assistance funds received by the State that convicted such individual of the prior offense before the distribution of the funds to the State. The Attorney General shall provide the State with an opportunity to select the specific Federal law enforcement assistance funds to be so reduced (other than Federal crime victim assistance funds).

(2) PAYMENT SCHEDULE.—The Attorney General, in consultation with the chief executive of the State that convicted such individual of the prior offense, shall establish a payment schedule.

(f) CONSTRUCTION.—Nothing in this section may be construed to diminish or otherwise affect any court ordered restitution.

(g) EXCEPTION.—This section does not apply if the individual convicted of murder, rape, or a dangerous sexual offense has been released from prison upon the reversal of a conviction for an offense described in subsection (c) and subsequently been convicted for an offense described in subsection (c).

(h) REPORT.—The Attorney General shall—

(1) conduct a study evaluating the implementation of this section; and

(2) not later than October 1, 2006, submit to Congress a report on the results of that study.

(i) COLLECTION OF RECIDIVISM DATA.—

(1) IN GENERAL.—Beginning with calendar year 2002, and each calendar year thereafter, the Attorney General shall collect and maintain information relating to, with respect to each State—

(A) the number of convictions during that calendar year for—

(i) any dangerous sexual offense;

(ii) rape; and

(iii) murder; and

(B) the number of convictions described in subparagraph (A) that constitute second or subsequent convictions of the defendant of an offense described in that subparagraph.

(2) REPORT.—Not later than March 1, 2003, and on March 1 of each year thereafter, the Attorney General shall submit to Congress a report, which shall include— *Deadline.*

(A) the information collected under paragraph (1) with respect to each State during the preceding calendar year; and

(B) the percentage of cases in each State in which an individual convicted of an offense described in paragraph (1)(A) was previously convicted of another such offense in another State during the preceding calendar year.

(j) EFFECTIVE DATE.—This section shall take effect on January 1, 2002.

SEC. 2002. PAYMENT OF CERTAIN ANTI-TERRORISM JUDGMENTS.

(a) PAYMENTS.—

(1) IN GENERAL.—Subject to subsections (b) and (c), the Secretary of the Treasury shall pay each person described in paragraph (2), at the person's election—

(A) 110 percent of compensatory damages awarded by judgment of a court on a claim or claims brought by the person under section 1605(a)(7) of title 28, United States Code, plus amounts necessary to pay post-judgment interest under section 1961 of such title, and, in the case of a claim or claims against Cuba, amounts awarded as sanctions by judicial order on April 18, 2000 (as corrected on June 2, 2000), subject to final appellate review of that order; or

(B) 100 percent of the compensatory damages awarded by judgment of a court on a claim or claims brought by the person under section 1605(a)(7) of title 28, United States Code, plus amounts necessary to pay post-judgment interest, as provided in section 1961 of such title, and, in the case of a claim or claims against Cuba, amounts awarded as sanctions by judicial order on April 18, 2000 (as corrected June 2, 2000), subject to final appellate review of that order.

Payments under this subsection shall be made promptly upon request.

(2) PERSONS COVERED.—A person described in this paragraph is a person who—

(A)(i) as of July 20, 2000, held a final judgment for a claim or claims brought under section 1605(a)(7) of title 28, United States Code, against Iran or Cuba, or the right to payment of an amount awarded as a judicial sanction with respect to such claim or claims; or

(ii) filed a suit under such section 1605(a)(7) on February 17, 1999, December 13, 1999, January 28, 2000, March 15, 2000, or July 27, 2000;

(B) relinquishes all claims and rights to compensatory damages and amounts awarded as judicial sanctions under such judgments;

(C) in the case of payment under paragraph (1)(A), relinquishes all rights and claims to punitive damages awarded in connection with such claim or claims; and

(D) in the case of payment under paragraph (1)(B), relinquishes all rights to execute against or attach property that is at issue in claims against the United States before an international tribunal, that is the subject of awards rendered by such tribunal, or that is subject to section 1610(f)(1)(A) of title 28, United States Code.

(b) FUNDING OF AMOUNTS.—

(1) JUDGMENTS AGAINST CUBA.—For purposes of funding the payments under subsection (a) in the case of judgments and sanctions entered against the Government of Cuba or Cuban entities, the President shall vest and liquidate up to and not exceeding the amount of property of the Government of Cuba and sanctioned entities in the United States or any commonwealth, territory, or possession thereof that has been blocked pursuant to section 5(b) of the Trading with the Enemy Act (50 U.S.C. App. 5(b)), sections 202 and 203 of the International Emergency Economic Powers Act (50 U.S.C. 1701–1702), or any other proclamation, order, or regulation issued thereunder. For the purposes of paying amounts for judicial

sanctions, payment shall be made from funds or accounts subject to sanctions as of April 18, 2000, or from blocked assets of the Government of Cuba.

(2) JUDGMENTS AGAINST IRAN.—For purposes of funding payments under subsection (a) in the case of judgments against Iran, the Secretary of the Treasury shall make such payments from amounts paid and liquidated from—

(A) rental proceeds accrued on the date of the enactment of this Act from Iranian diplomatic and consular property located in the United States; and

(B) funds not otherwise made available in an amount not to exceed the total of the amount in the Iran Foreign Military Sales Program account within the Foreign Military Sales Fund on the date of the enactment of this Act.

(c) SUBROGATION.—Upon payment under subsection (a) with respect to payments in connection with a Foreign Military Sales Program account, the United States shall be fully subrogated, to the extent of the payments, to all rights of the person paid under that subsection against the debtor foreign state. The President shall pursue these subrogated rights as claims or offsets of the United States in appropriate ways, including any negotiation process which precedes the normalization of relations between the foreign state designated as a state sponsor of terrorism and the United States, except that no funds shall be paid to Iran, or released to Iran, from property blocked under the International Emergency Economic Powers Act or from the Foreign Military Sales Fund, until such subrogated claims have been dealt with to the satisfaction of the United States.

(d) SENSE OF THE CONGRESS.—It is the sense of the Congress that the President should not normalize relations between the United States and Iran until the claims subrogated have been dealt with to the satisfaction of the United States.

(e) REAFFIRMATION OF AUTHORITY.—Congress reaffirms the President's statutory authority to manage and, where appropriate and consistent with the national interest, vest foreign assets located in the United States for the purposes, among other things, of assisting and, where appropriate, making payments to victims of terrorism.

(f) AMENDMENTS.—(1) Section 1610(f) of title 28, United States Code, is amended—

(A) in paragraphs (2)(A) and (2)(B)(ii), by striking "shall" each place it appears and inserting "should make every effort to"; and

(B) by adding at the end the following new paragraph:

"(3) WAIVER.—The President may waive any provision of paragraph (1) in the interest of national security.".

(2) Subsections (b) and (d) of section 117 of the Treasury Department Appropriations Act, 1999 (as contained in section 101(h) of Public Law 105–277) are repealed.

28 USC 1606, 1610 note.

SEC. 2003. AID FOR VICTIMS OF TERRORISM.

(a) MEETING THE NEEDS OF VICTIMS OF TERRORISM OUTSIDE THE UNITED STATES.—

(1) IN GENERAL.—Section 1404B(a) of the Victims of Crime Act of 1984 (42 U.S.C. 10603b(a)) is amended as follows:

"(a) VICTIMS OF ACTS OF TERRORISM OUTSIDE UNITED STATES.—

"(1) IN GENERAL.—The Director may make supplemental grants as provided in 1402(d)(5) to States, victim service organizations, and public agencies (including Federal, State, or local governments) and nongovernmental organizations that provide assistance to victims of crime, which shall be used to provide emergency relief, including crisis response efforts, assistance, training, and technical assistance, and ongoing assistance, including during any investigation or prosecution, to victims of terrorist acts or mass violence occurring outside the United States who are not persons eligible for compensation under title VIII of the Omnibus Diplomatic Security and Antiterrorism Act of 1986.

"(2) VICTIM DEFINED.—In this subsection, the term 'victim'—

"(A) means a person who is a national of the United States or an officer or employee of the United States Government who is injured or killed as a result of a terrorist act or mass violence occurring outside the United States; and

"(B) in the case of a person described in subparagraph (A) who is less than 18 years of age, incompetent, incapacitated, or deceased, includes a family member or legal guardian of that person.

"(3) RULE OF CONSTRUCTION.—Nothing in this subsection shall be construed to allow the Director to make grants to any foreign power (as defined by section 101(a) of the Foreign Intelligence Surveillance Act of 1978 (50 U.S.C. 1801(a)) or to any domestic or foreign organization operated for the purpose of engaging in any significant political or lobbying activities.".

42 USC 10603b
note.

(2) APPLICABILITY.—The amendment made by this subsection shall apply to any terrorist act or mass violence occurring on or after December 21, 1988, with respect to which an investigation or prosecution was ongoing after April 24, 1996.

Deadline.
42 USC 10603b
note.

(3) ADMINISTRATIVE PROVISION.—Not later than 90 days after the date of the enactment of this Act, the Director shall establish guidelines under section 1407(a) of the Victims of Crime Act of 1984 (42 U.S.C. 10604(a)) to specify the categories of organizations and agencies to which the Director may make grants under this subsection.

(4) TECHNICAL AMENDMENT.—Section 1404B(b) of the Victims of Crime Act of 1984 (42 U.S.C. 10603b(b)) is amended by striking "1404(d)(4)(B)" and inserting "1402(d)(5)".

(b) AMENDMENTS TO EMERGENCY RESERVE FUND.—

(1) CAP INCREASE.—Section 1402(d)(5)(A) of the Victims of Crime Act of 1984 (42 U.S.C. 10601(d)(5)(A)) is amended by striking "$50,000,000" and inserting "$100,000,000".

(2) TRANSFER.—Section 1402(e) of the Victims of Crime Act of 1984 (42 U.S.C 10601(e)) is amended by striking "in excess of $500,000" and all that follows through "than $500,000" and inserting "shall be available for deposit into the emergency reserve fund referred to in subsection (d)(5) at the discretion of the Director. Any remaining unobligated sums".

(c) COMPENSATION TO VICTIMS OF INTERNATIONAL TERRORISM.—

(1) IN GENERAL.—The Victims of Crime Act of 1984 (42 U.S.C. 10601 et seq.) is amended by inserting after section 1404B the following:

PUBLIC LAW 106–386—OCT. 28, 2000   114 STAT. 1545

"SEC. 1404C. COMPENSATION TO VICTIMS OF INTERNATIONAL TER-   42 USC 10603c.
RORISM.

"(a) DEFINITIONS.—In this section:
    "(1) INTERNATIONAL TERRORISM.—The term 'international
terrorism' has the meaning given the term in section 2331
of title 18, United States Code.
    "(2) NATIONAL OF THE UNITED STATES.—The term 'national
of the United States' has the meaning given the term in section
101(a) of the Immigration and Nationality Act (8 U.S.C.
1101(a)).
    "(3) VICTIM.—
        "(A) IN GENERAL.—The term 'victim' means a person
    who—
            "(i) suffered direct physical or emotional injury
        or death as a result of international terrorism occurring
        on or after December 21, 1988 with respect to which
        an investigation or prosecution was ongoing after April
        24, 1996; and
            "(ii) as of the date on which the international
        terrorism occurred, was a national of the United States
        or an officer or employee of the United States Govern-
        ment.
        "(B) INCOMPETENT, INCAPACITATED, OR DECEASED VIC-
    TIMS.—In the case of a victim who is less than 18 years
    of age, incompetent, incapacitated, or deceased, a family
    member or legal guardian of the victim may receive the
    compensation under this section on behalf of the victim.
        "(C) EXCEPTION.—Notwithstanding any other provision
    of this section, in no event shall an individual who is
    criminally culpable for the terrorist act or mass violence
    receive any compensation under this section, either directly
    or on behalf of a victim.
"(b) AWARD OF COMPENSATION.—The Director may use the
emergency reserve referred to in section 1402(d)(5)(A) to carry out
a program to compensate victims of acts of international terrorism
that occur outside the United States for expenses associated with
that victimization.
"(c) ANNUAL REPORT.—The Director shall annually submit to
Congress a report on the status and activities of the program
under this section, which report shall include—
    "(1) an explanation of the procedures for filing and proc-
essing of applications for compensation;
    "(2) a description of the procedures and policies instituted
to promote public awareness about the program;
    "(3) a complete statistical analysis of the victims assisted
under the program, including—
        "(A) the number of applications for compensation sub-
    mitted;
        "(B) the number of applications approved and the
    amount of each award;
        "(C) the number of applications denied and the reasons
    for the denial;
        "(D) the average length of time to process an applica-
    tion for compensation; and
        "(E) the number of applications for compensation
    pending and the estimated future liability of the program;
    and

"(4) an analysis of future program needs and suggested program improvements.".

(2) CONFORMING AMENDMENT.—Section 1402(d)(5)(B) of the Victims of Crime Act of 1984 (42 U.S.C. 10601(d)(5)(B)) is amended by inserting ", to provide compensation to victims of international terrorism under the program under section 1404C," after "section 1404B".

(d) AMENDMENTS TO VICTIMS OF CRIME FUND.—Section 1402(c) of the Victims of Crime Act 1984 (42 U.S.C. 10601(c)) is amended by adding at the end the following: "Notwithstanding section 1402(d)(5), all sums deposited in the Fund in any fiscal year that are not made available for obligation by Congress in the subsequent fiscal year shall remain in the Fund for obligation in future fiscal years, without fiscal year limitation.".

SEC. 2004. TWENTY-FIRST AMENDMENT ENFORCEMENT.

(a) SHIPMENT OF INTOXICATING LIQUOR IN VIOLATION OF STATE LAW.—The Act entitled "An Act divesting intoxicating liquors of their interstate character in certain cases", approved March 1, 1913 (commonly known as the "Webb-Kenyon Act") (27 U.S.C. 122) is amended by adding at the end the following:

27 USC 122a.

"SEC. 2. INJUNCTIVE RELIEF IN FEDERAL DISTRICT COURT.

"(a) DEFINITIONS.—In this section—

"(1) the term 'attorney general' means the attorney general or other chief law enforcement officer of a State or the designee thereof;

"(2) the term 'intoxicating liquor' means any spirituous, vinous, malted, fermented, or other intoxicating liquor of any kind;

"(3) the term 'person' means any individual and any partnership, corporation, company, firm, society, association, joint stock company, trust, or other entity capable of holding a legal or beneficial interest in property, but does not include a State or agency thereof; and

"(4) the term 'State' means any State of the United States, the District of Columbia, the Commonwealth of Puerto Rico, or any territory or possession of the United States.

"(b) ACTION BY STATE ATTORNEY GENERAL.—If the attorney general has reasonable cause to believe that a person is engaged in, or has engaged in, any act that would constitute a violation of a State law regulating the importation or transportation of any intoxicating liquor, the attorney general may bring a civil action in accordance with this section for injunctive relief (including a preliminary or permanent injunction) against the person, as the attorney general determines to be necessary to—

"(1) restrain the person from engaging, or continuing to engage, in the violation; and

"(2) enforce compliance with the State law.

"(c) FEDERAL JURISDICTION.—

"(1) IN GENERAL.—The district courts of the United States shall have jurisdiction over any action brought under this section by an attorney general against any person, except one licensed or otherwise authorized to produce, sell, or store intoxicating liquor in such State.

"(2) VENUE.—An action under this section may be brought only in accordance with section 1391 of title 28, United States

PUBLIC LAW 106–386—OCT. 28, 2000   114 STAT. 1547

Code, or in the district in which the recipient of the intoxicating liquor resides or is found.

"(3) FORM OF RELIEF.—An action under this section is limited to actions seeking injunctive relief (a preliminary and/ or permanent injunction).

"(4) NO RIGHT TO JURY TRIAL.—An action under this section shall be tried before the court.

"(d) REQUIREMENTS FOR INJUNCTIONS AND ORDERS.—

"(1) IN GENERAL.—In any action brought under this section, upon a proper showing by the attorney general of the State, the court may issue a preliminary or permanent injunction to restrain a violation of this section. A proper showing under this paragraph shall require that a State prove by a preponderance of the evidence that a violation of State law as described in subsection (b) has taken place or is taking place.

"(2) ADDITIONAL SHOWING FOR PRELIMINARY INJUNCTION.— No preliminary injunction may be granted except upon—

"(A) evidence demonstrating the probability of irreparable injury if injunctive relief is not granted; and

"(B) evidence supporting the probability of success on the merits.

"(3) NOTICE.—No preliminary or permanent injunction may be issued under paragraph (1) without notice to the adverse party and an opportunity for a hearing.

"(4) FORM AND SCOPE OF ORDER.—Any preliminary or permanent injunction entered in an action brought under this section shall—

"(A) set forth the reasons for the issuance of the order;

"(B) be specific in terms;

"(C) describe in reasonable detail, and not by reference to the complaint or other document, the act or acts sought to be restrained; and

"(D) be binding upon—

"(i) the parties to the action and the officers, agents, employees, and attorneys of those parties; and

"(ii) persons in active concert or participation with the parties to the action who receive actual notice of the order by personal service or otherwise.

"(5) ADMISSIBILITY OF EVIDENCE.—In a hearing on an application for a permanent injunction, any evidence previously received on an application for a preliminary injunction in connection with the same civil action and that would otherwise be admissible, may be made a part of the record of the hearing on the permanent injunction.

"(e) RULES OF CONSTRUCTION.—This section shall be construed only to extend the jurisdiction of Federal courts in connection with State law that is a valid exercise of power vested in the States—

"(1) under the twenty-first article of amendment to the Constitution of the United States as such article of amendment is interpreted by the Supreme Court of the United States including interpretations in conjunction with other provisions of the Constitution of the United States; and

"(2) under the first section herein as such section is interpreted by the Supreme Court of the United States; but shall not be construed to grant to States any additional power.

"(f) ADDITIONAL REMEDIES.—

114 STAT. 1548 PUBLIC LAW 106–386—OCT. 28, 2000

"(1) IN GENERAL.—A remedy under this section is in addition to any other remedies provided by law.

"(2) STATE COURT PROCEEDINGS.—Nothing in this section may be construed to prohibit an authorized State official from proceeding in State court on the basis of an alleged violation of any State law.

27 USC 122b. **"SEC. 3. GENERAL PROVISIONS.**

"(a) EFFECT ON INTERNET TAX FREEDOM ACT.—Nothing in this section may be construed to modify or supersede the operation of the Internet Tax Freedom Act (47 U.S.C. 151 note).

"(b) INAPPLICABILITY TO SERVICE PROVIDERS.—Nothing in this section may be construed to—

"(1) authorize any injunction against an interactive computer service (as defined in section 230(f) of the Communications Act of 1934 (47 U.S.C. 230(f)) used by another person to engage in any activity that is subject to this Act;

"(2) authorize any injunction against an electronic communication service (as defined in section 2510(15) of title 18, United States Code) used by another person to engage in any activity that is subject to this Act; or

"(3) authorize an injunction prohibiting the advertising or marketing of any intoxicating liquor by any person in any case in which such advertising or marketing is lawful in the jurisdiction from which the importation, transportation or other conduct to which this Act applies originates.".

27 USC 122a note. (b) EFFECTIVE DATE.—This section and the amendments made by this section shall become effective 90 days after the date of the enactment of this Act.

Deadline. 27 USC 122a note. (c) STUDY.—The Attorney General shall carry out the study to determine the impact of this section and shall submit the results of such study not later than 180 days after the enactment of this Act.

Approved October 28, 2000.

LEGISLATIVE HISTORY—H.R. 3244:

HOUSE REPORTS: Nos. 106–487, Pt. 1 (Comm. on International Relations) and Pt. 2 (Comm. on the Judiciary) and 106–939 (Comm. of Conference).
CONGRESSIONAL RECORD, Vol. 146 (2000):
    May 9, considered and passed House.
    July 27, considered and passed Senate, amended.
    Oct. 6, House agreed to conference report.
    Oct. 11, Senate agreed to conference report.
WEEKLY COMPILATION OF PRESIDENTIAL DOCUMENTS, Vol. 36 (2000):
    Oct. 28, Presidential statement.

○

H. R. 2620

One Hundred Eighth Congress
of the
United States of America

AT THE FIRST SESSION

Begun and held at the City of Washington on Tuesday,
the seventh day of January, two thousand and three

An Act

To authorize appropriations for fiscal years 2004 and 2005 for the Trafficking
Victims Protection Act of 2000, and for other purposes.

*Be it enacted by the Senate and House of Representatives of
the United States of America in Congress assembled,*

SECTION 1. SHORT TITLE.

This Act may be cited as the "Trafficking Victims Protection
Reauthorization Act of 2003".

SEC. 2. FINDINGS.

Congress finds the following:

(1) Trafficking in persons continues to victimize countless
men, women, and children in the United States and abroad.

(2) Since the enactment of the Trafficking Victims Protection Act of 2000 (division A of Public Law 106–386), the United
States Government has made significant progress in investigating and prosecuting acts of trafficking and in responding
to the needs of victims of trafficking in the United States
and abroad.

(3) On the other hand, victims of trafficking have faced
unintended obstacles in the process of securing needed assistance, including admission to the United States under section
101(a)(15)(T)(i) of the Immigration and Nationality Act.

(4) Additional research is needed to fully understand the
phenomenon of trafficking in persons and to determine the
most effective strategies for combating trafficking in persons.

(5) Corruption among foreign law enforcement authorities
continues to undermine the efforts by governments to investigate, prosecute, and convict traffickers.

(6) International Law Enforcement Academies should be
more fully utilized in the effort to train law enforcement
authorities, prosecutors, and members of the judiciary to
address trafficking in persons-related crimes.

SEC. 3. ENHANCING PREVENTION OF TRAFFICKING IN PERSONS.

(a) BORDER INTERDICTION, PUBLIC INFORMATION PROGRAMS,
AND COMBATING INTERNATIONAL SEX TOURISM.—Section 106 of the
Trafficking Victims Protection Act of 2000 (22 U.S.C. 7104) is
amended—

(1) by redesignating subsection (c) as subsection (f);

(2) by inserting after subsection (b) the following new subsections:

"(c) BORDER INTERDICTION.—The President shall establish and
carry out programs of border interdiction outside the United States.

Such programs shall include providing grants to foreign nongovernmental organizations that provide for transit shelters operating at key border crossings and that help train survivors of trafficking in persons to educate and train border guards and officials, and other local law enforcement officials, to identify traffickers and victims of severe forms of trafficking, and the appropriate manner in which to treat such victims. Such programs shall also include, to the extent appropriate, monitoring by such survivors of trafficking in persons of the implementation of border interdiction programs, including helping in the identification of such victims to stop the cross-border transit of victims. The President shall ensure that any program established under this subsection provides the opportunity for any trafficking victim who is freed to return to his or her previous residence if the victim so chooses.

"(d) INTERNATIONAL MEDIA.—The President shall establish and carry out programs that support the production of television and radio programs, including documentaries, to inform vulnerable populations overseas of the dangers of trafficking, and to increase awareness of the public in countries of destination regarding the slave-like practices and other human rights abuses involved in trafficking, including fostering linkages between individuals working in the media in different countries to determine the best methods for informing such populations through such media.

"(e) COMBATING INTERNATIONAL SEX TOURISM.—

"(1) DEVELOPMENT AND DISSEMINATION OF MATERIALS.—The President, pursuant to such regulations as may be prescribed, shall ensure that materials are developed and disseminated to alert travelers that sex tourism (as described in subsections (b) through (f) of section 2423 of title 18, United States Code) is illegal, will be prosecuted, and presents dangers to those involved. Such materials shall be disseminated to individuals traveling to foreign destinations where the President determines that sex tourism is significant.

"(2) MONITORING OF COMPLIANCE.—The President shall monitor compliance with the requirements of paragraph (1).

"(3) FEASIBILITY REPORT.—Not later than 180 days after the date of the enactment of the Trafficking Victims Protection Reauthorization Act of 2003, the President shall transmit to the Committee on International Relations of the House of Representatives and the Committee on Foreign Affairs of the Senate a report that describes the feasibility of such United States Government materials being disseminated through public-private partnerships to individuals traveling to foreign destinations."; and

(3) in subsection (f) (as redesignated), by striking "initiatives described in subsections (a) and (b)" and inserting "initiatives and programs described in subsections (a) through (e)".

(b) TERMINATION OF CERTAIN GRANTS, CONTRACTS AND COOPERATIVE AGREEMENTS.—Section 106 of such Act (as amended by subsection (a)) is further amended by adding at the end the following new subsection:

"(g) TERMINATION OF CERTAIN GRANTS, CONTRACTS AND COOPERATIVE AGREEMENTS.—

"(1) TERMINATION.—The President shall ensure that any grant, contract, or cooperative agreement provided or entered into by a Federal department or agency under which funds described in paragraph (2) are to be provided to a private

H. R. 2620—3

entity, in whole or in part, shall include a condition that authorizes the department or agency to terminate the grant, contract, or cooperative agreement, without penalty, if the grantee or any subgrantee, or the contractor or any subcontractor (i) engages in severe forms of trafficking in persons or has procured a commercial sex act during the period of time that the grant, contract, or cooperative agreement is in effect, or (ii) uses forced labor in the performance of the grant, contract, or cooperative agreement.

"(2) ASSISTANCE DESCRIBED.—Funds referred to in paragraph (1) are funds made available to carry out any program, project, or activity abroad funded under major functional budget category 150 (relating to international affairs).".

SEC. 4. ENHANCING PROTECTION FOR TRAFFICKING VICTIMS.

(a) AMENDMENTS TO TRAFFICKING VICTIMS PROTECTION ACT OF 2000.—

(1) COOPERATION BETWEEN FOREIGN GOVERNMENTS AND NONGOVERNMENTAL ORGANIZATIONS.—Section 107(a)(1)(B) of the Trafficking Victims Protection Act of 2000 (22 U.S.C. 7105(a)(1)(B)) is amended by adding at the end before the period the following: ", and by facilitating contact between relevant foreign government agencies and such nongovernmental organizations to facilitate cooperation between the foreign governments and such organizations".

(2) ASSISTANCE FOR FAMILY MEMBERS OF VICTIMS OF TRAFFICKING IN UNITED STATES.—Section 107(b)(1) of the Trafficking Victims Protection Act of 2000 (22 U.S.C. 7105(b)(1)) is amended—

(A) in subparagraph (A), by inserting ", or an alien classified as a nonimmigrant under section 101(a)(15)(T)(ii)," after "in persons"; and

(B) in subparagraph (B)—

(i) by inserting "and aliens classified as a nonimmigrant under section 101(a)(15)(T)(ii)," after "United States,"; and

(ii) by adding at the end the following new sentence: "In the case of nonentitlement programs funded by the Secretary of Health and Human Services, such benefits and services may include services to assist potential victims of trafficking in achieving certification and to assist minor dependent children of victims of severe forms of trafficking in persons or potential victims of trafficking.".

(3) CERTIFICATION OF VICTIMS OF A SEVERE FORM OF TRAFFICKING IN PERSONS.—Section 107(b)(1)(E) of the Trafficking Victims Protection Act of 2000 (22 U.S.C. 7105(b)(1)(E)) is amended by adding at the end the following new clause:

"(iv) ASSISTANCE TO INVESTIGATIONS.—In making the certification described in this subparagraph with respect to the assistance to investigation or prosecution described in clause (i)(I), the Secretary of Health and Human Services shall consider statements from State and local law enforcement officials that the person referred to in subparagraph (C)(ii)(II) has been willing to assist in every reasonable way with respect to the investigation and prosecution of State and local crimes

H. R. 2620—4

such as kidnapping, rape, slavery, or other forced labor offenses, where severe forms of trafficking appear to have been involved.".

(4) PRIVATE RIGHT OF ACTION.—

(A) IN GENERAL.—Chapter 77 of part I of title 18, United States Code, is amended by adding at the end the following new section:

"§ 1595. Civil remedy

"(a) An individual who is a victim of a violation of section 1589, 1590, or 1591 of this chapter may bring a civil action against the perpetrator in an appropriate district court of the United States and may recover damages and reasonable attorneys fees.

"(b)(1) Any civil action filed under this section shall be stayed during the pendency of any criminal action arising out of the same occurrence in which the claimant is the victim.

"(2) In this subsection, a 'criminal action' includes investigation and prosecution and is pending until final adjudication in the trial court.".

(B) CONFORMING AMENDMENT.—The table of contents of chapter 77 of part I of title 18, United States Code, is amended by adding at the end the following new item:

"1595. Civil remedy.".

(b) AMENDMENTS TO IMMIGRATION AND NATIONALITY ACT.—

(1) NONIMMIGRANT ALIEN CLASSES.—Section 101(a)(15)(T) of the Immigration and Nationality Act (8 U.S.C. 1101(a)(15)(T)) is amended—

(A) in clause (i)(III)(bb), by striking "15 years of age," and inserting "18 years of age,"; and

(B) in clause (ii)(I), by inserting "unmarried siblings under 18 years of age on the date on which such alien applied for status under such clause," before "and parents".

(2) ADMISSION OF NONIMMIGRANTS.—Section 214(n) of the Immigration and Nationality Act (8 U.S.C. 1184(n)) is amended—

(A) in paragraph (3), by inserting "siblings," before "or parents"; and

(B) by adding at the end the following:

"(4) An unmarried alien who seeks to accompany, or follow to join, a parent granted status under section 101(a)(15)(T)(i), and who was under 21 years of age on the date on which such parent applied for such status, shall continue to be classified as a child for purposes of section 101(a)(15)(T)(ii), if the alien attains 21 years of age after such parent's application was filed but while it was pending.

"(5) An alien described in clause (i) of section 101(a)(15)(T) shall continue to be treated as an alien described in clause (ii)(I) of such section if the alien attains 21 years of age after the alien's application for status under such clause (i) is filed but while it is pending.

"(6) In making a determination under section 101(a)(15)(T)(i)(III)(aa) with respect to an alien, statements from State and local law enforcement officials that the alien has complied with any reasonable request for assistance in the investigation or prosecution of crimes such as kidnapping, rape, slavery, or other forced labor offenses, where severe forms of trafficking in persons

H. R. 2620—5

(as defined in section 103 of the Trafficking Victims Protection Act of 2000) appear to have been involved, shall be considered.".

(3) ADJUSTMENT OF STATUS.—Section 245(l) of the Immigration and Nationality Act (8 U.S.C. 1255(l)) (as added by section 107(f) of Public Law 106–386) is amended—

(A) in paragraph (1)—

(i) by striking "admitted under that section" and inserting "admitted under section 101(a)(15)(T)(ii)"; and

(ii) by inserting "sibling," after "parent,"; and

(B) in paragraph (3)(B), by inserting "siblings," after "daughters,".

(4) EXEMPTION FROM PUBLIC CHARGE GROUND FOR INADMISSIBILITY.—Section 212(d)(13) of the Immigration and Nationality Act (8 U.S.C. 1182(d)(13)), as added by section 107(e)(3) of the Trafficking Victims Protection Act of 2000 (22 U.S.C. 7105(e)(3)), is amended—

(A) in subparagraph (A), by striking the period at the end and adding the following:

", except that the ground for inadmissibility described in subsection (a)(4) shall not apply with respect to such a nonimmigrant."; and

(B) in subparagraph (B)—

(i) by amending clause (i) to read as follows:

"(i) subsection (a)(1); and"; and

(ii) in clause (ii)—

(I) by striking "such subsection" and inserting "subsection (a)"; and

(II) by inserting "(4)," after "(3),".

(5) AGGRAVATED FELONY DEFINED.—Section 101(a)(43)(K)(iii) of the Immigration and Nationality Act (8 U.S.C. 1101(a)(43)(K)(iii)) is amended to read as follows:

"(iii) is described in any of sections 1581–1585 or 1588–1591 of title 18, United States Code (relating to peonage, slavery, involuntary servitude, and trafficking in persons);".

SEC. 5. ENHANCING PROSECUTIONS OF TRAFFICKERS.

(a) SEX TRAFFICKING OF CHILDREN OR BY FORCE, FRAUD, OR COERCION.—Section 1591 of title 18, United States Code, is amended—

(1) in the heading, by inserting a comma after "**FRAUD**";

(2) in subsection (a)(1), by striking "in or affecting interstate commerce" and inserting "in or affecting interstate or foreign commerce, or within the special maritime and territorial jurisdiction of the United States"; and

(3) in subsection (b), by striking "the person transported" each place it appears and inserting "the person recruited, enticed, harbored, transported, provided, or obtained".

(b) DEFINITION OF RACKETEERING ACTIVITY.—Section 1961(1)(A) of title 18, United States Code, is amended by striking "sections 1581–1588 (relating to peonage and slavery)" and inserting "sections 1581–1591 (relating to peonage, slavery, and trafficking in persons).".

(c) CONFORMING AMENDMENTS.—(1) The heading for chapter 77 of part I of title 18, United States Code, is amended to read as follows:

H. R. 2620—6

"CHAPTER 77—PEONAGE, SLAVERY, AND TRAFFICKING IN PERSONS".

(2) The table of contents for part I of title 18, United States Code, is amended in the item relating to chapter 77 to read as follows:

"77.   Peonage, slavery, and trafficking in persons".

SEC. 6. ENHANCING UNITED STATES EFFORTS TO COMBAT TRAFFICKING.

(a) REPORT.—

(1) IN GENERAL.—Section 105(d) of the Victims of Trafficking and Violence Protection Act of 2000 (22 U.S.C. 7103(d)) is amended by adding at the end the following new paragraph:

"(7) Not later than May 1, 2004, and annually thereafter, the Attorney General shall submit to the Committee on Ways and Means, the Committee on International Relations, and the Committee on the Judiciary of the House of Representatives and the Committee on Finance, the Committee on Foreign Relations, and the Committee on the Judiciary of the Senate, a report on Federal agencies that are implementing any provision of this division, or any amendment made by this division, which shall include, at a minimum, information on—

"(A) the number of persons who received benefits or other services under section 107(b) in connection with programs or activities funded or administered by the Secretary of Health and Human Services, the Secretary of Labor, the Board of Directors of the Legal Services Corporation, and other appropriate Federal agencies during the preceding fiscal year;

"(B) the number of persons who have been granted continued presence in the United States under section 107(c)(3) during the preceding fiscal year;

"(C) the number of persons who have applied for, been granted, or been denied a visa or otherwise provided status under section 101(a)(15)(T)(i) of the Immigration and Nationality Act (8 U.S.C. 1101(a)(15)(T)(i)) during the preceding fiscal year;

"(D) the number of persons who have been charged or convicted under one or more of sections 1581, 1583, 1584, 1589, 1590, 1591, 1592, or 1594 of title 18, United States Code, during the preceding fiscal year and the sentences imposed against each such person;

"(E) the amount, recipient, and purpose of each grant issued by any Federal agency to carry out the purposes of sections 106 and 107 of this Act, or section 134 of the Foreign Assistance Act of 1961, during the preceding fiscal year;

"(F) the nature of training conducted pursuant to section 107(c)(4) during the preceding fiscal year; and

"(G) the activities undertaken by the Senior Policy Operating Group to carry out its responsibilities under section 105(f) of this division.".

(2) CONFORMING AMENDMENT.—Section 107(b)(1) of the Victims of Trafficking and Violence Protection Act of 2000 (22 U.S.C. 7105(b)(1)) is amended by striking subparagraph (D).

H. R. 2620—7

(b) SUPPORT FOR THE TASK FORCE.—

(1) AMENDMENT.—The second sentence of section 105(e) of the Victims of Trafficking and Violence Protection Act of 2000 (22 U.S.C. 7103(e)) is amended by inserting at the end before the period the following: ", who shall be appointed by the President, by and with the advice and consent of the Senate, with the rank of Ambassador-at-Large".

(2) APPLICABILITY.—The individual who holds the position of Director of the Office to Monitor and Combat Trafficking of the Department of State may continue to hold such position notwithstanding the amendment made by paragraph (1).

(c) SENIOR POLICY OPERATING GROUP.—

(1) AMENDMENT.—Section 105 of the Victims of Trafficking and Violence Protection Act of 2000 (22 U.S.C. 7103) is amended by adding at the end the following new subsection:

"(f) SENIOR POLICY OPERATING GROUP.—

"(1) ESTABLISHMENT.—There shall be established within the executive branch a Senior Policy Operating Group.

"(2) MEMBERSHIP; RELATED MATTERS.—

"(A) IN GENERAL.—The Operating Group shall consist of the senior officials designated as representatives of the appointed members of the Task Force (pursuant to Executive Order No. 13257 of February 13, 2002).

"(B) CHAIRPERSON.—The Operating Group shall be chaired by the Director of the Office to Monitor and Combat Trafficking of the Department of State.

"(C) MEETINGS.—The Operating Group shall meet on a regular basis at the call of the Chairperson.

"(3) DUTIES.—The Operating Group shall coordinate activities of Federal departments and agencies regarding policies (including grants and grant policies) involving the international trafficking in persons and the implementation of this division.

"(4) AVAILABILITY OF INFORMATION.—Each Federal department or agency represented on the Operating Group shall fully share all information with such Group regarding the department or agency's plans, before and after final agency decisions are made, on all matters relating to grants, grant policies, and other significant actions regarding the international trafficking in persons and the implementation of this division.

"(5) REGULATIONS.—Not later than 90 days after the date of the enactment of the Trafficking Victims Protection Reauthorization Act of 2003, the President shall promulgate regulations to implement this section, including regulations to carry out paragraph (4).".

(2) CONFORMING AMENDMENT.—Section 406 of the Department of State and Related Agency Appropriations Act, 2003 (as contained in division B of Public Law 108–7) is hereby repealed.

(d) MINIMUM STANDARDS FOR THE ELIMINATION OF TRAFFICKING.—Section 108(b) of the Victims of Trafficking and Violence Protection Act of 2000 (22 U.S.C. 7106(b)) is amended—

(1) in paragraph (1)—

(A) by striking "that take place wholly or partly within the territory of the country" and inserting ", and convicts and sentences persons responsible for such acts, that take place wholly or partly within the territory of the country"; and

H. R. 2620—8

(B) by adding at the end the following new sentences: "After reasonable requests from the Department of State for data regarding investigations, prosecutions, convictions, and sentences, a government which does not provide such data, consistent with the capacity of such government to obtain such data, shall be presumed not to have vigorously investigated, prosecuted, convicted or sentenced such acts. During the periods prior to the annual report submitted on June 1, 2004, and on June 1, 2005, and the periods afterwards until September 30 of each such year, the Secretary of State may disregard the presumption contained in the preceding sentence if the government has provided some data to the Department of State regarding such acts and the Secretary has determined that the government is making a good faith effort to collect such data.";

(2) in paragraph (7)—

(A) by striking "and prosecutes" and inserting ", prosecutes, convicts, and sentences"; and

(B) by adding at the end the following new sentence: "After reasonable requests from the Department of State for data regarding such investigations, prosecutions, convictions, and sentences, a government which does not provide such data consistent with its resources shall be presumed not to have vigorously investigated, prosecuted, convicted, or sentenced such acts. During the periods prior to the annual report submitted on June 1, 2004, and on June 1, 2005, and the periods afterwards until September 30 of each such year, the Secretary of State may disregard the presumption contained in the preceding sentence if the government has provided some data to the Department of State regarding such acts and the Secretary has determined that the government is making a good faith effort to collect such data.".

(3) by adding the following new paragraphs at the end:

"(8) Whether the percentage of victims of severe forms of trafficking in the country that are non-citizens of such countries is insignificant.

"(9) Whether the government of the country, consistent with the capacity of such government, systematically monitors its efforts to satisfy the criteria described in paragraphs (1) through (8) and makes available publicly a periodic assessment of such efforts.

"(10) Whether the government of the country achieves appreciable progress in eliminating severe forms of trafficking when compared to the assessment in the previous year.".

(e) SPECIAL WATCH LIST.—Section 110(b) of the Trafficking Victims Protection Act of 2000 (22 U.S.C. 7107(b)) is amended—

(1) by redesignating paragraph (3) as paragraph (4); and

(2) by inserting after paragraph (2) the following new paragraph:

"(3) SPECIAL WATCH LIST.—

"(A) SUBMISSION OF LIST.—Not later than the date on which the determinations described in subsections (c) and (d) are submitted to the appropriate congressional committees in accordance with such subsections, the Secretary of State shall submit to the appropriate congressional committees a list of countries that the Secretary

H. R. 2620—9

determines requires special scrutiny during the following year. The list shall be composed of the following countries:

"(i) Countries that have been listed pursuant to paragraph (1)(A) in the current annual report and were listed pursuant to paragraph (1)(B) in the previous annual report.

"(ii) Countries that have been listed pursuant to paragraph (1)(B) pursuant to the current annual report and were listed pursuant to paragraph (1)(C) in the previous annual report.

"(iii) Countries that have been listed pursuant to paragraph (1)(B) pursuant to the current annual report, where—

"(I) the absolute number of victims of severe forms of trafficking is very significant or is significantly increasing;

"(II) there is a failure to provide evidence of increasing efforts to combat severe forms of trafficking in persons from the previous year, including increased investigations, prosecutions and convictions of trafficking crimes, increased assistance to victims, and decreasing evidence of complicity in severe forms of trafficking by government officials; or

"(III) the determination that a country is making significant efforts to bring themselves into compliance with minimum standards was based on commitments by the country to take additional future steps over the next year.

"(B) INTERIM ASSESSMENT.—Not later than February 1st of each year, the Secretary of State shall provide to the appropriate congressional committees an assessment of the progress that each country on the special watch list described in subparagraph (A) has made since the last annual report.

"(C) RELATION OF SPECIAL WATCH LIST TO ANNUAL TRAFFICKING IN PERSONS REPORT.—A determination that a country shall not be placed on the special watch list described in subparagraph (A) shall not affect in any way the determination to be made in the following year as to whether a country is complying with the minimum standards for the elimination of trafficking or whether a country is making significant efforts to bring itself into compliance with such standards.".

(f) ENHANCING UNITED STATES ASSISTANCE.—Section 134(b) of the Foreign Assistance Act of 1961 (22 U.S.C. 2152d(b)) is amended by adding at the end the following new sentence: "Assistance may be provided under this section notwithstanding section 660 of this Act.".

(g) RESEARCH RELATING TO TRAFFICKING IN PERSONS.—

(1) IN GENERAL.—The Victims of Trafficking and Violence Protection Act of 2000 (22 U.S.C. 7101 et seq.) is amended by inserting after section 112 the following new section:

H. R. 2620—10

"SEC. 112A. RESEARCH ON DOMESTIC AND INTERNATIONAL TRAF-
FICKING IN PERSONS.

"The President, acting through the Council of Economic
Advisors, the National Research Council of the National Academies,
the Secretary of Labor, the Secretary of Health and Human Services, the Attorney General, the Secretary of State, the Administrator
of the United States Agency for International Development, and
the Director of Central Intelligence, shall carry out research,
including by providing grants to nongovernmental organizations,
as well as relevant United States Government agencies and international organizations, which furthers the purposes of this division
and provides data to address the problems identified in the findings
of this division. Such research initiatives shall, to the maximum
extent practicable, include, but not be limited to, the following:
        "(1) The economic causes and consequences of trafficking
    in persons.
        "(2) The effectiveness of programs and initiatives funded
    or administered by Federal agencies to prevent trafficking in
    persons and to protect and assist victims of trafficking.
        "(3) The interrelationship between trafficking in persons
    and global health risks.".
    (2) CONFORMING AMENDMENT.—The table of contents of
the Victims of Trafficking and Violence Protection Act of 2000
is amended by inserting after the item relating to section 112
the following new item:

"Sec. 112A. Research on domestic and international trafficking in persons.".

    (h) SANCTIONS AND WAIVERS.—Section 110(d) of the Trafficking
Victims Protection Act of 2000 (22 U.S.C. 7107(d)) is amended—
        (1) in paragraph (4), by inserting after "nonhumanitarian,
    nontrade-related foreign assistance" the following: "or funding
    for participation in educational and cultural exchange pro-
    grams"; and
        (2) in paragraph (5)(A)(i), by inserting after "foreign assist-
    ance" the following: "or funding for participation in educational
    and cultural exchange programs".
    (i) SUBSEQUENT WAIVER AUTHORITY.—Section 110 of the Traf-
ficking Victims Protection Act of 2000 (22 U.S.C. 7107) is amended
by adding at the end the following new subsection:
    "(f) After the President has made a determination described
in subsection (d)(1) with respect to the government of a country,
the President may at any time make a determination described
in paragraphs (4) and (5) of subsection (d) to waive, in whole
or in part, the measures imposed against the country by the previous determination under subsection (d)(1).".

SEC. 7. AUTHORIZATION OF APPROPRIATIONS; RELATED MATTERS.

    Section 113 of the Trafficking Victims Protection Act of 2000
(22 U.S.C. 7110) is amended—
        (1) in subsection (a)—
            (A) by striking "105" and inserting "105(e), 105(f)";
        and
            (B) by striking "and $3,000,000 for each of the fiscal
        years 2002 and 2003" and inserting ", $3,000,000 for each
        of the fiscal years 2002 and 2003, and $5,000,000 for each
        of the fiscal years 2004 and 2005";

H. R. 2620—11

(2) in subsection (b), by adding at the end before the period the following: "and $15,000,000 for each of the fiscal years 2004 and 2005";

(3) in subsection (c)—

(A) in paragraph (1) to read as follows:

"(1) BILATERAL ASSISTANCE TO COMBAT TRAFFICKING.—

"(A) PREVENTION.—To carry out the purposes of section 106, there are authorized to be appropriated to the Secretary of State $10,000,000 for each of the fiscal years 2004 and 2005.

"(B) PROTECTION.—To carry out the purposes of section 107(a), there are authorized to be appropriated to the Secretary of State $15,000,000 for fiscal year 2003 and $10,000,000 for each of the fiscal years 2004 and 2005.

"(C) PROSECUTION AND MEETING MINIMUM STANDARDS.—To carry out the purposes of section 134 of the Foreign Assistance Act of 1961, there are authorized to be appropriated $10,000,000 for each of the fiscal years 2004 and 2005 to assist in promoting prosecution of traffickers and otherwise to assist countries in meeting the minimum standards described in section 108 of this Act, including $250,000 for each such fiscal year to carry out training activities for law enforcement officers, prosecutors, and members of the judiciary with respect to trafficking in persons at the International Law Enforcement Academies."; and

(B) in paragraph (2), by striking "for each of the fiscal years 2001, 2002, and 2003" and inserting "for each of the fiscal years 2001 through 2005";

(4) in subsection (d)—

(A) by adding at the end before the period the following: "and $15,000,000 for each of the fiscal years 2004 and 2005"; and

(B) by adding at the end the following new sentence: "To carry out the purposes of section 134 of the Foreign Assistance Act of 1961 (as added by section 109), there are authorized to be appropriated to the President, acting through the Attorney General and the Secretary of State, $250,000 for each of fiscal years 2004 and 2005 to carry out training activities for law enforcement officers, prosecutors, and members of the judiciary with respect to trafficking in persons at the International Law Enforcement Academies.";

(5) in subsection (e)—

(A) in paragraphs (1) and (2), by striking "for fiscal year 2003" each place it appears and inserting "for each of the fiscal years 2003 through 2005"; and

(B) by adding at the end the following new paragraph: "(3) RESEARCH.—To carry out the purposes of section 112A, there are authorized to be appropriated to the President $300,000 for fiscal year 2004 and $300,000 for fiscal year 2005.";

(6) in subsection (f), by adding at the end before the period the following: "and $10,000,000 for each of the fiscal years 2004 and 2005"; and

(7) by adding at the end the following new subsection: "(g) LIMITATION ON USE OF FUNDS.—

H. R. 2620—12

"(1) RESTRICTION ON PROGRAMS.—No funds made available to carry out this division, or any amendment made by this division, may be used to promote, support, or advocate the legalization or practice of prostitution. Nothing in the preceding sentence shall be construed to preclude assistance designed to promote the purposes of this Act by ameliorating the suffering of, or health risks to, victims while they are being trafficked or after they are out of the situation that resulted from such victims being trafficked.

"(2) RESTRICTION ON ORGANIZATIONS.—No funds made available to carry out this division, or any amendment made by this division, may be used to implement any program that targets victims of severe forms of trafficking in persons described in section 103(8)(A) of this Act through any organization that has not stated in either a grant application, a grant agreement, or both, that it does not promote, support, or advocate the legalization or practice of prostitution. The preceding sentence shall not apply to organizations that provide services to individuals solely after they are no longer engaged in activities that resulted from such victims being trafficked.".

SEC. 8. TECHNICAL CORRECTIONS.

(a) IMMIGRATION AND NATIONALITY ACT.—

(1) CLASSES OF NONIMMIGRANT ALIENS.—Section 101(a)(15) of the Immigration and Nationality Act (8 U.S.C. 1101(a)(15)) is amended—

(A) by moving the margins of subparagraphs (T) and (U) 2 ems to the left;

(B) in subparagraph (T), by striking "214(n)," and inserting "214(o),";

(C) in subparagraph (U), by striking "214(o)," and inserting "214(p),"; and

(D) in subparagraph (V), by striking "214(o)," and inserting "214(q),".

(2) CLASSES OF ALIENS INELIGIBLE FOR VISAS AND ADMISSION.—Section 212(d) of the Immigration and Nationality Act (8 U.S.C. 1182(d)) is amended by redesignating the paragraph (13) added by section 1513(e) of the Battered Immigrant Women Protection Act of 2000 (title V of division B of Public Law 106–386; 114 Stat. 1536) as paragraph (14).

(3) ADMISSION OF NONIMMIGRANTS.—Section 214 of the Immigration and Nationality Act (8 U.S.C. 1184) is amended by redesignating subsections (m) (as added by section 105 of Public Law 106–313), (n) (as added by section 107(e) of Public Law 106–386), (o) (as added by section 1513(c) of Public Law 106–386), (o) (as added by section 1102(b) of the Legal Immigration Family Equity Act), and (p) (as added by section 1503(b) of the Legal Immigration Family Equity Act) as subsections (n), (o), (p), (q), and (r), respectively.

(4) ADJUSTMENT OF STATUS OF NONIMMIGRANTS.—Section 245 of the Immigration and Nationality Act (8 U.S.C. 1255) is amended—

(A) in the subsection (l) added by section 107(f) of Public Law 106–386, by redesignating the second paragraph (2), and paragraphs (3) and (4), as paragraphs (3), (4), and (5), respectively; and

H. R. 2620—13

(B) by redesignating the subsection (l) added by section 1513(f) of Public Law 106–386 as subsection (m).

(b) TRAFFICKING VICTIMS PROTECTION ACT OF 2000.—(1) Section 103(7)(A)(i) of the Trafficking Victims Protection Act of 2000 (22 U.S.C. 7102(7)(A)(i)) is amended by inserting after "part II of that Act" the following: "in support of programs of nongovernmental organizations".

(2) Section 107(g) of the Trafficking Victims Protection Act of 2000 (22 U.S.C. 7105(g)) is amended by striking "214(n)(1)" and inserting "214(o)(2)".

Speaker of the House of Representatives.

Vice President of the United States and
President of the Senate.

I

109TH CONGRESS
1ST SESSION

H. R. 972

To authorize appropriations for fiscal years 2006 and 2007 for the Trafficking Victims Protection Act of 2000, and for other purposes.

IN THE HOUSE OF REPRESENTATIVES

FEBRUARY 17, 2005

Mr. SMITH of New Jersey (for himself, Mr. LANTOS, Mr. PAYNE, Mr. BLUNT, Mr. WOLF, Mr. CARDIN, Ms. ROS-LEHTINEN, Mr. PITTS, Mr. PENCE, and Mr. FALEOMAVAEGA) introduced the following bill; which was referred to the Committee on International Relations, and in addition to the Committees on Armed Services, Judiciary, and Energy and Commerce, for a period to be subsequently determined by the Speaker, in each case for consideration of such provisions as fall within the jurisdiction of the committee concerned

---

A BILL

To authorize appropriations for fiscal years 2006 and 2007 for the Trafficking Victims Protection Act of 2000, and for other purposes.

1   *Be it enacted by the Senate and House of Representa-*

2   *tives of the United States of America in Congress assembled,*

3   **SECTION 1. SHORT TITLE; TABLE OF CONTENTS.**

4   (a) SHORT TITLE.—This Act may be cited as the

5   "Trafficking Victims Protection Reauthorization Act of

6   2005".

2

1   (b) TABLE OF CONTENTS.—The table of contents for

2 this Act is as follows:

Sec. 1. Short title; table of contents.
Sec. 2. Findings.

TITLE I—COMBATTING INTERNATIONAL TRAFFICKING IN
PERSONS

Sec. 101. Prevention of trafficking in persons.
Sec. 102. Protection of victims of trafficking in persons.
Sec. 103. Enhancing prosecutions of trafficking offenses.
Sec. 104. Enhancing United States efforts to combat trafficking in persons.
Sec. 105. Additional activities to monitor and combat forced labor and child
        labor.

TITLE II—COMBATTING DOMESTIC TRAFFICKING IN PERSONS

Sec. 201. Prevention of domestic trafficking in persons.
Sec. 202. Establishment of grant program to develop, expand, and strengthen
        victim service programs for victims of domestic trafficking.
Sec. 203. Protection of victims of domestic trafficking in persons.
Sec. 204. Investigation by Federal Bureau of Investigation of acts of domestic
        trafficking in persons.
Sec. 205. Enhancing State and local efforts to combat trafficking in persons.
Sec. 206. Definitions.

TITLE III—AUTHORIZATIONS OF APPROPRIATIONS

Sec. 301. Authorizations of appropriations.
Sec. 302. Investigations by Federal Bureau of Investigations.

3 **SEC. 2. FINDINGS.**

4   Congress finds the following:

5   (1) The United States has demonstrated inter-

6   national leadership in combating human trafficking

7   and slavery through the enactment of the Traf-

8   ficking Victims Protection Act of 2000 (division A of

9   Public Law 106–386; 22 U.S.C. 7101 et seq.) and

10   the Trafficking Victims Protection Reauthorization

11   Act of 2003 (Public Law 108–193).

12   (2) The United States Government currently

13   estimates that 600,000 to 800,000 individuals are

3

1   trafficked across international borders each year and

2   exploited through forced labor and commercial sex

3   exploitation. An estimated 80 percent of such indi-

4   viduals are women and girls.

5   (3) Since the enactment of the Trafficking Vic-

6   tims Protection Act of 2000, United States efforts

7   to combat trafficking in persons have focused pri-

8   marily on the international trafficking in persons,

9   including the trafficking of foreign citizens into the

10   United States.

11   (4) Trafficking in persons also occurs within

12   the borders of a country, including the United

13   States.

14   (5) An estimated 100,000 to 300,000 children

15   in the United States are at risk for commercial sex-

16   ual exploitation in the United States, including traf-

17   ficking, at any given time.

18   (6) Runaway and homeless children in the

19   United States are highly susceptible to being domes-

20   tically trafficked for commercial sexual exploitation.

21   Every day in the United States, between 1,300,000

22   and 2,800,000 runaway and homeless youth live on

23   the streets. One out of every seven children will run

24   away from home before the age of 18.

4

1   (7) A comprehensive strategy is needed to pre-

2 vent the victimization of United States citizens and

3 nationals through domestic trafficking.

4   (8) A project by the United Nations Edu-

5 cational, Scientific and Cultural Organization

6 (UNESCO) in Southeast Asia has documented a

7 linkage between the spread of HIV/AIDS and traf-

8 ficking in women and girls. Scant other research or

9 statistical data exists regarding the interconnection

10 between trafficking in persons and HIV/AIDS. Fur-

11 ther research is needed to determine the extent to

12 which trafficking in persons contributes to the

13 spread of HIV/AIDS and to identify strategies to

14 combat this linkage.

15   (9) Following armed conflicts and during hu-

16 manitarian emergencies, indigenous populations face

17 increased security challenges and vulnerabilities

18 which result in myriad forms of violence, including

19 trafficking for sexual and labor exploitation. Foreign

20 policy and foreign aid professionals increasingly rec-

21 ognize the increased activity of human traffickers in

22 post-conflict settings and during humanitarian emer-

23 gencies.

24   (10) There is a need to protect populations in

25 post-conflict settings and humanitarian emergencies

5

1   from being trafficked for sexual or labor exploi-

2   tation. The efforts of aid agencies to address the

3   protection needs of, among others, internally dis-

4   placed persons and refugees are useful in this re-

5   gard. Nonetheless, there remains a lack of institu-

6   tionalized programs and strategies at the United

7   States Agency for International Development, the

8   Department of State, and the Department of De-

9   fense to combat human trafficking, including

10   through protection and prevention methodologies, in

11   post-conflict environments and during humanitarian

12   emergencies.

13   (11) International and human rights organiza-

14   tions have documented a correlation between inter-

15   national deployments of military and civilian peace-

16   keepers and aid workers and a resulting increase in

17   the number of women and girls trafficked into pros-

18   titution in post-conflict regions.

19   (12) The involvement of employees and contrac-

20   tors of the United States Government and members

21   of the Armed Forces in trafficking in persons, facili-

22   tating the trafficking in persons, or exploiting the

23   victims of trafficking in persons is inconsistent with

24   United States laws and policies and undermines the

6

1   credibility and mission of United States Government

2   programs in post-conflict regions.

3   (13) Further measures are needed to ensure

4   that United States Government personnel and con-

5   tractors are held accountable for involvement with

6   acts of trafficking in persons, including by expand-

7   ing United States criminal jurisdiction to all United

8   States Government contractors abroad.

9   (14) Communities in the United States are not

10   fully informed about sex offenders who are residing

11   or working within those communities because offend-

12   ers who are convicted in a foreign court of a sexually

13   violent offense, or a criminal offense against a child

14   victim, are not currently encompassed by the Jacob

15   Wetterling Crimes Against Children and Sexually

16   Violent Offender Registration Program carried out

17   under section 170101 of the Violent Crime Control

18   and Law Enforcement Act of 1994 (42 U.S.C.

19   14701), as amended by Megan's Law (Public Law

20   104–145;110 Stat. 1345).

7

TITLE I—COMBATTING INTER-NATIONAL TRAFFICKING IN PERSONS

SEC. 101. PREVENTION OF TRAFFICKING IN PERSONS.

(a) PREVENTION OF TRAFFICKING IN CONJUNCTION WITH POST-CONFLICT AND HUMANITARIAN EMERGENCY ASSISTANCE.—

    (1) AMENDMENT.—Section 106 of the Trafficking Victims Protection Act of 2000 (22 U.S.C. 7104) is amended by adding at the end the following new subsection:

    "(h) PREVENTION OF TRAFFICKING IN CONJUNCTION WITH POST-CONFLICT AND HUMANITARIAN EMERGENCY ASSISTANCE.—The United States Agency for International Development, the Department of State, and the Department of Defense shall incorporate anti-trafficking and protection measures for vulnerable populations, particularly women and children, into their post-conflict and humanitarian emergency assistance and program activities.".

    (2) STUDY AND REPORT.—

        (A) STUDY.—

            (i) IN GENERAL.—The Secretary of State and the Administrator of the United States Agency for International Develop-

8

ment, in consultation with the Secretary of
Defense, shall conduct a study regarding
the threat and practice of trafficking in
persons generated by post-conflict and humanitarian emergencies in foreign countries.

(ii) FACTORS.—In carrying out the
study, the Secretary of State and the Administrator of the United States Agency
for International Development shall examine—

(I) the vulnerabilities to human
trafficking of commonly affected populations, particularly women and children, generated by post-conflict and
humanitarian emergencies;

(II) the various forms of trafficking in persons, both internal and
trans-border, including both sexual
and labor exploitation;

(III) a collection of best practices
implemented to date to combat human
trafficking in such areas; and

(IV) proposed recommendations
to better combat trafficking in per-

9

1   sons in conjunction with post-conflict

2   reconstruction and humanitarian

3   emergencies assistance.

4   (B) REPORT.—Not later than 180 days

5   after the date of the enactment of this Act, the

6   Secretary of State and the Administrator of the

7   United States Agency for International Devel-

8   opment shall submit to the Committee on Inter-

9   national Relations of the House of Representa-

10   tives and the Committee on Foreign Relations

11   of the Senate a report that contains—

12   (i) the results of the study conducted

13   pursuant to subparagraph (A); and

14   (ii) specific recommendations to com-

15   bat trafficking in persons by departments

16   and agencies of the United States Govern-

17   ment that are responsible for post-conflict

18   and humanitarian emergency strategy and

19   assistance programs, including the Office

20   of Transition Initiatives and the Office of

21   Foreign Disaster Assistance of the United

22   States Agency for International Develop-

23   ment, the Office of the Coordinator for Re-

24   construction and Stabilization and the Bu-

25   reau of Population, Refugees, and Migra-

10

1   tion of the Department of State, and rel-

2   evant Department of Defense entities that

3   are carrying out or assisting in the conduct

4   of such programs.

5   (3) IMPLEMENTATION OF RECOMMENDA-

6   TIONS.—To the maximum extent practicable and in

7   consultation with the congressional committees spec-

8   ified in paragraph (2)(B), the Administrator of the

9   United States Agency for International Develop-

10   ment, the Secretary of State, the Secretary of De-

11   fense, and the heads of other relevant departments

12   and agencies of the United States Government shall

13   take such actions as are necessary to implement the

14   recommendations contained in the report under

15   paragraph (2)(B)(ii) as soon as practicable after the

16   date of the submission of the report.

17   (b) EXTENSION OF SEXUALLY VIOLENT OFFENDER

18 REGISTRATION PROGRAM TO FOREIGN OFFENSES.—

19   (1) IN GENERAL.—Subsection (b)(7) of section

20   170101 of the Violent Crime Control and Law En-

21   forcement Act of 1994 (42 U.S.C. 14071) is amend-

22   ed—

23   (A) in the matter preceding subparagraph

24   (A) by striking "convicted in another State"

11

1   and inserting "convicted outside that State";

2   and

3   (B) in subparagraph (A) by inserting after

4   "convicted in another State," the following:

5   "convicted of a foreign offense,".

6   (2)   GUIDELINES;   IMPLEMENTATION   BY

7   STATES.—Not later than one year after the date of

8   the enactment of this Act, the Attorney General

9   shall issue revised guidelines to implement the

10 amendments made by paragraph (1). For purposes

11 of subsection (g) of such section 170101, a State

12 shall have until two years from the date on which

13 the Attorney General issues revised guidelines pursu-

14 ant to the preceding sentence to implement the

15 amendments made by paragraph (1).

16 **SEC. 102. PROTECTION OF VICTIMS OF TRAFFICKING IN**

17   **PERSONS.**

18   (a) ACCESS TO INFORMATION.—Section 107(c)(2) of

19 the Trafficking Victims Protection Act of 2000 (22 U.S.C.

20 7105(c)(2)) is amended by adding at the end the following

21 new sentence: "To the extent practicable, victims of severe

22 forms of trafficking shall have access to information about

23 federally funded or administered anti-trafficking programs

24 that provide services to victims of severe forms of traf-

25 ficking.".

12

1   (b) ESTABLISHMENT OF GUARDIAN AD LITEM PRO-

2 GRAM.—Section 462(b) of the Homeland Security Act of

3 2002 (6 U.S.C. 279(b)) is amended by adding at the end

4 the following new paragraph:

5   "(4) APPOINTMENT OF GUARDIAN AD LITEM

6   FOR CHILD VICTIM OF TRAFFICKING.—

7   "(A) IN GENERAL.—If the Director of the

8   Office of Refugee Resettlement has reason to

9   believe that an unaccompanied alien child is a

10   victim of a severe form of trafficking in persons

11   (as defined in section 107(b)(1)(C)(ii)(I) of the

12   Trafficking Victims Protection Act of 2000 (22

13   U.S.C. 7105(b)(1)(C)(ii)(I))), the Director may

14   appoint a guardian ad litem who meets the

15   qualifications described in subparagraph (B) for

16   the child. The Director is encouraged, wherever

17   practicable, to arrange with a nongovernmental

18   organization for the selection of an individual to

19   be appointed as a guardian ad litem under this

20   paragraph.

21   "(B) QUALIFICATIONS OF GUARDIAN AD

22   LITEM.—No person shall serve as a guardian

23   ad litem under this paragraph unless the per-

24   son—

13

1   "(i) is a child welfare professional or

2   other individual who has received training

3   in child welfare matters; and

4   "(ii) has received training on the na-

5   ture of problems encountered by victims of

6   trafficking.

7   "(C) DUTIES.—The guardian ad litem

8   shall take such steps as may be necessary to in-

9   vestigate and report to the Director of the Of-

10   fice of Refugee Resettlement as to whether an

11   unaccompanied alien child is a victim of traf-

12   ficking. The guardian ad litem shall—

13   "(i) conduct interviews with the child

14   in a manner that is appropriate, taking

15   into account the child's age;

16   "(ii) investigate the facts and cir-

17   cumstances relevant to such child's pres-

18   ence in the United States, including facts

19   and circumstances arising in the country of

20   the child's nationality or last habitual resi-

21   dence and facts and circumstances arising

22   subsequent to the child's departure from

23   such country;

24   "(iii) work with counsel, if the child is

25   represented by counsel, to identify the

14

1   child's eligibility for relief from removal or

2   voluntary departure by sharing with coun-

3   sel information collected under clause (ii);

4   "(iv) develop recommendations on

5   issues relative to the child's custody, deten-

6   tion, release, and repatriation;

7   "(v) take reasonable steps to ensure

8   that the best interests of the child are pro-

9   moted while the child participates in, or is

10 subject to, proceedings or matters under

11 the Immigration and Nationality Act (8

12 U.S.C. 1101 et seq.); and

13 "(vi) take reasonable steps to ensure

14 that the child understands the nature of

15 the legal proceedings or matters and deter-

16 minations made by the court, and ensure

17 that all information is conveyed in an age-

18 appropriate manner.

19 "(D) DETERMINATION OF ELIGIBILITY

20 FOR BENEFITS AND SERVICES.—The Director

21 of the Office of Refugee Resettlement shall con-

22 sider the report provided by the guardian ad

23 litem in determining whether an alien child is

24 a victim of a severe form of trafficking in per-

25 sons eligible for services pursuant to section

15

107(b)(1)(A) of the Trafficking Victims Protection Act of 2000 (22 U.S.C. 7105(b)(1)(A)).

"(E) TERMINATION OF APPOINTMENT.—
The guardian ad litem shall carry out the duties described in subparagraph (C) until one of the following occurs:

"(i) Such duties are completed.

"(ii) The child departs the United States.

"(iii) The child is granted permanent resident status in the United States;

"(iv) The child attains the age of 18.

"(v) The child is placed in the custody of a parent, legal guardian, or licensed child welfare agency.

"(F) POWERS.—The guardian ad litem—

"(i) shall have reasonable access to the child, including access while such child is being held in detention, in the care of a foster family, or in any other temporary living arrangement;

"(ii) shall be permitted to review all records and information relating to such proceedings that are not deemed privileged or classified;

16

1   "(iii) may seek independent evalua-

2   tions of the child;

3   "(iv) shall be notified in advance of all

4   hearings or interviews involving the child

5   that are held in connection with pro-

6   ceedings or matters under the Immigration

7   and Nationality Act (8 U.S.C. 1101 et

8   seq.) or in connection with the investiga-

9   tion or prosecution of a severe form of

10   trafficking in persons (as defined in section

11   103 of the Trafficking Victims Protection

12   Act of 2000 (22 U.S.C. 7103)), and shall

13   be given a reasonable opportunity to be

14   present at such hearings or interviews;

15   "(v) shall be permitted to consult with

16   the child during any hearing or interview

17   involving such child; and

18   "(vi) shall be provided at least 24

19   hours advance notice of a transfer of that

20   child to a different placement, absent com-

21   pelling and unusual circumstances war-

22   ranting the transfer of such child prior to

23   notification.

24   "(G) TRAINING.—The Director of the Of-

25   fice for Refugee Resettlement is authorized to

17

1 provide training for all persons serving as
2 guardians ad litem under this section in the cir-
3 cumstances and conditions that child victims of
4 trafficking face and immigration benefits or
5 other rights under the Trafficking Victims Pro-
6 tection Act of 2000 (22 U.S.C. 7101 et seq.)
7 for which such child might be eligible.

8 "(H) AUTHORIZATION OF APPROPRIA-
9 TIONS.—There are authorized to be appro-
10 priated to the Secretary of Health and Human
11 Services such sums as may be necessary to
12 carry out this paragraph. ".

13 (c) ACCESS TO COUNSEL.—Section 107(c) of the
14 Trafficking Victims Protection Act of 2000 (22 U.S.C.
15 7105(c)) is amended by adding at the end the following
16 new paragraph:

17 "(5) ACCESS TO COUNSEL.—

18 "(A) ACCESS TO COUNSEL.—Victims of se-
19 vere forms of trafficking, while in the custody
20 of the Federal Government, shall not be denied
21 access to counsel in any proceeding or matter
22 relating to the investigation and prosecution of
23 the act of trafficking involved.

24 "(B) INFORMATION.—Victims of severe
25 forms of trafficking shall receive information

18

1   about their right to access to counsel under

2   subparagraph (A). To the maximum extent

3   practicable, victims of severe forms of traf-

4   ficking shall receive contact information for

5   nongovernmental organizations that receive

6   funding from the Federal Government to pro-

7   vide counsel or other assistance to victims of

8   trafficking.''.

9   (d) ESTABLISHMENT OF PILOT PROGRAM FOR RESI-

10 DENTIAL REHABILITATIVE FACILITIES FOR VICTIMS OF

11 TRAFFICKING.—

12   (1) STUDY.—

13   (A) IN GENERAL.—Not later than 180

14   days after the date of the enactment of this

15   Act, the Administrator of the United States

16   Agency for International Development shall

17   carry out a study to identify best practices for

18   the rehabilitation of victims of trafficking in

19   group residential facilities in foreign countries.

20   (B) FACTORS.—In carrying out the study

21   under subparagraph (A), the Administrator

22   shall—

23   (i) investigate factors relating to the

24   rehabilitation of victims of trafficking in

25   group residential facilities, such as the ap-

19

1 propriate size of such facilities, services to

2 be provided, length of stay, and cost; and

3   (ii) give consideration to ensure the

4 safety and security of victims of traf-

5 ficking, provide alternative sources of in-

6 come for such victims, assess and provide

7 for the educational needs of such victims,

8 including literacy, and assess the psycho-

9 logical needs of such victims and provide

10 professional counseling, as appropriate.

11 (2) PILOT PROGRAM.—Upon completion of the

12 study carried out pursuant to paragraph (1), the

13 Administrator of the United States Agency for

14 International Development shall establish and carry

15 out a pilot program to establish residential treat-

16 ment facilities in foreign countries for victims of

17 trafficking based upon the best practices identified

18 in the study.

19 (3) PURPOSES.—The purposes of the pilot pro-

20 gram established pursuant to paragraph (2) are to—

21   (A) provide benefits and services to victims

22 of trafficking, including shelter, psychological

23 counseling, and assistance in developing inde-

24 pendent living skills;

20

1   (B) assess the benefits of providing resi-

2   dential treatment facilities for victims of traf-

3   ficking, as well as the most efficient and cost-

4   effective means of providing such facilities; and

5   (C) assess the need for and feasibility of

6   establishing additional residential treatment fa-

7   cilities for victims of trafficking.

8   (4) SELECTION OF SITES.—The Administrator

9 of the United States Agency for International Devel-

10 opment shall select 2 sites at which to operate the

11 pilot program established pursuant to paragraph (2).

12   (5) FORM OF ASSISTANCE.—In order to carry

13 out the responsibilities of this subsection, the Ad-

14 ministrator of the United States Agency for Inter-

15 national Development shall enter into contracts with,

16 or make grants to, nonprofit organizations with rel-

17 evant expertise in the delivery of services to victims

18 of trafficking.

19   (6) REPORT.—Not later than one year after the

20 date on which the first pilot program is established

21 pursuant to paragraph (2), the Administrator of the

22 United States Agency for International Development

23 shall submit to the Committee on International Re-

24 lations of the House of Representatives and the

21

1   Committee on Foreign Relations of the Senate a re-

2   port on the implementation of this subsection.

3   (7) AUTHORIZATION OF APPROPRIATIONS.—

4   There are authorized to be appropriated to the Ad-

5   ministrator of the United States Agency for Inter-

6   national Development to carry out this subsection

7    $2,500,000 for each of the fiscal years 2006 and

8   2007.

9   **SEC. 103. ENHANCING PROSECUTIONS OF TRAFFICKING**

10   **OFFENSES.**

11   (a) EXTRATERRITORIAL JURISDICTION OVER FED-

12   ERAL CONTRACTORS.—

13   (1) IN GENERAL.—Part II of title 18, United

14   States Code, is amended by inserting after chapter

15   212 the following new chapter:

16   **"CHAPTER 212A—EXTRATERRITORIAL JU-**

17   **RISDICTION OVER FEDERAL CON-**

18   **TRACTORS**

"Sec.
"3271. Criminal offenses committed by Federal contractors outside the United States.
"3272. Definition.

19   **"§ 3271. Criminal offenses committed by Federal con-**

20   **tractors outside the United States**

21   "(a) Whoever, while an extraterritorial Federal con-

22   tractor, engages in conduct outside the United States that

23   would constitute an offense punishable by imprisonment

22

1 for more than 1 year if the conduct had been engaged

2 in within the special maritime and territorial jurisdiction

3 of the United States shall be punished as provided for that

4 offense.

5   "(b) No prosecution may be commenced against a

6 person under this section if a foreign government, in ac-

7 cordance with jurisdiction recognized by the United

8 States, has prosecuted or is prosecuting such person for

9 the conduct constituting such offense, except upon the ap-

10 proval of the Attorney General or the Deputy Attorney

11 General (or a person acting in either such capacity), which

12 function of approval may not be delegated.

13 **"§ 3272. Definition**

14   "As used in this chapter, the term 'extraterritorial

15 Federal contractor' means a person—

16   "(1) employed as a contractor (including a sub-

17   contractor at any tier), or as an employee of a con-

18   tractor (or subcontractor at any tier), of any Federal

19   agency;

20   "(2) present or residing outside the United

21   States in connection with such employment; and

22   "(3) not a national of or ordinarily resident in

23   the host nation.".

24   (2) CLERICAL AMENDMENT.—The table of

25   chapters at the beginning of such part is amended

23

1   by inserting after the item relating to chapter 212

2   the following new item:

"212A. Extraterritorial jurisdiction over Federal contractors .... 3271".

3   (b) NEW UCMJ OFFENSES.—

4   (1) IN GENERAL.—Subchapter X of chapter 47

5   of title 10, United States Code (the Uniform Code

6   of Military Justice), is amended by inserting after

7   section 920 (article 120) the following new sections:

"§ 920a. Art. 120a. Sex trafficking

9   "Any person subject to this chapter who knowingly

10   recruits, entices, harbors, transports, provides, or obtains

11   by any means a person, knowing that—

12   "(1) force, fraud, or coercion will be used to

13   cause that person to engage in a commercial sex act;

14   or

15   "(2) the person has not attained the age of

16   eighteen years and will be caused to engage in a

17   commercial sex act,

18   is guilty of sex trafficking and shall be punished as a

19   court-martial may direct.

"§ 920b. Art. 120b. Trafficking for labor or services

21   "Any person subject to this chapter who knowingly

22   recruits, harbors, transports, provides, or obtains by any

23   means a person for labor or services—

24   "(1) by threats of serious harm to, or physical

25   restraint against, that person or another person;

24

1   "(2) by means of any scheme, plan, or pattern

2   intended to cause the person to believe that, if the

3   person did not perform such labor or services, that

4   person or another person would suffer serious harm

5   or physical restraint; or

6   "(3) by means of the abuse or threatened abuse

7   of law or the legal process,

8 is guilty of trafficking for labor or services and shall be

9 punished as a court-martial may direct.".

10   (2) CLERICAL AMENDMENT.—The table of sec-

11   tions at the beginning of such subchapter is amend-

12   ed by inserting after the item relating to section 920

13   (article 120) the following new items:

"920a. 120a. Sex trafficking.
"920b. 120b. Trafficking for labor or services.".

14   (c) LAUNDERING OF MONETARY INSTRUMENTS.—

15 Section 1956(c)(7)(B) of title 18, United States Code, is

16 amended—

17   (1) in clause (v), by striking "or" at the end;

18   (2) in clause (vi), by adding "or" at the end;

19   and

20   (3) by adding at the end the following new

21   clause:

22   "(vii) trafficking in persons, selling or

23   buying of children, sexual exploitation of

24   children, or transporting, recruiting or har-

25

1   boring a person, including a child, for com-

2   mercial sex acts;".

3   (d) TRANSPORTATION OF MINORS.—Section 2423 of

4 title 18, United States Code, is amended by adding at the

5 end the following new subsection:

6   "(h) ENFORCEMENT AGAINST UNITED STATES CITI-

7 ZENS IN FOREIGN PLACES.—If a United States Govern-

8 ment official attached to a United States Embassy in a

9 foreign place becomes aware of a United States citizen or

10 an alien admitted for permanent residence in the United

11 States who is located in such foreign place and who has

12 traveled in foreign commerce in violation of subsection (a),

13 (b), (c), (d), or (e), the United States Embassy shall notify

14 local law enforcement authorities and shall encourage the

15 prosecution of the individual under applicable local laws

16 or the extradition of the individual to the United States

17 for the purpose of prosecution under this section.".

18 **SEC. 104. ENHANCING UNITED STATES EFFORTS TO COM-**

19   **BAT TRAFFICKING IN PERSONS.**

20   (a) APPOINTMENT TO INTERAGENCY TASK FORCE

21 TO MONITOR AND COMBAT TRAFFICKING.—Section

22 105(b) of the Trafficking Victims Protection Act of 2000

23 (22 U.S.C. 7103(b)) is amended—

26

1   (1) by striking "the Director of Central Intel-

2 ligence" and inserting "the Director of National In-

3 telligence"; and

4   (2) by inserting ", the Secretary of Defense, the

5 Secretary of Homeland Security" after "the Director

6 of National Intelligence" (as added by paragraph

7 (1)).

8   (b) REPORTING REQUIREMENT.—Section

9 105(d)(7)(D) of the Trafficking Victims Protection Act of

10 2000 (22 U.S.C. 7103(d)(7)(D)) is amended by adding

11 at the end before the semicolon the following: ", and with

12 respect to each case prosecuted under one or more of these

13 sections, the number of victims of trafficking identified in

14 each case and, of those victims, the number that have been

15 granted continued presence in the United States under

16 section 107(c)(3) or have been granted a visa under sec-

17 tion 101(a)(15)(T)(i) of the Immigration and Nationality

18 Act".

19   (c) MINIMUM STANDARDS FOR THE ELIMINATION OF

20 TRAFFICKING.—Section 108(b) of the Trafficking Victims

21 Protection Act of 2000 (22 U.S.C. 7106(b)) is amended—

22   (1) in paragraph (3), by adding at the end be-

23 fore the period the following: ", measures to reduce

24 the demand for commercial sex acts and for partici-

25 pation in international sex tourism by nationals of

27

1   the country, measures to ensure that its nationals

2   who are deployed abroad as part of a peacekeeping

3   or other similar mission do not engage in or facili-

4   tate severe forms of trafficking in persons or exploit

5   victims of such trafficking, and measures to prevent

6   the use of forced labor or child labor in violation of

7   international standards"; and

8   (2) in the first sentence of paragraph (7), by

9   striking "persons," and inserting "persons, including

10   nationals of the country who are deployed abroad as

11   part of a peacekeeping or other similar mission who

12   engage in or facilitate severe forms of trafficking in

13   persons or exploit victims of such trafficking,".

14   (d) RESEARCH.—Section 112A of the Trafficking

15 Victims Protection Act of 2000 (22 U.S.C. 7109a) is

16 amended—

17   (1) in the first sentence of the matter preceding

18   paragraph (1)—

19   (A) by striking "The President" and in-

20   serting "(a) IN GENERAL.—The President";

21   and

22   (B) by striking "the Director of Central

23   Intelligence" and inserting "the Director of Na-

24   tional Intelligence";

28

1   (2) in paragraph (3), by adding at the end be-
2   fore the period the following: ", particularly HIV/
3   AIDS";
4   (3) by adding at the end the following new
5   paragraphs:
6   "(4) Subject to subsection (b), the interrelation-
7   ship between trafficking in persons and terrorism,
8   including the use of profits from trafficking in per-
9   sons to finance terrorism.
10   "(5) An effective mechanism for quantifying the
11   number of victims of trafficking on a national, re-
12   gional, and international basis.
13   "(6) The abduction and enslavement of children
14   for use as soldiers, including steps taken to elimi-
15   nate the abduction and enslavement of children for
16   use as soldiers and recommendations for such fur-
17   ther steps as may be necessary to rapidly end the
18   abduction and enslavement of children for use as
19   soldiers."; and
20   (4) by further adding at the end the following
21   new subsections:
22   "(b) ROLE OF HUMAN SMUGGLING AND TRAF-
23   FICKING CENTER.—The research initiatives described in
24   subsection (a)(4) shall be carried out by the Human
25   Smuggling and Trafficking Center (established pursuant

29

1   to section 7202 of the Intelligence Reform and Terrorism

2   Prevention Act of 2004 (Public Law 108–458)).

3   "(c) DEFINITIONS.—In this section:

4   "(1) AIDS.—The term 'AIDS' means the ac-

5   quired immune deficiency syndrome.

6   "(2) HIV.—The term 'HIV' means the human

7   immunodeficiency virus, the pathogen that causes

8   AIDS.

9   "(3)   HIV/AIDS.—The   term   'HIV/AIDS'

10   means, with respect to an individual, an individual

11   who is infected with HIV or living with AIDS.".

12   (e) FOREIGN SERVICE OFFICER TRAINING.—Section

13 708(a) of the Foreign Service Act of 1980 (22 U.S.C.

14 4028(a)) is amended—

15   (1) in the matter preceding paragraph (1), by

16   inserting ", the Director of the Office to Monitor

17   and Combat Trafficking," after "the International

18   Religious Freedom Act of 1998";

19   (2) in paragraph (1), by striking "and" at the

20   end;

21   (3) in paragraph (2), by striking the period at

22   the end and inserting "; and"; and

23   (4) by adding at the end the following:

24   "(3) instruction on international documents and

25   United States policy on trafficking in persons, in-

30

1   cluding provisions of the Trafficking Victims Protec-

2   tion Act of 2000 (division A of Public Law 106–386;

3   22 U.S.C. 7101 et seq.) which may affect the United

4   States bilateral relationships.".

5   (f) PREVENTION OF TRAFFICKING BY PEACE-

6 KEEPERS.—

7   (1) INCLUSION IN TRAFFICKING IN PERSONS

8   REPORT.—Section 110(b)(1) of the Trafficking Vic-

9   tims Protection Act of 2000 (22 U.S.C. 7107(b)(1))

10   is amended—

11   (A) in subparagraph (B), by striking

12   "and" at the end;

13   (B) in subparagraph (C), by striking the

14   period at the end and inserting "; and"; and

15   (C) by adding at the end the following new

16   subparagraph:

17   "(D) information on the measures taken

18   by the United Nations, the Organization for Se-

19   curity and Cooperation in Europe, the North

20   Atlantic Treaty Organization and, as appro-

21   priate, other multilateral organizations in which

22   the United States participates, to prevent the

23   involvement of the organization's employees,

24   contractor personnel, and peacekeeping forces

31

1   in trafficking in persons or the exploitation of

2   victims of trafficking.''.

3   (2) PREVENTION OF TRAFFICKING IN CONNEC-

4   TION WITH PEACEKEEPING OPERATIONS.—

5   (A) CERTIFICATION BY SECRETARY OF

6   STATE.—At least 15 days prior to voting for or

7   otherwise officially endorsing a new, reauthor-

8   ized, or expanded peacekeeping mission under

9   the auspices of the United Nations, the North

10   Atlantic Treaty Organization, or any other mul-

11   tilateral organization in which the United

12   States participates (or in the case of a peace-

13   keeping mission to respond to an emergency, as

14   far in advance as is practicable), the Secretary

15   of State shall submit to the Committee on

16   International Relations of the House of Rep-

17   resentatives, the Committee on Foreign Rela-

18   tions of the Senate, and any other appropriate

19   congressional committee a certification that

20   contains—

21   (i) a determination that the organiza-

22   tion has taken appropriate measures to

23   prevent the organization's employees, con-

24   tractor personnel, and peacekeeping forces

25   serving in the peacekeeping mission from

32

1   trafficking in persons, exploiting victims of

2   trafficking, or committing acts of illegal

3   sexual exploitation and to hold accountable

4   any such individuals who engage in any

5   such acts while participating in the peace-

6   keeping mission; and

7   (ii) a detailed description of each of

8   the measures referred to in clause (i).

9   (B) PROVISION OF UNITED STATES

10   LOGISTICAL SUPPORT.—

11   (i) REQUIREMENT.—The United

12   States may provide logistical support for or

13   deploy personnel, including civilian police,

14   observers, or members of the United States

15   Armed Forces in support of a peace-

16   keeping mission under the auspices of the

17   United Nations, the North Atlantic Treaty

18   Organization, or any other multilateral or-

19   ganization in which the United States par-

20   ticipates only on or after the date on which

21   the Secretary of State submits to a Con-

22   gress a certification described in subpara-

23   graph (A).

24   (ii) EXCEPTION.—Notwithstanding

25   the failure of the Secretary of State to

33

1   submit a certification pursuant to subpara-

2   graph (A) with respect to a peacekeeping

3   mission described in such subparagraph,

4   support described in clause (i) may be

5   made available for the peacekeeping mis-

6   sion on or after the date on which the Sec-

7   retary of State submits to Congress a let-

8   ter that contains—

9   (I) an explanation as to why the

10   certification required by subparagraph

11   (A) has not been provided;

12   (II) a description of the steps

13   taken by the United States to encour-

14   age the organization to take the ap-

15   propriate measures described in sub-

16   paragraph (A); and

17   (III) a certification that, notwith-

18   standing the failure of the organiza-

19   tion to take the appropriate measures

20   described in subparagraph (A), the

21   Secretary of State has determined

22   that voting for or otherwise officially

23   endorsing the peacekeeping mission is

24   in the national interests of United

25   States.

34

1   (3) DEPARTMENT OF DEFENSE DIRECTOR OF

2   ANTI-TRAFFICKING POLICIES.—

3   (A) ESTABLISHMENT.—The Secretary of

4   Defense shall designate within the Office of the

5   Secretary of Defense a director of anti-traf-

6   ficking policies. The director shall be respon-

7   sible for overseeing the implementation within

8   the Department of Defense of policies relating

9   to trafficking in persons, including policies of

10   the Department and policies of the Federal

11   Government (including policies contained in Na-

12   tional Security Presidential Directive 22) as

13   they relate to the Department. The Secretary

14   may not assign to the director any responsibil-

15   ities not related to trafficking in persons.

16   (B) DUTIES.—The director designated

17   under subparagraph (A) shall, in consultation

18   with other relevant elements of the Depart-

19   ment—

20   (i) ensure that training materials and

21   instructional programs relating to traf-

22   ficking in persons are developed and used

23   by the military departments;

24   (ii) consult regularly with academi-

25   cians, faith-based organizations, multilat-

35

eral organizations, nongovernmental organizations, and others with expertise in
combating trafficking in persons, regarding
the Department's implementation of policies relating to trafficking in persons;

(iii) conduct surveys of members of
the Armed Forces and of employees of the
Department to assess attitudes and knowledge regarding trafficking in persons and
use the results of those surveys to develop
training materials and instructional programs relating to trafficking in persons;

(iv) ensure that trafficking in persons
is included as an intelligence requirement
in peacekeeping missions that track organized crime;

(v) ensure the proper handling of
cases in which a member of the Armed
Forces or an employee or contractor of the
Department is alleged to have engaged in
or facilitated an act of trafficking in persons and in such cases encourage, as appropriate, implementation of chapter 212
of title 18, United States Code (commonly
referred to as the Military Extraterritorial

36

1	Jurisdiction Act of 2000) and the Traf-
2	ficking Victims Protection Act of 2000;
3	(vi) ensure that the Department im-
4	plements the commitments relating to traf-
5	ficking in persons agreed to by the United
6	States in the context of the North Atlantic
7	Treaty Organization, the United Nations,
8	and other multilateral organizations, as
9	those commitments relate to the Depart-
10	ment;
11	(vii) establish a mechanism to ensure
12	that neither the Department nor any con-
13	tractor (or subcontractor at any tier) of
14	the Department rehires an employee of
15	such a contractor (or subcontractor) who
16	engaged in a severe form of trafficking in
17	persons while the contract is in effect;
18	(viii) include the subject of trafficking
19	in persons in military-to-military contact
20	programs;
21	(ix) in consultation with the Office of
22	the Inspector General of the Department,
23	investigate links between trafficking in per-
24	sons and deployments of members of the

37

1 Armed Forces and contractors of the De-
2 partment;

3 (x) consult with contractors of the De-
4 partment on programs to prevent traf-
5 ficking in persons and on accountability
6 structures relating to trafficking in per-
7 sons; and

8 (xi) perform such other related duties
9 as the Secretary may require.

10 (C) RESOURCES.—The director designated
11 under subparagraph (A) shall have sufficient
12 staff and resources to carry out the responsibil-
13 ities and duties described in this paragraph.

14 (D) RANK.—The director designated under
15 subparagraph (A) shall have the rank of assist-
16 ant secretary.

17 (g) FBI INVESTIGATIONS.—From amounts made
18 available to carry out this subsection (including amounts
19 made available pursuant to the authorization of appropria-
20 tions in section 302), the Director of the Federal Bureau
21 of Investigation shall investigate acts of severe forms of
22 trafficking in persons other than domestic trafficking in
23 persons (as defined in section 206).

38

1 **SEC. 105. ADDITIONAL ACTIVITIES TO MONITOR AND COM-**

2 **BAT FORCED LABOR AND CHILD LABOR.**

3   (a) IN GENERAL.—The Secretary of Labor, acting

4 through the head of the Bureau of International Labor

5 Affairs of the Department of Labor, shall carry out addi-

6 tional activities to monitor and combat forced labor and

7 child labor in foreign countries as described in subsection

8 (b).

9   (b) ADDITIONAL ACTIVITIES DESCRIBED.—The addi-

10 tional activities referred to in subsection (a) are—

11   (1) to monitor the use of forced labor and child

12   labor in violation of international standards;

13   (2) to provide information regarding trafficking

14   in persons for the purpose of forced labor to the Of-

15   fice to Monitor and Combat Trafficking of the De-

16   partment of State for inclusion in trafficking in per-

17   sons report required by section 110(b) of the Traf-

18   ficking Victims Protection Act of 2000 (22 U.S.C.

19   7107(b));

20   (3) to develop and make available to the public

21   a list of goods from countries that the Bureau of

22   International Labor Affairs has reason to believe are

23   produced by forced labor or child labor in violation

24   of international standards;

25   (4) to work with persons who are involved in

26   the production of goods on the list described in para-

39

1   graph (3) to create a standard set of practices that

2   will reduce the likelihood that such persons will

3   produce goods using the labor described in such

4   paragraph; and

5   (5) to consult with other departments and agen-

6   cies of the United States Government to reduce

7   forced and child labor internationally and ensure

8   that products made by forced labor and child labor

9   in violation of international standards are not im-

10   ported into the United States.

11   # TITLE II—COMBATTING DOMES-

12   # TIC TRAFFICKING IN PER-

13   # SONS

14   **SEC. 201. PREVENTION OF DOMESTIC TRAFFICKING IN**

15   **PERSONS.**

16   (a) PROGRAM TO REDUCE DEMAND FOR COMMER-

17   CIAL SEX ACTS.—

18   (1) PROGRAM.—The Secretary of Health and

19   Human Services shall identify best practices to re-

20   duce the demand for commercial sex acts in the

21   United States and shall carry out a program to im-

22   plement such best practices.

23   (2) REPORT.—The Secretary shall prepare and

24   post on the Internet Web site of the Department of

40

1 Health and Human Services a report on the best

2 practices identified under paragraph (1).

3 (3) DEFINITIONS.—In this subsection, the term

4 "commercial sex act" has the meaning given the

5 term in section 103(3) of the Trafficking Victims

6 Protection Act of 2000 (22 U.S.C. 7102(3)).

7 (b) TERMINATION OF CERTAIN GRANTS, CON-

8 TRACTS, AND COOPERATIVE AGREEMENTS.—Section

9 106(g) of the Trafficking Victims Protection Act of 2000

10 (22 U.S.C. 7104) is amended—

11 (1) in paragraph (1), by striking "described in

12 paragraph (2)"; and

13 (2) by striking paragraph (2).

14 **SEC. 202. ESTABLISHMENT OF GRANT PROGRAM TO DE-**

15 **VELOP, EXPAND, AND STRENGTHEN VICTIM**

16 **SERVICE PROGRAMS FOR VICTIMS OF DO-**

17 **MESTIC TRAFFICKING.**

18 (a) GRANT PROGRAM.—Subject to the availability of

19 appropriations, the Secretary of Health and Human Serv-

20 ices may make grants to States, Indian tribes, units of

21 local government, and nonprofit, nongovernmental victims'

22 service organizations to develop, expand, and strengthen

23 victim service programs for victims of domestic trafficking.

24 (b) SELECTION FACTOR.—In selecting among appli-

25 cants for grants under subsection (a), the Secretary shall

41

1 give priority to applicants with experience in the delivery

2 of services to runaway or homeless youth, including youth

3 who have been subjected to sexual abuse or commercial

4 sexual exploitation, and to applicants who would employ

5 survivors of commercial sexual exploitation as part of their

6 proposed project.

7   (c) LIMITATION ON FEDERAL SHARE.—The Federal

8 share of a grant made under this section may not exceed

9 75 percent of the total costs of the projects described in

10 the application submitted.

11 **SEC. 203. PROTECTION OF VICTIMS OF DOMESTIC TRAF-**

12   **FICKING IN PERSONS.**

13   (a) ESTABLISHMENT OF PILOT PROGRAM.—Not

14 later than 180 days after the date of the enactment of

15 this Act, the Secretary of Health and Human Services

16 shall establish and carry out a pilot program to establish

17 residential treatment facilities in the United States for

18 minor victims of domestic trafficking.

19   (b) PURPOSES.—The purposes of the pilot program

20 established pursuant to subsection (a) are to—

21   (1) provide benefits and services to minor vic-

22   tims of domestic trafficking, including shelter, psy-

23   chological counseling, and assistance in developing

24   independent living skills;

42

1   (2) assess the benefits of providing residential

2 treatment facilities for minor victims of domestic

3 trafficking, as well as the most efficient and cost-ef-

4 fective means of providing such facilities; and

5   (3) assess the need for and feasibility of estab-

6 lishing additional residential treatment facilities for

7 minor victims of domestic trafficking.

8   (c) SELECTION OF SITES.—The Secretary of Health

9 and Human Services shall select 3 sites at which to oper-

10 ate the pilot program established pursuant to subsection

11 (a).

12   (d) FORM OF ASSISTANCE.—In order to carry out the

13 responsibilities of this section, the Secretary of Health and

14 Human Services shall enter into contracts with, or make

15 grants to, nonprofit organizations with relevant expertise

16 in the delivery of services to runaway or homeless youth,

17 including youth who have been subjected to sexual abuse

18 or commercial sexual exploitation.

19   (e) REPORT.—Not later than one year after the date

20 on which the first pilot program is established pursuant

21 to subsection (a), the Secretary of Health and Human

22 Services shall submit to Congress a report on the imple-

23 mentation of this section.

24   (f) AUTHORIZATION OF APPROPRIATIONS.—There

25 are authorized to be appropriated to the Secretary of

43

1 Health and Human Services to carry out this section

2 $5,000,000 for each of the fiscal years 2006 and 2007.

3 **SEC. 204. INVESTIGATION BY FEDERAL BUREAU OF INVES-**

4   **TIGATION OF ACTS OF DOMESTIC TRAF-**

5   **FICKING IN PERSONS.**

6 From amounts made available to carry out this sec-

7 tion (including amounts made available pursuant to the

8 authorization of appropriations in section 302), the Direc-

9 tor of the Federal Bureau of Investigation shall inves-

10 tigate acts of domestic trafficking in persons.

11 **SEC. 205. ENHANCING STATE AND LOCAL EFFORTS TO**

12   **COMBAT TRAFFICKING IN PERSONS.**

13 (a) ESTABLISHMENT OF GRANT PROGRAM FOR LAW

14 ENFORCEMENT.—

15   (1) IN GENERAL.—Subject to the availability of

16   appropriations, the Attorney General may make

17   grants to States and local law enforcement agencies

18   to develop, expand, or strengthen programs to inves-

19   tigate and prosecute acts of domestic trafficking in

20   persons.

21   (2) MULTI-DISCIPLINARY APPROACH RE-

22   QUIRED.—Grants under paragraph (1) may be made

23   only for programs in which the State or local law en-

24   forcement agency works collaboratively with victim

25   service providers and other relevant nongovern-

44

1   mental organizations, including faith-based organiza-

2   tions and organizations with experience in the deliv-

3   ery of services to youth who have been subjected to

4   sexual abuse or commercial sexual exploitation.

5   (3) LIMITATION ON FEDERAL SHARE.—The

6   Federal share of a grant made under this subsection

7   may not exceed 75 percent of the total costs of the

8   projects described in the application submitted.

9   (b) IMPROVED INTERAGENCY COORDINATION TO

10 COMBAT DOMESTIC TRAFFICKING.—Section 206(a)(1) of

11 the Juvenile Justice and Delinquency Prevention Act of

12 1974 (42 U.S.C. 5616(a)(1)) is amended by inserting ",

13 the Director of the Office to Monitor and Combat Traf-

14 ficking of the Department of State" after "the Commis-

15 sioner of Immigration and Naturalization".

16 **SEC. 206. DEFINITIONS.**

17   In this title:

18   (1) DOMESTIC TRAFFICKING IN PERSONS.—The

19 term "domestic trafficking in persons" means a se-

20 vere form of trafficking in persons as defined by sec-

21 tion 103(8) of the Trafficking Victims Protection

22 Act of 2000 (22 U.S.C. 7102(8)), which occurs

23 wholly within the territorial jurisdiction of the

24 United States.

45

1   (2) VICTIM OF DOMESTIC TRAFFICKING.—The

2   term "victim of domestic trafficking" means a per-

3   son subjected to an act or practice described in

4   paragraph (1).

5   (3) MINOR VICTIM OF DOMESTIC TRAF-

6   FICKING.—The term "minor victim of domestic traf-

7   ficking" means a person subjected to an act or prac-

8   tice described in paragraph (1) who has not attained

9   18 years of age at the time the person is identified

10   as a victim of domestic trafficking.

11 TITLE III—AUTHORIZATIONS OF
12 APPROPRIATIONS

13 SEC. 301. AUTHORIZATIONS OF APPROPRIATIONS.

14   Section 113 of the Trafficking Victims Protection Act

15 of 2000 (22 U.S.C. 7110) is amended—

16   (1) in subsection (a)—

17   (A) by striking "and $5,000,000" and in-

18   serting "$5,000,000";

19   (B) by adding at the end before the period

20   the following: ", and $5,500,000 for each of the

21   fiscal years 2006 and 2007"; and

22   (C) by further adding at the end the fol-

23   lowing new sentence: "In addition, there are au-

24   thorized to be appropriated to the Office to

25   Monitor and Combat Trafficking for official re-

46

1   ception and representation expenses $3,000 for

2   each of the fiscal years 2006 and 2007.";

3   (2) in subsection (b), by striking "2004 and

4   2005" and inserting "2004, 2005, 2006, and 2007";

5   (3) in subsection (c)(1), by striking "2004 and

6   2005" each place it appears and inserting "2004,

7   2005, 2006, and 2007";

8   (4) in subsection (d), by striking "2004 and

9   2005" each place it appears and inserting "2004,

10   2005, 2006, and 2007";

11   (5) in subsection (e)—

12   (A) in paragraphs (1) and (2), by striking

13   "2003 through 2005" and inserting "2003

14   through 2007"; and

15   (B) in paragraph (3), by striking

16   "$300,000 for fiscal year 2004 and $300,000

17   for fiscal year 2005" and inserting "$300,000

18   for each of the fiscal years 2004 through

19   2007"; and

20   (6) in subsection (f), by striking "2004 and

21   2005" and inserting "2004, 2005, 2006, and 2007".

22   **SEC. 302. INVESTIGATIONS BY FEDERAL BUREAU OF INVES-**

23   **TIGATIONS.**

24   There are authorized to be appropriated to the Direc-

25   tor of the Federal Bureau of Investigation to carry out

47

1 sections 204 and 104(g) $15,000,000 for fiscal year 2006,

2 to remain available until expended.

○

The Athens Ethical Principals

We,

Members of the business community,

Being deeply concerned that the scourge of trafficking in human beings, especially women and children, inflicts enormous suffering in the world today,

Consider it unacceptable that millions of people are treated as commodities and slaves, and therefore denied their basic human rights and dignity,

Welcome the efforts of the international community to eradicate human trafficking, through the use of public-private partnerships, and envisage this initiative as an additional means to complement and reinforce such efforts,

Recognize the significant potential of the business community to contribute to the global fight against human trafficking and are inspired by business community members who are already applying ethical policies and codes of conduct concerning human rights,

Dissociate ourselves from such illicit practices by launching the following ethical principles in which we will:

1. Demonstrate the position of zero tolerance towards trafficking in human beings, especially women and children for sexual exploitation (Policy Setting).
2. Contribute to prevention of trafficking in human beings including awareness-raising campaigns and education (Public Awareness Raising).
3. Develop a corporate strategy for an anti-trafficking policy which will permeate all our activities (Strategic Planning).
4. Ensure that our personnel fully comply with our anti-trafficking policy (Personnel Policy Enforcement).
5. Encourage business partners, including suppliers, to apply ethical principles against human trafficking (Supply Chain Tracing).
6. In an effort to increase enforcement it is necessary to call on governments to initiate a process of revision of laws and regulations that are directly or indirectly related to enhancing anti-trafficking policies (Government Advocacy).
7. Report and share information on best practices (Transparency).

3

1. Establish a Zero Tolerance Policy: in order to explicitly demonstrate the position of zero tolerance towards trafficking in human beings, especially women and children for sexual exploitation, companies must:

- Craft and distribute a policy that incorporates all mandatory components listed in implementation guidelines one through seven;
- Implement a code of conduct with zero tolerance towards human trafficking which at a minimum:
  - ◊ Prohibits trafficking in persons, as defined by the United Nation's Protocol to Prevent, Suppress and Punish Trafficking in Persons, especially Women and Children: *"Trafficking in persons" shall mean the recruitment, transportation, transfer, harbouring or receipt of persons, by means of the threat or use of force or other forms of coercion, of abduction, of fraud, of deception, of the abuse of power or of a position of vulnerability or of the giving or receiving of payments or benefits to achieve the consent of a person having control over another person, for the purpose of exploitation. Exploitation shall include, at a minimum, the exploitation of the prostitution of others or other forms of sexual exploitation, forced labour or services, slavery or practices similar to slavery, servitude or the removal of organs... The consent of a victim of trafficking in persons to the intended exploitation set forth [above] shall be irrelevant where any of the means set forth [above] have been used."*
  - ◊ Ensures freedom of movement for employees and the right of employees to enter and leave employment willingly and voluntarily;
  - ◊ Publicly defines and prohibits excessive recruitment fees;
  - ◊ Prohibits patronizing persons in prostitution while on official business travel;
  - ◊ Makes engaging in any of the above behaviors a fireable offense.

It should be made clear that these standards apply to all enterprises in a company's supply chain(s) by taking the following actions, as appropriate:

- Ensure that all employees receive an orientation on the standards;
- Include prohibitions on trafficking in persons (as defined above) in any International Framework Agreements to which the company is a signatory;
- Promote the International Labor Organization's (ILO) four core labor standards in order to foster an environment that enables workers' protections and prevents human trafficking;
- Sign and implement the *Code of Conduct for the Protection of Children from Sexual Exploitation in Travel and Tourism* (as appropriate).

Companies are also encouraged to:

- Join existing multi-stakeholder initiatives focused on human trafficking or establish one for the company's industry sector if none exists;
- Publish a list of all labor recruiters, contractors, and sub-contractors in the company's supply chain(s).

2. Engage in Public Awareness Campaigns and Education: in order to contribute to prevention of trafficking in human beings including awareness-raising campaigns and education, companies must:

- Address any issues related to the company's supply chain(s) and inform employees and consumers about the measures or safeguards implemented;
- Publicly post hiring and recruiting procedures throughout the company's supply chain(s). (If a company uses labor recruiters, these procedures should be published in a manner that is accessible to people in countries of origin).

Companies are also encouraged to:

- Participate in larger government anti-trafficking workshops and ad campaigns;
- Cooperate with national governments to ensure that a national workshop or conference on human trafficking is held in every country in which there is a risk of trafficking in a relevant supply chain(s);
- Work with other companies to create and disseminate anti-trafficking public service announcements that include additional resources for seeking help/information (e.g. a hotline for victims);
- Show in-flight videos on all major human trafficking routes that inform trafficking victims of their rights and available resources, and inform travelers that child sex tourism is a crime (tourism and travel sector);
- Organize public education campaigns on the issue of human trafficking, including the distribution of written material and cooperation with chambers of commerce and employer- and employee-representative groups to disseminate information.

6

3. Strategic Planning: in order to develop a corporate strategy for an anti-trafficking policy which will permeate all our activities,[3] companies must:

- Engage in collective strategic planning that includes corporate social responsibility advisors, supply chain managers, and senior leadership to create an action plan to prevent/combat trafficking in the company's supply chain(s), including independent metrics for evaluation and disclosure to stockholders;
- Ensure that company standards meet or exceed national anti-trafficking laws or ILO standards, whichever is more stringent;
- Adopt recruitment and human resources practices (e.g. wages, working hours and employment contracts, etc.) that minimize the risk of forced labor;
- Map supply chain(s), beginning with the producer, and implement systems to trace commodities to raw materials;
- Monitor compliance with the code of conduct/standards and continually address any shortcomings found through monitoring;
- Submit company operations and those of supply chain(s) to independent external audits against a reputable standard;
- Ask "highest risk" suppliers to become certified against such reputable standards or agree to unannounced audits against the company's code of conduct/standards;
- Remedy violations when they are found, and establish a system for remediation, complete with a funding vehicle, aimed at preventing a recurrence of these problems throughout supply chain(s);
- Ensure that workers and other affected stakeholders have in place a transparent, safe, and accessible channel for communicating complaints, and that audits are conducted in response to whistleblower allegations;
- Incorporate the existence or non-existence of measures to combat trafficking into considerations regarding sourcing decisions and factory siting.

Companies are also encouraged to:
- Sign on to the UN Global Compact, making the Compact's 10 principles part of corporate strategy and day-to-day operations. Once part of the Compact, companies are required to issue an annual Communication on Progress (COP), a public disclosure to stakeholders (e.g. investors, consumers, civil society, governments, etc.) on the implementation of the 10 principles;
- Support or become involved in at least one project annually that aims to reduce vulnerability to human trafficking. Develop micro-credit schemes, poverty-alleviation, and economic-empowerment initiatives to provide social protection to vulnerable groups and direct attention and/or funding to the underlying causes of trafficking;

---

[3] For a business trying to uphold the Athens Ethical Principles, oftentimes the greatest challenge is not with its own workforce – a company can institute clear policies to ensure that its own workforce is free of trafficked persons – but rather with suppliers, particularly second- or third-tier suppliers or those further down the supply chain of raw materials operating in remote areas rife with corruption and weak on regulation. Remediation can also sometimes be a challenge, so the company should take steps to ensure that the "cure is not worse than the disease" – for example, that the trafficking victims are not left in worse circumstances once they are freed.

- Develop skills training and hiring schemes for trafficking survivors.

4. Employee Training: in order to ensure that personnel fully comply with our anti-trafficking policy, companies must:

- Seek independent external monitoring and verification of compliance with the company's code of conduct/standards at least annually, including unannounced audits, from a reputable/recognized organization. Those engaged in independent monitoring and verification should take all reasonable steps, such as securing anonymity of those interviewed, to ensure that the processes do not compromise the safety or job security of workers or others involved in the audits;
- Ensure that verifiers are accredited certification bodies, complying with either ISO/IEC 17021:2006 or ISO/IEC Guide 65:1996 or other relevant systems. Verifiers should have qualified and competent personnel skilled in identifying forced labor/trafficking and knowledgeable in the local anti-trafficking laws and relevant international standards;
- Develop a training module for all employees in the company's supply chain(s) on the basics of human trafficking and how to recognize and report it;
- Provide additional/advanced training on forced labor for social auditors, compliance personnel, human resource managers, supply chain managers, and other supervisors;
- Make available to the public monitoring and verification efforts undertaken by the company to combat human trafficking and make the results of those efforts available to relevant government organizations;
- Ensure that audits are conducted in response to whistleblower allegations and that protections are in place for whistleblowers.

5. Supply Chain Monitoring: in order to encourage business partners, including suppliers, to apply ethical principles against human trafficking, companies must:

- Conduct an initial risk assessment of the company's business partners and suppliers to determine the degree to which they adhere to national laws and employ practices consistent with good industry standards. Revise company code of conduct to address any deficiencies that may be discovered;

- Monitor all suppliers, contractors, and sub-contractors, tracing to raw materials to ensure that measures are in place throughout the company's entire supply chain(s) to prevent human trafficking;

- Promote agreements and codes of conduct by industrial sector, identifying the areas where there is risk of forced labor and take appropriate remedial measures;

- Include appropriate language in all partner and sub-contractor agreements throughout the company's supply chain(s) prohibiting exploitative activity and develop a policy of engagement and remediation to correct violations;[4]

- If the company produces or manufactures one of the products utilizing raw materials on the Department of Labor's "List of Goods Produced by Child Labor or Forced Labor," enhance auditing of those products in the company's supply chain(s) by an independent third-party monitoring or verification organization and make public the results of the audit;

- Require that sub-contractors who recruit labor share the contracts of those laborers with the entity that is monitoring the corporate strategy (whether an internal or external body) to ensure that no excessive fees that could result in a situation of debt bondage for employees are being charged; blacklist sub-contractors that have used abusive practices and forced labor; and share relevant information with industry colleagues;

- Include in the company's corporate policy a provision requiring that management under audit be absent during inspections;

- Prohibit the withholding of employee identity documents, including passports, by all suppliers and subcontractors;

- Ensure that all employees enjoy freedom of movement and are aware they have the right to enter and leave employment voluntarily and freely.

Companies are also encouraged to:

- Train or employ former human trafficking victims and provide skills development, mentorship, and internship programs;

- Create networks with other companies, sectoral associations, and employers' organizations to exchange information and ideas for the development of an industry-wide approach to combat

---

[4] Such measures could include: technical assistance to help suppliers address specific issues; positive incentives such as the creation of a preferred suppliers list, a price premium, purchase guarantees, access to financing, inclusion in national or country of origin trade promotion/registries, and/or public reporting that rewards compliance. Negative incentives for violations might include suspension/reduction/termination of contracts for repeated violations.

human trafficking, and to ensure that codes of conduct/standards are implemented across supply chain(s), and good practices are identified and promoted globally;

- Explore the creation of a consumer-facing label demonstrating adherence to the Athens Ethical Principles as outlined in these guidelines;
- Support grassroots community development in order to help eliminate the root causes of human trafficking;
- Publish labor recruiters' responsibilities;
- Pay a premium for innovative sub-contractors or suppliers that secure fair worker conditions.

6. Governmental Coordination: **In an effort to increase enforcement it is necessary to call on governments to initiate a process of revision of laws and regulations that are directly or indirectly related to enhancing anti-trafficking policies.** In order to achieve this, companies must:

- Cooperate with law enforcement whenever human trafficking is discovered in the company's supply chain(s);
- Leverage market power in sourcing decisions and factory siting to reward governments that enforce anti-trafficking laws and provide victim protection.

Companies are also encouraged to:

- Regularly engage with local and national governments in every country linked with the company's supply chain(s) to support effective anti-trafficking policies that address prevention of trafficking, protection of and assistance to victims, and prosecution of perpetrators;
- Build networks with stakeholders, including workers' organizations, law enforcement authorities, NGOs, and labor inspectors to develop approaches to combating human trafficking in the company's supply chain(s) that take into account prevention of trafficking, assistance to victims when violations are found, and cooperation with law enforcement to prosecute offenders;
- Work with national governments and employers' organizations to ensure that all relevant ILO and UN Conventions are ratified;[5]
- Support governments in the development of national legislation and any efforts to bring labor and criminal codes up to international standards;
- Support the development of an employers' National Action Plan against forced labor as part of key policy and institutional mechanisms to combat forced labor at the national level;
- Lobby Ministries of Labor to make labor inspection more regular, efficient, and effective through training, resourcing, and collaboration with business;
- Assist law enforcement in prevention measures where possible;[6]
- Engage with governments, international organizations, and/or local communities to promote the provision of social safety nets that prevent forced labor and provide services to victims and persons at risk;[7]
- Support victim assistance and protection mechanisms, such as funding to government shelters.

---

[5] To include: ILO Conventions 29, 105, 138, and 182, the UN Protocol to Prevent, Suppress, and Punish Trafficking in Persons, Especially Women and Children (often referred to as the "Palermo Protocol")

[6] For example, the transport sector can adopt special screening mechanisms to detect the illegal transport of human beings or the telecommunications sector can donate software or provide technical support to assist law enforcement in tracking victims and traffickers.

[7] For example, companies may choose to partner with other companies in their industry to pool remediation resources for greater potential impact.

7. **Transparency: in order to report and share information on best practices, companies must:**

- Publicly disclose to consumers the company's implementation of policies to incorporate best practices throughout supply chain(s);
- Include information on this issue and measures taken by the company in annual reports to investors;
- Provide information to potential investors, attracting them to products and services where there is a clear and sustainable commitment to the prevention of trafficking in persons in order for them to make socially responsible investments;
- Advertise the company's endorsement of the Athens Ethical Principles by clearly stating it on the company website with a link to actions taken to implement the principles;
- Publish the company's code of conduct/standards with regard to combating human trafficking on the company website;
- Mandate new employee orientations on the company's code of conduct/standards;

Companies are also encouraged to:

- Publish a list of suppliers, labor recruiters, contractors, and subcontractors as part of company's efforts to be transparent and to map supply chain(s) to raw materials;
- Partner on audits within the relevant industry to reduce costs;
- Join the Global Reporting Initiative (GRI) and submit a GRI Sustainability Report annually;
- Join the UN Global Compact and submit the annual Communication on Progress (COP), which is a public disclosure to stakeholders (investors, consumers, civil society, governments, etc.) on the implementation of the 10 principles.

Luxor Implementation Guidelines to the Athens Ethical Principles:
Comprehensive Compliance Programme for Businesses

In January 2006, Suzanne Mubarak Women's International Peace Movement, under the auspices of the Greek Ministry of Foreign Affairs, brought together CEOs from the private sector; representatives of non-governmental organizations (NGOs), international organizations, and governments; and individuals to share their expertise and develop measures to counter human trafficking. The meeting was co-sponsored by prominent international organizations in the fight against human trafficking: the International Organization for Migration (IOM), the United Nations Development Fund for Women (UNIFEM), the United Nations Office on Drugs and Crime (UNODC), the World Bank and the Geneva Centre for the Democratic Control of Armed Forces (DCAF). The group adopted a set of ethical principles against human trafficking, now known as the **"Athens Ethical Principles"** and launched the **"End Human Trafficking Now"** campaign to promote the Principles and facilitate their implementation by business companies.

The Athens Ethical Principles contain seven main values. Hundreds of companies have agreed to abide by these principles, but it is their **implementation** by businesses that will contribute to the eradication of human trafficking worldwide. Moreover, experience of many corporations suggests that the commitment to ethical business actually improves the bottom line.[1]

The four primary risk areas where companies may encounter human trafficking are:[2]

1. Exploitation within a company's supply chain, for example the use of forced labor by suppliers or sub-contractors;

2. Utilization of personnel supplied by third party agents (domestic or overseas) over which the company has limited oversight, as in labor brokers whose unscrupulous treatment of workers amounts to trafficking;

3. Traffickers' use of a company's products, facilities or services in the process of obtaining or maintaining someone in compelled service, such as the transport of trafficking victims via international airlines, shipping companies and others in the transportation sector;

---

[1] A Harvard University study found that "sales rose for items labeled as being made under good labor standards, and demand for the labeled products actually rose with price increases of 10-20% above…unlabeled levels." Michael J. Hiscox and Nicholas F. B. Smyth, *Is There Consumer Demand for Improved Labor Standards? Evidence from Field Experiments in Social Product Labeling, 2006*
[2] UNGlobal Compact: Human Rights and Business Dilemmas Forum

1

4. Traffickers' use of a company's properties, especially in the hospitality sector, to victimize individuals, particularly for sex trafficking.

In order to address these intersections between legal business operations and illegal trafficking, companies must implement the principles to which they have already pledged themselves. The following is a guide to help move beyond aspirational statements to the development of standard operating procedures – a way to move beyond principles to practice and implementation.

Senate Bill No. 657

CHAPTER 556

An act to add Section 1714.43 to the Civil Code, and to add Section 19547.5 to the Revenue and Taxation Code, relating to human trafficking.

[Approved by Governor September 30, 2010. Filed with
Secretary of State September 30, 2010.]

LEGISLATIVE COUNSEL'S DIGEST

SB 657, Steinberg. Human trafficking.

The federal Victims of Trafficking and Violence Protection Act of 2000 establishes an Interagency Task Force to Monitor and Combat Trafficking, as specified.

Existing state law makes human trafficking a crime. Existing state law also allows a victim of human trafficking to bring a civil action for actual damages, compensatory damages, punitive damages, injunctive relief, any combination of those, or any other appropriate relief.

Existing law generally regulates various business activities and practices, including those of retail sellers and manufacturers of products.

This bill would enact the California Transparency in Supply Chains Act of 2010, and would, beginning January 1, 2012, require retail sellers and manufacturers doing business in the state to disclose their efforts to eradicate slavery and human trafficking from their direct supply chains for tangible goods offered for sale, as specified. That provision would not apply to a retail seller or manufacturer having less than $100,000,000 in annual worldwide gross receipts. The bill would also make a specified statement of legislative intent regarding slavery and human trafficking. The bill would also require the Franchise Tax Board to make available to the Attorney General a list of retail sellers and manufacturers required to disclose efforts to eradicate slavery and human trafficking pursuant to that provision, as specified.

The people of the State of California do enact as follows:

SECTION 1. This act shall be known, and may be cited, as the California Transparency in Supply Chains Act of 2010.

SEC. 2. The Legislature finds and declares the following:

(a) Slavery and human trafficking are crimes under state, federal, and international law.

(b) Slavery and human trafficking exist in every country, including the United States, and the State of California.

93

(c) As a result of the criminal natures of slavery and human trafficking, these crimes are often hidden from view and are difficult to uncover and track.

(d) In recent years, significant legislative efforts have been made to capture and punish the perpetrators of these crimes.

(e) Significant legislative efforts have also been made to ensure that victims are provided with necessary protections and rights.

(f) Legislative efforts to address the market for goods and products tainted by slavery and trafficking have been lacking, the market being a key impetus for these crimes.

(g) In September 2009, the United States Department of Labor released a report required by the Trafficking Victims Protection Reauthorization Acts of 2005 and 2008 which named 122 goods from 58 countries that are believed to be produced by forced labor or child labor in violation of international standards.

(h) Consumers and businesses are inadvertently promoting and sanctioning these crimes through the purchase of goods and products that have been tainted in the supply chain.

(i) Absent publicly available disclosures, consumers are at a disadvantage in being able to distinguish companies on the merits of their efforts to supply products free from the taint of slavery and trafficking. Consumers are at a disadvantage in being able to force the eradication of slavery and trafficking by way of their purchasing decisions.

(j) It is the policy of this state to ensure large retailers and manufacturers provide consumers with information regarding their efforts to eradicate slavery and human trafficking from their supply chains, to educate consumers on how to purchase goods produced by companies that responsibly manage their supply chains, and, thereby, to improve the lives of victims of slavery and human trafficking.

SEC. 3. Section 1714.43 is added to the Civil Code, to read:

1714.43. (a) (1) Every retail seller and manufacturer doing business in this state and having annual worldwide gross receipts that exceed one hundred million dollars ($100,000,000) shall disclose, as set forth in subdivision (c), its efforts to eradicate slavery and human trafficking from its direct supply chain for tangible goods offered for sale.

(2) For the purposes of this section, the following definitions shall apply:

(A) "Doing business in this state" shall have the same meaning as set forth in Section 23101 of the Revenue and Taxation Code.

(B) "Gross receipts" shall have the same meaning as set forth in Section 25120 of the Revenue and Taxation Code.

(C) "Manufacturer" means a business entity with manufacturing as its principal business activity code, as reported on the entity's tax return filed under Part 10.2 (commencing with Section 18401) of Division 2 of the Revenue and Taxation Code.

(D) "Retail seller" means a business entity with retail trade as its principal business activity code, as reported on the entity's tax return filed under Part

10.2 (commencing with Section 18401) of Division 2 of the Revenue and Taxation Code.

(b) The disclosure described in subdivision (a) shall be posted on the retail seller's or manufacturer's Internet Web site with a conspicuous and easily understood link to the required information placed on the business' homepage. In the event the retail seller or manufacturer does not have an Internet Web site, consumers shall be provided the written disclosure within 30 days of receiving a written request for the disclosure from a consumer.

(c) The disclosure described in subdivision (a) shall, at a minimum, disclose to what extent, if any, that the retail seller or manufacturer does each of the following:

(1) Engages in verification of product supply chains to evaluate and address risks of human trafficking and slavery. The disclosure shall specify if the verification was not conducted by a third party.

(2) Conducts audits of suppliers to evaluate supplier compliance with company standards for trafficking and slavery in supply chains. The disclosure shall specify if the verification was not an independent, unannounced audit.

(3) Requires direct suppliers to certify that materials incorporated into the product comply with the laws regarding slavery and human trafficking of the country or countries in which they are doing business.

(4) Maintains internal accountability standards and procedures for employees or contractors failing to meet company standards regarding slavery and trafficking.

(5) Provides company employees and management, who have direct responsibility for supply chain management, training on human trafficking and slavery, particularly with respect to mitigating risks within the supply chains of products.

(d) The exclusive remedy for a violation of this section shall be an action brought by the Attorney General for injunctive relief. Nothing in this section shall limit remedies available for a violation of any other state or federal law.

(e) The provisions of this section shall take effect on January 1, 2012.

SEC. 4. Section 19547.5 is added to the Revenue and Taxation Code, to read:

19547.5. (a) (1) Notwithstanding any provision of law, the Franchise Tax Board shall make available to the Attorney General a list of retail sellers and manufacturers required to disclose efforts to eradicate slavery and human trafficking pursuant to Section 1714.43 of the Civil Code. The list shall be based on tax returns filed for taxable years beginning on or after January 1, 2011.

(2) Each list required by this section shall be submitted annually to the Attorney General by November 30, 2012, and each November 30 thereafter. The list shall be derived from original tax returns received by the Franchise Tax Board on or before December 31, 2011, and each December 31 thereafter.

(b) Each annual list required by this section shall include the following information for each retail seller or manufacturer:

(1) Entity name.

(2) California identification number.

O

ABOUT THE AUTHORS

Kelly Hyland Heinrich, J.D., and Kavitha Sreeharsha, J.D.
Working with a trafficked person is unforgettable and, for us, created a long-lasting commitment to addressing human trafficking. We were two of the first attorneys in the United States to provide legal services to trafficked persons—one of us on each coast, frequently relying on each other for both strategy and support. Each and every person we represented has given us a unique depth of understanding on an issue that is so often oversimplified.

In later years, we worked on federal and state legislation, regulations, national training programs, and government policy nationally and internationally. Our public policy work at times felt a bit more like pioneering, forging ahead without knowing what was over the next ridge. But we were and continue to be focused on creating solutions, whether within the federal government, consulting to multinational corporations, or engaging whole professions in anti-trafficking efforts.

This unique longevity and varied experience in a relatively new field gives us the vision to see the gaps and how to bridge them, which is how we came to found the Global Freedom Center. Working together, we have had the privilege to reach thousands of corporate, government, and nonprofit employees through training that leads to human trafficking identification and prevention.

About the Global Freedom Center
The Global Freedom Center's mission is to foster an expanded, knowledgeable, and mobilized global community against human trafficking that will identify and assist more trafficked persons and develop the policies and strategies required to prevent modern slavery. Our fully customized online and onsite trainings help clients identify and prevent human trafficking.

We have worked with a range of clients, including Fortune 500 companies, government agencies, nonprofit organizations, and universities.

Steeped in the complexities of human trafficking, our expert trainers and curriculum designers create basic and advanced courses that incorporate firsthand knowledge of trafficked persons. This informs the practices— indicators, screenings, policies, and procedures—incorporated into training that lead to victim identification and prevention.

Moreover, we work closely with clients to deliver a custom learning experience tailored to their industry, profession, role, and goals. Whether they are new to the issue and seeking to meet compliance requirements or want a larger impact of identifying and preventing human trafficking, our training simulations and interactive exercises prepare learners with practical scenarios to prepare them with experiential understanding of human trafficking. We create and deliver multidevice elearning, a one-time webinar or series of webinars, train-the-trainers courses, updates of existing trainings, or onsite trainings.

The Global Freedom Center is a 501(c)(3) nonprofit organization and a social enterprise. We rely on fees generated from government, corporate, and nonprofit clients as well as the royalties from this book, so thank you for your purchase! We also create free trainings for sectors less able to pay for services—such as social workers and school personnel—with support from private donors, grants, and corporate financial and in-kind contributions.

Please contact us about how we can help you start, assess, or improve your anti-trafficking efforts. We also welcome your tax-deductible donations to support our work at GlobalFreedomCenter.org.

NOTES

Introduction
1. Urban Institute & Northeastern University, Identifying Challenges to Improve the Investigation and Prosecution of State and Local Human Trafficking Cases (2012).

Chapter I
1. United States v. Toviave, Criminal No. 11-20259 (S.D. Mich. 2013).
2. United States v. Kil Soo Lee, Criminal No. 101-cr-00132-SOM-BMK (D. Haw. 2002).
3. Press Release, U.S. Dep't of Justice, Gang Leader Sentenced to 40 Years for Leading Juvenile Sex Trafficking Ring (Sept. 14, 2012), *available at* http://www.justice.gov/usao/vae/news/2012/09/20120914stromnr.html.
4. U.S. Dep't of State, Trafficking in Persons Report (2013) (supporting the research of Kevin Bales with an estimate of 27 million); Walk Free, The Global Slavery Index (2013) (citing 29.8 million enslaved from its own research).
5. Int'l Labour Org., Global Estimate of Forced Labour (2012).
6. U.S. Dep't of State, Trafficking in Persons Report (2014).
7. *Id.*
8. *Id.*
9. United States v. Navarrete, No. 09-10182, 2009 U.S. App. LEXIS 20609 (11th Cir. Sept. 16, 2009).
10. Chellen v. John Pickle Co., Nos. 02-CV-0085-CVE-FHM [Base File] and 02-CV-0979-CVE-FHM [Consolidated] (N.D. Okla. 2006).
11. Mazengo v. Mzengi, No. _____, 2007 U.S. Dist. LEXIS 99377 (D.D.C. Apr. 25, 2007).
12. Press Release, U.S. Dep't of Justice, Former Chicago Massage Parlor Operator Sentenced to Life in Prison for Human Trafficking of Four Women (Nov. 26, 2012), *available at* http://www.justice.gov/opa/pr/former-chicago-massage-parlor-operator-sentenced-life-prison-human-trafficking-four-women.
13. Press Release, U.S. Dep't of Justice, California Couple Plead Guilty in Alien Smuggling Scheme in Which Some Were Forced to Work at Elder Care Homes (Mar. 24, 2009), *available at* http://www.justice.gov/opa/pr/california-couple-plead-guilty-alien-smuggling-scheme-which-some-were-forced-work-elder-care.

14. Press Release, U.S. Dep't of Justice, Florida Couple Pleads Guilty to Forced Labor Conspiracy of 39 Filipino Guest Workers (Sept. 17, 2010), *available at* http://www.justice.gov/opa/pr/2010/September/10-crt-1048.html.

15. EEOC v. Trans Bay Steel, Inc., No. CV 06-07766 CAS (JTLx) (C.D. Cal. Dec. 7, 2006).

16. Press Release, Fed. Bureau of Investigation, Second Ukrainian Brother Sentenced to the Maximum for Human Trafficking Operation (July 17, 2012), *available at* http://www.fbi.gov/philadelphia/press-releases/2012/second-ukrainian-brother-sentenced-to-the-maximum-for-human-trafficking-operation.

17. Int'l Labour Org., Global Estimate of Forced Labour (2012); U.S. Dep't of State, Trafficking in Persons Report (2014).

18. Richard M. Locke, Promoting Labor Standards in a Global Economy: The Promise and Limits of Private Power (2013).

19. Human Rights Watch, Building a Better World Cup: Protecting Migrant Workers in Qatar Ahead of FIFA 2022 (2012) (updating readers at http://www.hrw.org).

20. *Id.*

21. United States v. Yarbrough, No. 4:09-cr-00584-HEA-FRB (W.D. Tenn. 2012).

22. United States v. Fields, No. 8:13-cr-00198-JSM-TGW, 2013 U.S. Dist. LEXIS 135763 (M.D. Fla. 2013).

23. United States v. Carslake, No. 06-CR-00317, 2009 U.S. Dist. Ct. Motions LEXIS 21531 (W.D. Mo. 2009).

24. Press Release, U.S. Dep't of Justice, Saudi Arabian National Charged with Fraud in Obtaining Visa for Domestic Employee (July 1, 2009), *available at* http://www.justice.gov/usao/txs/1News/Archives/Archived%20Releases/2009%20July/070109Al-Zehairi_print.htm.

25. United States v. McReynolds, No. 11-CR-8133 (D. Ariz. 2011).

26. United States v. Carreto, Nos. 06-2295-cr(L), 06-2344-cr, 06-5172-cr, 05-1406-cr, 05-1407-cr, 05-2229-cr, 05-2241-cr (E.D.N.Y. 2005).

27. United States v. Bello, No. 1:10-cr-00397 (N.D. Ga. 2011).

28. Yusuf v. Tjia, No. BC375866 (Cal. L.A. County 2009).

29. United States v. Akouavi Kpade Afolabi, No. 07-00785 (D.N.J. 2009).

30. United States v. Vasquez Valenzuela, No. 07-CR-00011, 2009 U.S. Dist. LEXIS 64070, 2008 U.S. Dist. LEXIS 105640, 2008 U.S. Dist. LEXIS 73137, 2008 U.S. Dist. LEXIS 75763 (C.D. Cal. 2009).

31. United States v. Evans, No. 05-CR-159 (M.D. Fla. 2007).

32. United States v. Kalu (D. Colo. 2013).

33. United States v. Garcia, Nos. 02-CR-110S-01, 05-3340, 2003 U.S. Dist. LEXIS 22088 (W.D.N.Y. 2004).

34. Int'l Labour Org., Global Estimate of Forced Labour (2012).

35. United States v. Soto-Huarto, 242 F. App'x 984 (S.D. Tex. 2004).

Chapter 2

1. *See* Victims of Trafficking and Violence Protection Act of 2000, Pub. L. No. 106-386, § 112, 114 Stat. 1464, 1486 (Oct. 28, 2000).

2. *Id.* § 102(a), 114 Stat. at 1466.

3. *See id.* § 108, 114 Stat. at 1480.

4. *See* Heather Clawson et al., Prosecuting Human Trafficking Cases: Lessons Learned and Promising Practices 24 (2008) (on file with authors).

5. *See* Amy Farrell et al., Identifying Challenges to Improve the Investigation and Prosecution of State and Local Human Trafficking Cases (2012) (on file with authors).

6. *See* U.S. Const. amend. XIII.

7. *See* 18 U.S.C. § 1581.

8. *See* 18 U.S.C. § 1584.

9. 18 U.S.C. § 1589.

10. United States v. Tran, No. 0:14-cr-00025-SRN (D. Minn. 2014).

11. 18 U.S.C. § 1591.

12. Anthony Marcus et al., *Conflict and Agency among Sex Workers and Pimps: A Closer Look at Domestic Minor Sex Trafficking,* 653 Annals Am. Acad. Pol. & Soc. Sci. 225, 231 (2014).

13. *See generally* Kate Walker, Cal. Child Welfare Council, Ending the Commercial Sexual Exploitation of Children: A Call for Multi-System Collaboration in California (2013) (on file with authors).

14. *See generally id.*

15. *See id.* at 13–14.

16. United States v. Cortes-Meza, 411 F. App'x 284 (11th Cir. 2011).

17. 18 U.S.C. § 1592.

18. United States v. Farrell, Nos. 08-1559, 08-1561 (8th Cir. 2009).

19. 18 U.S.C. § 1581.

20. 18 U.S.C. § 1584.

21. *See* United States v. Kozminski, 487 U.S. 931, 952 (1988).

22. *See* United States v. Lee, 472 F.3d 638 (9th Cir. 2006).

23. *See id.*

24. *See id.*

25. 18 U.S.C. § 1590.

26. 18 U.S.C. § 2421.

27. 18 U.S.C. § 2421(a).

28. 18 U.S.C. § 1952.

29. Amy Farrell et al., Identifying Challenges to Improve the Investigation and Prosecution of State and Local Human Trafficking Cases 1 (2012) (on file with authors).

30. *See generally id.*

31. *See generally id.*

32. *See generally* 18 U.S.C. § 3771.

33. *See* Amy Farrell et al., Identifying Challenges to Improve the Investigation and Prosecution of State and Local Human Trafficking Cases 8 (2012) (on file with authors).

34. *See* Victims of Trafficking and Violence Protection Act of 2000, Pub. L. No. 106-386, § 107, 114 Stat. 1464, 1474 (Oct. 28, 2000).

35. *See id.* § 107(b)(1)(E), 114 Stat. at 1476.

36. *See* 8 U.S.C. §§ 1101(a)(15)(T)(i), 1255(*l*).

37. 8 U.S.C. § 1101(a)(15)(T)(i)(III).

38. 8 C.F.R. § 214.11(f)(1).

39. *See* Victims of Trafficking and Violence Protection Act of 2000, Pub. L. No. 106-386, § 1513, 114 Stat. 1464, 1533 (Oct. 28, 2000).

40. 8 U.S.C. § 1101(a)(15)(U)(i)(III).

41. 8 U.S.C. §§ 1255(*l*)(c), 1255(m)(1).

42. 8 U.S.C. § 1101(a)(15)(T)(i)(III).

43. *See* Victims of Trafficking and Violence Protection Act of 2000, Pub. L. No. 106-386, § 112(a), 114 Stat. 1464, 1486 (Oct. 28, 2000).

44. United States v. Sabhnini, 599 F.3d 215 (2d Cir. 2010).

45. *Id.*

46. *Id.*

47. Victims of Trafficking and Violence Protection Act of 2000, Pub. L. No. 106-386, § 103(8), 114 Stat. 1464, 1469 (Oct. 28, 2000).

48. N.Y. Soc. Serv. Law § 483-bb(b).

49. *See generally* Padilla v. Kentucky, 130 S. Ct. 1473 (2010).

50. *See* Assemb. 7670, 232d Leg., Reg. Sess. (N.Y. 2010).

51. *See id.*

52. *See* Uniform Law Comm'n, Uniform Act on Prevention of and Remedies for Human Trafficking (2013).

Chapter 3

1. U.S. Dep't of Labor, List of Goods Produced by Child Labor or Forced Labor (2014), *available at* http://www.dol.gov/ilab/reports/pdf/TVPRA_Report2014.pdf.

2. United Nations, Guiding Principles on Business and Human Rights, *available at* http://www.ohchr.org/Documents/Publications/GuidingPrinciplesBusinessHR_EN.pdf.

3. Int'l Labour Org., Rules of the Game: A Brief Introduction to International Labour Standards (rev. ed. 2009), *available at* http://www.ilo.org/wcmsp5/groups/public/---ed_norm/---normes/documents/publication/wcms_108393.pdf.

4. United Nations, Guiding Principles on Business and Human Rights, *available at* http://www.ohchr.org/Documents/Publications/GuidingPrinciplesBusinessHR_EN.pdf.

5. Bureau of Int'l Labor Affairs, U.S. Dep't of Labor, Reducing Child Labor and Forced Labor: A Toolkit for Responsible Businesses (2010), *available at* http://www.dol.gov/ilab/child-forced-labor/index.htm.

6. The Inquisitor, Victoria's Secret Cotton Being Supplied by Slave Labor? (Jan. 15, 2012), *available at* http://www.inquisitr.com/181449/victorias-secret-cotton-being-supplied-by-slave-labor.

7. Electronista, Flextronics Accused of Using Slave Labor to Build iPhone 5 (Nov. 7, 2013), *available at* http://www.electronista.com/articles/13/11/07/apple.pulled.orders.from.malaysian.factory.because.of.low.yield.

8. Reuters, Hershey Sued for Info on Use of Child Labor in Cocoa Supplies (Nov. 1, 2012), *available at* http://www.reuters.com/article/2012/11/01/hershey-childlabor-idUSL1E8M1GSB20121101.

9. Forbes, Zara Accused of Alleged "Slave Labor" in Brazil (Aug. 17, 2011), *available at* http://www.forbes.com/sites/andersonantunes/2011/08/17/zara-accused-of-alleged-slave-labor-in-brazil.

10. The Examiner, Woman Finds Note from Chinese Labor Camp Prisoner in Kmart Decorations (Dec. 27, 2012), *available at* http://www.examiner.com/article/woman-finds-note-from-chinese-labor-camp-prisoner-kmart-decorations.

11. Athens Ethical Principles (adopted in Athens, Jan. 23, 2006), *available at* http://www.ungift.org/docs/ungift/pdf/Athens_principles.pdf.

12. Luxor Implementation Guidelines to the Athens Ethical Principles: Comprehensive Compliance Programme for Businesses, *available at* http://www.unglobalcompact.org/docs/issues_doc/human_rights/Resources/Luxor_Implementation_Guidelines_Ethical_Principles.pdf.

13. United Nations, Guiding Principles on Business and Human Rights, *available at* http://www.ohchr.org/Documents/Publications/GuidingPrinciplesBusinessHR_EN.pdf.

14. TheCode.Org, *available at* http://www.thecode.org/wp-content/uploads/2013/02/The-Code-NEW-Brochure-ENG-2013.pdf.

15. *See* http://www.kimberleyprocess.com.

16. California Transparency in Supply Chains Act of 2010, S.B. 657 (2010).

17. *Id.* § 2 (2010).

18. 15 U.S.C. §§ 78dd-1, 78dd-2, 78dd-3, 78m, 78ff.

19. Jones Day, The Foreign Corrupt Practices Act: An Overview (Jan. 2010), *available at* http://www.jonesday.com/files/Publication/3325b9a8-b3b6-40ff-8bc8-0c10c119c649/Presentation/PublicationAttachment/d375c9ee-6a11-4d25-9c30-0d797661b5ff/FCPA%20Overview.pdf.

20. Criminal Div. of U.S. Dep't of Justice & Enforcement Div. of U.S. Sec. & Exch. Comm'n, A Resource Guide to the U.S. Foreign Corrupt Practices Act (2012), *available at* http://www.sec.gov/spotlight/fcpa/fcpa-resource-guide.pdf.

21. U.S. Dep't of State, Trafficking in Persons Report (2005 to 2014).

22. United Nations Office on Drugs & Crime (UNODC), Issue Paper: The Role of Corruption in Trafficking in Persons (Vienna 2011), *available at* http://www.unodc.org/documents/human-trafficking/2011/Issue_Paper_-_The_Role_of_Corruption_in_Trafficking_in_Persons.pdf.

23. Conflict Minerals, 17 C.F.R. pts. 240, 249b (2012), *available at* http://www.sec.gov/rules/final/2012/34-67716.pdf.

24. Dodd-Frank Wall Street Reform and Consumer Protection Act, Pub. L. No. 111-203, 124 Stat. 1376 (July 21, 2010).

25. Combating Trafficking in Persons, 48 C.F.R. pt. 22, subpt. 22.17 (2006).

26. Combating Trafficking in Persons, 48 C.F.R. § 52.222-50 (2009).

27. Combating Trafficking in Persons, 48 C.F.R. pt. 222, subpt. 222.17 (2013).

28. Comm'n on Wartime Contracting in Iraq and Afghanistan, Transforming Wartime Contracting: Controlling Costs, Reducing Risks (Aug. 2011), *available at* http://www .wartimecontracting.gov/docs/CWC_FinalReport-lowres.pdf.

29. Exec. Order No. 13627, 77 Fed. Reg. 60029 (Oct. 2, 2012), *available at* http://www. gpo.gov/fdsys/pkg/DCPD-201200750/pdf/DCPD-201200750.pdf.

30. National Defense Authorization Act for Fiscal Year 2013, H.R. Res. 4310, 113th Cong. (2013) (enacted).

31. Ending Trafficking in Persons, 78 Fed. Reg. 59317 (Sept. 26, 2013), *available at* http://www.gpo.gov/fdsys/pkg/FR-2013-09-26/pdf/2013-23311.pdf.

Chapter 4

1. Int'l Labour Org., ILO Global Estimate of Forced Labour (2012) (on file with authors).

2. *See* Amy Farrell et al., Identifying Challenges to Improve the Investigation and Prosecution of State and Local Human Trafficking Cases (2012) (on file with authors).

3. *See* 8 U.S.C. § 1101(a)(15)(T)(i), (U)(i). See also Chapter 5 for an extensive discussion about unique immigration protections available to trafficked persons.

4. *See* Sheldon Zhang, San Diego State Univ., Looking for a Hidden Population: Trafficking of Migrant Laborers in San Diego County (2012) (on file with authors) (estimating that nearly one-third of all undocumented workers in San Diego County experienced human trafficking). *But see* Pew Research Ctr., Population Decline of Unauthorized Immigrants Stalls, May Have Reversed (2013) (on file with authors) (estimating a U.S. undocumented population of 11.7 million people). Between 2002 and June 2013, only 6,230 primary victim and family member T visas were granted in total. U.S. Citizenship & Immigration Servs., Form I-914—Application for T Nonimmigrant Status, Form I-918—Petition for U Nonimmigrant Status Receipts, Approvals, and Denials Fiscal Year 2013, Through Third Quarter (October 2012–June 2013) (2013) (on file with authors).

5. *See* 8 U.S.C. §§ 1101(i)(2), 1183(p)(3)(B).

6. William Wilberforce Trafficking Victims Protection Reauthorization Act of 2008, Pub. L. No. 110-457, § 205, 122 Stat. 5044, 5060 (Dec. 23, 2008).

7. *Id.* § 203(c)(1)(A), 122 Stat. at 5057.

8. As with other chapters, this chapter is intended to give a simple overview of civil litigation options and strategies. Attorneys intending to pursue civil litigation should seek additional resources and technical assistance, particularly given the novelty and lack of extensive case law in this area. *See* Dan Werner et al., Civil Litigation on Behalf of Victims of Human Trafficking (2008), *available at* http://www.splcenter .org/sites/default/files/downloads/splc_human_trafficking.pdf (last accessed Nov. 21, 2014), for a detailed manual guiding those interested in pursuing civil litigation for trafficked persons.

9. *See* Trafficking Victims Protection Reauthorization Act of 2003, Pub. L. No. 108-193, § 4(a)(4), 117 Stat. 2875, 2878 (Dec. 19, 2003).

10. 18 U.S.C. § 1589.

11. Shukla v. Sharma, No. 07-cv-2972, 2012 U.S. Dist. LEXIS 18392 (E.D.N.Y. Feb. 14, 2012).

12. 18 U.S.C. § 1590.

13. *Id.* § 1591(a).

14. William Wilberforce Trafficking Victims Protection Reauthorization Act of 2008, Pub. L. No. 110-457, § 221(2), 122 Stat. 5044, 5067 (Dec. 23, 2008).

15. 18 U.S.C. § 1582.

16. *Id.* § 1584.

17. *Id.* § 1592.

18. William Wilberforce Trafficking Victims Protection Reauthorization Act of 2008, Pub. L. No. 110-457, § 221, 122 Stat. 5044, 5067 (Dec. 23, 2008).

19. *See* 29 U.S.C. §§ 201–219.

20. Lucas v. Jerusalem Café, LLC, No. 12-2170 (8th Cir. July 29, 2013).

21. 29 U.S.C. § 255.

22. 42 U.S.C. § 2000e-2.

23. Chellen v. John Pickle Co., 434 F. Supp. 2d 1069 (N.D. Okla. 2006).

24. *See generally* Human Rights Watch, Cultivating Fear: The Vulnerability of Immigrant Farmworkers in the US to Sexual Violence and Sexual Harassment (2012) (on file with authors); PBS Frontline, Rape in the Fields (June 25, 2013), *available at* http://video.pbs.org/video/2365031455/ (last accessed Nov. 21, 2014).

25. *See* United States v. Botsvynyuk, No. 2:10-cr-00159 (E.D. Pa. 2012).

26. EEOC v. Henry's Turkey Serv., No. 3:11-cv-00041 (S.D. Iowa 2013).

27. EEOC v. Trans Bay Steel, Inc., No. 06-07766 CAS (JTLx) (C.D. Cal. 2006).

28. EEOC v. Global Horizons, Inc., No. 1:11-cv-00257-LEK-RLP (D. Haw. 2014).

29. 42 U.S.C. § 2000e-5(e)(1).

30. *Id.*

31. 18 U.S.C. § 1961(1).

32. *Id.* § 1961(5).

33. *Id* § 1962(a).

34. *Id.* § 1962(b).

35. *Id.* § 1962(c).

36. *Id.* § 1962(d).

37. *Id.* § 1964; Agency Holding Corp. v. Malley-Duff & Assocs., Inc., 483 U.S. 143, 155 (1987).

38. John Does I–V v. Rodriguez, No. 06-cv-805 (D. Colo. 2009).

39. 28 U.S.C. § 1350.

40. Kiobel v. Royal Dutch Petroleum Co., 133 S. Ct. 1659 (2013).

41. At the time of publication, Alabama, California, Colorado, Connecticut, District of Columbia, Florida, Hawaii, Illinois, Indiana, Maine, Massachusetts, Minnesota, Missouri, Ohio, Oklahoma, South Carolina, Tennessee, Texas, Vermont, Washington, and Wisconsin all had civil causes of action available to all victims of human trafficking.

42. *See* Trafficking Victims Protection Reauthorization Act of 2003, Pub. L. No. 108-193, § 4(a)(4), 117 Stat. 2875, 2878 (Dec. 19, 2003).

43. Among the organizations who advocate on behalf of domestic workers is the National Domestic Workers Alliance.

44. Violence Against Women and Department of Justice Reauthorization Act of 2005, Pub. L. No. 109-162, § 817, 119 Stat. 2960, 3060 (Jan. 5, 2006).

45. *See* 8 U.S.C. § 1367(a)(2), (b).

46. *See id.* § 1367(a)(1).

47. *See id.* § 1229(e).

48. S.B. 1193, 2011–2012 Gen. Sess. (Cal. 2012).

Chapter 5

1. Int'l Labour Org., ILO Global Estimate of Forced Labour (2012) (on file with authors).

2. Sheldon Zhang, San Diego State Univ., Looking for a Hidden Population: Trafficking of Migrant Laborers in San Diego County (2012) (on file with authors) (estimating that nearly one-third of all undocumented workers in San Diego County experienced human trafficking).

3. Recent reports place the U.S. undocumented population at 11.7 million. *See* Pew Research Ctr., Population Decline of Unauthorized Immigrants Stalls, May Have Reversed (2013) (on file with authors).

4. Names have been replaced to protect the identity of individuals.

5. *See* Victims of Trafficking and Violence Protection Act of 2000, Pub. L. No. 106-386, § 107(e), 114 Stat. 1464, 1477 (Oct. 28, 2000).

6. *See* Trafficking Victims Protection Reauthorization Act of 2003, Pub. L. No. 108-193, 117 Stat. 2875 (Dec. 19, 2003); William Wilberforce Trafficking Victims Protection Reauthorization Act of 2008, Pub. L. No. 110-457, 122 Stat. 5044 (Dec. 23, 2008); Violence Against Women Reauthorization Act of 2013, Pub. L. No. 113-4, 127 Stat. 54 (Mar. 7, 2013).

7. U.S. Citizenship & Immigration Servs., Form I-914—Application for T Nonimmigrant Status, Form I-918—Petition for U Nonimmigrant Status Receipts, Approvals, and Denials Fiscal Year 2013, Through Third Quarter (October 2012–June 2013) (2013) (on file with authors).

8. *See* Amy Farrell et al., Identifying Challenges to Improve the Investigation and Prosecution of State and Local Human Trafficking Cases (2012) (on file with authors).

9. U.S. Gov't Accountability Office, U.S. Government's Efforts to Address Alleged Abuse of Household Workers by Foreign Diplomats with Immunity Could Be Strengthened 3 (July 2008) (on file with authors).

10. *See, e.g.,* Michael A. Scaperlanda, *Human Trafficking in the Heartland: Greed, Visa Fraud, and the Saga of 53 Indian Nationals "Enslaved" by a Tulsa Company,* 1 Loy. U. Chi. Int'l L. Rev. 219 (2004) (describing the fraudulent facilitation of B1/B2 visas for the purposes of training and not the work ultimately performed by the workers in the Pickle case).

11. *See, e.g.*, Kiwanuka v. Bakilana, 844 F. Supp. 2d 107, 111 (D.D.C. 2012).

12. *See, e.g.*, Tanedo v. E. Baton Rouge Parish Sch. Bd., No. LA CV10-01172 JAK (MLGx), 2011 WL 7095434 (C.D. Cal. Dec. 12, 2011), in which teachers were recruited from the Philippines and compelled to teach in the United States, compelling their work through exhorbitant recruitment debts and confiscation of their passports.

13. *See generally* S. Poverty Law Ctr., Close to Slavery: Guestworker Programs in the United States (2013) (on file with authors).

14. *Id.*

15. *See generally* U.S. Dep't of State, Trafficking in Persons Report (2012) (on file with authors) (noting NGO reports of human trafficking within the J-1 program).

16. *See* Victims of Trafficking and Violence Protection Act of 2000, Pub. L. No. 106-386, § 107(c)(3), 114 Stat. 1464, 1477 (Oct. 28, 2000).

17. *See id.*

18. 28 C.F.R. § 1100.35 (2002).

19. *Id.* § 1100.35(b)(1).

20. Victims of Trafficking and Violence Protection Act of 2000, Pub. L. No. 106-386, § 107(b)(1)(E), 114 Stat. 1464, 1476 (Oct. 28, 2000).

21. Immigration law characterizes those without lawful permanent residence, including those with a clear path to permanent residence, as nonimmigrants. In the immigration application process, the authors will use the term nonimmigrants, and otherwise use immigrant.

22. 8 U.S.C. § 1182(d)(13).

23. *Id.* § 1184(o)(7)(A).

24. T visa applicants can also apply for their spouse and minor children, and T visa minor applicants can in addition apply for their parents and unmarried siblings under the age of eighteen; and T visa family member derivatives in some cases can also apply for their parent, unmarried sibling under age 18, or adult and minor children as derivatives. *Id.* § 1101(a)(15)(T)(ii).

25. U.S. Citizenship & Immigration Servs., Number of I-914 Applications for T Nonimmigrant Status (Victims of Severe Forms of Trafficking and Family Members) by Fiscal Year, Quarter, and Case Status 2008–2014 (2014).

26. *See* 8 U.S.C. § 1101(a)(15)(T)(i).

27. Victims of Trafficking and Violence Protection Act of 2000, Pub. L. No. 106-386, § 103(8), 114 Stat. 1464, 1470 (Oct. 28, 2000).

28. 8 U.S.C. § 1101(a)(15)(T)(i)(II).

29. 67 Fed. Reg. 4784, 4787 (Jan. 31, 2002).

30. *Id.*

31. Names and countries have been replaced to protect the identity of individuals.

32. 8 U.S.C. § 1101(a)(15)(T)(i)(III).

33. *Id.* § 1101(a)(15)(T)(i)(III)(cc).

34. *Id.* § 1101(a)(15)(T)(i)(III)(bb).

35. 67 Fed. Reg. 4784, 4788 (Jan. 31, 2002).

36. 8 C.F.R. § 214.11(s)(1)(iv).

37. 67 Fed. Reg. 4784, 4788 (Jan. 31, 2002).

38. 8 U.S.C. § 1101(a)(15)(T)(i)(IV).

39. 67 Fed. Reg. 4784, 4799–800 (Jan. 31, 2002).

40. *See generally* 67 Fed. Reg. 4784 (Jan. 31, 2002).

41. 8 U.S.C. § 1255(*l*).

42. *Id.* § 1255(*l*)(1)(A).

43. 73 Fed. Reg. 75540, 75543 (Dec. 12, 2008).

44. *Id.* at 75544.

45. *Id.*

46. *Id.*

47. *Id.* at 75544–45.

48. 8 U.S.C. § 1255(*l*)(1)(C).

49. *Id.*

50. 73 Fed. Reg. 75540, 75543 (Dec. 12, 2008).

51. *Id.*

52. 8 C.F.R. § 245.23(b)(1).

53. *See generally* Victims of Trafficking and Violence Protection Act of 2000, Pub. L. No. 106-386, 114 Stat. 1464 (Oct. 28, 2000).

54. *Id.* § 1513, 113 Stat. at 1533.

55. T visa applicants can also apply for their spouse and minor children, and minors can in addition apply for their parents and siblings under the age of eighteen; and T visa applicants can also apply for their adult and minor children as derivatives. 8 U.S.C. § 1101(a)(15)(T)(ii).

56. *Id.* § 1184(p)(4).

57. *Id.* § 1182(d)(14).

58. *Id.* § 1101(a)(15)(U)(i).

59. Adam Serwer, *24-Hour Shifts and Deportation Threats: The World of US Guest Workers*, Mother Jones (Apr. 25, 2013).

60. 8 U.S.C. § 1101(a)(15)(U)(i)(I).

61. 72 Fed. Reg. 53014, 53018 (Sept. 17, 2007).

62. 8 U.S.C. § 1101(a)(15)(U)(i)(III).

63. 72 Fed. Reg. 53014, 53023 (Sept. 17, 2007).

64. *Id.* at 53019.

65. *Id.* at 53023.

66. 8 U.S.C. § 1101(a)(15)(U)(i)(II).

67. *Id.* § 1101(a)(15)(U)(iii).

68. The U visa enumerated crimes include "rape; torture; trafficking; incest; domestic violence; sexual assault; abusive sexual contact; prostitution; sexual exploitation; stalking; female genital mutilation; being held hostage; peonage; involuntary servitude; slave trade; kidnapping; abduction; unlawful criminal restraint; false imprisonment; blackmail; extortion; manslaughter; murder; felonious assault; witness tampering;

obstruction of justice; perjury; fraud in foreign labor contracting (as defined in section 1351 of title 18, United States Code); or attempt, conspiracy, or solicitation to commit any of the above mentioned crimes." *Id.*

69. 8 C.F.R. § 245.24(b)(2).
70. *Id.* § 245.24(d)(8), (e).
71. *Id.* § 245.24(e)(1).
72. 73 Fed. Reg. 75540, 75548 (Dec. 12, 2008).
73. *Id.*
74. *Id.* at 75549.
75. 8 U.S.C § 1154(a)(1)(A).
76. *Id.* § 1229b(b)(2).
77. *Id.* § 1101(a)(27)(J)(i).
78. *Id.*
79. *Id.* § 1101(a)(27)(J)(iii)(II).
80. *Id.* § 1101(a)(27)(J)(ii).
81. *Id.* § 1158.
82. 42 U.S.C. §§ 2000d et seq. (1964).
83. *See* 8 U.S.C. § 1367(a)(2), (b).
84. *See id.* § 1367(a)(1).
85. *See id.* § 1229(e).
86. John Morton, DHS Immigration & Customs Enforcement, Memorandum: Prosecutorial Discretion: Certain Victims, Witnesses, and Plaintiffs (June 17, 2011).
87. *See generally* Victims of Trafficking and Violence Protection Act of 2000, Pub. L. No. 106-386, § 107(e), 114 Stat. 1464, 1477 (Oct. 28, 2000).
88. Since the enactment of the TVPA in 2000, the United States more than doubled the number of people deported. The United States deported 185,987 people in fiscal year 2000. The United States deported 419,384 in fiscal year 2012. U.S. Dep't of Homeland Sec., Yearbook of Immigration Statistics: 2003 (2003). *C.f.* U.S. Dep't of Homeland Sec., Yearbook of Immigration Statistics: 2012 (2012).
89. *See generally* Amy Farrell et al., Identifying Challenges to Improve the Investigation and Prosecution of State and Local Human Trafficking Cases (2012) (on file with authors).

Chapter 6

1. Protocol to Prevent, Suppress and Punish Trafficking in Persons, Especially Women and Children, Supplementing the United Nations Convention Against Transnational Organized Crime, U.N. Doc. A/53/383 (2000), *available at* http://www.uncjin.org/Documents/Conventions/dcatoc/final_documents_2/convention_%20traff_eng.pdf [hereinafter Trafficking Protocol].
2. May 18, 1904, 35 Stat. 426, 1 L.N.T.S. 83. The Agreement was created between Austria-Hungary, Belgium, Brazil, Denmark, France, Germany, Great Britain, Italy, the Netherlands, Portugal, Russia, Spain, Sweden, Norway, and Switzerland, and was ratified by the all but Austria-Hungary and Brazil. *Id.*

3. International Agreement for the Suppression of the White Slave Traffic, May 18, 1904, art. 1, 35 Stat. 426, 1 L.N.T.S. 83.

4. Jo Doezema, Trafficking and Controlling Borders: State's Interests Versus Women's Freedom of Movement (Feb. 1999).

5. May 4, 1910, 211 C.T.S. 45. The fourteen nations were Austria, France, Germany, Great Britain, Hungary, the Netherlands, Russia, Spain, Belgium, Brazil, Denmark, Italy, Portugal, and Sweden, though only the first aforementioned eight later ratified the Convention.

6. *Opened for signature* Sept. 30, 1921, 9 L.N.T.S. 415. The Convention was created by twenty-eight nations, ratified by ten, and acceded to by one nation and several British colonies.

7. *Opened for signature* Oct. 11, 1933, 150 L.N.T.S. 431. This Convention was created by twenty-five nations, ratified by five, and acceded to by four. *Id.*

8. *Id.* art. 1.

9. *Id.* art. 3.

10. Mar. 21, 1950, 96 U.N.T.S. 271.

11. *Id.*

12. *Id.* arts. 1–2.

13. Anne T. Gallagher, The International Law of Human Trafficking (Cambridge Univ. Press 2010).

14. Int'l Org. on Migration, Global Migration Trends: An Era of International Migration (2000).

15. Kelly Hyland Heinrich, *Ten Years After the Palermo Protocol: Where Are the Protections for Human Trafficking Victims?*, 18 Hum. Rts. Brief no. 1, at 2–5 (2011).

16. U.S. Dep't of State Office to Monitor and Combat Trafficking in Persons: Projects Funded During Fiscal Year 2013, *available at* http://www.state.gov/j/tip/rls/other/2013/215002.htm (last accessed Nov. 21, 2014).

17. UNODC, Human Trafficking, *available at* http://www.unodc.org/unodc/en/human-trafficking/what-is-human-trafficking.html?ref=menuside#UNODC's_Response (last accessed Nov. 21, 2014).

18. Vienna Declaration and Programme of Action, July 12, 1993, art. 18, U.N. Doc. A/CONF.157/23.

19. Beijing Declaration and Platform for Action, Fourth World Conference on Women, Sept. 15, 1995, U.N. Docs. A/CONF.177/20 and A/CONF.177/20/Add.1.

20. U.N. Comm. on the Elimination of Discrimination Against Women, "General Recommendation No. 19: Violence Against Women," Jan. 29, 1992, U.N. Doc. A/47/38.

21. Optional Protocol to the Convention on the Rights of the Child on the Involvement of Children in Armed Conflict, *entered into force* Feb. 12, 2002, G.A. Res. 54/263, annex I, 54 U.N. GAOR Supp. (No. 49) at 7, U.N. Doc. A/54/49, Vol. III (2000).

22. Optional Protocol to the Convention on the Rights of the Child on the Sale of Children, Child Prostitution and Child Pornography, *entered into force* Jan. 18, 2002,

G.A. Res. 54/263, annex II, 54 U.N. GAOR Supp. (No. 49) at 6, U.N. Doc. A/54/49, Vol. III (2000).

23. *See* http://www.ecpat.net.

24. Christopher Albin-Lackey, *Without Rules: A Failed Approach to Corporate Accountability*, Hum. Rts. Watch World Rep. 2013, *available at* http://www.hrw.org/world-report/2013/essays/112459?page=1.

25. G.A. Res. 158, U.N. GAOR, 45th Sess., 69th plen. Mtg., Supp. No. 49A, Annex, at 262, U.N. Doc. A/45/49 (1991).

26. *Opened for signature* July 28, 1951, 19 U.S.T. 6577, 189 U.N.T.S. 150 (1951).

27. *Opened for signature* Jan. 31, 1967, 19 U.S.T. 6223, T.I.A.S. No. 6577, 606 U.N.T.S. 267 (1967).

28. 8 U.S.C. § 1231(b)(3) (2004).

29. Pub. L. No. 96-212, 94 Stat 103 (1980); 8 U.S.C. § 208 (2005).

30. Trafficking Protocol, art. 14.

31. 8 U.S.C. § 1101(a)(42)(a) (2005).

32. UNHCR Guidelines on International Protection No. 7: The Application of Article 1A(2) of the 1951 Convention and/or 1967 Protocol Relating to the Status of Refugees to Victims of Trafficking and Persons at Risk of Being Trafficked (Apr. 2006).

33. Cece v. Holder, 733 *F.3d* 662 (7th Cir. 2013).

34. *In re* M-J (2001).

35. Trafficking Guidelines, *supra note* 32, para. 5.

36. Human Trafficking and Refugee Protection: UNHCR's Perspective, Conference Paper: Ministerial Conference on "Towards Global EU Action Against Trafficking in Human Beings" Brussels (Oct. 19–20, 2009).

37. UNHCR Guidelines on International Protection No. 7: The Application of Article 1A(2) of the 1951 Convention and/or 1967 Protocol Relating to the Status of Refugees to Victims of Trafficking and Persons at Risk of Being Trafficked (Apr. 2006).

38. Int'l Labour Org., Rules of the Game (2009), *available at* http://www.ilo.org/wcmsp5/groups/public/---ed_norm/---normes/documents/publication/wcms_108393.pdf.

39. Convention Concerning Forced or Compulsory Labour (ILO No. 29), *entered into force* May 1, 1932, 39 U.N.T.S. 55.

40. Abolition of Forced Labour Convention (ILO No. 105), *entered into force* Jan. 17, 1959, 320 U.N.T.S. 291.

41. Convention Concerning the Prohibition and Immediate Action for the Elimination of the Worst Forms of Child Labor (ILO No. 182), *entered into force* Nov. 19, 2000, 2133 U.N.T.S. 161.

42. Convention Concerning Decent Work for Domestic Workers (ILO No. 189), *entered into force* Sept. 5, 2013, U.N.T.S. ___.

43. U.S. Dep't of Labor, List of Goods Produced by Child Labor or Forced Labor (2014), *available at* http://www.dol.gov/ilab/reports/pdf/TVPRA_Report2014.pdf.

44. Bureau of Int'l Labor Affairs, U.S. Dep't of Labor, Reducing Child Labor and Forced Labor: A Toolkit for Responsible Businesses (2010), *available at* http://www.dol.gov/ilab/child-forced-labor/index.htm.

45. *See* Int'l Trade Union Confederation, How to Combat Forced Labour & Trafficking: Best Practices Manual for Trade Unions (Feb. 2009).

Chapter 7

1. *See* Victims of Trafficking and Violence Protection Act of 2000, Pub. L. No. 106-386, § 107(b)(1)(B), 114 Stat. 1464, 1475 (Oct. 28, 2000).

2. *See* Trafficking Victims Protection Reauthorization Act of 2003, Pub. L. No. 108-193, § 4(a)(2)(B), 117 Stat. 2875, 2877 (Dec. 19, 2003).

3. *See* Helaine M. Barnett, Legal Servs. Corp., Memorandum: Eligibility of Immigrant Victims of a Severe Form of Trafficking and Family Members for Legal Services (Oct. 6, 2005) (on file with authors).

4. *See* 45 C.F.R. § 1613.2.

5. *See* Victims of Trafficking and Violence Protection Act of 2000, Pub. L. No. 106-386, § 107(b)(1), 114 Stat. 1464, 1475 (Oct. 28, 2000).

6. *See id.* §§ 107(e)(1), 1513, 114 Stat. at 1477, 1533.

7. N.Y. Soc. Serv. Law § 483-bb(b).

8. Victims of Trafficking and Violence Protection Act of 2000, Pub. L. No. 106-386, § 107(b)(1)(E), 114 Stat. 1464, 1476 (Oct. 28, 2000).

9. Int'l Labour Org., ILO Global Estimate of Forced Labour (2012) (on file with authors).

10. *Id.*

11. *See, e.g.,* United States v. Botsvynyuk, No. 2:10-cr-00159 (E.D. Pa. 2012).

12. *See, e.g.,* Viji Sundaram, *How an Infamous Berkeley Human Trafficking Case Fueled Reform,* S.F. Pub. Press (Feb. 16, 2012), *available at* http://sfpublicpress.org/news/2012-02/how-an-infamous-berkeley-human-trafficking-case-fueled-reform (last accessed Nov. 22, 2014).

13. *See* Kate Walker, Cal. Child Welfare Council, Ending the Commercial Sexual Exploitation of Children: A Call for Multi-System Collaboration in California 13–14 (2013) (on file with authors).

14. *See id.*

15. Sheldon Zhang, San Diego State Univ., Looking for a Hidden Population: Trafficking of Migrant Laborers in San Diego County (2012) (on file with authors) (estimating that nearly one-third of all undocumented workers in San Diego County experienced human trafficking).

16. Recent reports place the U.S. undocumented population at 11.7 million. *See* Pew Research Ctr., Population Decline of Unauthorized Immigrants Stalls, May Have Reversed (2013) (on file with authors).

17. *See* Victims of Trafficking and Violence Protection Act of 2000, Pub. L. No. 106-386, § 107(e), 114 Stat. 1464, 1477 (Oct. 28, 2000).

18. U.S. Citizenship & Immigration Servs., Form I-914—Application for T Nonimmigrant Status, Form I-918—Petition for U Nonimmigrant Status Receipts, Approvals, and Denials Fiscal Year 2013, Through Third Quarter (October 2012–June 2013) (2013) (on file with authors).

19. *See* Amy Farrell et al., Identifying Challenges to Improve the Investigation and Prosecution of State and Local Human Trafficking Cases (2012) (on file with authors).

20. Int'l Labour Org., ILO Global Estimate of Forced Labour (2012) (on file with authors).

21. 67 Fed. Reg 4784, 4788 (Jan. 31, 2002).

22. 18 U.S.C. § 1591.

23. Los Angeles County Probation Department reported that 174 girls were arrested in Los Angeles County for prostitution-related crimes in 2010. *See* Abby Sewell, *Many Teen Prostitutes Come from Foster Homes, L.A. County Officials Say,* Los Angeles Times (Nov. 12, 2012), *available at* http://latimesblogs.latimes.com/lanow/2012/11/many-teen-prostitutes-come-from-foster-homes-group-homes.html (last accessed Nov. 22, 2014).

24. *See* Kate Walker, Cal. Child Welfare Council, Ending the Commercial Sexual Exploitation of Children: A Call for Multi-System Collaboration in California 13–14 (2013) (on file with authors).

25. *See id.*

26. *See* Unif. Law Comm'n, Uniform Act on Prevention of and Remedies for Human Trafficking § 15 (2013).

27. *See* Assemb. 7670, 232d Leg., Reg. Sess. (N.Y. 2010).

28. *See id.*

29. *See* Unif. Law Comm'n, Uniform Act on Prevention of and Remedies for Human Trafficking § 17 (2013).

30. Int'l Labour Org., ILO Global Estimate of Forced Labour (2012) (on file with authors).

INDEX

A

A-3 visa, 99, 128
ABA
  Model Business and Supplier Policies
    on Labor Trafficking and Child
    Labor, 79
  Rule of Law Initiative, 164–165
Agriculture, human trafficking in, 15
Alien Tort Claims Act (ATCA), 71, 111
American Apparel and Footwear
  Association (AAFA), 83
American Gateways
  National Legal Orientation
    Program, 126
Amnesty International, 168
Ancillary legal services, 200
Anti-trafficking victim services
  NGOs, 39
Arresting victims, 63–66
Asian American Legal Defense
  and Education Fund
  (AALDEF), 105
Asia Regional Trafficking in Persons
  (ARTIP) Project, 164
Asset forfeiture, 60
Asylum, 149–150, 170
Athens Ethical Principles, 80

B

B1/B2 visas, 128
Beijing Platform for Action, 166
Blackmail, 28
Bonded labor. *See* Debt servitude,
  Debt bodage, 30
Bureau of Democracy, Human Rights
  and Labor (DRL), 177
Bureau of International Labor Affairs
  (ILAB), 176
Business and human rights, 168–169

C

California Transparency in Supply
  Chains Act (S.B. 657), 80–83
  consumer tool, 81–82
  enforcement of, 83
  as model for future laws, 83
  risk and marketplace
    shame, 82–83
Caron, Cathleen, 169
Catholic Legal Immigration
  Network, 173
Catholic Relief Services, 177
CdeBaca, Luis, 162
Center for Gender and Refugee Studies
  (CGRS), 172
Chapter 77 offenses, 41, 44,
  45, 60, 105
Child(ren)
  human rights and humanitarian law,
    167–168
  labor, 31–32
  sex tourism, 2
  soldiering, 11
Child Soldiers International, 167
Chvotkin, Alan, 91–92
City Bar Justice Center
  Immigrant Women and Children
    Project, 62
Civil anti-trafficking litigation,
    practice of
  civil judgment, financial
    implications of, 115–116
  coordination with criminal
    case, 114–115
  diplomatic immunity, 116
  immigration exposure, 116–117
  safety planning, 113–114
  trafficked persons, building trust
    with, 112–113

Civil judgment, financial implications of, 115–116

Civil litigation, 63
   access to, 63
   cases and practices, building, 102–111
      Alien Tort Claims Act, 111
      civil causes of action, 103
      discrimination laws, 107–109
      Fair Labor Standards Act, 106–107
      Racketeer Influenced and Corrupt Organizations Act, 109–111
      Trafficking Victims Protection Act, causes of action under, 103–106

Civil Rights Act of 1964
   Title VI, 151

Code of Conduct for the Protection of Children from Sexual Exploitation in Travel and Tourism, 80

Coercion, human trafficking by, 26–30
   blackmail, 28
   bonding and dependency, 30
   criminal of unlawful acts, using, 26–27
   economic coercion, 29–30
   inhumane treatment, 27
   psychological coercion, 26, 42, 44, 51, 52, 97, 104, 142
   religious and cultural beliefs, 29
   shaming, 27–28
   social isolation, 28–29
   withholding identity documents and making threats, 26

"Combating Trafficking in Persons" clause, 88

Companies with forced labor, consequences for, 71–72

Compliance, 74
   and risk mitigation, 80–92

Continued Presence
   immediate access to, 130–131
   T nonimmigrants, 139–140
   U nonimmigrants, 146

Convention Concerning Decent Work for Domestic Workers, 176

Convention for the Suppression of the Traffic in Persons and of the Exploitation of the Prostitution of Others, 160

Convention on the Suppression of Traffic in Women and Children, 159

Convention to End Discrimination Against Women (CEDAW) Committee, 166

Corporate law, 69–92
   compliance and risk mitigation, 80–92
   damage control, 79–80
   risk mitigation, 75–79

Corporate policies, strengthening, 77–78

Corporate social responsibility (CSR), 5, 72–74, 75, 92

Corruption, human trafficking linked to, 85

Country clubs, human trafficking in, 17

Covenant House, 167

Criminalization of victims
   arresting victims, 63–66
   post-conviction relief, 66–67

Criminal justice response, 37–68
   asset forfeiture, 60
   criminalization of victims, 63–67
   federal laws, 40–47
   human trafficking task forces, 39–40
   immigrant victims, prosecutors and victim services attorneys collaborating, 56–59
   judges, role of, 67–68
   restitution, 59–60
   state anti-trafficking criminal statutes, 47–49
   victim-centered prosecution, 49–56

Cultural beliefs, human trafficking based on, 29

Culturally appropriate services, 152–153

D

Damage control, 79–80

Debt bondage. See Debt servitude

Debt servitude, 11, 129

Defense attorneys, 65, 66, 67, 68

Defense Attorneys' Bar Association, 39

Department of Homeland Security (DHS), 130, 153

Department of Justice (DOJ), 39, 153
   Human Trafficking Prosecution Unit, 40–41, 137

Diplomatic immunity, 116

Discrimination laws, 107–109

Document servitude, 44–45

Dodd-Frank Wall Street Reform and Consumer Protection Act of 2010, 86

DOL List of Goods Produced by Child Labor or Forced Labor, 76

Domestic servitude, 2, 11, 16

Domestic violence and sexual assault attorneys, 187–190
Due diligence, 204

E
Economic coercion, 29–30
ECPAT International, 167–168
EEOC v. Global Horizons, Inc., 108
EEOC v. Trans Bay Steel, Inc., 108
Elder care, human trafficking in, 16–17
Electronics Industry Citizenship Coalition (EICC), 168
"Ending Trafficking in Government Contracting," 89
Equal Employment Opportunity Commission (EEOC), 107, 108–109
Equity in labor/sex trafficking prosecutions, 48–49
Ethical sourcing, 73
Ethnicity, 152
Expanded identification of trafficked persons, benefits of, 183–185
Extreme hardship, 137

F
Fair Business Practices Act, 83
Fair Labor Association, 168
Fair Labor Standards Act (FLSA), 71, 106–107
Fair trade movement, 73–74
Fair Trade USA, 73–74
Federal Acquisition Regulation (FAR), 71, 88–92
"Combating Trafficking in Persons" clause, 88
enforcement of, 92
proposed rule, 89–92
Federal Bureau of Investigation (FBI), 137, 155
Federal Law Enforcement Agencies, 39
Federal laws, 40–47
document servitude, 44–45
forced labor, 41–42
involuntary servitude, 46
peonage, 45–46
sex trafficking, 42–44
Trafficking Victims Protection Act of 2000. *See* Trafficking Victims Protection Act of 2000
Federal Public Defender's Office, 39

Forced labor, 22–24, 41–42, 46–47, 104–105. *See* Labor trafficking
companies with, consequences for, 71–72
defined, 175
malnutrition, 24
physical assaults, 22–23
physical labor, 24
sexual violence, 23
surveillance, 23
threats of, 23
Foreign Corrupt Practices Act (FCPA), 71, 84–85
human trafficking linked to corruption, 85
Fraud, human trafficking by, 24–25
"Fraud in Foreign Labor Contracting," 90
Frydman, Lisa, 173

G
G-5 visa, 99, 128
Global Alliance Against Traffic in Women (GAATW), 169
Global Workers Justice Alliance, 169
Good World Solutions, 76

H
H1-B visa, 128
H2-A visa, 128
H2-B visa, 20, 128
Hagar International, 177
Herman, Nate, 83
Hotels, human trafficking in, 17
Human Rights First, 173
Human Rights Watch, 20, 168
Human trafficking. *See also individual entries*
case example, 9–10
definition of, 10–11, 48, 157–158
and immigration, nexus between, 122–124
in industries, 15–18
intersections with, understanding, 180–183
linked to corruption, 85
misconceptions about, 30–32
mitigating against, 117–118
physically present on account of, 133–134
root causes of, 19–21
scale of problem, 12–13
severe form of, 132–133
task forces, 39–40

Human Trafficking Pro Bono Legal
  Center, 103
Human Trafficking Prosecution Unit
  (HTPU), 40–41, 137
Human Trafficking Taskforce, 137

I
Identity documents, withholding, 26
Immigrant community NGOs, 39
Immigrant victims, prosecutors
  and victim services attorneys
  collaborating for, 56–59
Immigrant Women and Children Project, 62
Immigration
  attorneys, 190–193
  enforcement victims protections,
    153–154
  exposure, 116–117
  and human trafficking, nexus between,
    122–124
  protections, access to, 121–156
  relief and protections, 130–150
Immigration and Customs Enforcement
  (ICE), 57, 122, 154, 155
  Homeland Security
    Investigations (HSI), 137
Industries, human trafficking in, 15–18
  agriculture, 15
  country clubs, 17
  domestic servitude, 16
  elder care, 16–17
  hotels, 17
  janitorial services, 18
  manufacturing, 15–16
  prostitution, 16
  restaurants, 17
Inhumane treatment, 27
International Agreement for the
  Suppression of the White Slave
  Traffic (1904), 159
International Convention for the
  Suppression of the Traffic in
  Women of Full Age, 159
International Convention for the
  Suppression of White Slave Traffic
  (1910), 159
International Convention on the
  Protection of the Rights of All
  Migrant Workers and Members of
  Their Families, 169

International criminal law
  Palermo Protocol, 160–162
International Domestic Workers
  Network, 177
International human rights and
  humanitarian law, 165–169
  business and human rights, 168–169
  children, 167–168
  migrants, 169
  women, 166–167
International labor law, 175–178
International Labor Rights
  Forum (ILRF), 178
International Labour Organization (ILO),
  12, 77, 94, 121, 159, 175, 176
International law, history of, 158–160
International nongovernmental
  organizations (INGOs), 174
International Organization for Migration
  (IOM), 169, 174
International refugee law, 169–174
  asylum, 170
  causal link to grounds, 172–173
  IOs and NGOs, 174–175
  place of persecution, 171
  traffickers, as agents
    of persecution, 171
  United Nations High Commissioner for
    Refugees, role of, 173–174
  well-founded fear of persecution,
    170–171
International Rescue Committee (IRC),
  167, 174–175
International Trade Union Confederation
  (ITUC), 177
"Interstate and Foreign Travel or
  Transportation in Aid of
  Racketeering Enterprises," 47
Involuntary servitude, 46–47, 104–105

J
J-1 visa, 128
Janitorial services, human trafficking in,
  18
Judges, role of, 67–68
Juvenile justice attorneys, 193–196

K
Kimberley Process, 80
  Certification Scheme, 168–169

Kmart, 77
Kramer, Doug, 165

L
Labor and employment law attorneys, 196–198
Labor programs, designing
  ancillary legal services, 200
  checklist, 199
  collaboration, 200
  legal representation, providing, 198–199
  primary services, funding for, 199
  pro bono attorney, role of, 200–202
Labor trafficking, 11, 188
  myths and misconceptions in, 94–96
  prosecutions, equity in, 48–49
LaborVoices, 76
Language considerations, 150–152
Law enforcement coordination
  T nonimmigrants, 134–137
  trafficked immigrants, 154
  U nonimmigrants, 143–144
  in victim-centered prosecution, 53–55
Legal Services Corporation (LSC), 181–182
Limited English proficient (LEP), 150–151, 186
List of Goods Produced with Forced and Child Labor, 176–177
Local business coalitions, 40
Local Government Public Health Agencies, 39
Local law enforcement agencies, 39
Local prosecutors, 39
Local public benefits agencies, 40
Local public defender agencies, 39
Low-wage labor, 32
Lutheran Immigration and Refugee Services, 173
Luxor Implementation Guidelines, 80

M
Malnutrition, 24, 27
Mann Act, 47
Manufacturing, human trafficking in, 15–16
Mental abuse, 142–143
Mercy Corps, 167
Migrants
  human rights and humanitarian law, 169

Minors, sex trafficking of, 189, 194
Misra, Neha, 177
Moskowitz, Al, 164
Musalo, Karen, 172

N
National Center for Youth Law, 195
National Conference of Commissioners on Uniform State Laws. *See* Uniform Law Commission
National Defense Authorization Act (NDAA), 89, 90
National Legal Orientation Program, 126
Navarre, Michael, 85

O
Obama, Barack, 69, 89
Office of Refugee Resettlement, 187
Office of Temporary and Disability Assistance, 61
Office to Monitor and Combat Trafficking in Persons (J/TIP), 162
Optional Protocol on the Involvement of Children in Armed Conflict, 167
Optional Protocol to the Convention on the Rights of the Child on the Sale of Children, Child Prostitution and Child Pornography, 167

P
Padilla attorneys, 65
Palermo Protocol, 6, 157, 160–162, 163, 205
Peonage, 45–46, 104–105
Persecution
  place of, 171
  traffickers as agents of, 171
  well-founded fear of, 170–171
Physical abuse, 142–143
Physical assaults, 22–23
Physical labor, 24
Physically present on account of trafficking, 133–134
Policy against purchasing commercial sex, 77
"Possesses information" requirement, 143
Post-conviction relief, 66–67
Primary services, funding for, 199
Proactive identification, 96–102
  outreach and collaboration, 101–102
  screening process, implementing, 100–101

Proactive prosecution, 50–51
Pro bono attorneys, 62, 67, 103, 125, 185, 198
    role in designing labor programs, 200–202
Procurement of services, 77
Prosecutorial discretion, 154
Prosecutors
    collaborating for immigrant victims, 56–59
Protocol Relating to the Status of Refugees, 1967, 169–170, 173
Protocol to Prevent, Suppress and Punish Trafficking in Persons, Especially Women and Children. *See* Palermo Protocol
Psychological coercion, 26, 42, 44, 51, 52, 97, 104, 142
Public effort, harmonizing, 78
Public interest attorneys, 179–202
    domestic violence and sexual assault attorneys, 187–190
    expanded identification of trafficked persons, benefits of, 183–185
    immigration attorneys, 190–193
    intersections with human trafficking, understanding, 180–183
    juvenile justice attorneys, 193–196
    labor and employment law attorneys, 196–198
    misconceptions, overcoming, 180–183
Public interest expertise, leveraging, 185–186
Public interest lawyering, traditional, 186–187
P visa, 128

R
Racketeer Influenced and Corrupt Organizations Act (RICO), 109–111
Reducing Child Labor and Forced Labor: A Toolkit for Responsible Businesses, 177
Refugee, definition of, 170
Religious beliefs, human trafficking based on, 29
Request for Evidence (RFE), 138
Restaurants, human trafficking in, 17
Restitution, 59–60

Retrafficking, 171
Retribution, 171
Risk assessment, 75–76
Risk mitigation, 75–79
    compliance and, 80–92
    corporate policies, strengthening, 77–78
    policy against purchasing commercial sex, 77
    procurement of services, 77
    public effort, harmonizing, 78
    risk assessments, performing, 75–76
    supplemental audits, performing, 76
    training, 78
    transparency in policies, increasing, 76–77
    work across the company, 78–79
Ruggie Principles. *See* UN Guiding Principles on Business and Human Rights (UNGP)
Rule of Law Initiative (ROLI), 164–165

S
Safety planning, 113–114
Safeway, 77
Save the Children, 167
Screening process, implementing, 100–101
Securities and Exchange Commission (SEC), 83
Service providers, coordination with, 55–56
    Regulation on Conflict Minerals, 85–87
    impact of, 87
    purpose of, 86–87
Sex trafficking, 2, 11, 42–44, 100, 105, 188–189, 191
    distinguished from prostitution, 42–43
    of minors, 189, 194
    prosecutions, equity in, 48–49
Sexual abuse, 35, 43, 170
Sexual assault, 64, 95, 108, 145, 188–189
Sexual violence, 23, 94
Sex Workers' Project (SWP), 67
Shaming, 27–28, 152
Shelter NGOs, 39
Slavery, 104–105
Slavery Footprint, 76
Smuggling, 31

Social isolation, 28–29
Social service providers, coordination with, 118–119
Special Immigrant Juvenile (SIJ) Status, 148–149
State anti-trafficking criminal statutes, 47–49
  equity in labor/sex trafficking prosecutions, 48–49
  human trafficking, definition of, 48
State civil laws, 111–112
State Labor Department, 39
"Strengthening Protections Against Trafficking in Persons in Federal Contracts," 89
Supplemental audits, 76
Supply chain management, 72

T
T-1 visa, 138, 140, 141
T-2 visa, 138
Tahirih Justice Center, 166
Target, 77
Traditional public interest lawyering, 186–187
Trafficked immigrants, 13–14
  building trust with, 112–113
  considerations in representing
    coordinating with law enforcement, 154
    culturally appropriate services, 152–153
    immigration enforcement victims protections, 153–154
    investigation and prosecution, 155–156
    language considerations, 150–152
  financial consequences, impact of, 32–33
  identification of, 125–130
  indicators of, 127
  mental health, impact of, 34–35
  physical health, impact of, 33–34
  state of play for, 124–125
Traffickers
  as agents of persecution, 171
  tactics of, 21–30
    coercion, 26–30
    force, 22–24
    fraud, 24–25
Trafficking and Victims Protection Act (TVPA), 163, 164

Trafficking in Persons Action Plan, 163
Trafficking in Persons Report (TIP Report), 76, 85, 162
Trafficking Victims Protection Act of 2000 (TVPA), 37, 38, 41, 57, 59, 60, 68, 98, 105, 106, 124, 132, 149, 154, 172
  causes of action under, 103–106
Training, 78
Transparency in policies, increasing, 76–77
Tribal Governments, 39
Trust building, in victim-centered prosecution, 51–53, 54
Truth in Labeling Act, 83
T visa, for victims of trafficking, 6, 7, 57, 58–59, 66, 98, 107, 125, 131–132, 191–192
  adjustment of status, 139
  admissibility, 140
  age under eighteen when victimized, 140–141
  application process, 137–138
  assistance in investigation or prosecution, 140–141
  continuous physical presence, 139–140
  direct and indirect benefits of, 58
  extreme hardship, 137, 140–141
  good moral character requirements, 140
  law enforcement cooperation, 134–137
  physically present on account of trafficking, 133–134
  preparation for, 139
  severe form of trafficking, 132–133

U
UN Guiding Principles on Business and Human Rights (UNGPs), 74, 79, 80, 168
UNICEF, 163, 167
Uniform Act, 195
Uniform Law Commission, 66–67
United Nations Convention Against Transnational Organized Crime, 6, 157, 160
United Nations Convention Relating to the Status of Refugees, 1951, 169, 173
United Nations High Commissioner for Refugees, 170–171, 173–174

United Nations Office on Drugs and Crime (UNODC), 162, 163
United States v. Sabhnani, 60
Universal Declaration of Human Rights, 165
U.S. Agency for International Development (USAID), 88
U.S. Attorney's Office, 39
U.S. Citizenship and Immigration Services (USCIS), 58, 59, 124, 130, 131, 132, 133, 135, 137, 138, 139, 140, 141, 142, 144, 153, 191
U.S. Department of Defense, 88
U.S. Department of Health and Human Services (HHS), 187
  certification, 131
U.S. Department of Labor, 6, 70
  Bureau of Democracy, Human Rights and Labor, 177
  Bureau of International Labor Affairs, 176
  Toolkit for Responsible Business, 79
U.S. Department of State, 88
  Trafficking in Persons Report, 76, 85, 162
U.S. Equal Employment Opportunity Commission (EEOC), 5, 16, 17
U visa, for victims of crime, 6, 57, 58–59, 98, 107, 141–142
  adjustment of status, 146
  admissibility and discretion, 147
  assistance in investigation or prosecution, 146
  certifying agencies, 144
  continuous physical presence, 146
  criminal activity violated laws, qualifying, 144–145
  law enforcement cooperation, 143–144
  "possesses information" requirement, 143
  preparation for, 146
  substantial physical or mental abuse, 142–143

V
Vermont Service Center (VSC), 138, 141
Victim-centered prosecution, 49–56
  coordination with service providers, 55–56
  law enforcement coordination, 53–55
  proactive prosecution, 50–51
  trust building, 51–53, 54
Victim services attorneys
  access to civil remedies, 63
  collaborating for immigrant victims, 56–59
  counterpart, 60–63
Victims of Trafficking and Violence Protection Act of 2000 (VTVPA), 37, 71, 141
Vienna Declaration, 166
Violence Against Women Act (VAWA), 138, 141
  cancellation, 148
  confidentiality, 153
  self-petition, 147–148
Violence Against Women Services NGOs, 39
Vital Voices, 166

W
Walker, Kate, 195
Warnath, Stephen, 163
Wartime Contracting Commission, 89
Winrock International, 177
Women
  human rights and humanitarian law, 166–167
Work across the company, 78–79
Worker Rights NGOs, 39
World Diamond Council, 168
World Vision, 167